MW00851809

Sonidos Negros

ALEJANDRO L. MADRID, SERIES EDITOR
WALTER CLARK, FOUNDING SERIES EDITOR AND
SERIES EDITOR FOR CURRENT VOLUME

Sonidos Negros

ON THE BLACKNESS OF FLAMENCO

K. MEIRA GOLDBERG

OXFORD
UNIVERSITY PRESS

OXFORD
UNIVERSITY PRESS

Oxford University Press is a department of the University of Oxford.
It furthers the University's objective of excellence in research, scholarship,
and education by publishing worldwide. Oxford is a registered trade mark of
Oxford University Press in the UK and certain other countries.

Published in the United States of America by Oxford University Press
198 Madison Avenue, New York, NY 10016, United States of America.

© Oxford University Press 2019

All rights reserved. No part of this publication may be reproduced,
stored in a retrieval system, or transmitted, in any form or by any means,
without the prior permission in writing of Oxford University Press,
or as expressly permitted by law, by license, or under terms agreed with
the appropriate reproduction rights organization. Inquiries concerning
reproduction outside the scope of the above should be sent to the
Rights Department, Oxford University Press, at the address above.

You must not circulate this work in any other form
and you must impose this same condition on any acquirer.

Library of Congress Cataloging-in-Publication Data
Names: Goldberg, K. Meira, author.
Title: Sonidos Negros : on the blackness of flamenco / K. Meira Goldberg.
Description: New York, NY : Oxford University Press, [2019] | Includes
bibliographical references and index.
Identifiers: LCCN 2018006810 (print) | LCCN 2018028172 (ebook) |
ISBN 9780190466930 (updf) | ISBN 9780190466947 (epub) |
ISBN 9780190466916 | ISBN 9780190466916 (cloth : alk. paper) |
ISBN 9780190466923 (paper : alk. paper)
Subjects: LCSH: Flamenco. | Flamenco—Social aspects. | Dance and race.
Classification: LCC GV1796.F55 (ebook) | LCC GV1796.F55 G59 2019 (print) |
DDC 793.3/19468—dc23
LC record available at https://lccn.loc.gov/2018006810

3 5 7 9 8 6 4 2
Printed by Webcom, Inc., Canada

FOR LOVE:
MARJORIE AND BARBARA,
RUBY AND AMELIA,
AND ARTHUR

CONTENTS

LIST OF ILLUSTRATIONS

ACKNOWLEDGMENTS

I DEDICATE THIS BOOK TO three mothers, Marjorie, Barbara, and Brenda, who have spoken truth to power with love and grace, to two daughters, Ruby and Amelia, who carry feminist purpose into the future, and to Arthur, my beloved companion on the journey.

My story thus far has not been conventional—I never planned to do many of the most important things I have done, and this book, improbable in so many ways, is among those things. Throughout the years spent wading through a morass of disparate sources, fighting to weave wisps and suggestions and fleeting perceptions into a cogent and meaningful set of arguments, I have often been sustained quite simply by a sense of obligation to tell the story that my quirky path in life has opened before me. But this would have been utterly impossible without the embrace and support, moral and material, of those who share the reverence and passion for flamenco that has shaped my life.

I would like to thank my cherished elders, Izzie Weinzweig, Lois Torf, and Carol Gordon, and especially my stepfather, Malcolm S. Gordon, for telling me, when I approached the age my mother was when she died, that I had "a few books in me"—and the time is now! Thank you, Brenda Dixon Gottschild, my teacher and mentor, for showing me to do scholarship with my body and for always encouraging me to jump into the discussion when the time was right.

Thank you, Walter Clark, founder and founding editor of Oxford's series *Currents in Latin American and Iberian Music*, and Norman Hirschy, editor for dance, film, and media studies and music books at Oxford, for taking a chance on me. I am most grateful to Léonide Massine's heirs, Tatiana Weinbaum, Lorca Massine, and Theodor Massine, for their generosity in allowing my work with their father's footage of Juana Vargas, "La Macarrona," to be published. I am grateful to Margaret Heilbrun for deft, subtle, and discerning revisions, and to Joellyn Ausanka, senior production editor, Elizabeth Bortka, copy editor, and the entire production and editorial staff at OUP who had a hand in publishing this book. Thanks to Lynn Matluck Brooks for editing and publishing "Sonidos Negros: On the Blackness of Flamenco" in its embryonic form in *Dance Chronicle*. Antoni Pizà, a font of incredibly well-timed and erudite suggestions, opened a world of opportunity for me with a simple "yes." Thank you to the beautiful Michelle Heffner Hayes, for incisive brilliance, sage advice, and steadfast friendship. Kiko Mora, my life is infinitely richer for our long-standing, long-distance friendship, and for our shared enthusiasm for arcane detail and probing conversation. Thank you for your astonishing research, and for allowing me to publish our work on Jacinto Padilla, "El Negro Meri," here.

Thomas Baird's generous collaboration on the eighteenth-century fandango was the key to my understanding not only of the fandango, but also of the process of historical dance reconstruction. I am grateful to Tom and to our colleague Jared Newman for allowing me to reuse parts of our research here. Thank you to my friend and comrade-in-arms Anna de la Paz for her boundless generosity, energy, and curiosity, and most especially for collaborating with me on the villano, and for allowing me to publish that research here.

My thanks to Ruven Afanador for the gift of the striking image which I knew I wanted for the cover of this book from the moment I saw it. And thank you to Yolanda Heredia, the photograph's subject, for embracing its use here.

Thank you Carlota Santana for your leadership in the flamenco community, and for Flamenco Vivo's constant and bountiful support. Thanks especially to Hanaah Frechette, Flamenco Vivo executive director, for teaching me about images permissions and cool diplomacy, for noticing the *renverse en arrière* in an 1889 French press clipping, and for helping me reconstruct the two Macarrona clips. Thanks too to Leslie Roybal, director of the Center for Flamenco Arts at Flamenco Vivo Carlota Santana, for collaborating in this reconstruction, and for performing Macarrona's tangos in my conference presentation "*Tumulte Noir* and *Jaleo de Jerez*: Modernist Primitivism, Cakewalk and La Macarrona's Flamenco Dance" at the New Perspectives in Flamenco History and Research Symposium at the University of New Mexico, Albuquerque, June 8–9, 2014. Thank you Hans Rasch, Studio Manager at Flamenco Vivo, for being an ally in celebrating flamenco's spectacular diversity, and for cover design ideas, and thank you to my dear friend Michael Penland for taking my portrait—as an author!

I would like to thank my teachers, students, readers, and colleagues, over kitchen tables and in the studio, those who I chatted up and those who chatted me up, those I only know through email, and those I only know from reading their work: John Amira, Clara Mora Chinoy, Cristina Cruces Roldán, Sharina Marisela Doyle, Rafael Estévez, Raúl Fernández, Bronwen Heuer, Antonio

Hidalgo, Javier Irigoyen García, Benjamin Liu, Ariana Markoe, Mariano Parra, Jani Rodrigues, Craig Russell, Ramón Soler, and Ana Yepes. Alberto del Campo, Yvonne Daniel, Susannah Driver Barstow, Nick Jones, Peter Manuel, and Kiko Mora generously gave their time and deep knowledge to reading parts of the manuscript, and Nick also contributed to tricky translations and procured hard-to-obtain resources for me. Thank you Peter Manuel for telling me what a "hemiola" is, and for making me aware of José Luis Navarro García's *Semillas de Ébano*. Jesús Cosano sent me the 1709 villancico which forms the basis for Chapter 2, and Juan Vergillos sent me both of Daniel Pineda Novo's books on Macarrona and Ramírez. Thanks to Yinka Esi Graves and Miguel Ángel Rosales for friendship and inspiration. The brilliant Sybil Cooksey introduced me to Jayna Brown, black phenomenology, Afro-futurism and Afro-pessimism, and the rumba on West 3rd Street. I am especially grateful to Estela Zatania and Brook Zern for their friendship and wise counsel.

My gratitude to Rafael Abolafia, for the work, sweat, and tears I have shared with him goes much deeper than words, reminding me to walk always in the shadow of death and to choose love. And my life is equally enriched by Rafael's love, María Luisa Martínez, a woman of intelligence, grace, and impeccable eye who, among many kindnesses, did the incredible errand of sending me Manuel de Falla's correspondence with Diaghilev from 1916 to 1921 from the Archivo Manuel de Falla in Granada.

I would like to thank Robert Farris Thompson, whose book *Tango* was an epiphany for me, chewed up and digested slowly, for showing me that it is possible to trace the interweavings of Mother Africa, the Old World, and the New World inside my own dance, and for his beautiful writing that ranks right up there with Herman Melville, Fred Moten, and Elisabeth Le Guin. Le Guin's writing has taught me so much about taking the granular to the courageous and powerfully-written big insight.

Bless the librarians and book digitizers. I have made particularly extensive use of the Biblioteca Nacional de España, both their digitized library holdings and their amazing library of digitized periodicals. But I have also consulted the Bibliothèque Nationale de France, the Library of Congress, the Biblioteca Virtual de Madrid, the Biblioteca Virtual de Andalucía, the Biblioteca Virtual Miguel de Cervantes, the Real Academia de Bellas Artes San Fernando, the Biblioteca Virtual de Prensa Histórica, the Biblioteca Nacional de Perú, the Biblioteca Nacional de México, the Biblioteca Nacional de Portugal, and others. The digital archives of Google have been indispensable to my research, allowing me to access many primary documents such as dictionaries, travelers' accounts, histories, and literature.

At the New York Public Library for the Performing Arts, I am privileged to count Barbara Cohen-Stratyner, former curator of exhibitions, Shelby Cullom Davis Museum, and Tanisha Jones, director of the Jerome Robbins Archive of the Recorded Moving Image, as friends. My thanks also to Jay Barksdale, former director of the Wertheim Study at the New York Public Library, and François Bernardi, film editor for 100 *Years of Flamenco*.

Antoni Pizà, Director of the Foundation for Iberian Music at the Barry S. Brook Center for Musical Research and Documentation at the CUNY Graduate Center, has given me a loving home and an essential base of institutional support. I am grateful also for the support and consideration of William Mooney, Chair of the Department of Film, Media, and Performing Arts at the Fashion Institute of Technology, and that of all my FIT colleagues. But most especially to the Interlibrary Loan crew, headed by Peggy Murphy, who is as in love with books as I am, and without whose indefatigable support and patience this book could not have been written.

FOREWORD

Dr. Brenda Dixon Gottschild

IT'S 1986. I AM AN assistant professor at Temple University, hired in 1982 to flesh out the dance department's doctoral faculty, while also teaching studio and academic courses in the department's master's and undergraduate curriculum. I attend a departmental concert featuring a new student, Meira Weinzweig. I don't know her very well, but I know that her area is flamenco (which, back then, was Greek to me). I'm swept off my feet when this woman dares to pair her percussive dancing with the percussion accompaniment of "Papa" Joe Bryant, a revered professional known for his expertise in West African/Cuban/Brazilian genres—one of my areas of investigation. The correlations are revelatory! Before this event, it hadn't occurred to me that there was a meaningful relationship between flamenco and African endeavor. The thought crosses my mind that Meira is onto something big; she's actually dancing/embodying a *theory* that hasn't been researched—and I am enticed by the prospect of working with her.

Thus began a relationship that developed from student-teacher, to advisee-advisor, to mentee-mentor and, now, to colleagues-friends. While I continued my immersion in discovering "invisibilized" Africanist (namely, African and African American) presences in so-called white concert dance genres, Meira was in the initial stages of developing parallel premises in flamenco while at Temple, culminating in a brilliant doctoral dissertation that explored the Roma and African historical lines in flamenco—and the African part of this equation was as invisibilized as it was in my areas of investigation. Titled *Border Trespasses: The Gypsy Mask and Carmen Amaya's Flamenco Dance*, her dissertation was the first big step on the path leading to *Sonidos Negros: On the Blackness of Flamenco*. But this was no leap: there were many steps in between. In fact, this scholar-dancer continued studying flamenco in Seville with the reigning masters of the form. Furthermore, in addition to her doctorate, she completed her MFA, taking studio classes in modern dance and related areas, as well as conceiving, producing, choreographing, and dancing in her master's concert—the degree requirement at Temple. This is important information, because in the performing arts, whether it's dance, music, or theater, the theoretical propositions that are embodied in practice are the ones most likely to endure.

It must have been around 2003 or so. I make my way to one of the flamenco bistros in lower Manhattan to see Meira—now known professionally as "La Meira," now also a wife and mother—and, after almost two decades, I'm again swept off my feet. The rich texture of her dancing, now seasoned with years of practical and theoretical research, performance, and study, fills the tiny room and invades the space, enveloping spectators in a spirit that goes beyond words. That's the power of great performance, and of performance enriched by experience, research, practice, curiosity, creativity, commitment, perseverance, cultural immersion, and a deep desire to surrender to—rather than penetrate—the subject matter. To *Sonidos Negros* Meira brings this same hunger and thirst for getting to the heart and truth of the matter. In African American speak, we talk about "soul." In the flamenco lexicon, it's "duende." She gets it, and this book is full of it.

Sonidos Negros deals with the representation of race in flamenco—not to be confused with the flamenco appropriation of Africanisms, as its author points out. With the precise factual and historical clarity that characterizes her work, Meira shows the reader the eye-opening intertextuality that makes cognates of flamenco, circus, and African American forms such as the cakewalk and vaudevillian tap dance. Her chapters move us through the nuanced shades of a complex quest for Iberian identity—one that cannot be loosed from its Moorish (read Black) roots. In doing so, she is putting together the pieces of a puzzle long rendered asunder by colonialism and racism. She's plumbed early Spanish dance manuals and texts (thanks to her command of the verbal and somatic languages) and opens the work with a consideration of the "trope of the bumpkin shepherd," an interesting figure who grounds the culture in a national identity unbound by the restraint of imitating France or England, the reigning European super powers after Spain's fall from grace. That she utilizes "confusion and lasciviousness" as guiding premises in her quest is an epiphanic move. For centuries and into the new millennium, everywhere Africanist and Europeanist cultures have met they've both clashed and merged. This love-hate, exotic-erotic binary translates in culture-specific turns that the people who consider themselves white (and they will be the majority of the Oxford readership) are finally beginning to acknowledge. Each instance of this clash is sui generis and requires a unique investigation. Meira's exploration of race and the representation of blackness in flamenco is ripe and rife with epiphanies that give the reader a "dark side of the moon" perspective on flamenco, Spain, and the power of dance and dancing bodies to serve as a socio-cultural, political construct.

Inevitably, researching representations of race leads to unearthing racism.

Exploring the "purity of blood" trope of the Iberian Christian majority and its hegemonic tyranny over "Others"—be they Moors, Roma, Jews, or Muslims—is another way that this scholar has opened up her topic to novel scrutiny. Indeed, the Spanish were Northern Europe's "exotic desired Other" although they would be joined, if not replaced, by Americans of African lineage (Ada Overton Walker; Josephine Baker) through the international dissemination of African-American minstrelsy, followed by Black vaudeville. It becomes all the more significant, then, that this "Other"—Spain—was about the business of "Othering" the Others who had helped it establish its own proto-modern identity: namely, the Blacks, Gitanos, and non-Christians who were Spanish all along. Nevertheless, there'd always been an historical "special charm" in the regard of the French, Germans, and English for the "noble savage" of Spain—as opposed to the "brutish primitive" represented by Africans on display at carnivals, circuses, and early "anthropology" exhibits like the French and British events featuring the "Hottentot Venus." These are the contested narratives of race, race representation, and racism.

So now, again, I am swept off my feet by Meira Goldberg's doings. *Sonidos Negros* is a majestic work—readable, revelatory, and bringing to bear all her previous work in research and practice to reach this tome of truth. She speaks in a voice both personal and professional, inviting us in to share the insights of a life lived in flamenco, insights that may well shake up the ways in which scholars and lay readers alike perceive what it means to look at what we think we know, or realize we don't know, with new eyes.

Sonidos Negros

In the beginning God created the heaven and the earth. And the earth was without form, and void; and darkness was upon the face of the deep. And the Spirit of God moved upon the face of the waters. And God said, "Let there be light," and there was light. And God saw the light: that it was good, and God divided the light from the darkness. God called the light "day," and the darkness he called "night."...

—*Genesis 1:1–5a, Authorized Version*

Introduction

THE MOOR INSIDE

OW IS THE POLITICS of Blackness figured in the flamenco dancing body? Or, to put this question in another way, *What does flamenco dance tell us about the construction of race in the Atlantic world?* The idea of race, of Blackness as signifying religious confusion or misguidedness, and hence subjugated social status, evolved on the Iberian Peninsula during the *Reconquista*, the almost-eight-hundred-year struggle to expel Islam and Judaism. *Limpieza de sangre*, purity of blood, certified virtuous allegiance to the Catholic state, while non-Christian lineage equaled to depravity and abjection. Race was defined in terms of Christianity and its opposite, ranking ethnic and religious difference within a caste system whose governance served to simultaneously vanquish and incorporate the richly cosmopolitan Judeo-Islamic past. Aligned both socially and metaphorically with a substantial population of enslaved West and Central Africans, and with Roma immigrants, whose mysterious origins and dark looks lent them a sometimes useful, often dangerous ambiguity, early modern Spain's "Moors," that is, its Muslim inhabitants, became "Black," signifying moral turpitude as well as racial identity.

With the emergence of Spain as a Catholic empire founded upon the Atlantic slave trade, the religious imagery of the wars of Reconquista was deployed as justification for the brutal conquest of the Americas, and for the mass enslavement of Native Americans, Africans, and their descendants. As the ideology of blood purity became a governing principle of colonization and slavery, something more akin to modern ideas about race evolved. The conceptualization of ethnic West and Central African features, such as skin color, as defining the Blackness of abject social status operated through Christian theology: Blackness was seen, in the biblical sense, as being without light. For the Catholic state, that light was Jesus Christ, holding out the possibility of redemption from the primordial chaos.[1]

Spain's symbolic linkage of the Moor seen as Black with the enslavement of Africans, therefore, constituted visible proof of the morality and inevitability of Christian European dominance of the "Western" Hemisphere. Spain thus laid down an ideological framework that would be utilized by all the colonial slaving powers. And yet the Christian narrative of redemption, which, in tension with the racial determinism of limpieza de sangre, animates the dances traced here, cracks just slightly the carapace of racial ideology, an aperture through which flow, I will argue, subversive and indeed transformative bodily forces.

By the eighteenth-century, its empire in decline, Spanish dreams of sovereignty and autonomy were paradoxically achieved by performing—and eventually becoming, in the eyes of Europe—the Black Moor. Flamenco means "Flemish" (the Spanish Netherlands, held by the Crown from 1581 to 1714, were a lucrative, yet rebellious and troublesome part of the empire), but ironically inverts this term. Over the course of the eighteenth and into the nineteenth century, Spain, the once-feared conqueror and preeminent colonial power, became "flamenco"—a derisive comment on the patent absurdity of its claim to Europeanness. By the time flamenco emerged as a genre in the mid-nineteenth century, its disordered and raucous universe—the emblematic ¡Ole! of Gypsies, smugglers, fortune tellers, and prostitutes—described a long-demarcated and, I will argue, racialized zone within Spanish performance: of ostentatious satire, self-referential rhetoric of abjection, and acid social critique. Flamenco's essential qualities—its tumultuous sensuality, quixotic idealism, and fierce soulfulness—thus echo with the socio-political and aesthetic contests that trace the rise and fall of an empire. By the nineteenth century, flamenco performed Spain's outlaw-hero and his darkly beautiful, racially ambiguous consort. These two, born in exile and enslavement, under the lash and in shackles, held transgressive claims to personhood that paradoxically lent power and poetic resonance to flamenco as a theater for the expansion and play of modern possibilities for the self.

Sonidos Negros traces how, in the span between 1492—the year in which Christian reconquest of the Iberian Peninsula coincided with Christopher Columbus's landing on Hispaniola—and 1933—when Andalusian poet Federico García Lorca published his "Theory and Play of the *Duende*"—the Moor became Black, and how the imagined *Gitano* ("Gypsy," or Roma), intermediate between White and Black, Christian and non-Christian worlds, embodies the warring images and sounds of this process. By the nineteenth-century nadir of its colonial reach, Spanish resistance to European and U.S. cultural imperialism came to be enacted in terms of a minstrelized Gitano, who carried a hybrid of Spanish and American representations of Blackness directly into flamenco. As flamenco became a modernist form, this lexicon framed Spain's absorption of jazz, enacted through the body of the nation's racial Other.

Some Theoretical, Methodological, and Etymological Touchstones

I was a flamenco dancer long before I became a scholar. As one of a handful of foreigners immersed in the Madrid flamenco scene of the 1980s, I constantly negotiated the often treacherous and always ambiguous landscape of authenticity-as-action rather than as familial inheritance. The five years I spent performing nightly in flamenco clubs alongside a list of artists (Arturo Pavón, Antonio Canales, Manolo Soler, Diego Carrasco, Tony "El Pelao," "El Indio Gitano," Ramón "El Portugués," "Guadiana," "El Camborio" ∴.) that takes the breath away from flamenco aficionados remain my deepest flamenco education and point of reference. Therefore, the archive of the dancing body—*my* dancing body—is a principal reference here.

In seeking to describe the Blackness of flamenco I am not looking primarily for originary African movement, rhythmic/musical, aesthetic, or spiritual elements, though those elements are inevitably present here. Rather, I follow Toni Morrison, who, in *Playing in the Dark: Whiteness and the Literary Imagination* (1992), plumbs the "dark, abiding, signing Africanist presence" in her analysis of Whiteness.[2] Morrison's theorization of how white America navigated its "terror of human freedom—the thing they coveted most of all"—by casting enslaved black people as "surrogate selves"—founds my arguments with respect to flamenco's Blackness. Following Morrison, I will argue that flamenco represents Spain's fraught attempts to reclaim its lost stature among European nations—its Whiteness—by embodying its Blackness.

The first to apply Morrison's use of the term "Africanist" to dance was Brenda Dixon Gottschild in *Digging the Africanist Presence in American Performance: Dance and Other Contexts* (1996).[3] My work derives from Dixon Gottschild's foundational dance research, and I aspire here to emulate her deep hermeneutic analyses of the racialized dancing body. I aim to trace the many recurrent reflections within flamenco, its splendidly promiscuous and duplicitous unruliness, its archetypal narratives, myths, and gestures: terms and symbols preserved through time in a kaleidoscopic montage of inverted, mutating, and constantly realigning significations. I seek to illuminate the contradictions, the silences, the competing desires that flamenco so magnificently binds together. My purpose is to celebrate and foreground flamenco's hip-hop equivocations, its soulful intent, its sacred communal dimensions, the satiric arrows of its virtuosic spectacles. *Sonidos Negros* traces Blackness as a marker of cultural and national identity in a society that was rotting like a fallen tree into the forest floor. What remains? What sprouts anew? I wish to read in flamenco's *mestizaje*, its hybridity, a fragmentary portrait of the formation of race in what Paul Gilroy calls *The Black Atlantic*.[4]

Tracing genealogical relationships between embodied ideas migrating across great expanses of time and space is always a delicate, subjective, and conditional matter. Dance of the early modern era (roughly, the renaissance and the baroque) was recorded haphazardly and obliquely in literature, dance treatises, dictionaries, and similar bibliographic sources. Considering the ever-shifting winds driving cross-cultural pollination, how may we usefully extrapolate from the archive of the dancing body, proposing readings of textual dance references from the distant past?

Comparative literary analysis, and practice-based analyses of scripts in gesture and sound, structure my methodologies here. I often employ an etymological approach, comparing a number of sources to undertake a deep exegesis of a particular term. For example, I identify a constellation of dance terms related to the word *zapato*, or shoe. The first monolingual dictionary of Castilian Spanish, Sebastián de Covarrubias's *Tesoro de la lengua castellana o española* (1611), was published just two years after Felipe III began expelling Spain's *Moriscos* (Christians of Muslim descent), in a climate of widespread anxiety and paranoia over lineage and blood purity. Covarrubias makes clear the logic linking noisy and uproarious footwork with the doctrine of redemption, defining "zapato" as "the most humble thing there is, worn under the foot," and thus symbolic of the "humility and lowliness" of "Christ the Redeemer."[5] An eighteenth-century dictionary adds an illustration from one of the most important works of Spanish literature, Miguel de Cervantes's *Don Quixote de la Mancha* (published in two volumes, 1605 and 1615), which firmly identifies *zapateado* (percussive footwork) as a rustic dance of the common people, and categorizes it as a *baile de cascabel*, a bell dance.[6] Bell dances, with noisy footwork sometimes done wearing bells around the ankles or calves and sometimes in blackface, were used to represent Moors in the Spanish *morisca*, a dance also performed in France and England.[7] *Quixote*'s analogy between footwork dances and bell dances thus hints at noisy footwork's racial overtones.

Throughout this book, I explore "Blackness" as it is embodied in Spanish dance. I use the term "Blackness"—somewhat in counterposition to "Africanist"—as addressing not the positive cultural traits we all inherit from African ancestors, but rather the catastrophic dogma that non-Christians should be enslaved. In Genesis 1:1–5, the earth was a formless void, and the act of creation was a separation of darkness from light.[8] The association of darkness—Blackness—with evil dates from the Hellenized Jewish philosophy of the first century CE, "because pure evil has no participation in light, but follows night and darkness," and continues in the allegorical interpretations of the Bible by third-century Christian church fathers.[9]

In the epic struggle against Islam and Judaism on the Iberian Peninsula, Blackness was of the blood, of the soul—it was invisible. Sheep might be classified as white or black, but human beings could not be so easily distinguished. This problem created the pressure to represent Blackness by other means, as through dance. With the "discovery" of the New World, setting the stage for half a millennium of white Christian dominance, ideas about Blackness became overwhelmingly expressive of the drive to extract and expropriate wealth from the American colonies. And yet tensions intrinsic to European colonization—between concepts of Blackness as immutable bloodline, as opposed to an equivocal state of moral peril from which a soul might still emerge (or be forcibly wrested)—remain. From 1492 to the present day the countervailing forces within the term "Blackness" attach to these concepts.[10]

Similarly complicated and contradictory meanings lie inside the word *raza*, race, which in Spanish is opposed to *casta*, meaning both "caste" and "chaste," or virtuous. Raza denotes a stain or blemish: in the medieval sheep husbandry that provides this important vocabulary, the goal was to breed sheep with pure white wool, with raza denoting a flaw to be extirpated.[11] Fused with the canonical distinctions between darkness and light, good and evil, chaos and order, this lexicon of animal husbandry provided the language that founded and justified slavery. It also structured Spanish government in the colonies, and management of the population in the Iberian homeland.

A twist comes in the eighteenth century. Pressed by a new French dynasty, dissident Spaniards performed casta in terms of a racialized Other: Spain came to perform its Whiteness in terms of its Blackness. The intellectual skeleton I am excavating here reveals how, during the battle for religious domination over the Iberian Peninsula, the Moor became Black—but how, once that war was over, as it slipped from preeminence, Spain itself became Black. The Spain of *El Cid* (ca. 1040–99), champion in the war against the Moors, and of Hernán Cortés (1485–1547), who conquered the Aztecs, was reduced to performing itself for tourists. The toggle for this transfer is the figure of the Moor—African, Semitic, Roma, vanquished—yet, as the legendary Carmen Amaya sang, "the blood of kings flows / in the palm of my hand."[12] Flamenco embodies a Spanish self that is fraught with internal contradictions, dancing resistance to its abjection, and nostalgic longing for its past glory, in terms of Blackness.

One pervasive theme in this brief overview of etymological touchstones, and one of the greatest challenges in writing this book, is the slipperiness of the lexicon. Spanish dance, as we will see, was consistently condemned by moralists, legislated by the Crown, persecuted by the Inquisition—and just as consistently evaded such charges by changing names. As bolero dancer Antonio Cairón put it in his 1820 dance treatise, "the name might change again soon, but the form will not."[13] We will touch here upon *seguidilla*, *zarabanda*, *chacona*, *canario*, *guineo*, *encorvado*, *endiablado*, *jácara*, *polvillo*—these terms only partially cover the sixteenth and seventeenth centuries: another long list awaits as we consider later eras. Yet it is impossible to avoid this mushrooming web of terms, because, as Cairón says, pulling on a single fiber tends to involve the entire tissue. Aside from the ever-changing parade of dance names, however, certain terms of dance description appear consistently throughout the literature, and one of the most constant is *bulla*, which means ruckus or confusion.[14]

Bulla gestures toward the center of racialized concepts of dance. Principally, it signifies the confusion of not having accepted Christ and the concomitant peril of suspect bloodline. Bulla, holding the potential for damnation, thus constitutes the terms by which enslavement was justified. Ruckus and confusion fabricate the disturbing figure, which we will track from early-eighteenth-century Christmas pageants through "Jim Crow" and back to Spain again, of the compliant, "light-hearted" slave. Bulla, a consummately kinesthetic concept, also announces the noisy and unbridled ruckus of unselfconscious sensuality—lasciviousness is another universal indicator of Blackness, conceived as sinful misguidedness.[15]

But if bulla's danced deviance figures moral and racial aberration, it also performs the equivocation that can cloak resistance and dissent.[16] Suggestive, comic, and irrepressible confusion are, of course, key to the popular appeal of danced Blackness. Bulla enacts what performance theorist Jayna Brown describes as the "guileful ruse": the "multi-signifying practices of dissemblance" of the black performer, who plays "in the field of racialized fantasies."[17] Brown's point, that performance which exploits such racial imagery simultaneously enables a "space for satirical comment on the absurdity of such depictions," is related to what W. E. B. Du Bois calls "double consciousness," one of the most useful tools from Black performance theory to employ in looking at flamenco.[18]

Actually, regarding such dissembling practices, one might question whether it is the chicken or the egg that begins the cycle (for Spain, at least): the representation of purposeful or guileful confusion—paired with *desilusión*, disillusionment, the rupture of theatrical illusion—is one of the hallmarks of Spanish literature.[19] This is perfectly logical. For one thing, as the perilous stain of impure blood was invisible, appearances could not be trusted. For another, the economic explosion of Spain's American colonies, powered by slave labor, paradoxically sucked prosperity away from the metropole. *Don Quixote*, an impoverished knight, madly cleaving to his nobility of spirit in the harshest of real-world circumstances, founds his quest on the honorable ideals of *Dios, Patria, y Rey*—God, Country, and King—and yet in the wry asides of Quixote's squire Sancho Panza, as in the patent incongruence of their adventures (think of the familiar phrase "tilting at windmills") lies a skeptical and covertly critical attitude toward the state.

This equivocal perspective operates through a profound identification with picaresque figures, who voice widely felt dissent and disillusionment.[20] Sometimes male and sometimes female, sometimes urban and sometimes rural, refracted images of this figure emerge over and over, reflecting a "mobile, fragmentary, and contradictory" interpretation of the world.[21] The loutish shepherd, upon the approach of Goliath in Diego Sánchez de Badajoz's *Farsa del Rey David* (1554), turns to the audience to exclaim "¡Que me çurro...Que me meo!" (I am going to soil myself...I am going to pee on myself!)[22] Such super-dialogic and sharp-witted commentary was founded on "techniques of hiding and multiplying meaning."[23] The country bumpkins, enslaved characters, and outlaws of Spain were "disqualified from agency within the context of dramatic illusion," musicologist Elisabeth Le Guin powerfully observes, but "metatheatrical disjuncture and the attendant *desilusión*" gave them the "special power of throwing that entire illusion into question."[24]

Bulla covers nonsense: utterances, such as the uninhibited and sexually triumphant *cucurucucu* (cock-a-doodle-doo) of the cock's crow, which we will track as denoting Blackness in Spanish literature. Such nonsense is euphemistic: its semantic force lies in what is left unsaid.[25] Throughout this book, I align euphemistic verbal utterances with the corporeal deviance of jumping and footwork, both being equivocal expressions of racialized confusion and sonorous nonsense. Such nonsense covers the blasphemous curse; the powerful, if violently repressed, voice of resistance.[26] That is, if bulla embodies the Blackness of not having "seen the light" of Christ, it also voices forceful critique of and resistance to the Christian state.

Critique and dissent play within the semantic distinctions between two words for "dance": *danza* and *baile*. There is class distinction in these terms, with "danza" referencing the upright composure of the aristocracy, and "baile" referencing, as in the example from *Quixote* above, the unfettered gambols and noisy dances of villagers, enslaved blacks, and ruffian antiheroes alike. The salient difference is between confusion and clarity: in a social hierarchy legislated by race, aristocrats were expected to adhere to elevated standards, not only of education and comportment, but also of morality. Danza references order, legitimacy, refinement. By the same token, the universe of the outlaw and the outcast was danced in terms of baile—occasionally dramatized by an enslaved galley servant dancing under the lash, or a thief dancing at the end of the hangman's rope.[27]

How is the politics of Blackness inscribed on the flamenco body? Let us imagine, as Spain so often does, the other side of the Atlantic. In the early United States, founded on human trafficking and bondage as well as aspirations to freedom, the Christian narrative of redemption echoes in the antics of bumbling, "simple-minded," "light-hearted" blackface clowns, whose performances of confusion and ineptitude are obviously contradicted by their acrobatic feats of patent strength, discipline, and control. This ephebic Black body was most valuable in a society existentially dependent on slave labor; yet in its uncanny power, its magical ambiguity, we sense also the sheer eruptive force of the blasphemous curse, the potential for wrath and rage that strikes terror into the heart of the white man. This is the Black body, performance theorist Saidiya Hartman argues, which is "represented most graphically as the body in pain."[28] Flamenco's ancestors, dancing at the end of a hangman's rope or singing *soledades*, the lamentations of the Virgin Mary, share this body of pain and sorrow, vibrating with an underlying wrathful curse.[29] In flamenco's promiscuous conjugation of human suffering with its flip side, the "light-hearted slave" who supposedly has no thought or desire for rebellion against his shackles, I read a Du Boisian doubled consciousness that critiques and exploits racist stereotypes at the same time. The acute politics of the antebellum United States represented the figure of "Jim Crow" as immutably broken, incapable of redemption or transformation. But we will see the Black bodies of nineteenth-century flamenco pull on an older, Spanish thread, of virtuosic body power and insolent intensity, defying the blackface trope of "Jim Crow's" broken body and propelling Spanish culture toward modernism.

La ida y la vuelta

Sonidos Negros is divided into two parts. The first, "Changing Places: Figuring Race and Empire in the Eighteenth-Century Fandango," considers in the broadest terms what flamencos often call the *ida*, the "going": the reinvention or creolization of peninsular culture in the colonial world. The two chapters in this section describe the narrative of redemption as enacted by the *pastor bobo* or foolish shepherd, along with the continuum of secular-sacred performance along which he travels to the Americas and through which, I will suggest, Africanist spirituality flows back into what will become flamenco. Part II, "A Modernist Becoming: The Power of Blackness," considers the *vuelta*, or return: the reintegration of Americanness within Spanish identity. This section is comprised of four chapters. Chapter 3, "Parody and Sorrow," considers "El Tío Caniyitas" (1849), a Spanish manifestation of North American blackface tropes, in light of *Uncle Tom's Cabin* (1852). Moving back in time and across the Atlantic, Chapter 4, "Nonsense of the Body," looks at "Mungo," "Harlequin Friday," and "Jim Crow": figures which I argue are brought into focus as refracted images of the pastor bobo. Chapter 5, "Tilting Across the Racial Divide," looks at the transatlantic politics of representation of black men, through the lens of the strange disappearance and momentous rediscovery of a black flamenco equestrian clown, Jacinto Padilla, "El Negro Meri." And Chapter 6, "*Jaleo de Jerez* and *Tumulte Noir*," looks at the representation of Blackness in flamenco women, through the lens of the international debut of a luminary of early flamenco dance, Juana Vargas "La Macarrona."

Chapter 1. Good Shepherd, Bumpkin Shepherd: Distinction in Villano *Gambetas* and *Zapatetas*

The narrative of the pastor bobo forms the spine of this book. In Christmas pageants across the Spanish Empire, this shepherd clown enacts the drama of redemption: *Will he see the light of Christ, or won't he?* In order to emerge from his perilous yet comic confusion, the bobo must recognize that Christ is born. His addle, danced with clumsy jumps and noisy footwork, figures his unredeemed state. His progress toward epiphany, or lack thereof, is correspondingly enacted through transformations in and elevation of his deviant speech and ostentatiously muddled body language. Notions of racial difference thus constructed the rituals of Christmas: the pastor bobo's gambols and noisy footwork were codes for being of dubious and therefore suspect ethno-religious origin.

The bobo's tragi-comic teetering between biblical "darkness" and "light," confusion and epiphany, is a central narrative in the colonization of the New World and the racial hierarchy by which it was governed. In liturgical performances throughout the Spanish Empire, this figure's struggle to comprehend Catholic doctrine provided both comic entertainment and recapitulation of the canonical message.[30]

There were two somewhat contradictory theoretical tendencies regarding race in early modern Spain: one which emphasized the importance of adjudicating purity of blood as equating to social status and power, and the other, deriving from the teachings of Paul the Apostle, emphasizing the inclusiveness of Christianity and the central importance of evangelization to the colonial project.[31] These views had points of disagreement, but, woven together, the subjugation of the Americas was accomplished through evangelization, and access to power was governed by raza and casta, indemnifying bloodline and familial proximity to European nobility.

The pastor bobo's danced equivocations, teetering between Heaven and Hell, were transposed into the representation of racialized Others throughout the Spanish Empire.[32] The bobo's clowning enacted the central story of evangelization: epiphany, the acceptance of Christianity, leads to redemption, and the supposed proffer of citizenship. And yet, at the same time the transformation that epiphany wrought in this character's body language dramatized the possibility of redemption, it figured the caste distinctions that stratified Spanish society. The unbridled ruckus of the bobo's stomps and gambols was distilled in aristocratic Spanish dance academies into virtuosic jumps as marks of distinction, refinement, and training—depictions of the bobo who had shaken off his confusion ratified blood purity, citizenship, and social status. Virtuosic representations of the bobo thus paradoxically enacted religious, political, and racial legitimacy—foreshadowing the eighteenth-century embrace of this figure as a symbol of national identity.

But the bobo's representation of confusion often became less a bridge to redemption than an expressive end in itself, opening a space for enacting the most profound imperatives of resistance to slavery and genocide. Cloaked in bulla, in comic confusion, performances of the bobo preserved the cultures and religions of home in mighty syncretism, defying and denying abjection, and asserting the ancestral lineages of those enslaved. The bobo's antics thus enact equivocal devilry, but also the pathos of diasporic sadness and terrifying violence—those who do not accept Christ are doomed to exile, bondage, extirpation, and immolation. As Dominican friar Bartolomé de las Casas wrote in his *Short Account of the Destruction of the Indies* (1542),

It came to this pass, that the Indians should be commanded on the penalty of a bloody War, Death, and perpetual Bondage, to embrace the Christian Faith, and submit to the Obedience of the Spanish King; as if the Son of God, who suffered Death for the Redemption of all Mankind, had enacted a Law, when he pronounced these words: 'Go and teach all Nations...'

Such Inhumanity and Cruelty...merits nothing but Scandal, Derision, nay Hell itself.[33]

Chapter 2. Concentric Circles of Theatricality: Pantomimic Dances from the Sacred to the Secular

During the Enlightenment, the long tradition of Spanish skepticism and *desilusión* might have swept the fallacies of "race" away along with the absolute monarchies of the *Ancien Régime*, but that did not happen. Gold, washed by enslaved Natives and Africans in the streams of the Antilles, gave way to sugar, cotton, tobacco, and rice plantations.[34] Despite continual and successful revolts and abolitionist movements rising across the Atlantic world, Spain, existentially dependent on the revenue generated by those enslaved in the Americas, never developed a relevant abolitionist ideology.[35] Quite the contrary. If on the Iberian Peninsula Blackness could, at least in some circumstances, be danced into Whiteness through the accomplishment of Christian redemption, in the colonies the governing system of racial castes and forced labor promised freedom and redemption to those enslaved only after they had been worked to death.[36] As made abundantly clear in the intricacies of racial taxonomy depicted in casta paintings of eighteenth-century México, such as *torna atras* (return backward), and *tenete en el aire*, (hold-yourself-suspended-in-midair), blood purity determined social status—once there was a drop of raza there was no going back, no crossing the line to Whiteness, or to limpieza de sangre.[37]

And yet there is a telling racial dissonance at the heart of eighteenth-century Spanish identity.[38] The Habsburg dynasty, which ruled an empire upon which "the sun never set," died out in 1700, leaving Louis XIV's grandson to inherit the Spanish throne. Spain's situation grew increasingly precarious, with French replacing Spanish mores as the epitome of aristocratic fashion in Madrid, while, in the colonies, fraying regard for the rule of civil and ecclesiastical law signaled the empire's decline. New syncretic American forms, *fandangos*, wafted eastward across the Atlantic on a current of licentious exoticism.[39] The fandango fascinates, because this once renegade and exotic dance craze came to represent the quintessence of nationalism, and resistance to the French, in Spain.

Majismo, an aristocratic vogue for emulating the fashions and dances of the urban underclass, adopted the fandango as a sign of autonomous national identity. But the fandango danced the ideas of "purity of blood" that undergirded the conquest of an empire in reverse. A dance party of outcasts and outlaws that soon found its way into the ballrooms and stages of the elite, the fandango became an emblem of Spanishness. Here is an incremental and almost imperceptible shift leading to a total reversal in the magnetic poles of power, desire, and codes of meaning. Claiming and legitimizing expansive and freewheeling "bastard" American forms, eighteenth-century Spain resisted the French and advocated for its own untainted national essence in the figure of a dark Other, a Native-African-American, whose Blackness was now wrapped within the figure of an "indigenous" racial Other: the imaginary Gitano. This appropriation ironically evokes the wealth and power of the Spanish Empire while simultaneously providing the representational vocabulary for Spain's radical demotion on the global stage.

In a further delicious twist, given that it emanated from the cultures of those decimated and enslaved by Spanish conquerors, the fandango was adopted throughout the Western world as a symbol of freedom and class mobility, a metaphor that, by the nineteenth century, inflected every aspect of the world's perception of Spain. With the gradual loss of its global hegemony, Spain was marginalized and exoticized as Gitano, Moorish, and, in a transitive operation, Black—with the full and immense weight of that term as we are investigating it here. Spain's identification with this figure, often described euphemistically as a proto-romantic "exoticization" or even "orientalization," is in fact a racialized downgrade.[40]

Chapter 3. Parody and Sorrow

El Tío Caniyitas (Uncle Caniyitas) by Mariano Soriano Fuertes (1849), records the Spanish response to U.S. blackface minstrelsy in terms of its indigenous southern (Andalusian) musics and representational tropes. The stage Gitano of the Spanish nineteenth-century was paradoxically an assertion of wealth, culture, and liberal democratic values—that is, of membership (despite the declining fortunes of the nation) in the economic and political structures of colonial power. As in the United States, this vessel for the "soul" of the nation, voicing sorrow and loss, precariousness, and nostalgia for past glory, was the embodiment of Blackness—a parody of self-as-Other, of power as powerlessness. Perhaps in absorbing the heated rhetoric of American blackface, and perhaps because it was already inherent in the very Spanish equivocations of "swimmers under the lash," developing flamenco seems to resonate with these deep and deeply violent contradictions.

Chapter 4. Nonsense of the Body

This chapter examines several blackface representations of men. "Mungo," from Irish playwright Isaac Bickerstaff's *The Padlock* (1768), is based on a character from Cervantes and therefore, being both Spanish and English, is thoroughly European. Yet Mungo is an early and influential comic blackface character on the U.S. stage, emblematic, I argue, of the presence of Spain within the imaginary of elite European culture that is foundational to American aspirations to national identity.

"Harlequin Friday," from Richard Brinsley Sheridan's *Robinson Crusoe, or Harlequin Friday* (1781) adopts another European character, Harlequin, an astute servant performed in a black mask in early modern Italy's *commedia dell'arte*, but now become, in the words of performance theorist Elizabeth Maddock Dillon, "racially black"—performed in blackface.[41] Harlequin Friday is a fascinating mestizaje: his Friday aspect derives from the black Native character, an iteration of the "light-hearted slave" who welcomes colonization and enslavement, from Daniel Defoe's influential shipwreck novel, *Robinson Crusoe* (1719). But, although a blackface character, Harlequin Friday also has an aspect of Italian Harlequin, a comic country bumpkin like the Spanish bobo who is known, like the bobo, both for his rustic jumps and for his acerbic critiques of the powerful. Despite the fact that Italian Harlequin is secular while the Spanish bobo is at bottom a liturgical figure, the narrative these characters share is their essential ability to *become*: the bobo can be redeemed by accepting Christ, while, especially as reinterpreted in the eighteenth-century British harlequinades from which Harlequin Friday emerges, Harlequin is a consummately mutable character, magic in his transformational abilities. In line with the Enlightenment's egalitarianism, assessing social standing on merit and not birth, Harlequin enacts a drama of humanist individuation and self-actualization—despite the fact that he is a black character and his beloved Columbine is white. The narrative of Harlequin Friday, that a black character can magically recreate himself and thus win the hand of his white sweetheart, was an absurdity, an impossibility, in the racist societies of the eighteenth century. And yet the skeleton of this narrative, the possibility of redemption and transformation, is essential to eighteenth-century aspirations. To use Toni Morrison's argument, in Harlequin Friday we see a Black figure as a "surrogate self," figuring the United States' aspirations to freedom, autonomy, and to establishing itself as an equal to European nations. The deep question raised by Harlequin Friday, and by the Spanish bobo—whether Blackness can be redeemed—is answered with the body: able to take flight and thus transcend the limitations imposed by racism.

Harlequin Friday contrasts starkly with the final blackface character considered in this series: "Jim Crow," made famous by Thomas Dartmouth Rice in the early 1830s. In Rice's act, "Jump Jim Crow," the character is an enslaved man who is, above all, broken: "deformed" in body and crippled in spirit. There is no need to posit a direct line between the Spanish bobo, with his narrative of redemption, and "Jim Crow" of the 1830s United States in order to interrogate the genealogical relationships between European representations of Blackness and "Jim Crow." The bobo and Harlequin were both animated by the possibility of redemption and transformation which founded the colonial Americas. If redemption is not possible, if you can't convert Africans to Christianity and thus save their souls (and the same holds true, as Bartolomé de Las Casas decries above, for American First Peoples), then there is no justification for slavery—the entire colonial system falls apart.

But "Jim Crow" is permanently broken: the mid-nineteenth-century United States, on the brink of civil war, could admit nothing less. In the antebellum United States the white planter elite urgently sought to preserve slavery in the South and slave commerce with the North, and to expand slavery in the West—blackface minstrelsy did not merely play a part in these racial politics, writes social historian Eric Lott: "It *was* the racial politics of its time."[42] "Jim Crow's" body, as demanded by white slave society, was deformed and broken: he was an existentially "happy slave."[43]

But if "Jim Crow" is "light-heartedly" unconcerned with the ravages of violence his body displays, in his jumps (which, we recall, enact the accomplishment of redemption in early modern Spain), we also perceive a body full of power, ready for speed, ready to, in the words of Ta-Nehisi Coates, "achieve the velocity of escape."[44] In "Jim Crow," the essential narrative undergirding Spanish ideas about race—that, despite an "impure bloodline," there exists the possibility of redemption through Christ—was stripped away in favor of the racist ideology that leaves this character immutably broken. If "Jim Crow" can trace his lineage to these European notions of Blackness, how was the culture from which this character issued transformed by two hundred years of breeding human beings as if they were animals, a dehumanization and a fear so deep that it cancels or overrides Christian fears of Judgment?[45] Slavery's untenable dilemma is manifest in "Jim Crow's" broken body—as Saidiya Hartman determines, the exercise of power is inseparable from its display.[46]

Chapter 5. Tilting across the Racial Divide: Jacinto Padilla, "El Negro Meri," and the Flamenco Clown

Flamenco came into being as a performance genre in the mid-nineteenth century, spurred by an intense desire on the part of Spain's cultural and political elite to defend their status as European—precisely by asserting Spain's unique national identity, as personified by its last remaining Other (Moorish, Jewish, and Afro-descended Spaniards having long since "disappeared"): the Gitano.[47] Andalusian Gitanophilia, like the majismo out of which it developed, simultaneously appropriated and distanced itself (with a wink) from the persona of its fascinating alter-ego. Like the wave of romantic bohemianism then spreading across Europe, Spanish Gitanophilia paradoxically asserted the nation's preeminence within the structures of colonial power.[48] Thus, Spanish dancers pretending to be Gypsies on European ballet stages and performing dances such as the (Afro-Cuban) *tango* in Madrid "distilled" American dances of "delicious and lascivious" ancestry and, as Serafín Estébanez Calderón, one of the first flamenco chroniclers, wrote in 1847, dressed them "in Andalusian style."[49]

Yet in addition to their aspirations toward elite culture, nineteenth-century stagings of Spanish identity also absorbed the popular tropes of the equestrian circus, the tightrope daredevil, the Gitano exotic, and U.S. blackface minstrelsy. Spaniards easily apprehended "Jim Crow" and his ilk in terms of the pastor bobo. In fact, the bobo's narrative of transcendence and, we might even say, emancipation, weaves through the moving story of Jacinto Padilla, "El Negro Meri," a black man, long forgotten and erased from flamenco history.[50] In the first film of a flamenco *cuadro* (performing ensemble), recorded at the 1900 Paris Exposition Universelle by the Lumière brothers, Padilla, a well-known flamenco artist of the day, dances and sings. Padilla seems to have followed his father, a circus performer who was possibly born enslaved in Cuba, in a long and colorful career as equestrian acrobat, bullfighter, and flamenco performer. He invented and reinvented himself numerous times, bequeathing an important legacy not only to flamenco song, but also to dance: his virtuosic, acrobatic jumps in the 1900 film convey a body power highly prized in flamenco—a signature, for example, of the dynasty founded by Antonio Montoya Flores, "El Farruco" (1935–97).

The Spanish representations that become flamenco in the mid-nineteenth century encode Blackness: lasciviousness, confusion, and covert dissent. And yet, tracing the comic chaos of the Spanish bobo and the Italian Harlequin through the blackface character "Jim Crow" and into Jacinto Padilla's persona as "El Negro Meri," we note that Meri, in his magical body power, reclaims the right to *become*. In Jacinto Padilla, "El Negro Meri," an acrobat on a tightrope between European and American ghettoes of fictitious Blackness, we sense the veiled problematization of stereotype (what Houston Baker calls the "deformation of mastery"): the virtuosic body power, agency, and kinesthetic intensity that defied the blackface trope of the broken body and ironically propelled European culture toward a complicated modernism.[51]

Chapter 6. Jaleo de Jerez and Tumulte Noir: Juana Vargas "La Macarrona" at the Exposition Universelle, Paris, 1889

Juana Vargas "La Macarrona" (1870–1947) was one of the greatest flamenco dancers of all time. Yet audience response to her international debut at the 1889 Paris Exposition Universelle was fraught with competing concepts of what flamenco dance should be, with "distilled" French articulations of Spanishness vying for audience share with "authentic" performance. At the end of the Exposition Macarrona returned to an illustrious career in Spain, but she entered the French imagination as a profoundly sexualized figure: burlesque impersonations of her flourished in France for at least another decade.

The radical disjuncture between the reception of Macarrona's dance at the 1889 fair and her place in flamenco's pantheon today reveals much about the role played by race in the transition from romanticism to modernism—and Spain's part, as toggle, in this evolution. A generation before the Argentinian tango craze hit Europe, Macarrona's dances at the exposition were titled to emphasize their tango, or Afro-Cuban air. The reference was to nineteenth-century *tangos de negros* (black tangos), also called *tangos americanos* (Afro-American tangos), adapted and assimilated by Roma performers as *tangos gitanos* (Gitano tangos). The 1889 exposition was a theater in which European audiences could, as Spanish novelist and essayist Emilia Pardo Bazán put it, "penetrate the soul" of "the exotic element."[52] The strange and "natural" flamenco danced by Macarrona and *Les Gitanas de Granade* at the Grand Théâtre de l'Exposition was a landmark on the path to the progressive "Gypsification" of flamenco. Yet what a Spanish critic called the "bestial tangos of the Gitanos at the Exhibition" incorporated cosmopolitan references to the *can-can*, to Fanny Elssler's *Cachucha* and, in what French critics called Macarrona's "*déhanchements* (squirming, wiggling, lopsided or swaying walk) full of promise," to centuries of representations of Blackness in Spanish dance.[53]

In Macarrona's reception at the 1889 Paris exposition we see the conundrums of race being negotiated with the Gitana as an intermediary figure. As had been true from the first entry of the Roma into Spain in the early-fifteenth century, at the turn of the twentieth century, central to the conception of these "swarthy" people was their outlaw status, their defiance of social norms, and "their uneffaced suggestion of wildness, of freedom."[54] The Gitana casts her audacious glance backward to Spain and forward into the international arena, simultaneously representing Spain's Blackness and its Whiteness. The many Macarrona impersonations, not only in French burlesque but, as flamenco became a globalized art form, by deeply respectful and knowledgeable practitioners all over the world, reveal the "desire to become," the ability and the privilege to dream of a modern life, of autonomy, of freedom, as North American poet Walt Whitman writes, "immense in passion, pulse, and power."[55] As Pardo Bazán said, "Let us...believe in the authenticity of much of the exotic element," for what it reveals of "the enormity of beginning."[56]

A Body of Knowledge

José Luis Navarro García's *Semillas de ébano: El elemento negro y afroamericano en el baile flamenco* (1998), and Robert Farris Thompson's *Tango: The Art History of Love* (2005), provided the inspiration and impetus for this book. Reading descriptions of the fandango as "lascivious" (cited by Navarro from eighteenth-century sources), I wondered, *What movement are they describing?*

And then I realized, in repeated descriptions of erotic chases, that these sources were describing the ubiquitous flamenco step of changing places, the *pasada*. And that made we wonder, *Why, or how, is the pasada a sign of Blackness?*

I hope the answers will surprise you.

I wrote my doctoral dissertation under Brenda Dixon Gottschild. She was writing *Digging the Africanist Presence in American Performance* (1996) as I was reading Carmen Amaya, the first Roma performer to gain international renown, through the lens of Houston Baker Jr.'s *Modernism and the Harlem Renaissance* (1986). I have long felt that the tools invented by theorists of the Black experience are immensely useful in cracking the carapace of flamenco's weird stereotype—considering that it performs Spain's oh-so-*mestizo* Other—as Spanish in the sense of White. I garner courage to assert flamenco's relevance as a paradigm of Blackness from thinkers such as W. E. B. Du Bois (*The Souls of Black Folk*, 1903), Frantz Fanon (*Black Skin, White Masks*, 1967), Robert Farris Thompson (*Flash of the Spirit: African and Afro-American Art and Philosophy*, 1984), Toni Morrison (*Playing in the Dark: Whiteness and the Literary Imagination*, 1992), Paul Gilroy (*The Black Atlantic: Modernity and Double Consciousness*, 1993), Eric Lott (*Love and Theft: Blackface Minstrelsy and the American Working Class*, 1993), Saidiya Hartman (*Scenes of Subjection: Terror, Slavery, and Self-Making in Nineteenth-Century America*, 1997), Fred Moten, (*In the Break: The Aesthetics of the Black Radical Tradition*, 2003), Jayna Brown (*Babylon Girls: Black Women Performers and the Shaping of the Modern*, 2008), and Stefano Harney and Fred Moten (*The Undercommons: Fugitive Planning and Black Study*, 2013). I think these writers help us understand flamenco's pain, flamenco's soul—flamenco's power, through the experience of Blackness.

Attention to our Africanist cultural legacy evokes a painful need to face the racism that constructs and sustains our society; addressing these questions is inevitably and profoundly difficult. As flamenco scholars grapple with questions of identity raised by a relatively recent recognition of flamenco's African and Afro-American lineage, they sometimes dismiss and displace flamenco's Blackness. That is, there is a tendency in current flamenco scholarship to foreground flamenco's complicated mestizaje through the attempted erasure of Roma people, whose image is as central to flamenco as that of African Americans to jazz, rock 'n' roll, or hip-hop, and whose artists are of comparable importance to the form.

Critical race theorists writing on Blackness have long contended with this misconception by considering the image and the people separately and in dialogic relation. Du Bois describes black alienation as "double-consciousness," "a sense of always looking at one's self through the eyes of others," a feeling of "two-ness."[57] Fanon writes that "the white gaze" is "solely negating"—the image of one's body, for a person of color, is "an image in the third person."[58] Ralph Ellison is best known for *Invisible Man* (1952), a novel premised on this situation.[59] But Ellison later wrote "Change the Joke and Slip the Yoke" (1958), in which he addresses the "human ambiguities" behind the "ritual mask" that conforms our "national iconography" of Blackness, delineating a strategic "jiujitsu of the spirit, a denial and rejection through agreement."[60] Houston Baker develops this concept, exploring the liberating possibilities of such double-consciousness, such twoness or equivocation of artistic form, as "both a metadiscourse on linguistic investiture" and a lesson in "metaphorical 'worm holing.'"[61] Black performers like Bert Williams and George Walker, who, along with Ada Overton Walker, set new flamenco forms into motion when they brought the cakewalk across the Atlantic in 1897, converted "nonsense sounds and awkwardly demeaning minstrel steps into pure kinesthetics and masterful black artistry": a "mastery of form," writes Baker, which "conceals, disguises, floats like a trickster butterfly in order to sting like a bee." The flip side of "mastery of form," Baker continues, is "deformation of mastery," which has the magical ability to "transform an obscene situation, a cursed and tripled metastatus, into a signal self/cultural expression. The birth of such a self is…always, also, a release from BEING POSSESSED." The instantiation of modernist becoming, as Morrison describes, thus happens within black subjectivity. Performance theorist and poet Fred Moten writes, "Alienation and distance represent the critical possibility of freedom."[62] He quotes Edouard Glissant:

> Since speech was forbidden, slaves camouflaged the word under the provoca-
> tive intensity of the scream. It was taken to be nothing but the call of a wild
> animal. This is how the dispossessed man organized his speech by weaving it
> into the apparently meaningless texture of extreme noise.[63]

Jayna Brown adds that the "double consciousness" of people forced to view themselves "as if from the eyes of others" is a "salient place from which to intervene on this critical absence":[64]

> The artist's talent was her agile ability to navigate between and manipulate
> discursive terrains. Engaged in multiple directional strategies of perception,
> working within the hall of mirrors…As she is gazed upon, she also gazes
> back, and it is her body that questions.

Flamenco theorists who seek to erase the Roma people along with the Gitano stereotype strip from the flamenco body this ability to question. For example, in his 2008 *Guía comentada de música y baile preflamencos (1750–1808)*, Faustino Núñez acknowledges that flamenco is *música agitanada* (Gitano-styled music), but simultaneously denies that Gitanos constitute an ethnic group at all. He asserts instead that the "Gitanos" figured in these works were not Zincali, or Spanish Roma, but rather a category of "all the people of color that populated and populate Spain and that ended by calling themselves Gitano, grouping under this denomination the thousand dark-skinned races which populated the peninsula for centuries."[65] Núñez here follows Gerhard Steingress, who states in his *Sociología del cante flamenco* (1991):

> Clearly the existence of a "Gitano race" was a fiction of the eighteenth century: "to be Gitano" meant, more than belonging to one ethnicity among many, to belong to the lowest and most despised classes of Andalusian society. The decisive element in the situation of the Gitanos was not their "race" but their social position. After centuries of permanent assimilation, the Gitanos had lost many of their ethnic characteristics, becoming Andalusians. To "be Gitano" came to be a sign of individual characteristics of certain Andalusians, reinforced perhaps by family or neighborhood, and that little by little would lead to a "popular" way of being integrated by flamenco aficionados into the "exotic world of the Gitano."[66]

Steingress is a brilliant and seminal thinker on flamenco, for whom I have the utmost respect (as I do for Faustino Núñez). He is correct in pointing out the multiethnic character of Spain's marginalized classes. Numerous scholars, such as Reynaldo Fernández Manzano in *De las melodías del reino nazarí de Granada a las estructuras musicales cristianas* (1985), Christian Poché in *La Música Arábigo-Andaluza* (1997), and Cristina Cruces Roldán in *El flamenco y la música andalusí* (2003), have established that, despite the expulsion of Jews and Muslims in 1492, and of Moriscos in 1609, the lineages of Muslim and Jewish people and cultures persisted in Spain. In addition, despite the gradual decline in Afro-Spanish populations, Isidoro Moreno Navarro's essential study on *La antigua hermandad de los negros de Sevilla* (1997), along with Jesús Cosano Prieto's *Los invisibles. Hechos y cosas de los negros de Sevilla* (2017) document that the descendants of enslaved Ibero-Africans never "disappeared" either.[67]

The practice of enslavement in Spain, Antonio Domínguez Ortiz explains in *La esclavitud en Castilla en la Edad Moderna y otros estudios de marginados* (1952), encouraged the polyglot nature of the Spanish underclass. It was fairly common in Spain for an enslaved person to *ahorrar* (save money) to buy their freedom.[68] This "savings" accrued principally to slave owners: those enslaved in Spain often did not live with their masters, but instead lived in poor neighborhoods and were hired out as laborers.[69] Most of those who had purchased their freedom continued to labor in the homes of their former owners, and thus, if a former slave became unable to work, the former master was free and clear of any financial obligations.[70] "Enfranchisement was not a step toward economic and social betterment," explains Ruth Pike in *Sevillian Society in the 16th Century* (1972), for "ex-slaves continued to work in unskilled and menial jobs and to reside in the same neighborhoods as before their emancipation."[71]

Alfonso Franco Silva explains, in *La esclavidud en Andalucía, 1450–1550* (1992), that manumitted slaves frequently dedicated themselves to drinking, brawling, and robbery, swelling the tissues of the violent urban underbelly.[72] Marginal neighborhoods such as Triana, on Sevilla's Guadalquivir River (and, later, Madrid's Lavapiés), were, Cervantes writes in "El coloquio de los perros" (1613), refuges for outcasts and ruffians—cosmopolitan neighborhoods of black Spaniards, Spanish Roma, Moors, and Moriscos. Natalie Vodovozova's *Contribution to the History of the Villancico de Negros* (1996), culling detail from song texts, adds that some who lived in these neighborhoods were enslaved and some free, and that they made their living as muleteers and slaughterhouse workers, thieves, and sailors.[73] In *Libro de la gitaneria de Triana de los años 1740 a 1750*, "El Bachiller Revoltoso" describes a black constable married to a Roma woman; as Eduardo Molina Fajardo has suggested in *El flamenco en Granada: Teoría de sus orígenes e historia* (1974) with regard to Morisco populations, it certainly seems plausible that, through intermarriage and ethnic alliances, some black Spaniards found refuge in Roma communities.[74]

Richard Pym in *The Gypsies of Early Modern Spain* (2007) and Antonio Zoido Naranjo, in *La Ilustración contra los gitanos* (2009), document how, already by the early seventeenth century, Spanish Roma, many of whom refused to abandon their peripatetic ways, were widely seen not as an ethnic group but rather as a criminal class of thieves and bandits, outlaws and beggars. Roma dissention and ruffianism loomed large in the seventeenth-century Spanish imagination, epitomizing "the acute crisis of confidence that had by now begun to affect important sections of the nation's intellectual and religious élite" as, Pym writes, "after a series of debilitating setbacks," the Spanish Empire had, "it was feared, at last begun to falter."[75]

Steingress's analysis of the agglomeration of Spain's multi-ethnic underclasses within the image of the "Gitano" is thus correct, and essential to a complicated view of the mestizo image of the Gitano as holding Spain's Blackness. But the literature, not to mention the racist nationalism increasingly targeting Roma populations all over Europe, makes it overwhelmingly clear that Gitanos are not and have never been "assimilated."[76] In conflating class with ethnicity, in conflating the hegemonic view of race, whose objective is to create "slaves" in order to fuel colonial expansion, with the internal experience of identity and belonging, Steingress's influential argument slips into the position of denying Roma subjectivity—denying Roma people the right to define themselves as they so choose.

The argument that Gitanos are not an ethnic group but rather a class sounds tone deaf—and terrifyingly close to the language used in many royal edicts persecuting the Spanish Roma. There is, for example, the edict of 1619, forbidding Gitanos to call themselves such, or to use their own style of dress or their own Sanskrit-based language "in order that, forasmuch as they are not such by nation, this name and manner of life may be for evermore confounded and forgotten."[77] This edict articulates an essentially economic argument, which must be considered in light of competition for audience share even today.[78] In 2008, the Andalusian Provincial Government pushed back against renowned singer Antonio Mairena's long dominant theory that flamenco authenticity is closely held in the hearths of a few Andalusian Roma artistic dynasties, claiming flamenco instead as a Product of Cultural Interest (Bien de Interés Cultural, or BIC), an Andalusian patrimony regulated by the public administration that imposes a sort of "denomination of origin" label. Yet as of this writing the Spanish Constitution neither recognizes nor defines ethnic minorities such as the Spanish Roma.[79]

More nuanced conceptions of flamenco are slowly emerging. Queer flamenco artists and scholars are celebrating their diversity; flamenco's once rigid gender norms are becoming more fluid.[80] And Roma flamenco scholars are emerging, such as Gonzalo Montaño Peña, a member of the illustrious Peña lineage, Romani rights activist, musicologist, and curator of the interdisciplinary section on flamenco in *RomArchive, The Digital Archive of the Roma*.[81]

Alongside José Luis Navarro García (*Semillas de ébano*) and Jesús Cosano Prieto, (*Los invisibles*) the research of several other notable artists and scholars challenges the false oppositions between Blackness, Romaness, and Andalusianness within flamenco. Cosano Prieto's long-standing interest in these topics has inspired both Santiago Auserón (*El ritmo perdido: Sobre el influjo negro en la canción española*, 2012) and Raúl Rodríguez (*Razón de son: Antropomúsica creativa de los cantes de ida y vuelta*, 2014) to produce both performative and theoretical work. Steingress, José Luis Ortiz Nuevo and Faustino Núñez in *La rabia del placer: El nacimiento cubano del tango y su desembarco en España (1823–1923)* (1999), Cristina Cruces Roldán, in *Antropología y flamenco* (2003), Antonio Mandly Robles, in *Los caminos del flamenco: Etnografía, cultura y comunicación en Andalucía* (2010), and José Luis Ortiz Nuevo, in *Tremendo asombro* (2012), have applied what Fernando Ortiz, in *Contrapunteo cubano del tabaco y el azúcar* (1940), terms a transcultural approach to historiographical, musicological, sociological, and anthropological work. Historian Aurelia Martín Casares, in *La esclavitud en la Granada del siglo XVI: género, raza y religion* (2000), has broadened and deepened the historiography of enslavement in Spain, especially through her seminal research on enslaved women.

Performing artists who have broken the color barrier in Spain include Brazilian percussionist Rubem Dantas, whose groundbreaking work with guitarist Paco de Lucia in the 1970s introduced a variety of percussion instruments to flamenco, singer Concha Buika, from Palma de Mallorca, who melds flamenco, *cuplé* (torch songs), and jazz, Sevillano Raúl Rodriguez, who introduced the Cuban *tres* to flamenco, and British dancer Nicolia Morris, who performed in the Bienal de Sevilla in 2000 and 2004. Flamenco Latino, a New York-based company directed by Basilio Georges and Aurora Reyes, has been exploring the danced and musical intersections of flamenco and Afro-Latin forms for decades. Jani Rodrigues studied and performed in Sevilla for several years. Esther Weekes, based in Sevilla, is working between flamenco and jazz, and is touring a new exploration of Afro-Latin rhythm, *Cajones*, in Costa Rica. Agnes Kamya founded the Uganda Flamenco Project in 2014. Kevin LaMarr Jones directs Claves Unidos, which includes flamenco in its pan-diasporic dance explorations, and Aliesha Bryan won the 2016 flamenco Certamen in New York. Danish-Kenyan Phyllis Akinyi Olwande, based in Madrid, is exploring AfroFlamenco in performance and teaching practice.. Yinka Esi Graves is producing new work with Asha Thomas and Mbulelo Ndabeni and made her New York debut in 2017. Nora Chipaumire writes that Graves manifests the body as a site for urgent questions about the "burden of blackness" and how the body can be a "weaponized agent" challenging the racist economy.[82] Graves is featured in Miguel Ángel Rosales's documentary *Gurumbé: Canciones de tu memoria negra* (2016), a revelatory contribution to the contemporary discourse on race in Spain today. With all of this important shifting, extending, and pushing of flamenco performance in diaspora, is the very centrality of Spain as arbiter of authenticity and central cultural referent in question?

Researching this book has entailed a huge labor of synthesis, and I hope that its compilation of Spanish and English resources will be useful. I have drawn from many disciplines and have consulted a great number of primary sources. The literature of the *Siglo de Oro*, Spain's Golden Age, contains rich documentation for dance. For example, I reference Cervantes's *Don Quixote*, and several of his *Novelas ejemplares* (1613): *La gitanilla*, *La ilustre fregona*, *El celoso extremeño*, and *El coloquio de los perros*. Early dictionaries, such as Sebastián de Covarrubias Orozco's *Tesoro de la Lengua Castellana o Española* (1611) and *Diccionario de la lengua castellana* from the Real Academia Española (1726–39), describe the socio-religious dimensions of meaning within words such as *çapato* (*zapato*, or shoe), which are fundamental to my gloss of noisy footwork within the narrative of the pastor bobo. Rodrigo Caro's *Dias geniales ó Lúdicros* (ca. 1626), a book on folk customs and childrens' games, and Luis Vélez de Guevara's novel *El diablo cojuelo* (1641) helped me understand the subtle distinctions operating within racialized perceptions of dance, and particularly of jumping, during this period.

I have consulted a number of dance manuals, including *Escuela por lo vajo de Domingo González* (ca. 1650) whose *Villano Caballero por lo Vaxo*, the pastor bobo's dance done in a gentlemanly style, contains the jumped kick to the hat which is this character's emblematic gesture. Pablo Minguet é Irol's *Explicacion del Danzar a la Española* (1764) gives a villano choreography. Juan Antonio Jaque, *Libro de danzar de Don Baltasar de Rojas Pantoja* (ca. 1680) also contains a villano, although his choreography does not include the kick to the hat. Rodrigo Noveli's *Chorégraphie figurativa y demostrativa del arte de danzar en la forma española* (1708) and Bartolomé Ferriol y

Boxeraus, *Reglas útiles para los aficionados a danzar* (1745) document the *paso del amolador* (the knife-grinder's move), a suggestive pantomime performed, in Noveli, in shackles. Felipe Roxo de Flores's *Tratado de recreacion instructiva sobre la danza: su invencion y diferencias* (1793) sees both jumping and footwork, previously distinguished from each other (virtuosic jumps in the villano figuring as a distinguishing mark of aristocracy and perhaps racial purity), as essential to Spanish dance training, an indication of Spain's identification of the bobo as national symbol. I have used two sources from bolero dancer Antonio Cairón: *El encuentro feliz o Los americanos o La espada del mago* (1818) on the tango americano, and *Compendio de las principales reglas del baile* (1820) on fandango, *guaracha*, and zapateado. José Otero Aranda's *Tratado de Bailes de Sociedad* (1912) discusses tangos, *farruca*, *garrotín*, and zapateado in opposition to classically-oriented jumps and beats; Otero is central to my understanding of flamenco's response to the cakewalk in early-twentieth-century Spain, and his discussion of *panaderos* links the Africanist *vacunao* (vaccination), a flirtatious dance of sexual pursuit, with classical Spanish dance.

Luis Misón's *Tonadilla de los negros* (1761) describes Spain's emerging image of the hybrid Native-American-Afro-Gitano, danced in terms of footwork, which I argue incarnates Spanish identity in resistance to the French. *El Tío Caniyitas o El Mundo nuevo de Cádiz*, by Mariano Soriano Fuertes (1849), shows the accommodation of nineteenth-century Spanish theatricals to the influence of U.S. blackface minstrelsy in Spanish terms of Blackness.

I have cited a number of travel accounts, ranging from Marie Catherine Le Jumel de Barneville d'Aulnoy, who, in *The Ingenious and Diverting Letters of the Lady's—Travels into Spain* (1692), describes Gitanos singing in a tavern, to Jean-Charles Davillier, who toured Spain with illustrator Gustave Doré in 1862, and gives significant detail about the circus bullfights in which El Negro Meri performed. Gustavo Adolfo Bécquer, in "La Feria de Sevilla" (1869) and Emmanuel Chabrier, who visited Spain in 1882, articulate the Romantic image of the Gitano. In contrast, Emilia Pardo Bazán's chronicle of flamenco at the Exposition Universelle in 1889 Paris reveals how problematic flamenco was for the Spanish intelligentsia by the turn of the twentieth century.

Casiano Pellicer's *Tratado histórico sobre el origen y progresos de la comedia y del histrionismo en España* (1804) shows how Spain conceived its history at the dawn of the nineteenth-century. Emilio Cotarelo y Mori is one of the most prolific and foundational historians of Spanish theater; I reference six of his books here, most often citing his two-volume *Colección de Entremeses, Loas, Bailes, Jácaras y Mojigangas desde fines del siglo XVI à mediados del XVIII* (1911), an encyclopedia of early modern dances, a compilation of short theatrical pieces, and an invaluable historical analysis of these genres. Fernando Ortiz is the founder of Afro-Cuban musicology. His *Glosario de afronegrismos* (1924) and *Los instrumentos de la música afrocubana* (1952) illuminate the diasporic ramifications of zapateado and thus help make the connection between the Spanish bobo's ruckus and the vacunao's flirtatious chases in the New World.

I have relied where possible on English-language studies of Spanish sources, such as Robert Stevenson's "The Afro-American Musical Legacy to 1800" (1968), Maurice Esses's *Dance and Instrumental Diferencias in Spain during the 17th and Early 18th centuries* (1992), and Craig Russell's *Santiago de Murcia's Códice Saldívar No. 4: A Treasury of Secular Guitar Music from Baroque Mexico* (1995). Especially useful in my research has been the work of Lynn Matluck Brooks. *The Dances of the Processions of Seville in Spain's Golden Age* (1988) and *John Durang: Man of the American Stage* (2011) are important resources for understanding the disparate dance worlds of early modern Sevilla and the early United States, which I draw together here. *The Art of Dancing in Seventeenth-Century Spain: Juan de Esquivel Navarro and His World* (2003), Brooks's indispensable translation and commentary on a 1642 dance treatise, is the source for all translations from Esquivel here.

When I met Elisabeth Le Guin, I laughingly showed her my dog-eared copy of *The Tonadilla in Performance: Lyric Comedy in Enlightenment Spain* (2014), a porcupine of sticky notes, thick with underlining and emotional comments in the margins. Her theorization of this very complex historical moment is fundamental to my work.

My first inkling of the pastor bobo came from a conference presentation by Hispanist Benjamin Liu on Serranillas, medieval poetry of the borderland between Christian and Muslim Spain.[83] Liu's *Medieval Joke Poetry: The Cantigas d'Escarnho e de Mal Dizer* (2004) is an elegant analysis of the blasphemy, sly dissent, and racial equivocation cloaked in flamenco's literary ancestors. Javier Irigoyen García, in *The Spanish Arcadia: Sheep Herding, Pastoral Discourse, and Ethnicity in Early Modern Spain* (2014), undertakes a deep exegesis of the shepherd and sheep herding as central symbols in the ideation of blood purity, race, and national identity in Spain, allowing me to understand the villano's racial implications. Bronwen Jean Heuer's *The Discourse of the Ruffian in Quevedo's "Jácaras"* (1991) provided a further and essential link, between the pantomimic representations of profoundly religious and tragic themes, such as the *soledad* (solitude) of the Virgin, and the danced dissent, also pantomimic, of ruffian antiheroes in early modern Spain. I argue that the tradition of secular-religious danced pantomime, dating from at least the fifteenth century and still so essential in flamenco, conditions Spain's absorption of secular-sacred Africanist sexual pantomime. On the meaning and manifestations of the diasporic vacunao, I have consulted Maya Deren's *Divine Horsemen: The Living Gods of Haiti* (1983) and Yvonne Daniel's *Rumba: Dance and Social Change in Contemporary Cuba* (1995), and *Caribbean and Atlantic Diaspora Dance: Igniting Citizenship* (2011).

Charlotte Stern's "Fray Iñigo de Mendoza and Medieval Dramatic Ritual" (1965) and "The Coplas de Mingo Revulgo and the Early Spanish Drama" (1976), Juan José Rey's *Danzas cantadas del Renacimiento Español* (1978), and José María Díez Borque's "Liturgia-fiesta-teatro: órbitas concéntricas de teatralidad en el siglo XVI" (1987) clarify two essential aspects of Spanish dance: its interwoven origins in secular and liturgical performance, and the importance of danced pantomime in both contexts. Miguel Querol Gavaldá's *La música en la obra de Cervantes* (1948) is an important source on the villano. James Parakilas, in his "How Spain Got a Soul" (1998), posits Spain's "radical demotion" from world conqueror to tourist destination, which helped me grasp the complicated Spanish eighteenth century. Manuel Alvar's *Villancicos dieciochescos (la colección malagueña de 1734 a 1770)* (1973), and Danièle Becker's "El teatro lírico en tiempo de Carlos II: Comedia de música y zarzuela" (1989), contextualize the performance of dissent, in sung and danced pantomime, in popular settings such as Christmas festivities. Horacio Becco, in *El tema del negro en cantos: bailes y villancicos de los siglos XVI y XVII* (1951), Natalie Vodovozova's *A Contribution to the History of the Villancico de Negros* (1996), and Glenn Swiadon Martínez's *Los villancicos de negro en el siglo XVII* (2000) describe the representations of race in these Christmas festivities. Gabriel Saldívar, in *Historia de la música en México* (1934), Georges Baudot and M. Águeda Méndez, in *Amores prohibidos: la palabra condenada en el México de los virreyes: Antología de coplas y versos censurados por la inquisición de México* (1997), and Elena Deanda-Camacho, in " 'El chuchumbé te he de soplar:' Sobre obscenidad, censura y memoria oral en el primer 'son de la tierra' novohispano" (2007) trace the racialized and overtly political obscene pantomimes of American dances such as *cumbé*, *guaracha*, and *panaderos*, which would find their way onto Spanish stages. Rolando Antonio Pérez Fernández's *La binarización de los ritmos ternarios africanos en América Latina* (1986) and *La música afromestiza mexicana* (1990), and Antonio García de León Griego's *El mar de los deseos: el Caribe hispano musical historia y contrapunto* (2002) and *Fandango* (2006) provide theoretical, musicological, and historical context to such circulations.

On flamenco, Juan de la Plata's "Esclavos, moriscos, y gitanos: La etapa hermética del flamenco" (1990), and Luis Suárez Ávila's "Jaleos, Gilianas, versus Bulerías" (2004) planted the seeds for theorizing the Blackness of *bulla*, or ruckus, which runs throughout this book. Luis Lavaur, in *Teoría romántica del cante flamenco* (1976), and Alberto del Campo Tejedor and Rafael Cáceres Feria, in *Historia cultural del flamenco (1546–1910): El barbero y la guitarra* (2013) theorize nineteenth-century Gitanophilia in useful and nuanced ways. Daniel Pineda Novo's *Juana, "La Macarrona" y el baile en los cafés cantantes* (1996), *Silverio Franconetti: Noticias inéditas* (2000), and *Antonio Ramírez, el baile Gitano de Jerez* (2005) provide Macarrona's essential biography.

On El Negro Meri, I have referenced Kiko Mora's published research, "¡Y dale con Otero!...Flamencos en la Exposición Universal de París de 1900" (2016), and "Who Is Who in the Lumière Films of Spanish Song and Dance at the Paris Exposition, 1900" (2017), as well as a treasure trove of unpublished research which he has generously shared. Mora's identification of this Afro-Spanish flamenco artist is certainly one of the most significant contributions to flamenco studies of the past decade or more, and I am privileged to have participated in his research. Eusebio Rioja's "Un pinturero personaje del Flamenco decimonónico: *EL NEGRO MERI*" (2004) contains the only biographical sketch of Padilla of which I am aware. Ramón Soler Díaz, in "Del origen cubano de algunas letras flamencas" (1998), and, with Antonio El Chaqueta, in *Antonio El Chaqueta: Pasión por el cante* (2003), documents Meri's impact on flamenco song.

On Anglophone performances of Blackness, Elizabeth Maddock Dillon's *New World Drama: The Performative Commons in the Atlantic World, 1649–1849* (2014) provides an illuminating case study focused on Charleston, South Carolina. David Worrall, in *Harlequin Empire: Race, Ethnicity and the Drama of the Popular Enlightenment* (2007), tracks the transformational and aspirational Enlightenment narrative of Harlequin, which I see as connected to the potential for redemption in the bobo's evangelical narrative, as it becomes blackface. The bobo-Harlequin narrative of equivocal racial identity that can potentially be transformed into Whiteness through—in the case of the bobo—redemption, and—in the case of Harlequin—meritorious action, is suppressed in nineteenth-century blackface minstrelsy. However, it resurfaces in the modernist narrative of becoming. Beyond the flattened and brittle impersonations of blackface, I argue, the bobo and Harlequin are fertile sources for understanding modernism.

On race and representation in Spain and Spanish America, Baltasar Fra Molinero's *La imagen de los negros en el teatro del Siglo de Oro* (1995) opened my eyes. María Elena Martínez, David Nirenberg, and Max S. Hering Torres's *Race and Blood in the Iberian World* (2012) is an indispensable resource on race in Spain. Sylvia Wynter's "The Eye of the Other: Images of the Black in Spanish Literature" (1977) and David M. Goldenberg's *The Curse of Ham: Race and Slavery in Early Judaism, Christianity, and Islam* (2005) explore the Abrahamic ideation of Blackness. James Carroll's *Constantine's Sword: The Church and the Jews: A History* (2001) is a harrowing historiography of the Christian world's original racism: anti-Semitism. Gil Anidjar's *Blood: A Critique of Christianity* (2014) traces how Christianity, and particularly the conceptualization of Christianity as bloodline, permeates modern life and thought. Ilona Katzew's *Casta Painting: Images of Race in Eighteenth-Century Mexico* (2004) and Richard Aste's *Behind Closed Doors: Art in the Spanish American Home, 1492–1898* (2013) are gorgeous iconographies of race and identity in Latin America. Frida Weber de Kurlat's "El tipo del negro en el teatro de Lope de Vega: Tradición y creación" (1967), Lemuel A. Johnson's *The Devil, the Gargoyle, and the Buffoon: The Negro as Metaphor in Western Literature* (1971), and Thomas Foster Earle and K. J. P. Lowe's, *Black Africans in Renaissance Europe* (2005) provide iconographic, literary, and theoretical perspectives on race and Blackness in the Europeanist canon. Jody Blake's *Le Tumulte Noir: Modernist Art and Popular Entertainment in Jazz-Age Paris, 1900–1930* (1999), Annegret Fauser's *Musical Encounters at the 1889 Paris World's Fair* (2005), and Eva Woods Peiró's *White Gypsies: Race and Stardom in Spanish Musical Films* (2012) analyze the permutations of race in late-nineteenth- and early-twentieth-century Europe.

All translations are mine unless otherwise noted. I have used professional translations where possible (e.g., of Cervantes, Las Casas, Esquivel, Carpentier), but many of the sources used here have not to my knowledge been previously translated. I have only included the original Spanish text in endnotes in cases where there might be some doubt or nuance that the fluent Spanish reader might want to track. I follow Afro-Hispanist Nicholas Jones in capitalizing "Black" and "Blackness," "White" and "Whiteness" when referring to conceptual armatures and ideational systems, while when referring to people I use the lower case.[84] I also follow Jones in translating *habla de negros* (speech of blacks), a representational trope in early modern Spain, as "Black Talk."[85] When translating the Spanish word *negro* I have kept the italics in order to highlight its original ethos, rather than translating the word as either "negro" or "black." This is the exception for foreign words: in all other cases I italicize only until the word has been defined. In translations, I have kept the author's italics and to some degree have maintained archaic capitalization and punctuation.

I have substituted n****r in all quotations. I use "Gypsy" in quotations only; otherwise I use "Gitano" or "Roma."[86] Flamenco nicknames, such as "El Negro Meri," are in quotes the first usage only. I refer to "Jim Crow" and "pastor bobo" as "he," even though I know that they are "it." I have maintained the quotation marks around "Jim Crow" in order to emphasize the performativity of this character, while I use "pastor bobo" and "bobo" without quotation marks.

"The Gitanos are Ours, The Gitanos are We"

By the twentieth century, jazz age Spain's representations of Blackness, embodied in the imagined Gitano, became a nativized response to newer incursions of black culture from the now politically dominant Americas.[87] The cakewalk's Blackness, employed as a token of white privilege, reminded Spaniards of their subordinate, exoticized status in the eyes of Europe: Spaniards *shared* with Americans of African descent the "aspiration and inability to be European and modern."[88] In response, Spanish artists and intellectuals sought to elevate and dignify flamenco as an international art form, attempting to align Spain with the democratizing impulses of the modern world. The term *sonidos negros* (black sounds) in my title is drawn from poet Federico García Lorca's essay "Juego y teoría del duende" (1933), first given as a lecture on his way back from ten months in New York in 1929–1930. Lorca's experiences, particularly in Jazz Age Harlem, would indelibly mark his perception of racism and marginalization as an experience that he, doubly "queered" for not only his sexual orientation but for his suspect Granada (and therefore Moorish) origins, also suffered. In the essay, Lorca, quoting illustrious flamenco singer Manuel Torre, meditates on flamenco's complexly racialized well of sorrow.[89] Modernists like Lorca took the Gitano as embodying flamenco's sublime "pure instinct"—poetry that can evade the "riddle of metaphor," and "gulp down reality like a carnivorous flower."[90] Thus, in a play on words that simultaneously evokes the howl of Roma suffering, the blistering draft of flamenco song, and flamenco's Blackness, Lorca identified the Gitano in terms of flamenco's *sonidos negros*, its black sounds. As he said in 1931: "Being from Granada" (the last bastion of Muslim rule in Spain), "helps me understand those who are persecuted: the Gypsy, the black, the Jew...the Moor we all carry inside us."[91]

I | Changing Places

FIGURING RACE AND EMPIRE IN THE EIGHTEENTH-CENTURY FANDANGO

1 | Good Shepherd, Bumpkin Shepherd

DISTINCTION IN VILLANO *GAMBETAS* AND *ZAPATETAS*

There are few nations that have passion for music more than the Spaniards, as there is hardly [a person] there who does not know how to play a little the guitar or the harp, instruments which they employ to offer serenades to their mistresses. Thus every night in Madrid, as well as in the other cities of the kingdom, one observes an infinite number of lovers who run through the streets with their guitar and dark-lanterns. There is no artisan who after his work does not take the guitar in order to loosen up in the public squares, [nor] a laborer who goes to his work without hanging the guitar or harp on his back; there are few Spanish men and women of distinction who do not know how to accompany their voice with these instruments. In short, one can say that they have a natural inclination toward music.

—*Bourdelot-Bonnet's* Histoire de la musique et des ses effets *(1715)*

HOW, IN THE ERA of revolutionary republicanism and the elevation of the popular, of Diderot's 1751 *Encyclopédie* and Rousseau's 1762 *The Social Contract*, Mozart's 1786 *Le nozze di Figaro*, Jean Dauberval's 1779 *La fille mal gardée*, and Goya's 1777 *La maja y los embozados*, did Spain dance Blackness? We trace here two intersecting sets of footprints: the *gambetas and zapatetas*, the rambunctious gambols and noisy footwork of the *villano*, the country bumpkin's dance, and the traditions of danced pantomime, ranging from "unbridled sexual mimicry" in eighteenth-century fandango dances to the *pasos* of the *vía crucis*. Despite the dizzying panoply of changing names—from Siglo de Oro canarios, chaconas, seguidillas, zarabandas, and polvillos...to eighteenth-century *chuchumbés*, guarachas, and zapateados, for example—these intertwined lines embody Spanish notions of racial hierarchy, while at the same time masking the slippery transmutations of an Ellisonian joke.[1]

FIGURE 1.1 *Students Serenading*, by Gustave Doré, 1862. In Charles Davillier and Gustave Doré, *Spain* (London: Sampson Low, Marston, Low and Searle, 1876).

In medieval Nativity plays that would give rise to the Spanish theater, it was the *pastor bobo*, the foolish shepherd, who danced out the Christian narrative of redemption.[2] He is, John Brotherton writes, *pastor* (shepherd), *bobo* (fool), *villano* (villager), and *simple* (simpleton).[3] He speaks Spanish incorrectly, and his villano dance is described in terms of *gambetas* (gambols) and *zapatetas* (stamps): "explosive, funny, even grotesque movement," with "intense rhythms and loud music."[4] Performed in churches and churchyards, the dance depicts a lazy, cowardly, ignorant, gluttonous, lascivious, and often scatological clown "filled with terror at the sight of the angel and star," who eventually has an epiphany, offering a joyous sung and danced conclusion as he moves toward the manger with his simple gifts.[5] In *villancicos*, Christmas pageants, this character would "approach the altar and worship the Holy Family," dancing a "rustic *saltejón*" (a huge *salto*, jump), an "ecstatic dance" expressing "unrestrained joy and excitement."[6] Pastor Bobo asked rude and impertinent questions; his role was essential in making the "doctrines of Incarnation, Redemption, Transubstantiation, and the Immaculate Conception" comprehensible to "the humblest peasant in the audience."[7] His very figure and his narrative were thus tools of evangelization and thence of the colonization of the Americas, staged in religious pageants throughout the New World (see Figure 1.2).[8]

The pastor bobo's entertainment value, his ability to capture and thus indoctrinate an audience, lies in his comic confusion, his inability to see what his audience instantly recognizes: that Christ is born. *Will pastor bobo understand what he has seen or won't he? Will he be redeemed or not?* As Hispanist Charlotte

FIGURE 1.2 *Día de Reyes*, by Pierre Toussaint Frédéric (Federico) Miahle. Lithograph, 1855. In *Álbum Pintoresco de la Isla de Cuba Día de Reyes* (Habana: B. May y Ca., 1855).

Stern, writing about Fray Íñigo de Mendoza's ca. 1467–68 *Vita Christi* (*The Life of Christ*), puts it, the "Biblical-Spanish shepherds provoke with their songs and instrumental music the emotional outburst of the spectators, who surely do not remain passive listeners; rather they become animated participants in the adoration of Christ."[9] The "ritual function" of the bobo narrative, then, is not only to indoctrinate but also to intensify "the religious fervor of the audience through the animated demonstration of the shepherds' joy." Pastor bobo's confused racket is expressed in dance with "vigorous leaps" and zapatetas:

> The Biblical-Spanish shepherd, eyes agog and mouth agape, stands transfixed, a startled witness to the miracle of God's incarnation, and then is literally swept off his feet by the sheer wonder of it all, bursting into ecstatic dance to express his unrestrained joy and excitement: "*repica la çapateta* [let the zapateta ring out] / *ahuer de marras apuetro*" [outside doing deviant jumps like a colt].[10]

This adoration scene, performed in church, then spills out onto the street, a "'spiritualization' of the festive rejoicing of the villagers," in which "the boundary between the secular, village celebration and the sacred worship of Christ...is completely blurred."[11] Carnivalesque uproar is thus a tool of religious indoctrination. Stern cites philologist Carlos Clavería's exegesis of the word "*Belén*" (Bethlehem) as referring to "noisy, rowdy" Christmas celebrations.[12] "The central importance of the meanings 'confusion, disorder,'" from which derive all other uses of the word "*Belén*," Clavería writes, "originates in the tumult and noise of the Christmas Eve celebration, with villancicos and other uproarious demonstrations before the Nativity."[13]

In view of these overtones of confusion in the villano's dramatization of redemption, we note that, while jumps are associated with the innocent joy of shepherds, the ballet term *capriole*, a jump beating the legs together in the air, relates to the word *cabra*, or goat.[14] In Spain to be *como una cabra* is to be "crazy," but the goat also has sinister layers of meaning. The male goat does not simply represent sexual virility, but rampant lust, and even the devil himself.[15] As philologist Vicente Chacón Carmona has explained, the music in medieval pastoral plays was used to "distinguish between good and evil...Unredeemed characters and devilish creatures [had] poor musical aptitude...when compared with...angels."[16] In contrast, hell was depicted by "cacophonic sound and sheer noise," turning "nobility...into deformity," "song into lamentation," and "laughter into desolation." John Brotherton discusses Gil Vicente's *Auto pastoril castelhano* (1509), a Christmas play in which the "the boisterous, selfish *Pastores* [shepherds] have been completely transformed by the presence of their Saviour": the main character suddenly "reveals his knowledge of Latin," indicating "by his words that he has undergone a transformation, he has been fully awakened to the truth of God."[17]

The word *zapateado*, footwork, comes from *zapato*, or shoe. In *Tesoro de la lengua castellana o española* (1611), Sebastián de Covarrubias links the pastor bobo/villano's noisy and uproarious footwork to the narrative of redemption. He defines "zapato" (spelled *çapato*) as "the humblest thing there is, worn under the foot," and thus symbolic of the "humility and lowliness" of "Christ the Redeemer."[18] From this association flow a number of somewhat surprising glosses, such as "to get into a shoe is to be afraid," and "to shoe (*zapatear*) someone is to punish him in word or in deed." *Zapatear* is used in fencing, "when one has hit another with many flaccid hits," and *zapatear* is also "to dance hitting the palms of the hands on the feet, on the shoes, to the tune of some instrument, and that person is called a *zapateador: zapatetas* are those hits on the shoes." In 1739, the Real Academia Española (RAE) followed Covarrubias in defining *zapateado* as "the dance done with footwork" (*zapateando*).[19] Like Covarrubias, this dictionary defined *zapateta* as "the hit or clap of the hand on the foot or shoe," adding (and illustrating this with an example from Cervantes's 1605/1615 *Don Quixote de la Mancha*) "jumping at the same time [as hitting the shoe with the hand] as a sign of jubilation."[20]

The RAE definition of *zapateador* likewise follows Covarrubias: "one who does footwork," and the definition is again illustrated with a passage from the *Quixote*, which firmly identifies zapateado with *bailes de cascabel* (bell, or popular dances):

> [The patron of the village festival] has provided dancers too, not only sword- but bell-dancers, for in his own town there are those who ring the changes and jingle the bells to perfection; of shoe-dancers I say nothing, for of them he has engaged a host.[21]

RAE (1739) contains six definitions for the verb *zapatear*, all of which can be read through the lens of Christian evangelization, including "to hit someone with a shoe," "to shake some people up with word or deed," "in fencing, to trounce one's opponent," "to trip over something or run into something," and, in dance,

> To accompany the music by beating the hands together or hitting the hands one at a time on the feet, which are lifted to this end in various postures, always following the same rhythm. Most frequently used in the dance called the villano.[22]

The dictionary gives a Latin definition: "numeram saltare, percusso calceo crebris palmis" (to dance with frequent lifting and striking shoe), and an illustration from *Quixote* in which Sancho Panza, speaking to Don Quixote, emphasizes the contrast between zapateado as a dance of rustic innocents and cultivated, aristocratic dances:

> In an evil hour you took to dancing, master mine; do you fancy all mighty men of valour are dancers, and all knights-errant given to capering? If you do, I can tell you [that] you are mistaken; there's many a man would rather undertake to

kill a giant than cut a caper. If it had been the shoe-fling you were at I could take your place, for I can do the shoe-fling like a gerfalcon; but I'm no good at dancing.[23]

There are examples in Spanish literature of both gentlemanly and rude villanos. As an illustration of a sacramental villano, theater historian Emilio Cotarelo y Mori cites an early seventeenth-century *loa* (praise song) by Agustín de Rojas in which the characters "enter, and sing and dance a *villano*," and which includes the villano's characteristic *estribillo* (chorus), a didactic couplet about the Eucharist: "*Hoy al hombre se lo dan / á Dios vivo en cuerpo y pan*" (Today is given to man / God alive in body and bread).[24] Cotarelo cites a 1618 account of a fiesta in which this estribillo appears, with *villano* substituted for *hombre*: "Al Villano *que le dan*, etc."[25]

Cotarelo gives several seventeenth-century examples of this estribillo, which he calls a *letra tan zapateada*—a verse so often done with footwork.[26] Luis Briceño's 1626 treatise on Spanish guitar, Cotarelo tells us, contains another common variation on this tag: "Al Villano que le dan / la cebolla con el pan" (The villager is given / onions with his bread). Children performed zapateado in the feasts of Corpus Christi in seventeenth-century Toledo and Segovia, and the villano estribillo survives in children's songs today, sometimes substituting "Milano con el pan" for "El villano que le dan"; "pan" still figures in mouth-drummed footwork steps in, for example, Argentinian *malambo* (*salchicha con pan*, sausage with bread).[27]

However, the estribillo easily acquires a sarcastic overtone, commenting not on the miraculous gift of redemption but rather on the fact that villanos must work for their bread, and may not have enough to eat. Having only onions to eat with bread is a sign of poverty. In her magisterial *Nuevo corpus de la antigua lírica popular hispánica, Siglos XV a XVII*, folklorist Margit Frenk Alatorre lists another couplet from Briceño's villano: "Al villano testa rrudo / danle pan y açote crudo" (To the hard-headed villano / they give bread and a good beating).[28]

Despite the pastor bobo's evangelical purpose, then, the villano's noisy confusion also holds *desilusión* (disillusionment) and veiled critique. This figure's "pastoral landscape," Charlotte Stern writes, "is no Arcadia."[29] In his feigned foolishness and "volatile mixture of deference and disdain" the pastor bobo astutely voices "rivalry between squire and shepherd," and the "acute anxieties" and "rigors of an unsmiling nature" that "any Spanish herdsman, who has experienced the biting cold of winter or the scorching heat of summer, would appreciate." In one of the "most celebrated pieces of political satire" in Spanish literature, *Las Coplas de Mingo Revulgo* (ca. 1465) the narrator Mingo, a pastor bobo, impertinently critiques the King himself. Cloaked in this comic voice, the *Coplas* express Isabela I's criticism of her rival Enrique IV for not being a "good shepherd" in vigorously prosecuting the battle against

Muslim Iberia.[30] Medieval interest in pastoral allegories "derives essentially from the deeply held belief that they concealed religious or political meanings."[31] "Pastoral allegory...had behind it the awesome prestige of classical antiquity," and this "commingling of the learned and the popular," Sterns writes, "endowed the shepherd with a decidedly ambivalent profile."[32]

The pastor bobo often retains the name "Mingo," becoming, as we will see, euphemistically suggestive.[33] (We will presently trace this figure's migration to the eighteenth-century Anglophone theater as Mungo, perhaps the first blackface character on the U.S. stage, in Isaac Bickerstaff's *The Padlock* of 1768.) This "burlesque stage yokel" became indispensable in both sacred and secular orbits. From "pastoral Christmas dramas," writes musicologist Juan José Rey, "these customs pass...into the first *autos sacramentales*" (religious plays), and thence into secular theater. For example, Emilio Cotarelo y Mori documents an expense item from a 1554 festivity in Toledo: "from the villano dance, *zapateadores*," and from dances presented in 1561 in which "twelve young shepherds...dance and perform zapateado dressed in...white shoes and *cascabeles*" (bells).[34]

These bells, Miguel Querol Gavaldá has explained, when writing on the music described by Cervantes, are like the bobo's jumps and noisy footwork. They signal confusion in not simply a religious but also a racial sense, because they were used to represent *Moriscos* (Christians of Muslim descent): "during masquerades, buffoons' hats used to be decorated with cascabeles," and dancers dancing the *morisca* (moresca, morris dance) wore "strings of cascabeles tied to their calves with a leather thong....According to the size of the bells they were called *danza de cascabel gordo* (dance of the fat bell) or dance of the *cascabel menudo* (little bell)."[35]

These conventions migrated to England and France, where, Thoinot Arbeau's *Orchésographie* (1589) describes, the moresca dancer, "his face daubed with black," and wearing "leggings covered with little bells," performed "tapping the feet": "striking their feet together," "striking the heels only," or else "with *marque pieds* [stamps of the feet] and *marque talons* [heel stamps] intermixed."[36] Such blackface footwork was unholy: "Morisque dancers will not be admitted into the heaven imagined in the farce *Troys galans et un badin*," writes musicologist Howard Mayer Brown in *French Secular Theater 1400–1550*, "because their movements are likely to break through the floor."[37] Brown documents a representation of the bobo's ethnic and moral confusion as noisy, scatological, and even obscene in another French farce of this period, in which a character "refers to himself with '*le cul aussi decouvert / Comme un danseur de morisque*'" (with the ass uncovered / Like a moresca dancer).

Rambunctious gambols and noisy footwork (sometimes enhanced by bells around the calves), the danced terms of the bobo's confusion, thus imply suspect ancestry. To be confused is to be unredeemed: the bobo's commotion precisely describes these early modern notions of ethno-religious difference.

"Blood purity" is "an inner trait that cannot be seen," Javier Irigoyen-García states, "projected into a repertoire of highly ritualized objects and cultural practices."[38] Villano scenes in the Spanish theater thus typically included "naming the generations": a burlesque of the certification of one's purity of blood, which Hispanist Lucas Marchante-Aragón calls an "exercise...popular among the Spanish Renaissance new nobility who needed to cleanse their past from...Semitic taint."[39] The bobo speaks a "debased dialect, dresses poorly," and "devours pork and wine"—ostentatiously demonstrating that he is neither Muslim nor Jew. He "boasts of possessing blood purity that makes him superior to *conversos* (converted Jews)," flaunting his "rustic genealogies, reciting long lists of relatives and ancestors with ridiculous names."[40] The equivocations of these ridiculously overblown genealogies, Irigoyen writes, "clearly link...the dramatic shepherd to the doctrine of blood purity."

The stakes in such early representations of the shepherd were not simply religious, but also, even before the world-changing events of 1492 (the expulsion of Jews and Muslims from the Iberian Peninsula and the opening of the Americas to Spanish colonization), political and economic. Hispanist Benjamin Liu examines fourteenth- and fifteenth-century poems set in the border zone between Islamic Granada and Christian Jaen, which illustrate how the shepherd as a figure of questionable lineage is based in historical fact.[41] One poem, by the Arcipreste de Hita, begins, "The other day I saw a *mestizo* shepherdess...." The shepherds and shepherdesses in this region, inhabited by a highly mobile population of Muslim workers and artisans, ambassadors, beggars, and merchants, followed their herds—heedless of the border dividing Christian from Muslim land. The term *mestizo*, Liu explains, was first used in Spain in the mid-twelfth century, signifying a person of mixed—perhaps Muslim and Christian—parentage: "demarcation in Spain first refers to the border between Christians and Muslims."[42] Irigoyen writes that in such Christian-Muslim borderlands, "there was always the possibility that these shepherds were *Mudéjares* (Muslims living under Christian rule), or even Muslims who converted and were integrated into the Christian fold."[43] The anxiety caused by the suspect lineage and hence suspect allegiance of these medieval shepherds illuminates the economic stakes of Reconquest: by the fifteenth century, the humble sheep of these medieval shepherds had become Castilla's most valuable Merino wool.[44]

As the ideology of blood purity fed the maelstrom of colonization of the Americas and the Atlantic slave trade, the pastor bobo's danced equivocations, his ethno-religious confusion encoded in gambols and noisy footwork, were transposed into the representation of racialized Others throughout the Spanish Empire. Moriscos, *negros*, Gitanos, and Native Americans became "Native Comic Types," represented in deviant "jargon" and transgressive dance language.[45] As pictured in the image of a Kings Day celebration in 1855 Cuba, such colonial festivities opened a portal through which diasporic African performance could flow toward the Iberian Peninsula (see Figure 1.2).

We see this representational scramble appear in the *chacona*, one of the first Spanish dance crazes to arrive from the Americas. In *La Ilustre Fregona* (The Illustrious Kitchen Maid) of 1613 Cervantes describes the chacona as an *Indiana amulatada*, a mixed-race woman of the Indies.[46] The best known and first published of the chacona texts, musicologist Louise K. Stein writes, in 1624 Rome by Juan Arañés, is "erotic, exotic, satirical… and celebratory all at once."[47] In Stein's translation of this dance song, we read a biting critique of the "good life," with the transgressive Mingo, a pastor bobo, here accentuating his obscene side, veiled in the *respingos* (the startled jumps) of an ass.[48]

Entraron treinta Domingos	Thirty Sundays [Dominicans?]
con veinte lunes a cuestas,	came with twenty Mondays [?] on their backs
y cargó con es[as] zestas,	and all these baskets were carried by
un asno dando respingos.	a stubbornly kicking donkey.
Juana con tingo lo[s] mingos,	Juana with Tingolomingos
salió las bragas enjutas,	came out in tight-fitting pants
y más de quarenta putas	and more than forty whores
huiendo de Barcelona.	fleeing from Barcelona.
Y la fama lo pregona:	And everyone is talking about it…
A la vida, vidita bona,	To the good life, the very good life,
vida, vámonos a chacona.	Let's all go to Chacona[49]

"Tingolomingos" is euphemistic nonsense, suggesting that Juana possesses a quality that tickles the Mingos—perhaps her tight pants—the possibilities of word play here, such as "mingo, *mango* [a handle]," may more pornographically suggest male genitalia being tickled.[50]

Irigoyen explains that in 1624, with the general imposition of statutes of blood purity during the reign of Felipe II (1556–98) having led in 1609 to Felipe III's decree of expulsion of the Moriscos from Spain, the pastor bobo's "hermeneutical uncertainty seems to have been decided… in favour of Old Christians" (the state's designation for Christians deemed untainted by Muslim or Jewish ancestry).[51] Felipe II had ordered "censuses based on genealogy," compiling "massive information about Spain's population," and the Habsburg state had thus bureaucratized ethnic difference, assuming "a completely new role in which detailed and substantive information about its subjects was used to manage the population." Some 275,000 to 300,000 Moriscos were forced into exile in the years between 1609 and 1614, while the state mandated that they leave behind all their children under the age of five, and in most circumstances below the age of ten.[52] Such cruelty increased the pressure on Moriscos to assimilate, "to learn to speak 'in Christian' [*hablar en cristiano*], abandon their traditional dress, or intermarry with Old Christian families" in order to remain, in hiding, or to return to Spain.

Irigoyen analyses a painting of the *Adoration of the Shepherds*, commissioned from court painter Juan Pantoja de la Cruz to commemorate the 1609 expulsions, depicting Felipe III as a good shepherd. "Pastoral iconography" is here "a viable representational trope of royal power."[53] The monarch, Marchante-Aragón writes, like the shepherd, is a faithful intermediary, "the rightful link between God and the people," and "the source of harmony between the world of men and God."[54] Felipe III's shepherd disguise, Irigoyen adds, predicates "a symbolic identification between the king and 'the people,' conceived as the constituency that legitimates power" (see Figure 1.3).[55] Citing Noël Salomon's study of the villano in Siglo de Oro theater, Marchante-Aragón notes, "if the *villano* claim of blood purity had been used originally as a comical feature in the theater for an urban audience," "the motif of the dignified *villano* whose honor resides in his purity of blood, in contrast with those nobles who could not always prove such origins," emerged at the precise moment of the 1609 expulsions: "around 1608–1610."[56]

In his discussion of the villano, Cotarelo tells us that Juan de Esquivel Navarro, in his 1642 *Treatise on the Art of Dancing*, "gives some curious notices about this dance."[57] While most of the aristocratic dances treated in

FIGURE 1.3 *El nacimiento de Cristo* (Felipe III as shepherd at left), by Juan Pantoja de la Cruz. Painting, 1603. © Photographic Archive Museo Nacional del Prado.

Esquivel's *Discursos* begin with a courtly and elegant bow, Esquivel describes the villano's unusual opening bow, with "shepherdlike" jumps imitating village dances.[58] In this bow, the dancer, having removed his hat with two hands, does a *puntapié*, which RAE (1737) defines as "a hit given with the toes," such as "kicking on a door."[59] The dancer kicks his leg up to touch the hat, Esquivel says, before returning the hat to his head and his leg to the floor. Another spectacular jump "performed in the *villano*" is *voleo* or *boleo*, which Esquivel also calls a "puntapié."[60] Lynn Matluck Brooks writes that puntapié for Esquivel is a *vacío*, or kick, "close to the balletic *degagé* or *grand battement*."[61] Puntapié seems to be a more generic term for a kick, and, as RAE indicates, the salient difference between puntapié and vacío seems to be that the puntapié kicks something, such a door, or the hat in the villano's opening bow. The voleo (*volear* is to propel an airborne object by hitting it), Esquivel writes, is executed "flying, in the air."[62] Brooks translates voleo as "hurtling step," a "flying leap-turn" about which Esquivel "remarks that some have knocked themselves flat on their backs attempting this feat," and that while performing this step "one adept kicked a lamp hanging two handspans above his head."

Brooks proposes that, while Esquivel's description lacks precision, the Italian *salto del fiocco*, described in Cesare Negri's 1602 treatise *Le gratie d' amore*, is "a possible match for the *voleo*."[63] In the Italian *salto del fiocco*, Brooks writes, the dancer begins with the "left leg somewhat raised forward, then with great strength" lifts "off into a jump with the right leg, which rises until it kicks the tassel, crossing the right over the left leg, as the body turns to the left." Dancers practicing this step trained to jump higher and higher by kicking a tassel raised incrementally to provide an increasingly challenging target; perhaps this is why Esquivel thinks of the voleo as a puntapié.[64] This virtuosic jumped turn, which can involve the body making a complete revolution in the air while also performing a spectacular feat such as removing "the hat from the hand of a very tall man standing on a chair with his hand stretched up high" remained in the classical Italian vocabulary in 1779, when Gennaro Magri recorded it in his chapter on caprioles.[65]

Negri, who maintained his influential school of dancing in Milan under Spanish domination from 1550 to 1604, is a reliable authority on Spanish popular and court dances, according to dance historian Mabel Dolmetsch.[66] Indeed, Negri's treatise contains a *villanicco* (although Rey complains that Negri's "*Il villanicco*" has neither melody, harmony, nor any rhythmic similarity to the Spanish villano).[67] Negri's is the earliest villano choreography I know of, and, unlike the morisca, canario, zarabanda, and chacona, which propagated through the European courts as moresca or morris, *canarie*, *sarabande*, and *chaconne* or *ciaccona*, it is the only European export, that I know of, of this dance.[68] (We will see that the villano figure and dance vocabulary were ubiquitous in the Spanish colonies, but not with this name.) Dolmetsch transcribes and translates Negri's *villanicco*, "a cheerful and convivial" couples dance: although it contains "hopped flourishes in retreat," it contains no special bow, no shepherd-like kick to the hat.[69]

The same is true for Juan Antonio Jaque's 1680 *Libro de danzar de Don Baltasar de Rojas Pantoja*, a dance manual written for a nobleman who was a councilman of Toledo, a confidante of Felipe V, and the first Marqués de Valcerrada.[70] Although Jaque's villano (which he spells "Billano") does include several jumped kicks, such as a "capriole ending with the foot in the air," and *floreo*, "a kick and a rebound...[with] a jump," Jaque's villano neither includes the virtuoso voleo described by Esquivel, nor does it include the more generic puntapié, or kick to the hat, that Esquivel describes as particular to the villano bow.[71] Engraver Pablo Minguet é Irol's 1758 *Arte de danzar a la francesa* (Art of French Dance), with its 1764 appendix *Explicacion del danzar a la española*, describing "all the steps and movements of Spanish dance," and his 1764 *Breue tratado de los passos del danzar a la española* (Brief Treatise of the Steps of Spanish Dance) also omit the voleo.[72] Minguet's 1764 *Explicacion* does give a complete choreography for the villano, however, including a step called *puntillazo* (a big blow with the toes), similar to the kick to the hat in Esquivel's bow, which is used several times in the dance, toward the end of each *mudanza*, or phrase.[73] The spectacular ending of the last villano mudanza in Minguet is: "Drop to the knees, and get up on the heels, and upon rising give a puntillazo with the right foot."[74] It is clear from these sources that the sorts of jumps used in the villano and taught in dance academies demanded great strength and skill, and disciplined practice.

Domingo González, a student, like Esquivel, of Antonio de Almenda, dance master to Felipe IV from 1639 to 1654, also has a villano choreography.[75] His treatise, which baroque dance authority Ana Yepes dates to ca. 1650, was, like Jaque's, written as an instruction manual for distinguished gentlemen, further confirming that Spanish aristocrats danced the villano.[76] Titled *Villano cavallero por lo vaxo*, which translates roughly as "Gentlemanly Villano in the Low Style," Gonzalez includes castanets in his choreography, and he specifies that they are played with the "arms low, without movement."[77] González does include the special villano kick to the hat described in Esquivel: in the opening bow, the dancer takes his hat off, stamping the floor with the left foot, while holding the hat, and doing a puntapié with the right foot, kicking the hat. González's villano also includes other jumped kicks (*quatropeados*, *floretas*, and *campanelas sacudidas*) throughout.[78] González's description of the villano bow is almost identical to Esquivel's; dance historian Diana Campóo Schelotto speculates that both villanos may come from the same source: their teacher Antonio de Almenda.[79]

Villano Caballero por lo Vaxo. Hazese esta pieza con castañuelas los brazos bajos, sin movimiento. Advertencia. A la cortesía en este tañido no en otro se quita el sombrero con entreambas manos aun tiempo dando antes y al principio del tañido una patadita en el suelo con el pie siniestro volviendo el perfil

izquierdo delante, quitandose el sombrero levantando este otro pie de pun-
tapié, y dando con la punta de él en el sombrero sosteniendose sobre el otro.
Cortesia breve: juntar y pino, paso ael lado, juntar y pino, otro paso ael lado
Juntar y pino: dos pasos breves quedando en planta y poniendoos sombrero.

(Gentlemanly Villano in the low style. This piece is done with castanets,
the arms low, without movement. Notice. In the bow[80] of this music and in no
other the hat is taken off with two hands at once, having given before and at
the beginning of the music a little stamp on the floor with the left foot while
turning the left profile to the front, taking the hat off lifting this other foot in a
puntapié, and hitting with the tip of it [the foot] on the hat while standing on
the other [foot]. Short bow: bring the feet together and do a *pino*[81] [rise up onto
the half-toe], step to the side, bring the feet together and do a pino, another
step to the side. Bring the feet together and do a pino. Two short steps holding
the stance[82] gracefully and putting the hat back on.)

As Benjamin Liu describes in his work on medieval *Serranillas*, before 1492,
when there were encounters between Muslim raiders and shepherds along the
Christian-Muslim border in Andalucía, in order to repopulate frontier lands,
livestock owners were granted privileges and titles of nobility in exchange
for taking the obligation to defend their territories from Muslim raids.[83]
Irigoyen adds:

> These newly-minted nobles were called *caballeros villanos* (commoner
> knights or nobles), an apparent oxymoron that underscores that the combina-
> tion of sheep herding and the fight against the Muslim was one of the instances
> in which the expansion of Christian kingdoms to the south allowed for upward
> social mobility.[84]

It is fascinating to learn from Gonzalez's ca. 1650 *Villano cavallero* that, generations after the 1609 expulsion of Moriscos from Spain, this incongruous
gentlemanly villano was a virtual *lingua franca* of aristocratic dance academies. As Brooks points out, while Negri's 1602 dance treatise addresses "a
noble audience," Esquivel's 1642 treatise "is addressed to an aspiring middle-
class audience, many of whom hoped to climb yet higher socially."[85] Gonzalez's
Villano Cavallero, contemporary with Esquivel's unusual discussion of the
villano in a treatise emphasizing the "excellent qualities"—while "reproving
dishonest actions"—in dance seems to epitomize what Marchante calls "the
motif of the dignified *villano* whose honor resides in his purity of blood."[86]

The virtuosic jumps in Esquivel's and González's villanos are marks of distinction, refinement, and training. They are also marks of accomplishment;
perhaps, given the politics of ethno-religious difference, the distinction here is
that the bobo villano remains dramatically holding his confusion in tension,
while the gentleman villano's virtuosity, like the Latin spoken in Gil Vicente's
1509 *Auto pastoril castelhano*, signals his accomplishment of redemption.

The distinction between virtuosic jumping and noisy footwork in the seventeenth-century villano may thus serve as an exercise through which aspiring new nobility could demonstrate their pure-blooded lineage, and through which the Catholic aristocracy could advertise its legitimacy in terms of the Old Christian bloodline.

Compellingly, these jumps are found in staged representations of folk dances from northern Spain today. For example, the often-staged *jota aragonesa* (a Spanish folk dance and music from the province of Aragón in northeastern Spain) features the *salto albalate*, a jump in which, like the voleo, the dancer with one leg in the air jumps off from the supporting leg, kicks the airborne leg and lands again on the same supporting leg—even without the added difficulty of the voleo's body rotation, this jump requires great athleticism and practice—and similar jumps are found in the Basque jota. The staged jota often ends with a spectacular sequence of eight bell hops, called in Spanish dance *batudas*.[87] Such spectacular jumps in staged Aragonese and Basque folk dances seem consistent with the idea of the "dignified villano": the union of Castilla and Aragón in the 1469 marriage of Isabel I and Fernando II led to the 1492 Reconquest, and Basques, among the Spanish peoples whose land had never been conquered by Muslim armies, could claim the elevated social status of purity of blood.[88] (Basques were considered half French, and so enjoyed an exceptional political status on French stages as well.[89]) Further, stagings of northern folk dances eschew noisy footwork: I think it is possible, therefore, that jota jumps reference the villano's demonstrations of Old Christian lineage in seventeenth-century dance academies.

And yet, the wobbliness of the pastor bobo figure reveals enduring fault lines in the Catholic state's interpretation of the concepts of blood purity with regard to slavery. The alliance between the Pauline/Imperial agenda of colonization through evangelization, whose rationale depends upon the idea that the bobo can be redeemed, and the equally central ideology of social hierarchy as determined by blood purity, a system in which one drop of "bastard" lineage could disinherit, remains uneasy.[90] Irigoyen writes,

> in many cases it is almost impossible to determine whether the figure of the shepherd is used to defend the statutes of blood purity or to criticize them.... [S]hepherding becomes again and again the trope in which blood purity can be promoted but also denied, and therefore the shared symbolic space in which competing versions of the Spanish people and the Christian community collide.[91]

In the aftermath of the 1609 expulsions, "the national 'Self,'" writes Marchante-Aragón, "now stands in contrast with the bastard genealogy of the interloper 'Other'"—and yet "it draws upon the presence of the newly fashioned 'Other' in order to establish its existence and the origins of its authenticity."[92] These contradictions would only be exacerbated and complicated in the eighteenth century.

FIGURE 1.4 *El paseo de Andalucía o La maja y los embozados*, by Francisco de Goya. Oil on canvas, 1777. Courtesy of the Museo Nacional del Prado.

Resisting the Bourbons

Crippled by the inherited effects of generations of inbreeding, with a series of regents and favorites governing in his stead, Carlos II died in 1700 without an heir, and the Habsburg crown passed into the hands of the Bourbons. Enlightenment Spain stood at the precipice, in danger of slipping from its preeminent perch atop the imperial stage. Having during the Siglo de Oro "assumed the hegemony of European culture," writes Malcolm K. Read in *The Body in Spanish Literature and Linguistics*, Spain now "faced, for the first time…a singular rift between itself and the transpyrenean tradition."[93]

Felipe V, the first Bourbon monarch, was Louis XIV's grandson; French fashions in dance, music, and dress, along with French political ideas filtered through society. Felipe V ruled from 1700 to 1746, but the War of Succession (1701–1714), a European but also a civil conflict between Habsburg and Bourbon partisans, marked the first decade and more of his reign. Raised in France, Felipe V worked to gain the trust of his Spanish subjects, to learn their language, and to " 'hispanicize' the court as much as possible," explains musicologist Rainer Kleinertz, "avoiding cultural imports such as Italian opera" and elevating traditional *zarzuela*, spoken and sung theatricals which included danced *entremeses* (interludes, "jocular, waggish plays in one act"), to a prominent position at court performances.[94]

Felipe V attempted to turn Spain into a modern nation-state in the French model, moving it out of "a feudal conglomeration of counties" and "into a modern absolutist monarchy, with a unified system of legislation and taxes and without internal customs barriers."[95] Professional administrators replaced grandees, creating an economic boom. Despite Felipe's hispanicizing efforts, a cosmopolitan culture at court prevailed, especially after the king's second marriage in 1714 to Isabela de Farnesio, who personally curated Italian and Italian-influenced opera, thus importing Italian balletic influences as well.[96] The famed Italian *castrati* Farinelli arrived in Madrid in 1737, performing privately as the king's personal servant and, after Felipe's death in 1746, serving Felipe's son and successor Fernando VI as director of court productions. Fernando's queen, Bárbara de Braganza, brought her harpsichord teacher, composer Domenico Scarlatti, to Spain in 1729, where he would remain until his death in 1757.[97] A series of French dance masters arrived to instruct the royal family. In 1725, Felipe founded the *Real Seminario de Nobles de Madrid*, a royal seminary where the nobility was trained in both French and Spanish dance.[98]

Felipe V, Fernando VI (reigned 1746–1759), Fernando VI's half-brother and successor, Carlos III (reigned 1759–1788), and Carlos III's son and successor Carlos IV (reigned 1788–1808) all ruled in the enlightened absolutist mode. They gradually dismantled feudal *señoríos* (land holdings), and guarded against powerful religious orders such as the Jesuits, who wielded enormous influence in the colonies and were suspected of being more loyal to the pope than to the Spanish Crown.[99]

Bourbon reforms improved conditions on public roads and sought to ensure safety from marauding bandits.[100] An increasing number of foreign visitors chronicled their experiences, elaborating a new vision of Spain as an exotic destination. Tourists might see, as in the 1715 Bourdelot-Bonnet epigraph above, "lovers who run through the streets with their guitar and dark-lanterns." They might taste, as Casanova did at a masked ball in Madrid in 1767, the "wild" and "truly seductive" "national gestures" of the fandango, danced "to perfection" by "Gitanas" with "attitudes [in] which nothing more lascivious could possibly be seen, those of the man indicated love crowned with success, those of the woman consent, ravishment, the ecstasy of pleasure."[101] Concurrent with Spain's declining stature on the global political stage, then, was its rise in the European imagination as a sensuous—even wanton—fandango playland. Thus, writing "On National Characteristics," Immanuel Kant uses an *auto da fé* (the Inquisition's public burning of a sinner at the stake) to illustrate his characterization of Spaniards as haughty, amorous, "odd and exceptional"—Spanish bloodlust ranking below German equanimity on the scale of racially superior Whiteness.[102]

To add injury to insult, the endless wars that marked Felipe V's reign drained the economy of labor, leading to food shortages, and increasing impoverishment and disenfranchisement of the laboring classes. Responses to these circumstances engendered what historian Antonio Zoido Naranjo calls a "great dislocation of ideas": a tendency toward seeing enlightened ideas as foreign impositions, leading often to a reversal in the roles of progressivism and conservatism.[103] In his book on the *Gran Redada* (the genocidal Roma mass imprisonment) of 1749, Zoido describes the reception of Enlightenment ideas in Spain:

> The Enlightenment opposed traditional ways of life...and tried to change them without also changing the conditions in which people lived. On the contrary, these conditions—the loss of imperial and colonial power coinciding with the decadence of the territory which had been the center of the empire—Andalucía—were each day filled with greater hardship.[104]

Sevilla had been the center of the empire and thus a major commercial center for the Western Hemisphere, but by the eighteenth century the city's stature was greatly diminished, causing indignation, Zoido says, in a society "anchored to the past."[105] Such social and economic realignments left Spain torn between supporters of *casticismo*, cleaving to traditional Spanish cultural values, and the fops who followed Bourbon fashion.

Majismo, images of which spread through the world on the wings of painter Francisco de Goya's brush, adopted Andalusian Gitano fashions in dance, music, and dress, not only in resistance to French custom but, weirdly, as an evocation of Spain's glorious and "unrecoverable" past (see Figure 1.4).[106] The impulse that led "shabby rascal[s]" to dance with "gaudy women," as tourist Joseph Baretti describes in 1760, and granted low-class fandangos admission to aristocratic ballrooms and theater stages also led to majos dressing up as Roma.[107] In Sevilla, for example, the 1768 regulations governing masked balls prohibited "indecent and dirty costumes, which make the gathering ugly and cause tedium and disgust"; it was explicitly prohibited "to dress in the costume of low people such as Gitanos."[108] Nonetheless, this was still in vogue in 1818, as Richard Bright records in his account of *Travels from Vienna Through Lower Hungary*: "In Andalusia particularly it is a kind of fashion amongst the inferior nobility to Gitanise themselves...imitating their manners, using their phrases, and entering into all their diversions."[109]

In an intriguing cast backward, not only to the glory days of empire but inevitably toward Muslim Andalucía as well, many traditional modes of Spanish public life were nostalgically designated as southern—Andalusian.[110] If in the seventeenth century, as philologist Frida Weber de Kurlat explains, theatrical works featuring *negros* and *mulatos* were set in Andalucía, and above all in Sevilla, the slaving capital of the peninsula, these figures were replaced with Gitanos during the eighteenth century.[111]

And majismo's uptake of southernness was, already in the eighteenth century, almost flamenco. Even the majos of Madrid adopted this persona, as Julio Caro Baroja writes: "the Madrid-Sevilla axis is fundamental to understanding the essential characteristics of popular Spanish culture."[112] In his 1861 book on Old Madrid, Ramón de Mesonero Romanos writes that the "low-class neighborhood" of Lavapiés, the home of the quintessential Madrileñan majo, was populated by immigrants from all the "celebrated sites on the map of picaresque Spain," including Triana, and Málaga's equally ill-reputed neighborhood, El Perchel.[113] "The majos of Madrid" learned their "ingeniousness and devilishness…their carelessness and arrogance" from "boastful Andalusians."[114]

Mesonero Romanos's "exalted yet scandalous" majos were urban dandies, street vendors, servants, *cigarreras* (like Mérimée's 1845 *Carmen*, whose title character worked in a tobacco factory in Sevilla), or *Manolos*, figured in Ramón de la Cruz's eponymous 1769 *sainete* (one-act farce).[115] The streets, plazas, and taverns in lower class neighborhoods such as Triana or Lavapiés were stages where aristocrats in majo disguise could "slum," and where neighborhood residents, imitated in *tonadillas* (lyric comedies) and impersonated by the restive nobility, could claim their own Spanish citizenship.[116] Pelayo Vizuete's extensive 1887 dictionary of arts and sciences links majo fandangos with flamenco (by then in its "Golden Age"), and southern identity with eighteenth-century casticismo, explaining that Spanish theatrical dance is Andalusian popular dance. "The *fandango*," Pelayo Vizuete writes, is "Andalusian *por excelencia*"—"its surname is *flamenco*."[117]

Discussing Unamuno's 1902 essay *En torno al casticismo* (which he translates as "*On Castillian National Essence*"), Irigoyen powerfully argues that the word *casticismo*, and the cultural efflorescence it describes, define a radical dissonance at the heart of Spanish identity.[118] Casticismo comes from the word *casta*, meaning chaste, or caste. If, in early modern Spain, *raza*, or race, signified the stain of Blackness, casta signified and certified nobility and purity of blood—Whiteness.[119] Eighteenth-century majismo asserted its untainted Castillian national essence by dressing up as a dark Other, whose Semitic and south-Saharan African antecedents were now wrapped within an imaginary Gitano.

In early modern Spain the ruffian *jaque* (figured in the dance-song and literary form called *jácara*), the pastor bobo, the villano, the *negro* (black slave), and the Gitano emerged as astute and potentially subversive voices, whose noisy confusion and narrative of redemption added depth, dramatic tension, and sardonic wit to the great works of the Siglo de Oro. The sharp-tongued metatheatrical commentary of these stage characters ruptured the dogma of *Dios, Patria, y Rey* (God, Country, and King) precisely by enacting the possibility of redemption—thus calling into question the crown and church's rule based on *limpieza de sangre*, or blood purity.[120] If Spaniards had long identified with the equivocations of race attendant on skepticism and *desilusión*, during the eighteenth century this alternate reflected self became darker and more "exotic" (see Figure 1.2). Under the Bourbons, both enlightened followers of French mores and *casticistas*, or Spanish traditionalists, saw the Spanish Roma, indomitable, unintegratable, and long associated with the outlaw and outcast life, as emblematic of Otherness.[121] Spain's identification with this figure, often described euphemistically as a proto-romantic "orientalization," is in fact a racialized downgrade. With the fandango, "Andalusian *por excelencia*" and flamenco—that is, Roma—eighteenth-century Spain danced Blackness for Europe.[122]

2 | Concentric Circles of Theatricality
PANTOMIMIC DANCES FROM THE SACRED
TO THE SECULAR

A man and a woman dance together, sometimes one couple, sometimes more.
They move to the music, arousing lust in every way imaginable: by curving
their arms in extremely soft gestures, moving their buttocks again and again,
twitching their thighs, and provoking each other suggestively. They engage in
all kinds of unbridled sexual mimicry with the greatest skill and fervor. You can
see the man thrust his hips while the woman moans and writhes....

— *Manuel Martí Zaragoza, Deacon of Alicante,*
describing a public dance in Cádiz, 1712

BOURBON REFORMS WERE INEFFECTIVE in ameliorating the precarious
circumstances in which much of the Spanish population lived, and such
afflictions exacerbated majismo's nationalistic indignation. Liberalization
of the grain trade, for example, implemented by Carlos III's Italian prime
minister, Leopoldo de Gregorio, the Marqués de Esquilache, led to rising
bread prices.[1] In 1766, Esquilache crafted an edict prohibiting men of the royal
household from wearing the traditional long capes and broad-brimmed hats
that were part of the majo's costume.[2] Such modes of dress, it was claimed,
facilitated criminal behavior: the cloak could conceal a weapon; the broad-
brimmed hat could conceal a person's identity (see Figure 1.4). Under pain of
arrest, royal functionaries were required to adopt French-style short capes and
smaller three-cornered hats. (Léonide Massine's ballet *Tricorne* of 1919 references these strictures.) Esquilache then imposed these measures on the general
population; Francisco Goya, a witness to the ensuing riots, recorded them in
his 1766 painting *Motín de Esquilache.*

Of course the value of dance education for the Spanish nobility (as for other
European nobility) had always lain in teaching manners, elegance, and decorum, as the distinctive villano bow makes clear. But in the latter third of the

eighteenth century the official standards for the proper dance decorum to be taught at the Royal Seminary, founded in 1725 by Felipe V, recorded growing concerns over majismo.[3] Majismo ran afoul of the fundamental principles of Spanish government, in which the privileges accorded the nobility were seen as a consequence of their supposed moral superiority, implying an obligation to model virtue and piety for the common people. Aristocratic betrayal of social status constituted a violation of this obligation (consider Goya's renowned paintings of the nude and clothed *Maja*, which led to an Inquisitional tribunal for their owner, Carlos IV's minister Manuel de Godoy, and for the painter himself).[4]

Carlos III's advisers blamed the 1766 Esquilache riots on the Jesuits, who were expelled, and their missions in the Americas dismantled the following year. These actions had important consequences all across the empire, but one in particular illuminates the identity politics of eighteenth-century dance. As the nobility thought that Jesuit education represented the finest option, enrollment at the Royal Seminary declined drastically following the Jesuit expulsion in 1767. In 1770 a naval officer took over, refocusing the curriculum on military training.[5] Spanish dances and guitar were no longer taught, only violin and French ballet. By 1798 a royal decree concerning the proper education of the nobility expressly prohibited the *bolero*, a fandango dance popular among majos, to members of the aristocracy.[6] Nonetheless, reflecting majismo's large political and cultural footprint, in 1799 it was decreed that all dramatic works, music, and dance in public theaters should be "national" in style, giving rise to the *escuela bolera* or bolero school, the Spanish school of classical dance (see Figure 2.1).[7]

"In the two years immediately following the Esquilache rebellion," Hispanist Rebecca Haidt writes, "three percent of Madrid's population" was "detained and accused of vagrancy," which is to say that they have been conscripted as free labor.[8] "Manolo has been sent to the African presidios ten times, while his friends and relatives in the low-class neighborhoods have been sent to workhouses." Casticismo and majismo, weaving cultural symbols resistant to France into Spain's developing eighteenth-century identity, emerged from this feeling of dissidence and disillusionment. But such themes are far from unique to the majos of the eighteenth century; they thread continuously through Spanish sensibility, from the ruffians of picaresque sixteenth-century literature to the jaques figured in seventeenth-century jácaras.[9] As Bronwen Heuer argues in *The Discourse of the Ruffian in Quevedo's Jácaras*, many read in the figure of the "shackled and imprisoned" ruffian-hero, pressed into service as galley slave and transatlantic colonist, "a metaphor for how one saw oneself."[10] In a nation where many were of mixed ethnicity, statutes of blood purity fostered unease and anxiety in great swaths of the population; this pressure only intensified under the Bourbons.

If dance during the Habsburg dynasty reflected both the evangelical purpose of imperial expansion and the astute insinuations of picaresque figures, under the Bourbons Spanish dance took on new layers of meaning. The ruckus

THE FANDANGO AT THE THEATRE SAN FERNANDO, SEVILLE. *To face page 302.*

FIGURE 2.1 *The Fandango at the Theatre San Fernando, Seville,* by Gustave Doré, 1862. In Charles Davillier and Gustave Doré, Spain (London: Sampson Low, Marston, Low and Searle, 1876).

of the potentially transgressive yet childlike bobo, whether in the person of a villano or a "light-hearted" black slave, was adopted by the urban swank, the self-conscious majo who donned ruffian disguise in defiance of Bourbon attempts at cultural cleansing. If eighteenth-century Spain precipitously declined on the global stage, the territory which had been the nerve-center of the empire, Andalucía, was now cast, as in the Countess d'Aulnoy's travel memoir

Voyage en Espagne (1691), as a place where blind singers sang *romances* (ballads) on the streets for pennies, and at the inns you would find Gitanos,

> Men, and...women blacker than Devils, nasty and stinking like swine, and clad like beggars...impudently grating on a sorry guitar, and singing like a cat roasting. The woman have all of 'em their hair about their ears, and you would take 'em for *Bedlamites*, they have glass necklaces, which hang twisted about their necks like ropes of onion...they are urgent to serve you only to have an opportunity to steal something of you, even though it be just a pin.[11]

Song and dance are uniquely important to Spanish theater, given Spain's tradition of singing and dancing actors performing both comedy and tragedy, just as flamenco artists do today. Spanish players drew from "a large, constantly circulating orally transmitted repertory" of sung poetry: the romances and seguidillas that constitute flamenco's archive. These were both "'high' courtly music, preserved in written polyphonic songbooks, and popular music performed by everyone," writes Louise K. Stein, "from the skilled improviser to the amateur at home, and from street musicians to professional actors and actresses" (see Figure 2.2).[12]

FIGURE 2.2 "Soledad con una canasta al brazo," by Emilio Beauchy. Photograph, 1889 (?). Courtesy of the Biblioteca Nacional de España.

As in the case of the villano, these music and dance forms had deep roots in liturgical performance. Philologist José María Díez Borque argues that we should consider Spanish liturgy, popular festivals, and theater as "concentric circles" within a single "orbit of theatricality."[13] Despite aspersions continually cast upon its morality, such performance embodies both the evangelical work of Catholicism, as in the villano narrative, and also the glories of Spanish wealth, in representations of the vast empire's exotic subjects, such as the canario, a representation of Canary Islanders, or the chacona, a mixed-race American woman.[14] Referencing their secular/sacred repertoire of music and dance, then, eighteenth-century Spaniards cast a longing glance backward, to a time when Spain was in the victorious religious vanguard against the Moor and the Turk, and Spanish artistic traditions set the standards for taste in Europe.

In his foundational 1804 history of Spanish theater, written during the reign of Carlos IV and on the eve of the sovereignty-shattering Napoleonic invasion, Casiano Pellicer enunciates this position. He lingers over Spain's seminal importance to the theatrical traditions of both France and Italy, quoting from Voltaire's preface, written a century earlier, to his translation of the medieval Spanish epic poem *El Cid*, that "in European theater as in public business, Spain's taste dominates just as its politics does."[15]

The inbreeding that affected Carlos II and precipitated dynastic change was a result of close familial relations between Spain and other monarchies, including France. Felipe V, grandson of Louis XIV, ascended to the Spanish throne via these alliances: Felipe III's daughter, Ana Mauricia, had married Louis XIII, while Felipe III's son and successor Felipe IV's daughter, Maria Teresa, married Louis XIII's son and successor, Louis XIV. (Carlos II's parents Felipe IV and Mariana of Austria were likewise first cousins, and both were children of marriages between first cousins.) Spanish players, then, present in the entourages of Spanish queens and princesses, influenced style at the French court.[16] For example, Louis XIV's court composer and choreographer Jean-Baptiste Lully's *Ballet des Muses* (1666) includes an *entrée* titled "Mascarade espagnole," in which artists from the queen's retinue danced, sang, and played instruments.[17]

Danzas habladas (spoken dances) had a long history in Spain, such as the sixteenth-century *Danza de los pecados* (Dance of Sins), and *Historias* (Stories), in which a musician relates a story in song, and the characters—villanos, nymphs, Indians, and giants—act it out in pantomime.[18] But the seventeenth-century *bailes cantados* (sung dances) growing out of these Spanish traditions were unusual in France. Pellicer pointedly notes that Lully's frequent collaborator, the illustrious playwright Molière, owed a clear debt to Spanish theater.[19] Molière's "novel genre of comédie-ballet, which mixes ballet with comedy, is modeled directly on the paradigm of the Spanish *comedia*...in which 'music and dancing were...standard elements of theatrical performances.'"[20]

Spanish theater originates, Pellicer writes, in sixteenth-century dramatist Lope de Rueda's "charming *pasos*, which can be taken out of the plays and dialogues and placed into other works."[21] These pasos were secular, stand-alone *entremeses* performed between acts.[22] Small regional touring companies of the Siglo de Oro, Cotarelo says, always included dance as a "sort of appendix" to the entremés itself, but soon "poets and playwrights understood the advantage of...making of an accessory a principal attraction."[23] Cotarelo speculates that dance became a separate theatrical element because, while "it was easy for music to transcend its popular roots," dance "became more and more technical," as we saw in the villano, and thus "harder to integrate with other scenic arts." From 1616 these *bailes*, separate dance pieces that could be inserted into a larger performance and had become the "principal attraction" rather than an "accessory," began to be published.

Luis Quiñones de Benavente (1581–1651), the author of these earliest published bailes, elevated their literary cachet by calling them *entremeses cantados* (sung entremeses).[24] Benavente published twenty bailes, all satirical, all both sung and danced.[25] Many bailes, although secular, nonetheless had the poetic form of the villancico—a combination of estribillos and *coplas* or verses—and were danced with the villano's characteristic gambetas and zapatetas which, as we have seen in Chapter 1, enacted the pastor bobo's ethno-religious confusion.[26] For example, Cotarelo cites the 1616 "Baile del Sotillo de Manzanares:" "¡Qué bien brincan de aquí para alla zagalas del Manzanares!" (How well the shepherdesses of the Manzanares [Madrid's river] jump from here to there!") And "El Baile de Leganitos":

Bailo, brinco, zapateo,	I dance, I jump, I do footwork
doy vueltas de dos en dos,	I do turns two by two
cabriolas y floretas	caprioles and *floretas* (similar to *pas de basque* in ballet)
á tan delicada voz.[27]	in such a delicate voice.

As in flamenco today, seventeenth-century performers' artistry was measured by their ability to dance the verse.[28] Cotarelo quotes the "famous humanist" Don Jusepe Antonio González de Salas (1588–1654), who, in his preamble to Quevedo's *Terpsícore* describes these bailes, or entremeses cantados, as the

harmony of the dances, which is the same as saying...the versification with which the measures [of music] and the movements [of the dance] should correspond...poetry that with discernment and assisted by the music of the voice gives soul and life to the actions and [elegant] movements of the dance.[29]

Writing in 1633, Salas adds "We see...in our theaters...dancers [who] sing at the same time: this sharpness and elegance, introduced in the past few years [is] extremely difficult." Esquivel (1642) concurs: "To dance well, one must have a good ear, because lacking this, it is extremely difficult to dance to the measure."[30]

A century later, at the court of Felipe V, successful actors in Italian-styled works still had also to be accomplished dancers and musicians, able to harmoniously integrate music, verse, and movement.[31] In a 1723 work by an Italian composer and a Spanish librettist, stage directions required the "actors to move in rhythm with the music," with "Hercules on a horse on whose facade were two golden drums marking the [musical] air softly and continuously"; this rhythm was echoed by "two harpies fighting in the air such that their clashes matched the rhythm of Hercules."[32]

Like flamenco today, these sung and danced performances, viewed by Louis XIV's court as uniquely Spanish, could range dramatically from comedy and burlesque to the most serious and tragic themes, with overlapping circles of secular and liturgical performance. Díez Borque sees medieval troubadors, early modern Nativity dramatizations, and these dramatized dance-songs within a continuous tradition. He cites Diego Pérez de Valdivia's *Discussion Or Lesson About Masking, in Which the Question of Whether It Is a Mortal Sin to Do Masking Is Discussed*: "It is well known," states this tract, written before 1589, "that in recitations and songs minstrels evoke with their facial expressions and with their gestures the characters of the songs."[33] Further, religious and elevated subject matter was not merely permitted in Spanish theater; it was compulsory. For a theatrical performance to be sanctioned depended, writes Pellicer, on performing only "ancient" and "gallant" dances, with "rigor and order."[34]

Recall that Lope de Rueda's innovative integration of music and dance in sixteenth-century secular theatricals, precursors of the secular bailes or entremeses cantados of the seventeenth century, were called *pasos*. A paso (literally, step), as a performative element in Spain references the *Vía Crucis*, or the Stations of the Cross, a meditation following the suffering steps of Christ on his way to Crucifixion.[35] In her book on the processional dances of early modern Sevilla, Lynn Matluck Brooks translates *pasos* as "floats," carried by penitents from each parish brotherhood in the religious processions of Easter Week.[36] As Nativity celebrations evoked fervid expressions of adoration and joy, the ritual function of Easter processions was to move participants to vividly experience the suffering of the Crucifixion, and the awe of the Resurrection. Easter processions enacted the Passion of Christ in multiple and interrelated ways, including dialogues, dramatic scenes, dance, and *plantos* (the Virgin's sung lamentations), voicing "la soledad y las angustias de nuestra Señora" (the solitude and anguish of Our Lady) in a manner that reminds us of *saetas* sung today during Holy Week in Andalucía.[37] (Flamencos, for whom soleares, from soledades, is one of the principal forms, will find this fascinating.) Like the bobo's comic antics, these laments, performed in religious contexts, migrated to secular performance, as for example, in the "novel introduction" of a lament sung by Cupid in Luis de Ulloa y Pereira's comedia *Pico y Canente* (1656).[38] They migrated also into flamenco, as we will see in the *queja de Galera*, the galley-slave's lament, accompanying Gitano dance performances in 1742 Sevilla.

In his beautiful book on eighteenth-century villancicos in Málaga, philologist Manuel Alvar describes the various pasos, starting with a request for silence, an elegy or introduction (this part was known as a *tonada*, a tune, suggesting another flamenco form: *tonás*), and an estribillo, which made up the villancico as an "independent literary-musical unit."[39] Villancicos, religious pageants, were "primitive sung and danced entremeses": with pastoral scenes and burlesque dialogues as well as the most plaintive *cris de cour*, they had something to please and to move every audience, from commoners to aristocrats.[40] The chapel master served as the church music director; he produced these villancicos, and set their verses, which were often published as *pliegos* (gazettes) *de cordel*, a genre of literature so named because they were made up of a few leafs tied together with twine (*cordel*), to music.[41]

The chapel master's prestigious position granted him credit on the cover of the published villancicos, but the verses themselves were unattributed (see Figure 2.5). Although they utilized popular strophes, Alvar explains, the verses were actually the "product of cultivated and educated men," but the theatrical librettists who wrote them were widely viewed with disdain.[42] Some of the suspicion directed at these eighteenth-century writers stemmed from the satirical dissentions of the "familiar and instantly recognizable" sub-genre of seventeenth-century jácaras "made wildly popular by Quevedo in his [ca. 1610] 'Carta del Escarramán a la Méndez,'" an acid satire yet also an elegy to a ruffian antihero, Escarramán, which, as we will examine presently, had spurred countless imitations.[43] In view of the long-standing debates over theater's morality or lack thereof, then, it is not surprising to find dramatists, working anonymously, cycling in and out of writing liturgical villancicos.[44] Likewise, it is not surprising that political commentary might find veiled expression in these liturgical songbooks.

During the dysfunctional reign (1665–1700) of the last Habsburg, the disabled Carlos II, pliegos of villancicos written by dramatists and featuring popular characters proliferated.[45] In addition, blind beggars began versifying the last confessions of violent criminals, graphic crime reports which, taking their name from the earlier literary and theatrical forms, were called *xácaras* (jácaras). Like the *ciegos* (blind men) who lend their name to the Spanish lottery vendors even today, these xácaras were peddled around the city; their vulgar language and ephemeral medium made them perfect for masking political satire.[46] Not only did these gazettes—the beginnings of journalism in Spain— subvert their purported aim of deterring crime, by making popular heroes (as the earlier seventeenth-century literary jácaras had) of the condemned ruffians, but these figures' continued popularity in eighteenth-century dance songs provides us with yet another example of how Spanish taste for the picaresque antihero had long masked widespread dissatisfaction and dissidence.

Villancicos' oscillations between sacred and secular spheres, then, should be considered in this light. The establishment of secular performance spaces in the mid-sixteenth century had coincided with the rise of controversy over the cathedral as a theatrical space, yet those very controversies had also led to repeated suppression of theater, forcing such theatricals to periodically retreat back to the safe haven of the church.[47] In the eighteenth century, villancicos that had been performed in churches "flowered in the *tonadilla escénica*"— secular lyric comedy.[48] Yet "the oldest *tonadillas escénicas* (1761)" of the second half of the eighteenth century, writes musicologist José Subirá in his foundational work on the genre, "are associated with the tonadillas 'a lo divino' (sacred tonadillas) of the first half of the eighteenth century." In Málaga, for example, epidemics in 1741 and 1751 resulted in the theater being closed, its building demolished, and a hospital erected on the site, leading to the efflorescence of liturgical villancicos documented in Alvar's book.[49]

The Bourbons looked askance upon Spanish traditions of liturgical performance. Carlos III prohibited *autos sacramentales*, sacramental plays, because they were indecorous, in 1765 and again in 1780, decreeing that

> In no Church in my Kingdom, whether it be Cathedral, paroquial, or plain, shall there be from this day forward dances, nor giants, but rather this practice must cease in the processional and all other ecclesiastic events, as they are not suited to the gravity and decorum which they require.[50]

But villancicos were simply too popular to stamp out entirely.[51] In fact, in religious festivals across the empire—such as the 1855 Christmas celebration in which black Cubans, in ceremonial dress and playing ceremonial instruments of diasporic Africa, figure the Three Kings—the dramatic and musical structure of the villancico, lushly and exotically garbed, proliferated (see Figure 1.2).[52] Villancicos such as the *villancicos de negros*, written in Black Talk and staged throughout Old and New Worlds, were popular in their depictions of rustic bobos and exotics, from Gitanos, barge workers, postmen, scribes, and ruffians, to Congolese blacks and parrots from Havana, regaling the Christ child in the manger with dance and song.[53] Secular eighteenth-century tonadillas drew from this villancico repertoire, and their dances, "black dances that are actually creole," and Native American dances "that are actually black dances," exoticized the pastor bobo's familiar danced tropes of gambetas and zapatetas.[54]

Thus, Díez Borque argues, whether in cathedrals, street festivals, or theaters, we must reconstruct the possibilities of early modern Spanish performance within the framework of an "ideological, or ritual scene."[55] Liturgical dramatizations throughout the Spanish Empire often treated catechism from the jocular and satirical perspective of the pastor bobo, the *negro*, or the villano, whose confusion and struggle to comprehend Catholic doctrine provided both comic entertainment and recapitulation of the canonical message.[56] Yet, as sociolinguist Glenn Swiadon Martínez emphasizes in his study of the *villancicos de negro*, those enslaved throughout the Spanish-speaking world never ceased to resist their subjugation.[57] In fact, it is precisely the dramatic tension intrinsic to the villano/bumpkin shepherd's narrative of redemption—*will he see the light, or remain confused?*—that opens up an equivocal space allowing for the satirical expression of dissent within the catechism.

And while the *bulla*, the uproar, and the confusion which signifies all of these characters tends toward the comic, the liturgical aspects of Spanish dance traditions also allow for the expression of the depths of human suffering, of the sublime freedom of those with nothing to lose. Such is the cry to the Mother and for the Mother, foreshadowing today's flamenco repertoire, in this verse for the Ascension of the Virgin Mary, sung in Black Talk in 1685 México:[58]

Mas ya que te va,	But since you are leaving,
ruégale a mi Dios	beg my God
que nos saque lible	to free us
de aquesta plisión.	from this prison.

Nadadores de Penca (Swimmers under the Lash) and *Bailadores en la Horca* (Dancers on the Hangman's Noose)

Writing about what is most influential about Spanish theater, Casiano Pellicer not only highlights Lope de Rueda's sixteenth-century bailes, with their integration of music, dance, and gesture, but also Lope de Rueda's ability to present nature with detail and realism as a way of "evoking tenderness in the souls of the audience," "provoking tears" as well as laughter.[59] In the Siglo de Oro, popular characters were likewise depicted with gestural detail and realism. In his chronicle of life at the court of Felipe IV (reigned 1621–1665), playwright Juan de Zabaleta writes, "if in the theater there is a depiction of agony, the actor must throw himself down onto that slimy stage, muddy with saliva, [and] studded with crooked nails and splinters."[60] Cotarelo quotes an anonymous critic of immorality in the theater, writing in 1618:

> [A]fter Our Lady came an entremés in which a woman tavern-keeper... sings and dances an indecent *Carretería* [racing around] also called *Lavandería de paños* [laundry] in which all the *rufianerías* [ruffian behaviors] done at a laundry are represented," and to make matters worse, the actor "who had just played Our Lord comes out to sing and dance *Allá va Marica* (There Goes Marica)."[61]

Marica in today's usage means an effeminate man, raising the question of whether this actor who had just played Christ then followed up with a drag performance.[62]

Writing on the bailes of the seventeenth century, Cotarelo states that they not only included *indios* (Native Americans) and *negros*, courtly galliards and pavannes, but also pantomimic dances of swimmers, fencers, and galley slaves. These pantomimes were new in the early-seventeenth century:

> Neither aristocratic dances, nor folk dances, nor processions of *negros* and *indios*; they were figures and movements done by the actors throughout the entire work, expressing the plot or its subtext (which consisted of amorous solicitations, disdain, jealousy and other emotions), through *paseos* [walking about the stage], turns, *cruces* [crosses]...changes of partners and other turns and capricious mimicries, which with strange names figure in the notes of these new dances.[63]

Pantomime could be off-color, and even sexually explicit, as in the zarabanda, a theater dance which moralist Juan de Mariana describes in 1598 as performing "in public the most stupid and dirty acts that are done in bordellos, representing kisses and embraces and everything else with the mouth and arms, thighs and the whole body," or the fandango dances featuring "unbridled sexual mimicry" described in 1712 Cádiz in the epigraph above.[64]

One such pantomimic dance gesture is the *mudanza del amolador*, the knife grinder's move. "The *amolador* was a person who sharpened knives with a pedal-operated grindstone," explains Ana Yepes, adding that the amolador was probably "a variation known by everyone."[65] The step appears in a 1643 entremés by Benavente called *El Amolador*, whose suggestive estribillo is: "Oh, grinder, dear little grinder! / Oh, sharpen me that knife!" and in Domingo González's ca. 1650 *Jácara por lo vaxo* (Jácara in a low-class style).[66] In Jaque's 1680 dance manual, Yepes notes, this step appears in the only dances which include indications of space: *Jácaras* and *Paradetas*. These clues, taken together, Yepes suggests, might hint at a theatrical use for this step. The amolador is recorded in Beauchamp-Feuillet notation in Rodrigo Noveli's 1708 dance treatise—"*con grillos*" (in shackles)—a theatrical convention evoking the world of the jaque.[67] This seventeenth-century step, Yepes notes, was preserved well into the eighteenth century among dance masters teaching in the French school: Bartolomé Ferriol y Boxeraus, a disciple of Pierre Rameau and author of a 1745 dance treatise, describes the amolador as "making circles with the hand and index finger, at the same time that the foot on the same side lowers and lifts, while also imitating with the mouth the sound that the stone makes in this practice."[68] As an example of the way that gestures such as the amolador, "known by everyone" in seventeenth- and eighteenth-century Spain, may, like spoken language, persist and migrate, visualize the gesture accompanying "tsk-tsk-tsk," and consider its underlying suggestiveness.

Among Spanish dance historians it is widely observed that "baile" and "danza" both refer to dance, with "baile" staking out the more popular and noisier end of the spectrum and "danza" tending toward the gentility of aristocratic dances.[69] But Heuer points out "a curious polysemy" in the word "baile": "Its primary meaning is dance, music, and a verse form, but its secondary meaning is thief."[70] In mid-sixteenth-century romances written in *germanía* (thieves' slang), "baile" means "ladrón, que baila en la horca" (a thief, dancing at the end of the hangman's rope). "Looking at the context in which 'baile' is used," Heuer continues, "a very amplified meaning of the word can be derived. In *'Cortes de los bailes'* [The Tribunal of the Bailes]," ruffians

> are called by the trumpet of judgment to gather and perform. Here, as in the other *bailes,* movements and gestures include knife fights, squirming or shuddering (the chattering of teeth is equated with castanets) under torture or punishment, and the quick moves of thieving: cutting purses, picking pockets. The many "dances of life" parallel the many types of criminals or delinquents in their crafts.[71]

Heuer points out a similar play in Quevedo's use of the word *cantar* (to sing), "given that not to confess, that is, not to sing, or squeal on one's friends is a paramount virtue of the ruffian."[72] "The word 'cantar' and words signifying musical instruments and accompaniment," she adds, "are used for torture devices and punishment methods to elicit a confession." "*'Bailar'* [to dance]," Heuer continues, "can mean the dance or song which [the ruffians] are in the midst of, or it may be a more general kind of dance of life, in their case, thieving which results in punishment or dancing under the lashings of the whip."[73] In fact, perhaps echoing the devilish overtones within the word "capriole" (from *cabra,* or goat), in his bailes, Quevedo similarly plays on the word *salto,* meaning both "jump" and "robbery."[74] "Inventing the phrase *'nadador de penca,'* " Heuer writes, Quevedo

> creates the image of the condemned swimming through lashings of the whip as if in a dance....Curiously, another *baile* by Quevedo is called "Los Nadadores" and in it the many characters of the *hampa* [ruffian world] become "swimmers"...they are equated with various kinds of fish for their acts of thieving and their forms of loving.[75]

Cotarelo discusses Quevedo's *Baile de la galera* (ca. 1614), also known as *Los galeotes,* set on a galley ship and featuring ruffians and a dancer who acts as *oficia de cómitre* (the person who directs the rowers in a galley ship).[76] One character, Pironda, asks another, Santurde, "Have you forgotten how to dance amidst afflictions and sorrows?" Santurde answers, "He who dances late forgets." A third character, Juan Redondo (which is both the name of a dance and an everyman villano figure), says:

Bailaré mortificado.	I will dance even if I am tortured.
Puede tanto el natural,	Easy grace,[77] rhythm, movement, and
el son, la mudanza, el garbo,	style are so powerful,
que bailamos el azote,	That we dance the whip, the galley, and
la galera y el trabajo.	the hard labor.

"Imitating the sounds and movements and hard labor of the galleys," Cotarelo continues, "the four begin to dance, finishing with some satirical seguidillas, like all the ones [Quevedo] always puts at the end of his bailes."[78]

Cotarelo documents another odd seventeenth-century danced dramatization: the *Baile del Mellado en jácara* (a baile done as a jácara, that is, as a dialogue), by Juan de Matos Fragroso (1608–ca.1689).[79] Like Escarramán, the ruffian immortalized in Quevedo's famous jácara, El Mellado de Antequera was a well-known jaque.[80] These popular jácaras, Hispanist Ted Bergman writes, "evoke the standard procedures of…prosecution with which the audience must have been familiar."[81] Ruffians like Escarramán and Mellado "must have been hunted down, thrown into a dark prison, interrogated and probably tortured for a confession." Such figures would then "be led on a 'walk of shame'" to the gallows. The procession represented in Matos Fragroso's *Baile del Mellado* is, Heuer states, "a strange mixture of the sacred and profane."[82] A savage yet ironic critique of the theocratic state, it parodies the liturgical dramatizations of the Stations of the Cross even as it compares the ruffian's torture and execution to Christ's suffering, and his prostitute-consort's grief to that of Mary Magdalene, or perhaps even the Soledades of the Virgin Mary on Holy Saturday.[83] This trope was already established in the parade of beggars depicted in the anonymous picaresque novel *Lazarillo de Tormes* (1554), which was banned for heresy, Heuer writes, quoting Javier Herrero on "Renaissance Poverty,"

> In the *Lazarillo*…the seat of power is no longer the castle, but the town council, as befits the bureaucratic administration of the absolute monarchy. It is an all-powerful body from which fearsome laws emerge. Such power is seen through the eyes of a beggar…whipped by unspecified torturers, representing a remote authority. The beggars are called "a procession"; the term is used here to signify directly a line or two of prisoners. But nothing is accidental in this masterpiece of sarcasm, and underlying this signification, and shadowing it with a religious evocation, we find the meaning of the Easter parades in which the suffering and passion of Christ were (and still are in Spain) commemorated. The beggars, then, whipped by the powerful, are covered with Christ's image, and in their suffering we see renewed the passion of him who said that what was done to one of these poor was done to him.[84]

Perhaps unlike the last confessions of executed criminals made into jácaras by blind singers during this era, late-seventeenth century jácaras such as Matos Fragroso's *Baile del Mellado* were "not meant to simulate any type of bold public declaration on the part of the criminal before death."[85] Rather, Mellado's consort is seen sobbing over her lover's impending execution in verse, expressing a "cynical and strange *jácara*-love"; her loudly professed grief "contains a modulation between melodrama and farce," an equivocal yet vivid moral lesson. Matos Fragroso's "*Baile en jácara*," Cotarelo writes, "a dialogue" with song and dance at the end performed by jaques and their prostitute consorts, enacts "the torment, whipping, and later the death on the gallows of that ruffian."[86]

Calenda, Chica, Cumbé, Chuchumbé, Panaderos, Fandangos: Spanish Pantomime and Africanist Vacunao

> Almost every Spanish dance...[is] of Moorish origin. [Spanish dances] are also
> branches and imitations of the African Chica or Fandango; they are all,
> therefore, more or less marked by that looseness, I might even say obscenity.
> —*Carlo Blasis*, Notes Upon Dancing, 1828

Writing on the "Afro-American Musical Legacy" in Spanish America before 1800, eminent musicologist Robert Stevenson discusses the *calenda*, which in the Americas became, like the fandango, both a dance and a festivity.[87] Stevenson quotes cleric Jean-Baptiste Labat's *Nouveau Voyage aux isles de l'Amerique (1693–1705)*, describing the calenda as a "Spanish creole diversion" in the villancico mode, "danced Christmas Eve on a stage constructed inside the choir grille of even the most respected Spanish American cathedrals, 'so that the people can take joy in the Saviour's birth.'" Covarrubias (1611) defines "calenda" (also spelled "kalenda")—its English cognate is "calendar"—in Latin, addressing its ritual role as a link to the cycle of religious celebrations.[88] The "function and liturgical context" of the calenda is the "Martilology," the calendar for celebrating the saints' days throughout the year.[89] But Labat continues his account with an odd and surprising observation: "The Spaniards took it from the Negroes, and dance it everywhere in the Americas after the true Negro fashion."[90]

In his article on the kalenda's "Tangled Roots," anthropologist Julian Gerstin translates the Labat passage, written in 1698 in Martinique. The dancers

> approach...each other, they leap back on the beat, until the sound of the drum tells them to join and they strike their thighs...that is, the men's against the women's....It seems that they beat their bellies together, while it is however only their thighs that support the blows. They back away immediately, pirouetting, to recommence the same movement with completely lascivious gestures, as often as the drum gives them the signal, which it does several times in succession.[91]

A sexily allusive "vaccination" or "injection," the *vacunao*'s possession of the woman by the man, according to dance scholar Yvonne Daniel, is signaled through "an aggressive hand movement, a kick, movement of handkerchief, or pelvic thrust."[92] This "erotic pelvic gesture, the object of male pursuit and female flight," is the essence of the dance's intentionality: "dancers reveled in mounting the attack and in preparing the defense." As Dulce María Morales Cervantes, "La Perla Negra," described it to the Spanish press in 1917,

The man stands in front of the woman and runs toward her, doing beautiful *trenzados* (braids, filigrees, with his feet) in order to catch her, and the woman enfuriates him, pretending to yield, and she escapes, also doing trenzados. The role of the man is to hit against the belly of the woman, and the role of the woman consists in defying him as if he were a bull and in impeding his bumping her, giving him instead her hips. In Cuba, the audience goes crazy with enthusiasm, yelling as the man advances, "¡Vacuna a esa morena, valiente! (Vaccinate that dark woman, brave man!) And they applaud when the dance ends and the man conquers the woman.[93]

Labat's description of a flirtatious and sexually pantomimic dance of "completely lascivious gestures," in which men and women, dancing together, repeatedly approach each other and leap back, seeming to beat their bellies together (although Labat takes care to observe that "only their thighs...support the blows"), vividly recalls not only the dance still done in Martinique, *Bèlè*, but also the Cuban rumba *guaguancó*, the *umbigada* of Brazilian *batuque*, the *ombligada* that Robert Farris Thompson describes in Argentinian tango, the nineteenth-century *resbalosa* danced by "black men and zamba women" on a beach in Lima, Perú, the eighteenth-century Mexican chuchumbé that we will examine presently and, as musicologist Antonio García de León Griego argues, "all the cumbé" (consider Venezuelan and Colombian *cumbia*, *joropo*, and *currulao*) "dances done belly-to-belly."[94]

The *cumbé* to which García de León refers figured Blackness in Spain. RAE defined "cumbé" in 1732 as "a dance of *negros*, done to a happy tune...and consisting of many *meneos* (wiggles) from side to side."[95] In his essential work on *Santiago de Murcia's Códice Saldívar No. 4*, musicologist Craig Russell writes, "the syllable *umbé*...identifies [an] entire class of dances (the *cumbé*, *paracumbé*, *chuchumbé*, etc.)."[96] Thus, an early Christmas song, "La Negrina" of Mateo Flecha (ca. 1535) includes an estribillo which rhythmically plays on the (to the Spanish ear) African-sounding expression: "gugurumbé."[97] Like the chacona's sarcastic *a la vida bona* (to the good life), cumbé dances have a characteristic estribillo: "¡Gurrumé, gurrumé, gurrumé!/que fase nubrado y quiele yové" (*Gurrumé, gurrumé, gurrumé!* / it's getting cloudy and the rain's gonna fall—in Black Talk).[98] The second line of this estribillo seems to echo the well-known verse "Esta noche ha llovido / mañana hay barro / Pobre del carretero / que va en carro" (It rained tonight / tomorrow the roads will be muddy / Poor cart driver / who travels those roads). But (and perhaps this is a subtext of both the cumbé estribillo as well as the verse we sing today), in a 1597 description of a ruffian's execution, "llovió muy bien" (it rained very well), which, philologist Elena Di Pinto suspects, may allude to the release of bodily fluids as an external sign of death by hanging.[99]

The first line of the cumbé estribillo is nonsense, although its suggestive onomatopoeia, sometimes shortened to *guuú, guuú* (which we will further examine in Chapter 3) recalls the uninhibited and sexually triumphant *cucuru-cucu* of the cock's crow. An obscene 1588 Neapolitan moresca, translated by art historian Donald Posner, makes clear the suggestiveness implicit in this utterance, expressed in movement as jumping:[100]

O Lucia, ah Lucia, Lucia mia
. . .
Come forward with your lips and glue them here.
Look at this heart of mine surging and bounding,
Lift your foot for I am jumping Canazza!
Cock-a-doodle-doo! [*cucurucucu* in Spanish]
Now jump up!
Look at me leap and turn and jump;
I am jumping Lucia,
Now you jump too, for here I am dancing...

Mexican nun and poet Sor Juana Inés de la Cruz (1651–95) wrote a *villancico de negros* including the expression *gulungú, gulungú*. Sor Juana seems to represent the Black Talk of the "light-hearted" African slaves singing this song by changing the "guru" prefix into "gulu," using Quevedo's recipe for representing African-accented Spanish: "If you write theater and are a poet, show your knowledge of the Guinean tongue by changing the r's into l's and the l's into r's," writes Quevedo.[101] The second line of the cumbé estribillo likewise follows this recipe: *nublado* (cloudy) becomes *nubrado* and *quiere* (wants) becomes *quiele*.

As in the "jumping Canazza" of the obscene 1588 moresca, the cumbé lyrics' impropriety and equivocation clearly has a bodily correlate. In the earliest published cumbé in Spain, the *Baile del Paracumbé* (1708), a *gracioso* (clown) dressed as a villano, proclaims himself "*El Paracumbé de Angola*," which Russell translates as the "stud" from Angola.[102] But these dances not only represent Blackness as "light-hearted" confusion and a suggestive lack of inhibition. Blackness is not only corporeal transgression, Aurelia Martín Casares and Marga Barranco argue in their article "Popular Literary Depictions of Black African Weddings in Early Modern Spain," but also—like the Spanish concept of raza itself—"corporeal flaw." Martín Casares and Barranco illustrate this performative concept with Francisco de Avellaneda's *Bayle entremesado de negros* (1663), in which all the participants are "defective": mute, "lame, one-armed, left-handed, or hunchbacked."[103] Likewise, a vicious eighteenth-century depiction of a black wedding in Cádiz reminds us of the moresca "with the ass uncovered" in renaissance France. This theatrical ends with the female protagonist, "a good dancer who knew how to sing the cumbé,"

on the floor with unkempt hair, her breast showing, a scratched face, and her bottom "in the air," and therefore uncovered... attended [not] by a doctor, but by a veterinarian who administrates a boiling enema, which results in her dying in her own faeces.[104]

These depraved depictions of the black body attest to an intense desire to enjoy the benefits that slave labor provides, and, in eighteenth-century Spain, perhaps the longing for past prosperity that slave labor represents. As Brenda Dixon Gottschild writes, the "black dancing body...elusive, fantacized, imagined, loved, hated," ever Other, is "the last word in white desirability."[105]

Let us examine what evidence we have of movement in these cumbé dances. Labat's vivid 1698 account of a belly-to-belly dance resonates strikingly with Martí's above-quoted 1712 description of a dance in Cádiz:

- A man and a woman dance together, sometimes one couple, sometimes more
- curving their arms in extremely soft gestures
- moving their buttocks again and again
- twitching their thighs
- provoking each other suggestively
- sexual mimicry
- the man thrust[s] his hips
- the woman moans and writhes.[106]

In 1796, a century after Labat's description of a vacunao in Martinique, Médéric Moreau de Saint-Méry published *De la danse*, documenting a dance called *chica* in Saint Domingue (present-day Haiti).[107] (As bolero dancer Antonio Cairón writes in his 1820 dance treatise, "the name might change again soon, but the form will not."[108]) Musicologist Ned Sublette adds that, similar to Labat's comment that Spaniards took the calenda "from the Negroes, and dance it everywhere in the Americas after the true Negro fashion," Moreau ascribes the chica "to the Congos of Saint-Domingue, noting that it was performed throughout the Antilles and the Spanish American continent."[109] Moreau's description clearly describes a cumbé dance, a voluptuous "struggle where all the ruses of love" are depicted, the female dancer moving her hips, while the man "throws himself at her suddenly, almost touching her, withdrawing, and throwing himself at her again."

In his glossary of Afro-Spanish words, Fernando Ortiz comments that the cumbé "must have been danced a lot in Cuba, considering that the word has engendered...common Afro-Cubanisms."[110] "The root *kumb* is very common in West Africa," Ortiz writes, and "the African character of the word is confirmed in the information we have about the dance...*paracumbé*." "We should not exclude the possibility of an ethnic or geographical origin of the word *cumbé*," Ortiz adds, "as the 'sevillanas' are from Sevilla."

Reading William Holman Bentley's *Dictionary and Grammar of the Kongo Language* (1887), Ortiz notes that *kumba* means "to make a noise, to roar, rumble, grunt," "to marvel (giving vent to the sound of surprise)," and "to talk behind one's back, slander, vilify, calumniate, scandalize."[111] *Kumbu* is a "rumbling sound, roar, grunt," *kemba* is "to rejoice, make merry, put on fine things and go out merry-making," *kembela* is to "praise," "celebrate," "extol," and "sing praises of." *Nkumba* in Congo is also "belly button," and *nkumbi* is a "drum used when libations of blood are being poured out at the grave of a great hunter," as well as a "slanderer," and a "vassal chief."[112] Ortiz's erudite dissertation goes on to consider the word *cumba* among other African groups, concluding, "it seems that the word *kumba* was related both to place and to lineage or nation of origin, and was widely used in Africa, from northern Guinea to the Congo."[113]

In sum, the cumbé dances that became widely popular throughout the Spanish-speaking world in the late-seventeenth and the eighteenth centuries are called by an African word used among slaves. I think this flirtatious chase is what Labat meant when in 1698 he commented that Spaniards dance the calenda "everywhere in the Americas after the true Negro fashion."[114] In its pan-West-African meaning, *kumb* is not only cognate with belly button, and not only with the noisy confusion and ostentation that we are tracking as encoding Blackness for Spain. Ortiz's research into the etymology of this root prompts a further question: does the aspect of "praise" and veneration present in this word gesture toward, as Robert Farris Thompson argues, veiled Africanist spirituality activated within pan-Hispanic cumbé dances?

The intent of cumbé dances is, Thompson says, "to emphasize life," to enact an "ideal communion," and to affirm "that the world cannot exist without marriage."[115] This profound gesture of hope and affirmation, then, is also a powerful political gesture of resistance to imperial Spain's aims of dehumanization and cultural annihilation. We will see these politics articulated in a shockingly brazen manner in yet another member of the cumbé family: the *chuchumbé* (see Figure 2.3).

In 1766, writes eminent musicologist Gabriel Saldívar in his history of Mexican music, a fleet from Europe via Havana arrived in the Mexican port of Nueva Veracruz.[116] Some of the immigrants aboard were of *color quebrado* (people of "broken color," of mixed blood) who, because they didn't have money to go inland, stayed in Veracruz, working as sailors and servants.[117] Their music, an "indecent song" called the *chuchumbé*, quickly became all the rage, and, thankfully for dance history, attracted the attention of the Mexican Inquisition.[118] The Inquisition's documents record that, to obscene sung verses, men and women danced together with *ademanes* (gestures), *meneos* (wiggles), and *sarandeos* (shakes), contrary to decency because they include *manoseos de tramo en tramo*, (touches climbing up the body), *abrazos*, (embraces), and *dar barriga con barriga* (hitting belly against belly).[119]

In the verses recorded by the Inquisition in 1766 the word *chuchumbé* means "penis":

FIGURE 2.3 "Negro Fandango Scene, Campo St. Anna, Rio De Janeiro," by Augustus Earle (1793–1838). Watercolor, ca. 1822. Courtesy of the National Library of Australia.

En la esquina está parado	On the corner stands
un fraile de la Merced,	A friar of *la Merced,*
con los hábitos alzados	With his habit pulled up
enseñando el chuchumbé.[120]	Showing his *chuchumbé.*

Elisabeth Le Guin describes the sense of "precariousness and longing" that the vagaries of transatlantic shipping might have engendered in eighteenth-century Spain, dependent on American exports.[121] From the Cuban perspective, Ortiz explains, the "absurd Spanish commercial monopoly, which created shortages and interfered with the export of many agricultural products" made smuggling unavoidable.[122] Musicologist Rolando Pérez Fernández adds that across the Spanish colonies illegal trading of enslaved people was an important part of this underground economy.[123] This social distortion, Ortiz observes, "not only corrupted civil, military, and ecclesiastic functionaries, who were in charge of administering justice and imposing order, but also created a mentality that to violate the law was not wrong, because the law was unjust."[124] Spaniards looking across the Atlantic at the Americas in the eighteenth century thus saw societies in which "in one way and another, all the laws were broken, be they arbitrary or necessary."

Elena Deanda-Camacho explores the lawless society recorded in the chuchumbé verses collected by the Mexican Inquisition. They depict priests sexually exploiting their parishioners (as alluded to in the above verse), Afro-Mestizo soldiers "whose geographic mobility led them to form multiple informal families," and abandoned women forced to turn to prostitution in order to support themselves and their children.[125] The large number of soldiers, sailors, and other unstable and mobile men, Deanda-Camacho writes, meant that women often found themselves as single mothers in a society in which trading on sex, either through prostitution or by establishing more permanent yet still licentious relationships (such as becoming the second "wife"), was one of the only viable modes of survival.[126] "To dance the chuchumbé" is "to dance to the music 'belly-to-belly' ... or literally to 'dance to the penis' and obtain food through sex." At a time when independence movements were stirring across the Americas, the chuchumbé's representation of the "sexual practices of free Afro-Mestizos, loose women, and friars" attracted the attention of the Inquisition "because it attacked the implementation of Catholic morals and imperial hegemony."

The Mexican Inquisition collected and preserved forty verses as well as vivid witness testimony making clear that the chuchumbé was an Africanist "belly-to-belly" dance.[127] But, as with the slippery and ever-changing dance names in Spain, the chuchumbé was only one among many such licentious dance musics censured by the Mexican Inquisition.[128] I am not aware of the chuchumbé being danced on the eighteenth- or nineteenth-century Spanish stage, but a related cumbé dance, *Los panaderos* (the baker's dance), has been canonized in the repertoire of the bolero school.[129] The Mexican Inquisition denounced panaderos in 1779 as a scandalous and sacrilegious dance. From the cited verse, it is easy to understand why:[130]

Esta sí que es Panadera	She really is a baker
que no se sabe chiquear	who doesn't indulge herself.
quítese usted los calsones	Take off your underpants,
que me quiero festejar.	because I want to party.
	And the man answered:
Este sí que es panadero	He really is a baker
que no se sabe chiquear	who doesn't indulge himself
lebante usted mas las faldas	Lift your skirts higher
que me quiero festejar.[131]	because I want to party[132]

In Spain, panaderos, danced with heelwork and castanets, was considered a dance of *jaleo*, or bulla, ruckus. In his 1912 dance treatise, Maestro José Otero (1860–1934) calls panaderos "a classic Andalusian dance" from Cádiz.[133] *Panaderos de la Flamenca*, a bolero school dance, eventually became *Alegrías*, says Otero, a cornerstone of today's flamenco repertoire (see Figure 2.4). Otero includes several verses of panaderos, which he comments are "allusive of dance"—though he elides their sexual allusions:

Qué bien amasa la panadera	How well the panadera kneads
y qué bien muele la molinera.	and how well the *molinera* (miller's wife) grinds.
La panadera fué y se embarcó	The panadera set sail
en una lancha y se mareó.	on a launch and fainted.

FIGURE 2.4 *"Panaderos de la Flamenca.*—Posición al dar las vueltas ó rueda diciendo que 'no' la bailadora al bailador." In José Otero Aranda, *Tratado de Bailes de Sociedad, regionales españoles, especialmente andaluces, con su historia y modo de ejecutarlos* (Sevilla: Tip. de la Guía Oficial, Lista núm. 1, 1912), 207. Courtesy of the Biblioteca Nacional de España.

And Otero gives the panaderos ending verse, sung, like the chuchumbé, in the voice of an abandoned woman; this verse is now firmly established in the flamenco songbook:

Tú no me pagas la casa;	You don't pay my household expenses
tú no me das de comer;	you don't give me money to eat
me vienes pidiendo cuentas…	now you come to ask me for an accounting
¿á fundamento de qué?	on the basis of what?

Otero devotes thirteen pages and four photographs to the panaderos, including one image recording the dancing couple about to change places, the man leaning in toward the woman, his focus directed desirously toward her face, neck, and chest, even though his shoulder girdle turns away from her and his leading arm is held out in front of him protectively (see Figure 2.4).[134] The woman gives him the side of her body: not her hip or thigh, as Labat described in 1698, but rather inclining her shoulder toward him from the waist; the only body parts possibly colliding in this encounter are the leading arms, which act as bumpers. Thus panaderos, a lascivious cumbé dance in 1779 México, was indeed absorbed, perhaps via the port of Cádiz, into the repertoire of what Otero calls "classical Andalusian dance."

I have argued elsewhere that the flirtatious fandango dances described by tourists in eighteenth-century Spain clearly describe the *pasada*—the step of changing places that flamencos know from dancing *sevillanas*—and just as clearly echo the descriptions of cumbé dances that we have been discussing here.[135] For example, Joseph Baretti, in 1760, writes, "men and women...dance close to each other, then wheel about, then approach each other with fond eagerness, then quickly retire, then quickly approach again."[136] In 1765 Pierre Agustín Caron de Beaumarchais describes how "the man turns about [the girl]," coming and going "with violent movements, to which she responds with similar gestures."[137] Jean-François Bourgoing writes in 1797,

> The fandango is danced only by two people, who never touch one another, not even with their hands; but to see them provoke one another, by turns retreating to a distance, and advancing closely again; to see how the woman, at the moment when her languor indicates a near defeat, revives all at once to escape her pursuer; how she is pursued, and in turn pursues him.[138]

And Étienne Françoise de Lantier, in 1799:

> [T]he two dancers approach each other, they run away from each other, they chase each other in succession...The lovers seem just at the point of falling into each other's arms; but, suddenly, the music ceases and the art of the dancer is to remain immobile.[139]

Today, sevillanas are the only couple dance in the flamenco repertoire, and the pasada is part of the sevillanas choreography in all its variants. But in the vocabulary of the bolero school, the pasada is called *panaderos*.[140] The memories of its American origins have been wiped away, and the sharp edges of the vacunao have been blurred and Whitened through equivocation. But the sexy intentionality of the panaderos step, the quintessential step of the eighteenth-century fandango, remains.[141] As photo's caption (see Figure 2.4, above) states: this is the position in which "the *bailaora* (woman dancer) is saying 'no' to the *bailaor* (man dancer)."[142]

In light of Spain's loss of status on the eighteenth-century imperial stage it is fascinating to consider Moreau's 1796 comment that the Spanish fandango "is nothing but the chica"—that is, for Moreau, the fandango is an Africanist belly-to-belly dance.[143] As musicologist Alejo Carpentier comments,

> *El Chuchumbé* was not invented on the boat traveling from Havana to Veracruz....It formed part of a vast and motley family of *paracumbés*...close of kin to the sarabande and the chaconne mentioned by the poets of the Spanish Golden Age, always accompanied by the "kicking of the apron," the gesture of "the lifted skirt," the choreographed pursuit of the female by the male. The latter is an eternal theme and basis of the fandango.[144]

In the original Spanish, Carpentier's "kicking of the apron" is *puntapié al delantal*.[145] That is, the vacunao's kicking gesture has the same name as the kick to the hat of the villano's special opening bow—illuminating, perhaps, some of the color of both the term and the danced action. We have seen the *puntapié al delantal* in Spain, for example, in a 1643 entremés by Benavente, in which Melisendra dances "dando al aire castañetas / puntapiés al delantal" (giving castanets to the air/kicks to the apron)."[146] Cotarelo explains that in this entremés we learn that "it is characteristic of these dances" for women to "sacudir las piernas" (shake their legs) to move their skirts. As Claudia Jeschke documents in her fascinating book on the *Hispanomania of 19th Century Dance*, it was the fandango, seen as a lascivious dance from the Indies, and specifically the fandango's flirtatious pasada, a manifestation of the vacunao of Afro-American cumbé dances, that embodied Spain's Otherness for Europe, providing imagery for performances of Spanishness on ballet stages.[147] Thus, Italian ballet master Carlo Blasis quotes Moreau in his *Notes Upon Dancing* (1847) that "the Fandango...is no other than the Chica," adding that "when the Chica is danced with its most expressive characteristics, there is, in the gestures and movements of the two dancers...a kind of contest, in which every amorous trick, and every means of conquest are put into action."[148]

A Ruptured Mirror: The Ethics and Politics of Dancing Schools

In the political and social schisms of the latter half of the eighteenth century, such as the 1766 Esquilache riots, followed by the removal of Spanish dance from the curriculum of the Royal Seminary in 1770, aristocratic decorum, indicating moral superiority and thus noble privilege, found itself in direct opposition to, and in condemnation of, Spain's long-standing predilection for the popular and the picaresque. This is the backdrop of the Royal Decree of 1798 that prohibited the bolero to members of the aristocracy.[149] It is also the subtext in Juan Jacinto Rodríguez Calderón's acerbic *Description of the Schools of Bolero Dancing, as They Were in* 1794 *and* 1795 *in the Capital of Spain*, a satirical "moral history" published in Philadelphia in 1807.[150] In the bolero academy, even before finding young women with their bloomers "pulled up nearly to their knees" practicing caprioles with a rope and supported by young men who often found themselves "with the ladies' skirts over their heads" and in full view of "what respect and modesty does not permit me to say," Rodríguez Calderón records the first hint that he was entering a den of "ills of body and soul": "I put my hand on my hat in order to correctly greet the gathering, but unfortunately no one deigned to answer me." These are the politics of exile (the former cadet, presumably now in Philadelphia, calls himself a "new Robinson") embodied in majismo's uptake of the villano, danced, with intensely self-conscious irony, in newly reintegrated terms of noisy zapateado and ebullient jumping.

The dances interwoven in casticismo's semantic web—fandangos, boleros, seguidillas, chuchumbés, cumbés, panaderos, and guarachas (to name a few)—long considered sinful and transgressive, were now "castas"—pure-blooded Spanish. This shift is illustrated by a subtle mistake in a nineteenth-century quotation of a seventeenth-century work. In his 1804 history of Spanish theater, Pellicer discusses the late-fifteenth and early-sixteenth century polemic about whether theater, with its dances, should be considered a mortal sin. Pellicer quotes Rodrigo Caro (1573–1647), a priest, poet, lawyer, and historian, whose work·Días geniales (ca. 1626) is an essential source documenting seventeenth-century folk customs, including dance. In attributing to Caro a long list of popular dances that entered Siglo de Oro theater, Pellicer indicates that the dances villano and zapatetas, and canario and zapateado were synonymous: "The shameless and clownish dances of the common folk that were introduced into the theaters and later spread among the people were," Pellicer quotes Rodrigo Caro: "the *Guineo* (Guinean), the *Perra Mora* (Moorish female dog), the *Guiriguirigay* ...the villano or zapatetas...the canario, or zapateado."[151] But Pellicer's list quotes Caro inaccurately. In 1626, Caro in fact wrote:

> It seems that the Devil has brought these lascivious dances from Hell, and the insolence that in the gentile republic was not tolerated is viewed with applause and pleasure by Christians, unconcerned by the ruin of their customs and the sweet poison, for it kills at least the soul, of lasciviousness and dishonesty that the youth gently drink; and it is not only one dance but many, to the extent that it seems there is as great a lack of names as there is a surfeit of dishonesties: such were the *Zarabanda*, the *Chacona*, the *Carretería*, the *Tapona*, *Juan Redondo*, *Rastrojo*, *Gorrona*, *Pipirronda*, *Guiriguirigai*, a huge troupe of this ilk, which the ministers of idleness, musicians, poets, and actors invent each day without punishment.

That is, Pellicer in 1804 adds several dances to Caro's 1626 list of "dances from Hell," including a Black dance (guineo), a Moorish dance (perra mora), and "villano or zapatetas," "canario or zapateado." It is Pellicer in 1804, and not Caro in 1626, who makes canario and zapateado equivalent; Caro does not mention either one. In his 1820 dance treatise Cairón, citing Pellicer, makes this linkage explicit: "[T]he canario came from the Canary Islands: it was later called guaracha, and lately zapateado: the name might change again soon, but the form will not."[152] Caro does mention villano, and does associate it with zapatetas, and with extirpation: in a discussion of Ezekiel's prophesy (Ezekiel 25:6–7, "Because you have clapped your hands and stamped your feet, rejoicing with all the malice of your heart against the land of Israel," says the Lord to Ammon, "I will...give you as plunder to the nations"), Caro comments that this must be a "dance playing castanets, doing zapatetas and capers, as in the villano."[153]

In the seventeenth century, jumps—unlike percussive footwork—became part of a dancer's training in the aristocratic context. The seventeenth-century gentlemanly villano included the puntapié, used in the villano's rambunctious bow to kick the hat, in the voleo to kick the tassel, and in the "kicks to the apron" in Benavente's 1643 entremés.[154] But by the eighteenth century these jumped kicks, a mark of distinction in the seventeenth-century gentlemanly villano, seem to have become characteristic of, even definitive of, Spanish dance as a whole. In Minguet's series of dance manuals—published perhaps beginning as early as 1725, and continuing through 1774—Minguet's increasingly bourgeois readership is instructed on how to dance the French-influenced *contradanzas* of the day, and also, perhaps reflecting the 1725–1770 curriculum of Felipe V's Royal Seminary, the Spanish dance steps "used in Seguidillas, Fandango, and Other Musics."[155] Alan Jones notes that many of Minguet's Spanish steps "involve vigorous jumping, and, in particular, kicking: a forward kick (*puntapié arriba*), a backward kick (*coz arriba*) and combinations of the two (*floreo, cargado*, and others)."[156]

In 1793, Felipe Roxo de Flores's treatise on *recreational dance* lists "*cabriolas* (caprioles), *taconéos* (heelwork), zapatetas, and other weaving and interlacing steps of the feet" as fundamental elements to the "preparation or training for Spanish dance."[157] (Flamenco dancers will not be surprised to read this, as our fancy moves are called *patadas*, or kicks.) This passage is the first time of which I am aware that percussive footwork (taconéos and zapatetas) is listed among the formal techniques of Spanish dance training. That is, in Roxo's short phrase, we note a key shift in seeing these "weaving and interlacing steps," broadly conceived, as particular to Spanish dance: Roxo sees caprioles, the jumps that two centuries earlier were a mark of aristocratic education, as equivalent to taconeos and zapatetas, the footwork that had previously signified the pastor bobo's potentially damning noisy confusion.

I cannot resist raising here another intriguing yet obfuscating "dust cloud," referring to the bobo's rambunctious appetite for dance, and for unbridled sex. If Rodrigo Caro in 1626 saw the villano's zapatetas as potentially inviting the Lord's wrath, Pellicer's augmented 1804 list of the "shameless and clownish dances of the common folk" included not only "villano or zapatetas" and "canario, or zapateado," but another Siglo de Oro footwork dance, not mentioned in Caro: the *Polvillo* (little dust cloud). Cotarelo tells us that Cervantes often figures Gitanas dancing and singing the polvillo, with its estribillo:[158]

Pisaré yo el polvico	I will step in the dust
atan menudico;	so delicately;
pisaré yo el polvo	I will stamp the dust
atan menudo.	so lightly.

The emphasis here is on charm and light-footedness, a "concealment of passion and ease of demeanor" that hints at good breeding: in Cervantes's novela, *La gitanilla*, the title character turns out to be an aristocrat, kidnapped by Gitanos, who marries a nobleman in the end. But we should also recall that in

Spanish, *echar un polvo* refers to coitus.[159] Cotarelo quotes several early modern characterizations of the polvillo as "sinful," "gross and insolent," including the suggestive word play of Francisco Navarrete y Ribera's 1640 entremés *La escuela de danzar* (The Dance School), in which the maestro asks his gentlewoman pupil, "¿Quiere un *polvillo?*" ("Would you like a polvillo?").[160] Perhaps it is even possible, then, to read the polvillo estribillo as referencing stereotypical Roma adroitness, the ability to transgress with subtlety and impunity.

Rodrigo Noveli's 1708 treatise on Spanish dance seems to reference the polvillo, in describing both the canario and the villano as *golpeados* (stamped): their aim is "to raise dust and to cover oneself with it."[161] Cairón, in 1820, seems also to reference this abandon in his curious note that in the villano "one adopts various postures traveling from one spot to another, and sometimes seated on the ground the feet are lifted in a sort of spasm of anger [*patala-tilla*]."[162] Perhaps we should recall here the French Renaissance characterization of footwork in the moresca as breaking through the floor, as it were, to hell.

The shift from the seventeenth century's distinction between virtuosic, aristocratic caprioles and the dust raised by raucous Gitanos, criminal actors, and black slaves, to the eighteenth century's integration of jumping and footwork within a single body of, as Roxo de Flores says in 1793, the fundamental elements to the "preparation or training for Spanish dance," is subtle. Yet this shift reveals a great deal about the embodied politics of majismo as it took up the mestizo image of the Gitano body.

As we saw in Chapter 1, the complicated politics of the villano, danced in the context of paranoia about blood purity, engaged indirectly and symbolically with the heavy questions of slavery and race, colonization, and empire building. The villano was danced everywhere, from aristocratic dance academies, to cathedrals, to popular religious festivals. However, with the bureaucratization of blood purity statutes leading in 1609 to the expulsion of the Moriscos, the peasant/slave aspect of the villano came to be distinguished from the aristocratic *villano caballero* (gentlemanly villano) by an emphasis on bawdy, noisy footwork in the former, and virtuosic, refined jumping in the latter.

The distinction between raucous footwork, signifying the bobo's confusion and hence indeterminate or equivocal status, and virtuosic jumping, gesturing toward the accomplishment of epiphany and redemption, is of essential political significance. If the bobo can be truly redeemed from his abject status, then the entire imperial system founded upon slavery falls apart.[163] By the same token, if aristocrats playing the role of a humble villano do not clarify their exemplary choreographic and hence moral status, they call into question their own privilege. Founded on the dogma that non-Christians should be enslaved, colonization of the Americas was predicated on the medieval Iberian belief that Christianity was heritable. "Pastoral performances served to naturalize the notion of an idealized community of Old Christians," Irigoyen writes, "and provided the symbolic means for excluding Moriscos (as well as Jews and Gypsies) from the representation of Spanish identity. The aestheticization of the figure of the shepherd is...inherent to racism."[164]

And yet, in enacting a narrative of redemption, the bobo shepherd fundamentally calls into question those very notions of blood purity. Although pastoral performances "aimed at opposing the Moorish cultural and genealogical legacy," Irigoyen writes, they simultaneously promoted "a homogeneous conception of national identity that subsumes class difference."[165] The play of possibilities enacted by the bobo, then, embodies another aspect of sixteenth- and seventeenth-century polemics over slavery: if there is *not* the possibility of redemption through evangelization and cultural assimilation, then the colonial project, based on slavery, loses its moral footing and thence its indispensable backing from the Catholic Church.[166] One signal moment in this discourse was the 1550 debate before Carlos V between Dominican friar Bartolomé de las Casas, whose *Short Account of the Destruction of the Indies* was published in 1542, arguing that even non-Christians were part of Christendom, and Juan Ginés de Sepúlveda, who had translated Aristotle's *Politics* in 1548, arguing that Native Americans were "natural slaves" in the Aristotelian sense.[167]

In taking up fandango dances such as the profane Mexican panaderos, an Africanist cumbé dance which became part of the bolero school, eighteenth-century majismo internalizes this intrinsic dissonance. On the one hand, the pastor bobo figures the pure-blooded Christianity of Spain's idealized self (embodied in the gentlemanly villano's accomplished jumps). On the other, the possibility of redemption is implicit in the bobo's pre-epiphany inchoate and equivocal state. This deeply political incongruence is the toggle through which majismo, adopting dances of jaleo or confusion such as panaderos as emblems of casticismo—national essence—comes to assert its Spanishness through the figure of the pastor bobo, the ruffian, and the Gitano—its Whiteness figured in its Blackness. And so, in the eighteenth-century, majo dances of jaleo and confusion enter not only the repertoire of what will become the bolero school but also the tonadilla stage. Part of this process, as Roxo de Flores reveals in 1793, is that the distinction between noisy footwork and virtuosic jumping begins to break down. Writing a hagiography in 1852 of the noble house of Azara, who trace their Old Christian line to ninth-century Aragón and Navarra, Basilio Sebastián Castellanos de Losada traces the continuity between the villano's footwork and the zapateados of the stage majo. From the villancico, "a sacred dance," he writes, and precursor of the "*Villano*, in which the dancer carried the rhythm strongly in his feet," came the "*Zapateado*, which is danced in theaters by the Manolos and Manolas of low-class Madrid neighborhoods, and by the curros of Sevilla."[168]

The old villano trope, danced with zapateado as representing the humility of Christ the Redeemer, ironically references the successful evangelization of the

New World, and hence the grandeur of an empire upon which the "sun never set." Eighteenth-century Spain was considered exotic, passionate (sub-rational), musical, and so on. With the empire waning and national values denigrated and soon to be under assault by the French, majos cloaked the villano's sly dissentions in the figure of a mixed-race, and therefore debased, Andalusian Gitano. Reflecting the villano's confounded notions of blood purity and opting for the equivocal or subaltern side of the equation, majismo critiques the racist and imperialist hierarchy within which its status is precipitously falling. As we will see in the next section, with this move, majismo prefigures the coming appropriations of abjection that characterize the advent of modernism.

"Neglita gitana huachi": The Guaracha as a Mixed-Race Villano

> In vain new songs and dances of distinct, though always delicious and lascivious, ancestry arrive in Cádiz from the two Indies; they will never acclimate there, if before passing through Sevilla they do not leave behind in vile sediment whatever exaggerations are too stupid, tiresome and monotonous. A dance...leaves the school of Sevilla, as from a crucible, distilled and dressed in Andalusian style...
>
> —*Serafín Estébanez Calderón "El Solitario," Escenas andaluzas, 1847*[169]

In 1709, in the Cathedral of Cádiz, the villancico verses sung in the "Kalenda, Noche, y Días del NACIMIENTO de N. Sr. IESU-Christo" (the Calenda, Night, and Days of the birth of our Lord Jesus Christ), under the direction of chapel master Gaspar Ubeda y Castellò, were published (see Figure 2.5).[170] In the introduction to "Villancico IX" from this pliego, the conflicted imagery of Blackness as confused and jumbled, strange, and not human, is immediately established:

Los negros de monicongo	The blacks of Monicongo[171]
vienen à la noche buena,	Come on Christmas eve,
a dar calor al pesebre,	To warm the manger,
con todas sus chimeneas.	With all their chimneys.
. . .	. . .
Al portal llegan festivos,	They arrive at the gate [of Bethlehem] festively
y al revèz todo lo ostentan,	And they display everything backwards
pantorrillas en los labios,	Calves on their lips,
y en ambas paticas geta.	And on each leg a snout.[172]

The estribillo of this villancico, in Black Talk, contains two more assemblages of this chimera: an Italian *Arará* (a Cuban religious tradition of Dahomeyan ethnic groups), and a black-skinned *flamenco* (the Spanish word for "Flemish").

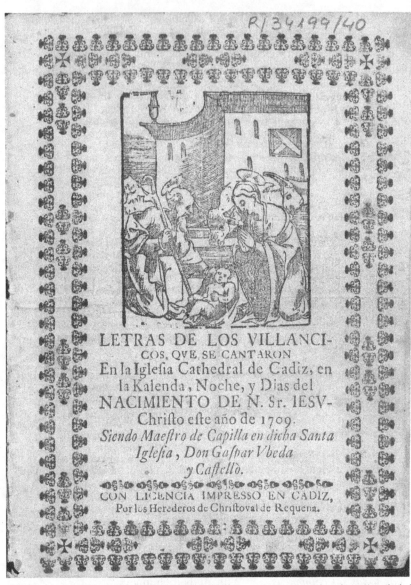

R/34199/40

LETRAS DE LOS VILLANCI-
COS, QVE SE CANTARON
En la Iglesia Cathedral de Cadiz, en
la Kalenda, Noche, y Dias del
NACIMIENTO DE N. Sr. IESV-
Christo este año de 1709.
Siendo Maestro de Capilla en dicha Santa
Iglesia, Don Gaspar Vbeda
y Castello.

CON LICENCIA IMPRESSO EN CADIZ,
Por los Herederos de Christoval de Requena.

FIGURE 2.5 *LETRAS DE LOS VILLANCICOS que se cantaron en la Iglesia Catedral de Cadiz, en la Kalenda, Noche, y Días del NACIMIENTO de N. Sr. IESU-Christo este año de 1709. Portada, 1709.* Courtesy of the Biblioteca Nacional de España.

Plimo, plimo, glande fliesta,	*Primo, primo, grande fiesta,*	Cousin, cousin, big fiesta,
fliesta glande plimo mio,	*fiesta grande primo mio,*	Big party cousin of mine,
flamenquiyo en calbonara	*flamenquiyo en carbonara*	Little carbonized *flamenco*
Ginoveso de Arara	*Ginoveso de Arara*	Genovese from Arará[173]

The play of words here is to ridicule the idea of black Europeans. It certainly makes one wonder about the identity of the singers: were they black Spaniards, or Spaniards in blackface? Felipe V's claim to the Spanish Netherlands, a significant, if difficult to govern, parcel in Spain's European holdings, was ceded just four years later, under the Treaty of Utrecht (1713), finally settling the War of the Spanish Succession, which had begun almost immediately after the Bourbons inherited the throne in 1700.[174] This song, above, makes flamencos, the Flemish who loomed large amid anxieties about Spain's standing within Europe, black. In the miscegenation posited in the words *flamenquiyo en calbonara*, then, like the disturbingly jumbled bodies of the *negros de monicongo*, we sense the political charge of Blackness, shaping flamenco's emergence out of precisely these kinds of performance.

The *negros de monicongo* sing "Let's go to Bethlehem," and ask "Y siolo Maetlo duelme?" (And señor Master is asleep?) Their answer is enigmatic: "No, que se asista en Iglesia, / y con la mano que azota, / lo compasso, le golbiena" (No, he should go to Church, / and with the hand that whips, / I measure [in the sense of suffering, or bearing witness to] it, Christ governs [or perhaps stays] the whipping hand.)[175] These lines are purposefully ambiguous. The last line establishes the object as "the whipping hand" ("*lo compasso*," "I measure it"). Then, with "*le golbiena*," "it governs him," the verse raises the possibility, in the equivocation between the capitalized "Master," Christ, and the master whose hand holds the whip, of a divine calling to account. The plight of these enslaved Africans is voiced in the first person, indicating a deep identification on the part of the church's parishioners with their suffering. The deformed bodies of the *negros de monicongo*, swimming as it were beneath the lash, thus prefigure flamenco's corporeal ethics of "kinesthetic and emotional dynamics as felt, suffered, or received—and bodily contained with grace and majesty."[176] The irony voiced here, a deep and deeply racialized response to the nation's decline, is that Spain saw itself in the image of a dispossessed and fractured black body.

Figuring assiduously the program of the "light-hearted slave," a perhaps dissembling promotion of the vicious fiction that enslaved people are too confused to be free, the *negros* sing "with much respect," and compare themselves to a "bueye mansa," a tame mule, singing with the angels from heaven. They break into a Latin catechism, singing "Ay Jesu dominas tecam": as in the trope of the pastor bobo, epiphany is dramatized through the metamorphosis in their speech from Black Talk to elevated Latin. They list exotic parrots that they will bring the Christ Child: a "cotorra" and a "papagayo from Havana." And they sing rhythmic series of equivocal nonsense: "tu, tu, turu, tu, tu," imitating the trumpet sound, "zumba, zumba, zumba, zambo," "ge, ge, ge, garagaja," and "guachi, guachi, guachi."

Zambo, Anglicized as "Sambo," was, in the system of racial categories that governed Spanish colonial society, a person of mixed African and Amerindian heritage.[177] I have argued that utterances such as the cumbé estribillo's "gurrumé" suggest the sexually triumphant "cucurucucu" of the cock's crow. Some equivocal utterances, such as "achí, achí," in Antonio Rosales's tonadilla *La jitanilla en el coliseo* of 1776, seem able to invoke the psychic violence—in this case the despective sneezes uttered by whites—suffered by black people in the Spanish-speaking world. Simultaneously, they invoke powerful Africanist retentions, such as *axé* or *ashé* (spiritual command), which Robert Farris Thompson has argued bloom inside American notions of the cool.[178]

While some of the terms in the 1709 villancico are familiar today, its "guachi, guachi, guachi" is not. This curious word also appears in Luis Misón's *Tonadilla de los Negros* (1761), where it is spelled "huachi" (but pronounced the same).[179] In Misón's tonadilla, a *neglita jitana*—a "little black Gitana," pronounced in Black Talk—and her companions (a "black man" and a "white woman," with all three characters played in drag by white actresses), enact a comic love triangle. They dance *con taconeo* (with heelwork), and they sing "neglita jitana huachi / que me robas el alma huachi" (little black Gitana *huachi* / you have stolen my soul *huachi*; in flamenco today this affection might be expressed as "gitana mía," "primo mío," or "mi negro.")

RAE gives the derivation of *huacho/a* or *guacho/a* as Native American, from the Chilean Quechua *huaccha* or *huacchu* (orphan or illegitimate child).[180] In his *Glosario de afronegrismos*, Fernando Ortiz writes that the American word *guaricha*, which he thinks must have been spread by the colonizers, is in Colombia a "detestable delicacy." RAE adds that in Colombia and Ecuador *guaricha* is a synonym for *rabona*, a female camp follower—and in Venezuela a "young single Indian woman."[181] "The guaracha was an American dance," Ortiz says, "which some have said was done by women alone."[182]

The *guaracha* was a Spanish dance as well, which Pellicer in 1804 calls a "lively and dangerous" descendant of the zarabanda, that scandalous late-sixteenth century dance that Juan de Mariana described as enacting "kisses and embraces and everything else," using "the mouth and arms, thighs and the whole body."[183] Roxo de Flores, who in his 1793 treatise lists zapatetas and taconeo among the "weaving and interlacing steps of the feet" that are essential to the "preparation or training for Spanish dance," mentions the guaracha as a contemporary dance, like the bolero.[184] Yet, as quoted above, Cairón writes in 1820 that "the *canario*...was later called guaracha, and lately zapateado: the name might change again soon, but the form will not."[185] There is a discrepancy here: Pellicer in 1804 sees the guaracha as a lascivious sexual pantomime, while Cairón in 1820 sees the guaracha as a footwork dance, like canario and zapateado.

The indigenous people of the Canary Islands are called "Guanches"; perhaps Cairón, in associating the canario with the guaracha, had this in mind. Although Cotarelo does not mention the guaracha, he does define zapateado as "a Spanish dance which, like the old *canario*, is danced using...charming *zapateo* (footwork)."[186]

This association of zapateado techniques with the canario is important to dance historians because, like the zarabanda and chacona, the canario was widely adopted in European courts. Thus there exists a great deal of documentation about the dance, its music, and its steps.[187] The canarios described in Fabritio Caroso (1581, 1600), Thoinot Arbeau (1589), and Cesare Negri (1604) all describe the most salient footwork techniques used in flamenco today: stamps (*golpes*), use of the toes and heels (*punta y tacón*), and brushes of the metatarsal (*escobilla*, little broom, a synonym for flamenco zapateado).

In Cuba as in Spain, Fernando Ortiz explains, the guaracha is "a dance of stamping of the feet."[188] Like zapateado from zapato, the guaracha's "name is derived from the meaning of this word in México, a certain kind of...shoe or sandal." "*Guarache* and *guaracha*," Ortiz continues, "are still Mexican names for a certain kind of popular shoe," and the guaracha, "an old Spanish dance," was a dance "in which the sound of the *guarachas* on the ground played a role."

> In Cuba...the dance called *guaracha* was marked by the rhythmic sound of this popular shoe, introduced to Cuba by blacks, or by the numerous...*guachinangos* who made up the troops of the fortress of Havana, the so-called *Llave de las Indias* (Key to the Indies); or by the rabble and soldiers of the fleets and armadas which passed through the port of Havana and stayed for up to six months.[189]

"*Guachinango*," Ortiz writes, "is an old Cuban word for someone from Veracruz and, by extension, Mexican."[190] In his *Human Factors of Cubanidad* (1940), Ortiz adds that "continental Indians [of Yucatán and México], victims of slavery imposed by the conquerors," arrived in Cuba "as slaves or soldiers" and appear in Cuban "histories as campechano and guachinango Indians."[191] The Cuban word "guachinango," in other words, references indigenous Mexicans who were enslaved by Spaniards and carried to Cuba. But Stevenson, citing Saldívar, notes that in México the guaracha was seen as a "negroid dance of supposedly Cuban provenance."[192] That is, Cubans saw the guaracha as Mexican, and vice versa—in addition, the word is of pre-Columbian provenance.

In a dissertation on Cuban percussive footwork, Ortiz discusses the guaracha. Recalling Covarrubias's 1611 references to the humility of Christ the Redeemer within the word "zapato," Ortiz's observations are worth considering in detail. "*Guarachear* is to *zapatear*," Ortiz says, which is to say that the verb comes from the footwear, as *taconeo* comes from the sound of *tacones*, or heels, and *chancleteo* comes from the sound of *chancletas*, or sandals.[193] But Ortiz reveals a world of Bourdeausian distinctions within these overlapping footwork dances:

> Taconeo is more than chancleteo. The chancleta...and the guaracha do not have a heel. This [heel] is required by a zapato and it asserts itself not only in the dimension of sound but also in the social dimension. Where people didn't wear shoes with heels there was no place for taconeo...In Cuba the blacks have not done

taconeo; they didn't bring shoes from Africa…if on the feet of a black man you hear the sound of heelwork in dance it is in its role of participant in the shoemaking apparatus imposed by whites, not to meet the demands of traditional styles.[194]

Further, Ortiz adds,

In taconeo the sound tries to express a figure of presumptuousness and cynicism, overly strident and lacking *sandunga fina* [stylish and refined charm]. Chancleteo can mean sensuality and grace, in the street as in dance; but in Cuba taconeo is crude and tasteless, flirtatious noise.[195]

Spanish dance historian María José Ruiz Mayordomo quotes a verse from the guaracha sung by the famous *tonadillera* (tonadilla performer) María Antonia Fernández "La Caramba" (1751–1787) in Antonio Rosales's *Tonadilla a solo de la Gitana*, performed in Madrid in 1783.[196]

Ay, guacharita	Ay, little *guachara*
que guachara estás	how *guachara* you are
que tu guacharo	your *guacharo* (male *guachara*)
te esguacharça	does the *guachara* to you[197]

"The author here is making a play on words," Ruiz Mayordomo explains, alternating the term *guacharo*, which in Quechua may mean orphan or small animal, but in this context means "crybaby" or "whiner," with *esguachar/esguazar*, which is "to ford a river."[198]

The double entendre may be equivocal, but it makes perfectly clear what is essential to this exotic impersonation: the figure of a young, vulnerable, exotic, and sexually available woman. The dark-skinned American guaracha fulfilled a fantasy of Spanish colonial domination that was no longer real, and everyone knew it. Majismo would annex and resignify this exotic *neglita jitana huachi*, this Afro-Native-American Gitana, as an eighteenth-century villano, its unbridled jumps and noisy footwork leaving "the school of Sevilla," like panaderos did, "as from a crucible, distilled and dressed in Andalusian style."[199]

Bourbon rule exiled Spain from itself, demanding it give up its unique national character in order to retain its status as European. In opposition, majismo adopted the image of the exotic and rebellious Gitano, holding in tension the sense of precariousness and longing for Spain's colonial riches, and nostalgia for its Afro-Islamic past, as self.

This appropriation enacts a fantasy of wealth and domination fulsome in its wry self-awareness and its disillusioned sense of its own diminution. Casticismo figures a national identity imbued with self-conscious irony, laughing derisively at its own mirror image. And yet, in this solipsistic reflection that, as I have argued elsewhere, evokes "the overwhelmingly salty-acid taste of grasping a radical incongruence," we sense also flamenco's tragic essence, its sense of loss and of pain—its tormenting spirit—its *duende*.[200] If Goya's majos depict the dewy pastoralist fantasies of dissolute aristocrats, his brutal *Saturn Devouring his Son* (1819–23) depicts, in the words of art historian Robert Hughes, the torment of lust for power in a society "so reactionary that 'tradition'" justifies an "unthinkable incest," where "fathers eat the young," and the future is murdered.[201] Like the victims of the public *autos da fé* (burning heretics at the stake) that led Kant to characterize Spain as "odd and exceptional," there is something of the sacred and the sublime in Spain's suffering antiheroes, publicly enduring "torture and a degrading death, or the galleys, from which they would not emerge alive"—an exaltation of what philologist Felipe Pedraza Jimenez calls "the morality of resistance."[202]

The Spanish Roma have long been willing purveyors of their own ambivalent image, "playing," as critical race theorist Jayna Brown says, "in the field of racialized fantasies."[203] In the eighteenth century, as Henry Swinburne writes in 1776, they danced the "lascivious and indecent" *mandingoy*, "imported from the Havannah…of negro breed."[204] Already in 1742 El Bachiller Revoltoso had described aristocratic majos crossing the river from Sevilla to the gitanería of Triana to see dances of the *cascabel gordo* (big bells).[205] "There is no denying that the Gitanas are very talented dancers," wrote El Bachiller, "in demand" to perform the *Manguindoi* at the principal houses of Sevilla "because it is so daring." And yet, in what might be considered a radically incongruent addition to its daring pantomimes, this 1742 performance also voiced Roma pain and suffering: the dancer

> is accompanied by two men playing guitar and tambourine and a third sings, while she dances, a long breath called *queja de Galera* (lament of the galley), because a Gitano *forzado* (pressed into service) wailed in this way while he was rowing and from him it passed to other benches and from there to other galleys.

In Misón's *Tonadilla de los Negros* (1761), a "neglita jitana huachi" dances "con taconeo" (with heelwork). In Rosales's 1783 tonadilla we have "guachara" as a sexy euphemism. In 1793, Roxo de Flores lists "cabriolas, taconéos, zapatetas, and other weaving and interlacing steps of the feet" as essential to Spanish dance training.[206] Rodríguez Calderón describes a bolero academy in 1794–1795, where young women practiced caprioles with their bloomers "pulled up nearly to their knees," as a den of "ills of body and soul."[207] In 1798 a royal decree prohibited the bolero to members of the aristocracy. And Cairón in 1820 says that zapateado is a contemporary manifestation of the guaracha, which he characterizes as a footwork dance. If, as we saw, in the seventeenth century, unbridled stamping, a sign of ethno-religious confusion, was distinguished from virtuosic jumping, the elevated language signaling epiphany, in the eighteenth century we see the wobbly and blurry intermingling of these two aspects of the villano.

Zapateado on the Spanish-speaking stage of the nineteenth century seems to emanate from eighteenth-century dances such as the guaracha. It is therefore

FIGURE 2.6 "El zapateado, the celbrated [*sic*] Spanish dance, as danced by Mlles Fanny & Theodore Elssler, arranged by Henri Rosellen." Lithograph (New York: Firth & Hall), 1840. Jerome Robbins Dance Division, The New York Public Library. NYPL Digital Collections. http://digitalcollections.nypl.org/items/2762b400-9d9f-0131-a40d-58d385a7bbd0

perhaps not surprising that the first mention of Gitano dance on the Spanish stage, in 1806, is a performance of "El Zapateado."[208] Along with the fandango's flirtatious pasadas, zapateado provided the language evoking Spain's eroticism and exoticism on the nineteenth-century ballet stage. In 1828, Théophile Gautier wrote about a Spanish dancer dancing the guaracha in Paris, and by 1840 a piano arrangement of "El Zapateado," published in New York, featured the famed Paris Opera ballerina Fanny Elssler and her sister Thérèse on its cover (See Figure 2.6).[209]

Meanwhile, Ned Sublette explains, in Cuban comic theater the dominant musical genre "was the up-tempo *guaracha*: a satiric, topical, or situational humorous song" which "replaced the Spanish *jácara* as between acts entertainment."[210] Though not specifically as a footwork dance, the guaracha in Cuba was captured in the orbit of U.S. blackface minstrelsy, and would move, as we will see in the next chapter, toward new Spanish appropriations of American Blackness (see Figure 2.7).[211]

FIGURE 2.7 "Guayaba-Guaracha para piano. Por Ruperto Ruiz de Velasco. Extrenada con extraordinario éxito en los bailes de máscaras del Teatro Principal el año 1885 y eje-cutada con general aplauso en el baile nominado, La Fiesta en el Harem. Así como en los bailes de la Sociedad, La Diva. En el Teatro de Goya." Musical score (Zaragoza: Imp. y Lit de Villagrasa, January 28, 1886). Courtesy of the Biblioteca Nacional de España.

Fernando Ortiz articulates the politics of the various warring imaginaries within percussive footwork dances such as guaracha and zapateado. But he also takes care to delineate some of the concentric and overlapping circles of sacred and secular, indigenous American and diasporic African worlds,

FIGURE 2.8 "The Planting of the Tabla in Huetamo (Michoacán)," by Raquel Paraíso. Photograph, June 11, 2011. The dancer is David Durán Barrera. In the past, in the Tierra Caliente region of Central Mexico, fandangos used to take place where a wooden sounding board could be planted under a shade tree by digging a hole in the ground and placing the *tabla* (platform) on top of it. Musical groups such as Los Jilguerillos del Huerto are working to reclaim and recontextualize these lost cultural traditions. Photo courtesy of Raquel Paraíso.

present within these dances. Ortiz describes several traditions of percussive footwork found among Natives throughout the Spanish- and Portuguese-speaking Americas. The Aruacas, or Arawak, indigenous peoples of the Antilles and the Caribbean, place a plank of wood "on the ground to dance on top of and in this way to be able to make the stamps of the feet sound" (See Figure 2.8).[212] "Certain Caribbean tribes," Ortiz continues,

> make a huge plank out of the root of a certain tree and they place it over a deep open hole in the ground, in which a sacred object has been deposited. Afterwards, the plank is covered with earth and so becomes a resonating platform upon which to dance. In this way the sound of the dancing feet can be heard over a long distance, and creates the rhythm for the flute. The plank thus serves as a drum, but this is not its primary function; rather it is to communicate to the deity that the dance is being done.[213]

Ortiz notes, "similar to this *tabla sonora*," or soundboard, "is the *tambor de tierra* (earth drum) used by the Catuquinarú Indians of Central Brazil," and, in México, from the Huasteca to the Mixteca regions and into many other parts of México "they dance the *mestizo huapango*."[214]

Ortiz is circumspect about teasing apart Native from diasporic African cultural elements in these footwork dances. What is clear, however, is that slavery links the guarachas of Spain, Cuba, and México. As Saldívar says, Afro-Mexican music and dance "followed the route those enslaved were forced to travel."[215] Thus, the earliest guaracha we know of is from México, a guaracha by Juan García de Céspedes, Chapel Master of the Cathedral in Puebla, dated 1674.[216] It is, unsurprisingly, a Christmas song.[217]

En la guaracha, ay	In the guaracha, ay
le festinemos, ay	we celebrate him, ay
mientras el niño, ay	while the baby, ay
se rinde al sueño, ay.	surrenders to sleep, ay.
Toquen y baylen, ay	Let them play and dance, ay
porque tenemos, ay	because we have, ay
fuego en la nieve, ay	fire in the snow, ay
nieve en el fuego, ay.	snow in the fire, ay.
Ay, que me abraso, ay	Ay, he embraced me, ay
divino Dueño, ay	divine Master, ay
en la hermosura, ay	in the beauty, ay
de tus ojuelos, ay....	of your eyes, ay....

What, in this guaracha's carnal shivers of love and desire, may we sense of the precariousness and longing that a declining and utterly dependent Spain might have felt toward its rising and soon to be independent colonies? And what, in the guaracha's oscillations of identity between *negra*, Gitana, and Native American, between Christ the Redeemer and the hand that whips, do we sense of the bobo villano's teetering between redemption and eternal damnation? The transgressive vacunao was absorbed into majo fandangos as an eroticized game of changing places with the Other. In flamenco, unlike other diasporic manifestations of this movement idea, this dance ritual is rarely consummated.[218] Nonetheless, in flamenco's whispers of sensual abandon, and in its pounding feet, I hear echoes of the highest spiritual and political imperatives of Africanist and perhaps also Native American aesthetic and spiritual values—to deny abjection and genocide and to affirm the unbreakable continuity and strength of their lineage—and their unbreakable resistance.

II | A Modernist Becoming
THE POWER OF BLACKNESS

I say unto you: one must still have chaos in oneself to be able to give birth to a dancing star.

—*Nietzsche,* Thus Spoke Zarathustra

3 | Parody and Sorrow

F OR SPAIN, WHAT SOME historians call the "long nineteenth century" began with the Peninsular War, also known as the Spanish War of Independence (1808–1814), in fierce guerilla warfare against invading Napoleonic forces. Taking advantage of turmoil on the Iberian Peninsula, Bolivia, México, Venezuela, Chile, Argentina, Uruguay, Perú, Ecuador, Panamá, Guatemala, El Salvador, Costa Rica, and Honduras all progressed with successful revolutions for independence between the years 1809 and 1825. Spain endured three civil wars over the course of the nineteenth century (the Carlist dynastic struggles of 1833–1840, 1846–1849, and 1872–1876), and lost its last remaining Caribbean and Pacific possessions—the islands of Philippines, Puerto Rico, Guam, and Cuba—in the Spanish-American War of 1898.

It is strange to consider that during this era of burgeoning republicanism and capitalist enterprise in Europe and the Americas, Spaniards only enjoyed the benefits of constitutional democracy for the briefest of periods: first, with the Constitution of 1812, promulgated in the midst of war and abrogated when Fernando VII was restored to the throne after the expulsion of French forces in 1814; then during the *Trienio Liberal* (1820–1823) following war hero General Rafael del Riego's uprising; next, with the First Republic of 1873–1874; and then during the Second Republic of 1931–1939. Not until after dictator Francisco Franco's death in 1975 did a stable democratic society emerge, fully formed as if from the head of Zeus, with the Spanish Constitution of 1978.

Yet the local networks, the regional and the international alliances that successfully repulsed Napoleon's armies in 1814 also supported and gave refuge to those thinking and working toward a new Spain, independent of the crippling demands of sustaining and defending its colonial enterprises. In what was certainly a long-standing custom across England and France (where many Spanish *liberales* found refuge after the war), and especially in Andalucía (the epicenter of defense against the French), the local café, the neighborhood bar, and the roadside tavern were gathering places where patrons could discuss politics, sing patriotic and nationalistic songs, and conceive and plan mercantile projects.[1] The *Himno de Riego*, honoring the general, became the national anthem during the Trienio Liberal, as well as during the First and Second Republics, and popular wartime songs such as "Trágala" ("Swallow It") survive in well-known flamenco verses such as this one, from *alegrías*:[2]

Con las bombas que tiran	With the bombs that
los fanfarrones	the French show-offs throw
Se hacen las gaditanas	The women of Cádiz
Tirabuzones	tie their hair in ringlets

During the Constitutional period of 1812–1814, liberal and propagandistic *sainetes* (picaresque one-act farces or tidbits), recalling perhaps the old trope of the pastor bobo in their aim of simultaneously edifying and entertaining audiences, set democratic indoctrination, rustic speech, and comic antics to music and dance.[3] Spanish guerilla fighters and ruffian antiheroes like Escarramán not only famously sired the characters in Prosper Mérimée's *Carmen* (1845) but also the earlier "Polo del Contrabandista" (Smuggler's Song), written and performed by celebrated tenor Manuel García in 1805, and reprised at Madrid's Teatro de la Cruz in 1813 on the occasion of Fernando VII's birthday (this was before Fernando vacated the Constitution and executed all of its partisans the following year).[4]

At the same time, from the dying embers of majismo, the national characters and musical forms staged in eighteenth-century tonadillas and villancicos ceded favor to Italian *bel canto*. Luis Lavaur, seminal scholar of the impact of Romanticism on flamenco's development, writes that *bel canto* acquired a unique and local character in early-nineteenth-century Spain: Italian *dilettanti* had their counterparts in the Andalusian *aficionados* who passionately discussed their favorite singers and sang their songs in cafés and taverns.[5] (Flamenco aficionados still do.) Sentimentalism, and Romantic interest in the feminine, the uncanny, and the irrational may have been an "aesthetic register" all across the map of Western sensibility.[6] But flamenco's "rending songs," while reflecting this taste, conveyed a unique response, conditioned in particular by Spain's ordeal as one of the battlegrounds upon which Napoleon's domination of Europe was decided. Flamenco is a form of nineteenth-century casticismo, Lavaur argues; a forceful nationalistic repudiation of foreign interference, which paradoxically reveals the influence of these foreign invaders.

Leading thinkers of the Enlightenment had viewed Spanish "passion," and its penchant for bloody rituals such as *autos da fé* (public immolations), as ranking Spain beneath other European nations on the scale of racially superior Reason and Whiteness.[7] Attributing such gruesome displays (and bullfighting must certainly be included in this list) to the peninsula's Muslim and African past was, of course, an old and enduring theme. Prefiguring the mid-nineteenth-century aphorism often attributed to novelist Alexandre Dumas that "Africa begins at the Pyrenees," French ambassador Dominique Dufour de Pradt states in his 1816 account of the Peninsular War, "blood, manners, language, the way of life and making war, in Spain everything is African...If the Spaniard were Mohammedan, he would be completely African."[8]

Nonetheless, partisan heroism during the Napoleonic Wars inspired widespread admiration and piqued incipient Romantic interest, attracting foreign tourists inclined toward Orientalism. Consequently, the ironic self-consciousness and desilusión that impart to Spanish literature and theater its deliberate ambiguity grew, in nineteenth-century nationalistic music and dance, increasingly self-exoticized. Whereas Spain's political and economic decline had been gradual, musicologist James Parakilas argues, its acquisition of a "national soul" was sudden, almost as if it were "compensation offered to the powerless."[9]

Gitanos, along with *negros* and Moriscos, were stock characters of the eighteenth-century tonadillas, but Spanish Roma performers rarely set foot on the professional stage until well into the nineteenth century.[10] And yet, in what Lavaur terms a "Wildean paradox of the natural imitating the artificial," Gitano artists acted as the embodiment of Spanish "soul," pulling national musics toward the exotic, the intuitive, and the spectral.[11] Tourists such as Washington Irving (whose *Tales of the Alhambra* are thought by many to have sparked romanticism's fascination with Spain) in 1829, Prosper Mérimée (who wrote *Carmen*) in 1830, French poet and dance critic Théophile Gautier in 1840, Hungarian composer Franz Liszt (Isaac Albéniz's teacher) and Russian composer Mikhail Glinka (who sparked the movement called "Symphonic Alhambrism") in 1845, and French banking scion Baron Charles Davillier (who attended a *zarandeo*; *zarandear* is "to shake") in 1862, sought out Gitano performance in alternate venues, "slumming," as aristocratic majos had a century before, in Triana and Granada's Albaycín.[12]

In sixteenth-century seguidillas and moriscas, seventeenth-century jácaras, zarabandas, and chaconas, and eighteenth-century villancicos, fandangos, and cumbés, the performance that would constitute flamenco was often identified with the marginal worlds of those enslaved and those pressed into service: Gitanos, Moriscos, *curros negros* (black toughs), *barateros* (gangsters), prostitutes, gamblers, ruffians, and smugglers. But Jews and Muslims had been expelled in 1492, Moriscos in 1609 and, already in the eighteenth century, Afro-Spaniards too had largely "disappeared" from the population. Now, the romantic Gitano, host for those vanished Others, became the focal point of this imagery.

Of course the Roma had never been considered even remotely "Spanish" until 1783, when Carlos III rescinded the genocidal policy of detention and forced labor for "those whom they call Gitanos."[13] English author George Borrow records in 1831 that the Spanish Roma so hated the associations of the word "Gitano" that they eschewed its usage in favor of calling themselves "foreigners": "flamencos," or Flemish.[14] Recall that in the 1709 Calenda in Cádiz, the trope of a "black flamenco" was already established within the villancico, inspiring both derision and, in line with eighteenth-century Spain's generalized sense of precariousness and identification with those "pressed into service," profound empathy. Thus it was understood at all social levels in nineteenth-century Spain that to sing *por lo flamenco* (in a flamenco style) meant to sing not in a foreign style (Italian *bel canto* would fill that niche) but in a "Gitano" style. As performed by Gitanos and non-Gitanos alike, in Spanish Roma neighborhoods and on distinguished theatrical stages, emerging flamenco performance made reference to what performance theorist Diana Taylor calls the "repertoire" of the stage Gypsy—the *neglita jitana huachi* that I have described as a complex mestizaje.[15]

In fact, bohemianism flavored mid-century musical nationalism across Europe. And Romantic audiences—along with the desire to participate in elite European cultural and political discourse—pulled Spaniards toward these stylistic inclinations.[16] Yet despite its populist and its exotic aspects, in Europe and also in the United States (where blackface minstrelsy was emerging), such staged nationalism was couched in elite rhetoric. For example, the blackface performer Thomas Dartmouth "Daddy" Rice performed as a supernumerary in *Bombastes Furioso* at New York City's Park Theatre before he first played and popularized the blackface persona of "Jim Crow" in the late 1820s; in 1833 at the Park Theatre "Signora Adelaide Ferrero" danced in a "new ballet entitled 'The Festival of Bacchus,'" followed by one Mr. Blakely, singing the "Comic Extravaganza of Jim Crow."[17] Spanish dancers such as María Mercandotti, adopted by a British aristocrat during the Spanish War of Independence and classically trained under Auguste Vestris at the Paris Opera, circulated internationally.[18] And in 1818, at the Madrid Teatro del Príncipe, Antonio Cairón choreographed and performed in the premiere of a baile *de medio carácter* called *El encuentro feliz o Los americanos o La espada del mago* (The Happy Encounter, or The Americans, or The Magician's Sword).[19]

Cairón, whose 1820 treatise we saw in Chapter 2, was a bolero dancer, and in categorizing this piece "*de medio carácter,*" he references European ballet's categories of *danse noble*, *demi-caractère*, and *comique* (in the French tradition) or *grottesco*, (in the Italian school).[20] Historian Basilio Sebastián Castellanos de Losada discusses the Spanish usage of these categories in theater dances: "*grotesco*" (grottesco), depicting villano-esque "lowly people, villagers and country people" dancing with "extraordinary jumps and strange and ridiculous gestures"; "*cómico*" (comique), vivacious, quick, and agile dance, though "less free" than baile grotesco; "baile *serio*," which should only express serious and grand characters, sentiments, and themes; and "baile *de medio carácter*," which requires the speed and agility of baile cómico, but "demands elegance, refined and pleasant manners, and exquisite taste."[21] *The Happy Encounter*, above, contains four scenes with set changes and popular special effects, such as a tempest, and lightning, two bailes "*de negros*," and a tango (understood in nineteenth-century Spain as an Afro-Cuban dance, this is the earliest identified score of a tango in Spain).[22] In classifying these dances representing *negros* as "de medio carácter," rather than cómico or grotesco, Cairón distinguishes their elegance, refinement, and impeccable taste from the "extraordinary jumps" and "ridiculous gestures" of the dance of "lowly people."[23]

Nonetheless, nineteenth-century stagings of national identity also absorbed the popular tropes of the equestrian circus, the tightrope daredevil, the Gypsy exotic, and the blackface clown.[24] In a dizzying circuit reflecting the increasing ease of transatlantic travel, by the 1830s and 1840s, prima ballerina Fanny Elssler's interpretations of Spanish dances had traveled to the United States, and blackface minstrel parodies of her performances were exported back to Europe.[25] In nineteenth-century Cuba, considered the "jewel" of the Spanish Empire, European minuets, contradanzas, and zapateados signified Whiteness, as Fernando Ortiz explains, on stages, ballrooms, and at country picnics.[26] And black and blackface artists of Cuban musical theater, performing guarachas shaped by the dance, music, language, and religious traditions of enslaved Africans continually arriving "a full generation after anywhere else in the hemisphere," carried a new wave of Africanist music and dance ideas back to Spain, profoundly impacting, as in the case of the tango, flamenco's development.[27]

The ricocheting back and forth of such representational conundrums nonetheless served elemental economic and political imperatives on both sides of the Atlantic. The population of African descendants in Spain had declined in inverse proportion to the metastasizing Atlantic slave trade. Traffickers no longer conveyed African captives through distribution centers in Sevilla and Lisbon. Instead they took them directly through the Middle Passage, from "factories" off the West African coast directly to American ports such as Havana, Cartagena de Indias, New Orleans, and Veracruz.[28] Domínguez Ortiz records the last mention of a slave in Madrid in 1799, and while in 1812 there were still slaves in Cádiz (once known as a "West African metropolis" and "emporium of African commerce"), by 1836 the importation of those enslaved from overseas was prohibited.[29] Slavery was quietly abolished in Spain in 1837, although this was never announced publicly, so as not to anger Cuban sugar plantation owners.[30] The 1861 *ley del suelo libre* (the Free Soil Act) decreed that slaves from colonial territories who were brought to the Spanish metropolis by their masters had to be released, simply because they had stepped on Spanish free soil—but such laws were rarely enforced.

Like the Spanish economy, the U.S. economy depended existentially on "two and a half *billion* hours of uncompensated labor" from those enslaved in the Anglophone colonies between 1650 and 1800.[31] (As an illustration of how interpenetrated Spanish slavery was and is with our own history, the brand used to mark slaves, often on their faces, was the word *esclavo* (slave), symbolized as an "S" and a "*clavo*" (nail) in this manner: "$.") Ta-Nehisi Coates, building his powerful "Case for Reparations" (2014), writes that in 1860, "the nearly 4 million American slaves were worth some $3.5 billion, making them the largest single financial asset in the entire U.S. economy, worth more than all manufacturing and railroads combined."[32] In the antebellum United States, the white planter elite urgently sought to preserve slavery in the South and slave commerce with the North, and to expand slavery in the West—blackface minstrelsy did not merely play a part in the racial politics of its time, writes Eric Lott: "It *was* the racial politics of its time."[33]

The blackface performance of this era was a "derisive celebration of the power of blackness," Lott argues, placing "blacks, for a moment, ambiguously, on top."[34] At a time when the United States teetered on the brink of civil war, this ludicrous reversal shored up white allegiances, encouraging white working class audiences to join the wealthy elite in imagining their superior stake vis-à-vis enslaved African Americans in the socio-economic hierarchy.[35] The mid-nineteenth-century "culture of feeling" pursued a similar agenda, often featuring the figure—consider Harriet Beecher Stowe's widely disseminated and translated abolitionist novel *Uncle Tom's Cabin; or, Life Among the Lowly* (1852)—of a "passive, sentimentalized, often-male slave."[36] As the cultural historian Saidiya Hartman says in her discussion of Isaac Brinckerhoff's 1864 tract *Advice to Freedmen*, "the 'backbreaking' regimen of slave labor" was imagined in the black man's body as a "sentimental ethic of submission," a "cheerful genuflection, bending the back joyfully and hopefully to the burden."[37] But the threat of violence undergirds such nineteenth-century melodrama, notes Hartman—a "force of evil" which also drives the parodic reversals of blackface.[38]

Spaniards reckoned with and took up the tropes of U.S. blackface minstrelsy in terms of their own history of violent racial conflict. If U.S. performance figured Blackness as an "essentially pained expression of the body's possibilities," this expression of pain and sorrow reminds us of Quevedo's seventeenth-century swimmers under the lash, "imitating the sounds and movements and hard labor of the galleys," dancing out "torment, whipping, and...death on the gallows."[39] In Spain, the huge profits gained in the American colonies, powered by slave labor, paradoxically sucked prosperity away from the metropole. Into this vacuum flowed the distinct cultures and manifestations of Spanish identity that we are following here. And the outlaws whose danced sufferings evoked the suffering of Christ on the *Vía Crucis* became national symbols in eighteenth century Spain, and then flamenco in the nineteenth century, precisely because of their implicit critique of the Catholic state, whose persecution and enslavement of its most humble and vulnerable classes is (equivocally) represented as antithetical to its own Christian values. This metaphor aligns rather precisely with the sentimental depiction in *Uncle Tom's Cabin* of the Black body as a body in pain—as opposed to a body filled with righteous wrath. Spanish ruffian antiheroes, of questionable lineage, dancing a savage yet ironic critique of power at the end of the hangman's rope in the seventeenth century, or in shackles in Rodrigo Noveli's 1708 dance treatise, represented and contended with state violence through parody, irony, and equivocation.

By the nineteenth century, "Andalusian Gitanophilia," to use Lavaur's term, like the eighteenth-century majismo out of which it developed, had become, paradoxically, an assertion of wealth, culture, and liberal democratic values—that is, of membership (despite the declining fortunes of the nation as a whole) in the economic and political structures of colonial power.[40] From flamenco folklorist Antonio Machado y Álvarez (Demófilo)'s *Colección de cantes flamencos* (1881) to musicologist Felipe Pedrell's manifesto *Por nuestra música* (1897) and his song collection *El cancionero popular español* (1922), we see the effort to place an articulated Spanish musical identity alongside those of other European countries and in opposition to what many saw as impoverishing foreign stereotypes. Some sectors of the elite were increasingly resentful of their entanglement with this folkloric image, but others claimed "authentic" flamenco performance as the essence of Spanish *volkgeist*.[41] "A songbook is infinitely valuable," writes Demófilo in 1859, "because it reveals the Humanity of the common folk...uncovering the often hidden but never lost individualism in the rich manifestations of the spirit of the people."[42] These fault lines were revealed in a fascinating polemic that played out in the Spanish press in 1866 around Francisco Arderius's blackface troupe, the *Bufos Madrileños* (The Madrid Clowns).[43] The Barcelona periodical *La España musical* wrote on September 6:

In the old days Spain had fewer people but more Spaniards than now.... Artistically we have reached the extreme of disdaining Spanish *zarzuela* in favor of the *Bufos madrileños*, descendents of those *Bufos parisienses* (Parisian comic operas) which are so famous in our country. The most Spanish theater of Madrid has been converted into a local branch of the French theater. Mr. Dumas was right when he said something about Africa and the Pyrenees, but when he said that, he should have considered how much in Spain is French.[44]

To which, in the context of intense back-and-forth about Barcelona (in its urbanity, often suspected of harboring more sympathy for French culture than the rest of Spain) versus Madrid, Spanish versus French, both versus Italian theater—and the shadow of Africa hanging over the discussion—the Madrid periodical *El Pensamiento Español* (*Spanish Thought*) chimed in sarcastically on September 20:

Vaudeville in Spanish, that the low class calls *zarzuela*...Is Paris not the capital of the civilized world?[45]

Flamenco's development in the nineteenth century was thus spurred by an intense desire on the part of Spain's cultural and political elite to defend their status as European, precisely by asserting Spain's unique national identity, personified by its last remaining Other (Moorish, Jewish, and Afro-descended Spaniards having long since "disappeared"): the Gitano.[46]

As Lavaur puts it, flamenco developed as a "radically urban pseudo-folklore": pessimistic, melodramatic, and *desmelenado* (disheveled).[47] During an era in which rationalist and liberal republicanism was abhorred along with the French invaders, yet simultaneously emulated and admired by those resisting these selfsame invasions, mid-nineteenth-century flamenco songs, expressing a clichéd "vague, profound, and timeless pain," were nostalgic laments for Spain's glorious and unrecoverable past.[48] Ironically, the emergence of flamenco, both representing and protagonized by professional Roma artists, pulled Andalusian popular music away from the truly working-class performance of aficionados singing *bel canto*–influenced songs and toward a dramatization of Gitano stereotypes.[49] Like American blackface, *gitanismo*—fictionalized self-representation—had become a bona fide commercial enterprise.

El Tío Caniyitas

> Gone too from the world, Averroes and Moses Maimonides, dark men in mien and movement, flashing in their mocking mirrors the obscure soul of the world, a darkness shining in brightness which brightness could not comprehend.
>
> *James Joyce*

For Spain, Luis Misón's 1761 *neglita jitana huachi* represents what Hartman terms the "metaphorical aptitude" of Blackness as an "imaginative surface upon which the master and the nation came to understand themselves."[50] She quotes a chilling observation from Toni Morrison's *Playing in the Dark*: "The slave population, it could be and was assumed, offered itself up as surrogate selves for meditation on problems of human freedom." Lott genders this in a useful way, adding, "The black mask offered a way to play with collective fears of a degraded and threatening—and male—Other while at the same time maintaining some symbolic control over them."[51] In the male travesty of Spanish productions such as Francisco Asenjo Barbieri's 1859 *Zarzuela-disparate* (zarzuela-folly) *Entre mi mujer y el negro* (Between my Wife and the Negro), (in which multiple layers of comic disguise are set in motion by a white suitor's terror of a murderous Cuban slave, ludicrously in love with his mistress), or Soriano Fuertes's 1849 *El Tío Caniyitas* (featuring an Englishman in Gitano drag), we see these knotty issues playing out on the mid-nineteenth century Spanish stage.[52]

FIGURE 3.1 *Scene from the "Tio Caniyitas,"* by Gustave Doré, 1862. In Charles Davillier and Gustave Doré, Spain (London: Sampson Low, Marston, Low and Searle, 1876).

On April 30, 1848, E. V. de M. penned an article in the Madrid periodical *La España* titled "Musical Choreography Revue...Death of Spanish opera before it was born."[53]

In the past few weeks preceding the new theater season, the public has been entertained with a thousand and one notices about the opera companies that will be performing at the Teatro de la Cruz and the Teatro del Circo...The theater watchers of the Circo noted the arrival of a Frenchified Italian company, while on the stage of the Cruz there rang out a ceaseless exclamation of *¡ópera nacional!* [national opera!] As often occurs in these cases, two bands soon formed and began fighting, *Crucicistas* and *Cirquistas*...

The advocates of the Teatro de la Cruz...have found it impossible to accomplish their project. The *ópera nacional* thus has been postponed, that is, the national opera that the professors and composers of music...might have composed...In place of the operas that the most notable Spanish composers might have written, we have *El tango americano*, the *Sa pi tu sé* and the *Neguita* [*Negrita*, little black woman, in Black Talk] sung by señores Pardo and Guerrero, both actors belonging to the company of this theater. People of good taste, those who are truly interested in our national treasures, have lost out in this transaction; but there are many other people for whom these songs are equivalent and even superior to the most select melodies of composers with names like Rossini, Bellini, and Donzeti [sic], and they go ecstatic and haywire with pure pleasure when the above-named actors sing the little song that says:

Pobe neguito,	Pobre negrito,	Poor little black man,
que titi etá...	qué triste está...	how sad he is...
Tabaja mucho	Trabaja mucho	He works hard
y no gana naa	Y no gana nada	and he doesn't earn anything

And they get delirious with excitement when the following verse, which we think comes from the song *Sapitusé*, gets an encore:[54]

Si tu boquita fuera ciruela verde	If your little mouth were a green plum
toda la noche anduviera	all night long I'd be
muerde que muerde.	biting and biting.

Si tu boquita fuera terron de azúcar,	If your little mouth were a jar of sugar
toda la noche estuviera	all night long I'd be
chupa que chupa.	sucking and sucking.

This *tango americano* (American tango) called *sapitusé* was all the rage in the summer of 1848, with several newspaper articles writing that "the entire country is singing it," and one article reporting that the scandalous song was prohibited; it remained in vogue through 1852.[55] In 1850, at the same time the French ballerina Marie Guy-Stéphan was performing *Giselle* in Madrid, singer-dancers Manuel Guerrero and Francisco Pardo, who, as we have read above, were actors at the Cruz, performed this tango in a *comedia de costumbres andaluzas* (play of Andalusian customs).[56]

One wonders whether Guerrero and Pardo's comic duet, two men singing a song of sexual innuendo, was performed in drag, or in blackface, or both. In 1848, the duo sang accompaniment to several dancing couples, but the following year the duo sang a tango americano in a piece with the intriguing title "He Who Dresses as Another."[57] In this latter performance, Guerrero and Pardo's tango was followed by a dance called *Guayabito* (little guava, which seems a reference to Caribbean exoticism), danced by two men: Carlos Atané and Manuel Guerrero. Atané was a pioneering choreographer of the emerging *bailables*, which Kiko Mora calls "minstrelizing" performances, oscillating between the academic language of the bolero school and the race mimicry of flamenco performance, emerging at this precise moment.[58] It seems noteworthy, considering eighteenth-century villancicos de negros such as the 1709 Calenda in Cádiz examined in Chapter 2, that this tango "dressed as another," was performed on Christmas day—and that the same song billed in Madrid as a "tango americano" was titled a "Tango de Guinea," a Guinean tango, in 1849 Málaga.[59]

Flamenco historian Eusebio Rioja quotes Rafael Marín y Reus's *Método para guitarra* (1902), the first published flamenco guitar method, describing the burlesque pantomimes that were part of these nineteenth-century tangos.[60] *"Tangueros,"* tango performers, Marín writes, "tend to be, among the flamencos, what the *'excéntricos'"* (eccentric dancers) "are to the Circus." They "make people laugh with their contortions and their songs of ambiguous intention," and so "they are called *'gracioso* (clown), *chuflón,'"* (a huge *chufla* or burlesque).[61]

In 1849, Mariano Soriano Fuertes, composer, musicologist, and founder of *La Iberia Musical y Literaria* (Musical and Literary Iberia), premiered a zarzuela that over its long and influential term on the Spanish stage would disseminate and popularize this burlesque image.[62] Soriano Fuertes wrote about *El Tío Caniyitas o El Mundo nuevo de Cádiz: Opera cómica española, en dos actos* (Uncle Caniyitas or The New World of Cádiz: Spanish Comic Opera, in Two Acts) in volume four of his 1855–1859 *Historia de la Música Española desde la venida de los fenicios hasta el año de 1850* (History of Spanish Music from the Arrival of the Phoenicians until the Year 1850):

> In November of 1849 *Caniyitas* was performed for the first time, with a happy result, at the Teatro de San Fernando in Sevilla, by the actors Doña Rita Revilla and Don Francisco Luna, and the Spanish singers Don Manuel Carrión, a tenor celebrated throughout Europe today…just a little over a year after its premiere it had been performed 130 nights in a row in the three Cádiz theaters at the same time, and in theaters in Gibraltar, Málaga, Valencia, Madrid, Granada, and afterwards in all the other theaters of Spain and America, with satisfying success.

Cotarelo writes about the premiere of *Caniyitas* at Madrid's renovated Teatro del Circo:

> *El Tío Caniyitas*…is written in such thick *caló* (Spanish Roma dialect) that it is a wonder that the audience could understand a word of what was sung, and still less what was spoken, we might add. Nonetheless, it seems to have been well received, because it was performed eight nights in a row, and was later often shown…The music of *El Tío Caniyitas*, which on the whole might be considered a rhapsody or arrangement of a multitude of old and more-or less-known modern Andalusian airs, as the composer himself admits, consists of fifteen pieces, according to the arrangement for piano and voice published at its premiere.[63]

El Tío Caniyitas was condemned by Madrid critics, but nonetheless became popular and was widely repeated; some critics called the piece *casticista* (nationalist), revealing its implication in the still highly charged politics of eighteenth-century *majismo*.[64] Gerhard Steingress quotes from an 1850 review of *Caniyitas* in Jerez, which remarks on how the innovation of centering the plot on a Gitano brought "the most popular songs to the stage with the object of introducing and extending among all the classes of society the taste and *afición* for the national opera."[65] The review continues, "In society and having fun at home . . . Gitano jokes are repeated everywhere, and the original airs that the gentleman [composer] Soriano Fuertes has figured out how to combine with the already known vulgar songs that resound among all classes of people."

Several elements of this comic opera survive in flamenco today. For example, the first scene includes a song now known in the flamenco canon as a variant of cantiñas (which, as referenced in *Caniyitas*'s title, come from Cádiz): *mira-brás*, with its *pregón* (cry of a hawker at an open-air market):

Vengasté a mi puesto, hermosa	Come to my stand, lovely girl
no se vaya usté, salero	don't go away, salty one
Castañas de Galarosa	Chestnuts from Galarosa [Huelva province]
peros y camuesas, peros![66]	pears and pippins, pears!

In the memoir of his 1862 tour of Spain, Charles Davillier recorded his impressions of *Caniyitas*:

> There are certain of the *zarzuelas* [that are] imitations of the French comic operas . . . As an example of a purely Spanish *zarzuela*, we may take the *Tio Caniyitas* . . . whose hero is an Englishman in love with a gipsy, who disguises himself as a *majo*. This opera had a most unparalleled success; in less than two years it made the tour of the Peninsula, and . . . in America the *Tio Caniyitas* became so much the fashion that its incidents were reproduced in a hundred different ways in lithographs, engravings, or cigarette papers, cigar-holders, and even on the *abanicos de calaña*—fans mounted in willow, and sold at two *cuartos* [quarters] on féte days.[67]

Steingress also documents a number of performances of *Caniyitas* in Granada and Córdoba, including parodies (of what some thought was already a parody) that took the piece into the realm of the bullfighting circus.[68]

Caniyitas parodied Andalucía's ridiculous and stereotypical vision of foreigners, particularly Englishmen.[69] That is, the work is not a parody of the English, but of the Andalusian—it parodies not the foreigner, but the foreigner's vision of the self—as Gitano Other, depicted with an assemblage of Spanish images of Blackness. Beginning with its opening scene, the chorus announces the *bulla* or confusion that inevitably characterizes Blackness for Spain:

Ay qué bulla	Oh what a ruckus
qué confusión	what confusion
hay en la plaza	there is in the plaza
de S. Juan de Dios![70]	of San Juan de Dios!

In this scene, the chorus also sings a verse echoing the suggestive onomato-poeic endings that we traced in Chapter 2 as allusions to lascivious Blackness. Evoking the cock's *cucurucucu* in the obscene 1588 Neapolitan moresca, or the *¡Gurrumé, gurrumé, gurrumé!* estribillo of cumbé dances, the chorus sings:[71]

Tú serás paloma blanca,	You will be a white dove,
yo seré palomo azul,	and I will be a blue dove,
vente al campo y haremos	come with me to the countryside and we will do
guuú, guuú, guuú...[72]	*guuú, guuú, guuú...*

Just as the above-quoted *Sapitusé* verses of tangos are known through the voices of two flamenco legends, Pepe de la Matrona (1887–1980), who re-corded them in 1910, and José Monge Cruz "El Camarón de la Isla" (1950–92), who recorded them in the title track of *Como el agua* (1981), the "gurugú" tag is famous as sung by legendary flamenco singer Pastora Pavón "La Niña de los Peines" (1890–1969).[73] Another tango which we will presently examine, the 1875 "Gangú Gangú," sung by El Negro Meri, also echoes these utter-ances. Thus, in the Black Talk nonsense syllables of these tag lines in *El Tío Caniyitas* (1849) there sparks a synapse, centuries-old representations of Blackness streaming inside this parody of self-as-Andalusian.

We consider here this sorrow and sense of loss, this pessimistic, disheveled, and self-parodying body, set alongside the overwrought grins and broken bodies of American blackface minstrel characters that would succeed Italian songs as the contested object in Spain's nineteenth-century culture wars. In the powerful words of black feminist theorist bell hooks, "Mournful imperialist nostalgia constitutes the betrayed and abandoned world of the Other as an accumulation of lack and loss."[74] For Spain, Gitano music had long performed this range of feeling, characterized, for example, in a 1799 poem by the Count of Noroña as *quejumbroso*, or plaintive.[75] In an article published in 1869, poet and playwright Gustavo Adolfo Bécquer used the same word:

> ...the slow and rhythmic sound of *palmas* [hand-claps] is heard from far away, and a plaintive and sorrowful voice that intones sad songs or the segui-dillas of [illustrious flamenco singer Francisco Ortega Vargas] "El Fillo." It is a group of flamenco people of pure race around a rickety table and an empty jug who sing *lo hondo* (deep song) without guitar accompaniment, grave and ecstatic like priests of an abolished cult, who gather in the silence of the night to remember the glories of past days and to sing crying, like the Jews, *super fluminem Babiloniae* (by the rivers of Babylon)."[76]

As flamenco commoditized the stage Gitano that hosted centuries-old representations of Blackness, it paradoxically absorbed the foreign blackface tropes from the Americas that it simultaneously sought to resist. Flamenco was masked, perhaps not overtly in burnt cork, but in a similarly thick bark, covering

FIGURE 3.2 "Sensation among 'Our Colored Brethren' on ascertaining that the Grand Performance to which they had been invited on New Year's Day, was *unavoidably postponed to the year* **1900**!" by J. M. D. 1862. Art and Picture Collection, The New York Public Library. NYPL Digital Collections. https://digitalcollections.nypl.org/items/510d47e1-3faa-a3d9-e040-e00a18064a99

slippery, derisive, and doubled meanings. The resistance implicit in "texts wrought by toil, terror, and sorrow," songs containing " 'unsayable claims to truth' that can never be communicated," is to be found precisely in their opacity, Hartman writes, their "veiled and half-articulate messages," the ghosts of whose imperceptible intentions we somehow nonetheless sense.[77] And, while I have often thought about the female body as the object of desire, the politics surrounding the black man's body are most pertinent to our considerations of the characters "Tío Caniyitas," "Mungo," "Harlequin Friday," and "Jim Crow"—constituents of the semantic field out of which Jacinto Padilla, "El Negro Meri," would launch his influential flamenco career.

The thrill and terror of porous boundaries between Black and White, order and chaos, civilization and savagery—the warp and weft of desire for and fear of the Other out of which twentieth-century modernism would issue—had a different life in Spain, itself the object of the covetous gaze of conquering armies and foreign tourists.[78] Yet perhaps in absorbing the heated rhetoric of American blackface, and perhaps because it was already inherent in the very Spanish equivocations of "swimmers under the lash," developing flamenco seems to resonate with these deep and deeply violent contradictions. Only by playing the Gitano could Spain be, in the nineteenth century, on top.

4 | Nonsense of the Body

...considering the ridiculous figure of servants
when they offer drinks to their masters, dancing the Coliseo, the Guineo,
excessively inclining their bodies in a notably dangerous and disgusting
manner; and though they are mute, they are chatterboxes with their feet...

—*Francisco de Quevedo, 1627*

WRITING IN 1951 ON the figure of the *negro* in sixteenth- and seventeenth-century Spanish song, dance, and villancicos, Horacio Becco observed that this character, "like a photographic negative, inculcated fetishism against shadow, terror of witchcraft," and wonder at "its sonorous half language," whose dislocated, inciting, yet irrational words were infinitely suggestive.[1] The function of skipping words (doing *guuú, guuú, guuú* alone together in the countryside, as in *El Tío Caniyitas*) is euphemistic, explains Benjamin Liu, in his monograph on *Medieval Joke Poetry*. Language that is "literally devoid of meaning," Liu writes, quoting semiotician Émile Benveniste, "makes reference to a profanation in language without going through with it, thus fulfilling its psychical function while diverting it and disguising it."[2]

Philologist José Manuel Pedrosa describes the euphemistic "nonsense" syllable tags such as the *guuú, guuú, guuú* of *Caniyitas* as "an exuberant harvest" of related words found in popular poetry all over Spain, "never identical but all reminiscent of one another."[3] The suffixes "–mango, –ango, –tango, –dango" illustrate the "more than equivocal" meanings of these utterances: *mango*, a handle, suggests male genitalia.

As an example, Pedrosa discusses an old folkdance from Asturias called the "perlindango," whose racy verses play on the nonsense "dango, dingo," given to me by "my love Mingo."[4] Such is the equivocating "poetry of 'sins of language,'" writes Liu: the "forked tongue" with which this poetry speaks instantly disrupts "conventions of the 'what' and 'how' of acceptable discourses."[5]

Mingo, as we have seen, has a long and suggestive history in Spain. We first met him in the *Coplas del Mingo Revulgo* (ca. 1465) as an astute pastor *bobo* prototype, a *villano* or villager impertinently critiquing Enrique IV himself. As we saw at play in Domingo González's *Villano cavallero por lo vaxo* (ca. 1650), the *bobo*'s transgressive equivocations potentially imply non-Christian blood. Thus, if the virtuosic *caprioles* of the *Villano cavallero por lo vaxo* certified good standing within the Church, the "surging and bounding" jumps in the obscene 1588 Neapolitan *moresca* discussed in Chapter 2 imply religious as well as racial "confusion"—and purposeful obfuscation from what we might consider a Black perspective. Thus, in the obscene depiction of a priest "showing his *chuchumbé*" in eighteenth-century México, dissent is given voice by people of *color quebrado*, or mixed blood. Perhaps, then, as in the deadpan obscenity and irony critiquing the "good life" enjoyed by "Thirty Sundays" (or perhaps Dominican friars) in Juan Arañés's *chacona* (1624) we may read coded Blackness within Mingo's euphemisms:[6]

...*un asno dando respingos.*	...an ass jumping up and down
Juana con tingo lo[s] mingos...	Juana with *tingo* the *mingos*...

Nonsense of the body, like verbal nonsense, weaves constantly through Spanish performances of race. And, while T. D. "Daddy" Rice's late-1820s-to-1830s "Jim Crow" act is an icon of specifically nineteenth-century U.S. racist imagery, many elements of this character clearly echo earlier European and Latin American imaginaries.

Otherness of the body on the Iberian Peninsula was a sign of impure blood—non-Christian lineage—and so making Otherness visible was an important representational device in figuring Blackness as religious deviance. Circumcision, for example, indicating Muslim or Jewish practice, was ridiculed in medieval Spanish joke poetry as a physical defect.[7] In the 1709 *Calenda* in Cádiz examined in Chapter 2, the invisible stain of *raza* was visualized in the *negros de monicongo* not in the color of their skin, but in terms of misassembled bodies, with calves on their lips and snouts on their legs, while the wedding guests in Avellaneda's *Bayle entremesado de negros* (1663) were all either "lame, one-armed, left-handed, or hunchbacked."[8]

Since Otherness of the body performed defective, or non-Christian lineage, it also signified a state of moral peril. Such is the *encorvada* (hunchback), which Covarrubias's 1611 dictionary defined as a *dança descompuesta* (an immodest and discourteous dance) "done by twisting the body and the limbs."[9] An *entremés* published in 1691 lists the *encorvada* along with the *endiablada* (literally bedeviled: ugly, disproportionate, perverse):[10]

Entra la comezón por los zancajos	The itch starts in my heels
y pongo larenzados unos ajos	And I put on some garlic *larenzados* [?]
mas con la picazón con que me veo	But with the temper I find myself in

bailo la Zarabanda y el Guineo	I dance the *Zarabanda* and the *Guineo*
las Folías, Canario y Encorvada	the *Folías*, *Canario* and *Encorvada*
el Villano, *las Vacas, la*	the *Villano*, the *Vacas*, the
Endiablada	*Endiablada,*
la Pavana, Capona y Saltarelo	the *Pavana*, *Capona* and *Saltarelo*
hasta caer de nalgas en el suelo.	until I fall on my ass on the floor.

In his exhaustive compendium, *Dances and Instrumental Diferencias in Spain*, Maurice Esses writes that moral critics described "generally uninhibited and openly erotic" dances such as these "as being works of the devil which would lead one straight to Hell."[11] Interestingly, in the 1691 entremés, the "itch" to dance the *endiablada*, whose successor, Covarrubias says, was the zarabanda and whose grandchild was the chacona, starts in the heels.

In view of the Spanish representations of race as embodied defectiveness, or nonsense, it is fascinating to note that "Jim Crow" is similarly "deformed, the right shoulder being drawn high up, the left leg stiff and crooked at the knee, giving him a painful, at the same time laughable limp."[12] "Jim Crow's" Black Talk likewise resonates with the garbled language that dramatizes the Spanish bobo's unredeemed state.

> *Wheel about, turn about*
> *Do jis so,*
> *An, ebery time I wheel about,*
> *I jump Jim Crow!*

When Rice brought his "Jim Crow" act to Europe in 1836, therefore, the blackface clowns of Spain may well have encountered their own reflection. But, although the overwhelming itch that deforms the (dancing) body in the seventeenth-century *endiablada* holds, at the heart of its comic narrative, the possibility of redemption, in the context of the overwhelming white anxieties of the 1830s United States there is none for "Jim Crow." He is existentially broken, in both body and in will, and cannot resist his subjugation.

What does "Jim Crow's" deformed and broken body tell us, then, about the way he reflects earlier European performative constructs of race (see Figure 4.1)? In colonial Spanish society, Whiteness was certified as a condition of membership in the elite. Notwithstanding, both enslavement and forced conversion to Christianity were advertised as spiritual boons to those in bondage.[13] The system of colonization was built on the prospect of redemption. Such was the context of the 1550 debate before Carlos V between Dominican friar Bartolomé de las Casas and Juan Ginés de Sepúlveda, who had translated Aristotle's *Politics* two years earlier. Sepúlveda's argument that some people were "natural slaves" (a term used by Aristotle) permeates and animates the ubiquitous trope of the "light-hearted" slave; we undoubtedly

FIGURE 4.1 *Thomas Rice as Jim Crow at the Bowery Theatre.* Artotype, 8.5 in. × 6.5 in., New York, 1833. From PR 104 (Theatrical Portrait File). Box 33-R Misc; folder: Ri; image #48912, New-York Historical Society.

recognize this image in "Jim Crow."[14] But recall, too, that the Spanish pastor bobo's raucous equivocations embody desilusión; his suffering beneath the lash, "covered with Christ's image," is an implicit critique of worldly power.[15] And what about Casas's argument that enslaving fellow members of the Kingdom of Christ—taking away the promise of redemption—would damn Spain itself?[16]

If, as I believe, "Jim Crow" can trace his lineage to these European notions of Blackness, how was the culture from which "Jim Crow" issued transformed by two hundred years of breeding human beings as if they were animals, a dehumanization and fear so deep that it overwhelms Christian fears of Judgment?[17] Slavery's untenable dilemma is manifest in "Jim Crow's" broken body, and yet "Jim Crow," "light-heartedly" unconcerned with the ravages of violence that his body exhibits, simultaneously shows us, with his jumps, a body full of power, ready for speed, ready to, in the words of Ta-Nehisi Coates, "achieve the velocity of escape."[18]

We examine here some of the channels through which this repertoire wandered. In the antecedents to blackface, we find colonial America's aspirations to emulate European elite culture. Yet in opposition to the clarity of redemption, the nonsense of *guuú, guuú, guuú* purposefully sews confusion, covering the "veiled and half-articulate messages" implicit in "texts wrought by toil, terror, and sorrow" with a travesty of Blackness, whose "deformed" body and speech nonetheless represent the gravest threat to racial hierarchy.[19] As we have already observed here, all of this cheerfulness in early-nineteenth-century blackface emerged from a social, political, and economic context which was becoming increasingly dire. By 1852, Frederick Douglass, in a speech "What to the slave is the Fourth of July?" said,

> It is not light that is needed, but fire; it is not the gentle shower, but thunder. We need the storm, the whirlwind, and the earthquake. The feeling of the nation must be quickened; the conscience of the nation must be roused.[20]

Mungo, the Blackface Clown

> Yet, with all my being, I refuse to accept this amputation. I feel my soul as vast as the world, truly a soul as deep as the deepest of rivers; my chest has the power to expand to infinity. I was made to give and they prescribe for me the humility of the cripple.
>
> *Franz Fanon, Black Skin, White Masks, p. 119*

In the fourteenth century, the royal courts of the British Isles, the Iberian Peninsula, and what are now France and Italy—all of them Catholic—were locked in battle with the forces of Islam for control over the Mediterranean. "Blackamoors" were performed at British court, as at folk festivals and May Games, all the way from then through the arrival of Rice's "Jim Crow" impersonation in 1836 London.[21] In *The Negro as Metaphor in Western Literature* Lemuel Johnson writes, "when the Negro makes his literary appearance" in Elizabethan England "he is not differentiated from the Moor," but by 1601, "to distinguish between the Moor as Moor and the Moor as Negro," the expressions " 'Black Moore,' 'Blackmoore' and the slightly derogatory 'Blackamoore' " have been recorded.[22] In England, as in Spain, and as we saw in the French moresca as well, the figure of the "blackman" had a "diabolic connotation"; in *Things of Darkness* Kim Hall writes, "from the middle ages on, Mohammed and 'Mohammedism' had been a sign for sexual and moral depravity."[23] In England, as in Spain, this spiritual deviance was performed through interwoven depictions of licentiousness and misshapen bodies. For example, George F. Rehin describes a May Day 1823 procession in England "led by 'two men with blackened faces, one dressed as a woman in rags, the other, with a large artificial hump on his back, carrying a birch broom.' "[24] (See Figure 4.4.)

Mr. DIBDIN, in the Character of . MUNGO in the PADLOCK .
Me wish to my Heart me was Dead.Dead.Dead .
London Publish'd as the Act directs, 1769 . Printed for Carington Bowles, N.º 69 St Pauls Church Yard.

FIGURE 4.2 *Mr. [Charles] Dibdin in the Character of Mungo in The Padlock.* Mezzotint, London, 1769. Courtesy of The Rare Book & Manuscript Library, University of Illinois at Urbana-Champaign.

Perhaps we may wonder here whether "Jim Crow" alludes in dance not only to the English "Blackamoor," but also to a Spanish iteration of this imaginary Blackness: the *diablo cojuelo,* or limping devil.[25] Listing many of the same dances named in the diabolical *Encorvada* (1611), the devil protagonist in Spanish dramatist Luis Vélez de Guevara's *El diablo cojuelo* (1641) brags of having invented all the infernal dances:

Yo truje al mundo la	I brought into the world the
çarabanda, el deligo, la	zarabanda, the *deligo*, the
chacona, el bullicuzcuz, las	chacona, the *bullicuzcuz*, the
cosquillas de la capona, el	*cosquillas* [tickles] *de la capona*, the
guiriguirigay, el çambapalo,	guiriguirigay, the *zambapalo*, the
la mariona, el auilipinti, el	*mariona*, the *auilipinti*, the *pollo*
pollo, la carreteria, el	[chicken], the carreteria, the
hermano bartolo,	*hermano bartolo* [Brother Bartolo],
el carcañal, el guineo, el	the *carcañal*, the guineo, the
colorín colorado; yo inventé	*colorin colorado*; I invented
las pantorgas, las jácaras,	the *pantorgas*, the jácaras,
las papalatas, los comos, las	the *papalatas*, the *comos*, the
mortecinas, los títeres, los	*mortecinas*, the puppet shows, the
bolatines, los saltambancos,	acrobats, the mountebanks,
los maesse corales, y al fin,	the magic tricks, and in the end,
yo me llamo el Diablo Cojuelo.[26]	I am called the Limping Devil.

The chacona and guineo are, as we have seen, explicitly Afro-identified, but many of the other dances in this list, such as the zarabanda with its sexual pantomime, and the *guiriguirigay*, which means "obscure and difficult to understand language," also hint at encoded Blackness. Guiriguirigay, or *guirigay* means *bulla*, ruckus and confusion, such as a gathering where everyone is shouting at the same time, creating a babel in which no conversation is possible. And a *guiri* is a foreigner, "mute," as in the Quevedo epigraph above, because he is unable to speak the native tongue. The connection between Blackness and unholy transgressiveness is made explicit in the limping devil's sarcastic boast that "I am a man privileged to have been baptized and to be free of the power of witchcraft, with which the princes of infernal Guinea have made a pact."[27]

The Spanish diablo cojuelo certainly did make an appearance on both European and American stages by the mid-nineteenth century. Alain-René Lesage based his 1707 novel *Le diable boiteux* on Vélez de Guevara's *Diablo cojuelo* of 1641.[28] In turn, Jean Coralli and Edmund Burat de Gurgy based their eponymous 1836 ballet, whose *Cachucha* provided the vehicle for Fanny Elssler's rise to international stardom, on Lesage's 1707 novel. As in Victor Hugo's *The Hunchback of Notre Dame* (1831), also fashioned into ballet, we observe the conjugation of devilish deformity and indomitable sexual appetite, for example, in the titillating suggestion of ravishment revealed in Théophile Gautier's description of Fanny Elssler's *Cachucha*: "Her wasp-like figure is boldly arched back...How she twists! How she bends!... Her swooning arms flutter about her drooping head, her body curves back, her white shoulders almost brush the floor."[29] Poets called the devil in *Le Diable*

Boiteux "Cupid," explains dance historian Joellen Meglin: "In Lesage's view, a misbegotten creature incites desire, and desire underlies the human comedy."[30]

Drawing from the villano dance vocabulary of unbridled jumps and noisy footwork, the Spanish limping devil is, perhaps counterintuitively, a figure of physical prowess and voracious appetites. In this he resembles Harlequin, the black-masked country bumpkin and astute servant of the Italian *commedia dell'arte* (see Figures 4.3 and 4.4). Discussing Gennaro Magri's *Trattato teorico-practico di ballo* (1779), dance historian Linda Tomko notes that, similarly to the way gambols might depict the bobo's scatological or obscene antics in Spanish dance, "large-scale caprioles" were employed in such dancing "*commedia* figures" as Harlequin, in representing "gluttony and excess."[31] The parodic "Drunk Dance" in Jean Favier's *Le Mariage de la Grosse Cathos* (1688), according to historians of early dance Rebecca Harris-Warrick and Carol G. Marsh, also references Harlequin choreographies in its "mock bravura sequence[s] of backward and forward jumps."[32] In ballet, the characters represented with the *grotteschi*'s jumps evolved over the course of the eighteenth century away from the masked characters of the Italian *commedia dell'arte* and toward the folkloric imagery of character dance. Dance historian Bruce Alan Brown describes how, on mid-eighteenth-century ballet stages, " 'natural characters' in national dances" began to replace the "indecent antics 'of Harlequins, of Pulcinellas, of Guangurgolos, etc.' "[33] In the United States, the acrobatic buffoonery of such Harlequinades was incorporated into the "naturalistic" representations of early blackface minstrelsy.

The blackface clown made his way from English to North American stages in the latter half of the eighteenth century. Foster Damon, in his chronicle of "The Negro in Early American Songsters" (1934), records a " 'negro dance in character' performed by one Mr. Tea on April 14, 1767": Damon calls this the first evidence of blackface impersonation on the American boards.[34] Two years later, "the first negro song presented on the American stage was sung in New York, May 29, 1769, by Lewis Hallam the younger, as Mungo, in Bickerstaffe's *Padlock*."[35]

The Padlock: A Comic Opera as It Is Performed by His Majesty's Servants at the Theatre-Royal in Drury-Lane had been first performed in 1768 London, under the management of Britain's leading actor, playwright, and producer David Garrick. The program had included *Hamlet*, with Garrick himself playing that title role.[36] For *Padlock*, Charles Dibdin, then just beginning his career as a prolific composer, songwriter, novelist, and actor, wrote the score and also played the role of Mungo, in blackface, and costumed in a garish striped suit (see Figure 4.2). It is perhaps fitting, in light of Eric Lott's concise summary of blackface minstrelsy as a tale of *Love and Theft*, that the libretto, written by Irish playwright Isaac Bickerstaff, told a story of love and jealousy. Based on one of Cervantes's novellas, *El celoso extremeño* (The Jealous Extremeñan,

1613), *Padlock* told the story of an old miser who kept his young fiancée locked away from other suitors behind a "formidable padlock."[37]

The main comic character in *El celoso extremeño* was the miser's black slave, Luis, in the classic role of a servant as confidant and romantic intermediary. Robert Stevenson writes, Luis "loved music so violently that he was willing to risk life itself if only he could study with someone able to teach him the *guitarra* [guitar], *clavicímbano* [clavichord], *órganos* [organ], or *harpa* [harp]."[38] Luis is "droll, literally burning with a love for music, by no means disdainful of a drink, and not too heroic in the face of danger." Luis was a eunuch, and this seems a crucial detail in making this character sufficiently non-threatening to be charming.[39] Like other Cervantine heroines, the poor but noble Leonora is drawn with a sympathetic brush, and Cervantes's descriptions of popular music and dance (as, for example, the seguidillas in *La gitanilla*, and chacona in *La ilustre fregona*) are also present in *El celoso extremeño*.[40]

In *The Padlock* (1768), the "Luis" character is called "Mungo."[41] Mungo's name, Hans Nathan writes, "suggests those of Jumbo, Sambo and Gumbo in American blackface minstrel songs." And, if Mungo reminds us also of the Spanish Mingo, "Sambo" is an Anglicization of *zambo*, a person of mixed African and Amerindian heritage in the system of racial categories that governed Spanish colonial society.[42]

Mungo is a West Indian slave; his master is Don Diego, a planter.[43] Here again remain traces of a tale of *Love and Theft*. Bickerstaffe had planned for the Irish actor John Moody, who had lived for a time in Jamaica, to play the role of Mungo, and so he wrote the libretto in Black Talk, with a West Indian lilt. But, as Charles Dibdin recounts dryly in his memoir, "I knew…that Moody would never perform [the role], and I knew he never could. Perhaps I had taken some care in the composition of the songs."[44] Dibdin got the role, and his blackface portrayal of the "bumbling, drunken, singing-and-dancing black servant named Mungo" was a stunning success, netting £3000 for the London theater managers, consolidating his own successful career, and paving the way for a new North American industry.[45]

The caption of the 1769 mezzotint of "Mr. Dibdin in the Character of Mungo in the Padlock" reads, "Me with to my Heart me was Dead. Dead. Dead" (see Figure 4.2). The Bickerstaffe verse is:

> Dear heart! What a terrible life I am led!
> A dog has better, that's shelter'd and fed;
> Night and day 'tis the same
> My pain is dere game;
> Me wish to de Lord me was dead.[46]

In *Dan Emmett and the Rise of Early Negro Minstrelsy*, Hans Nathan observes that in the context of heated debates about the slave trade in England during the era not only of the American Revolution but also of intensifying slave revolts in the Caribbean, "the Negro had become not only an object of national concern but, so to speak, a fashionable commodity."[47] Culminating in the Haitian Revolution (1791–1804), which sent shock waves outward toward both sides of the Atlantic, these uprisings brought slavery to the fore of late-eighteenth-century British political discourse.[48] In 1799, Scottish explorer Mungo Park published his *Travels in the Interior Districts of Africa...in the Years 1795, 1796, and 1797*, recounting an incident when, " 'weary and dejected' in a village in search of shelter...[he] was asked into a hut, given food, and provided a place to sleep."[49] Park's expedition inspired a raft of sentimental and Europeanized representations of Blackness, such as a collection of "Minuets, Cotillions & Country German Dances for the Violin, Mandolin, Flute & Harpsichord. Composed by an African." Pathetic and melancholy songs such as "The Desponding Negro" (1792), "The Negro's Lamentation" (1800), and "The Dying Negro," which opens "O'er my toil-wither'd limbs sickly languors are shed," were written in standard English—not Black Talk.[50] British abolitionist sympathies would decline in the nineteenth century, as unrest in the former colonies led to shortages of commodities such as sugar and cotton.[51] In the United States, meanwhile, such sentimental ballads would give way, especially after the War of 1812, to representations of the stage negro "as a comic figure in uniform fighting, willy-nilly, for the British."[52]

The Padlock's Mungo is "fond of music and wine."[53] He is shiftless and cowardly, an astute servant who alternates "servility and humorous impertinence." He sings euphemistic and rhythmic tag lines:

> *Let me when my heart a-sinking*
> *hear the sweet guitar a-clinking*
> *when de tring peak such music he make*
> *I soon am cured of tinking*
> *then the toot toot toot of the merry flute*
> *and Cymbalo and Tymbalo*
> *and Cymbalo and Tymbalo*[54]

Likewise, in the best tradition of the Spanish bobo, he speaks impertinences to power. Encountering a drunken Mungo unexpectedly in the dead of night, his master demands: "Wretch, do you know me?" To which Mungo replies, "Know you?—damn you," adding "dere young gentleman wid young lady; he play on guitar, and she like him better dan she like you. Fal, lal, lal...you old dog."[55]

Harlequin (Friday)

Robinson Crusoe or Harlequin Friday, a "pantomimical revolution" in two acts, was written by Richard Brinsley Sheridan and first performed in London in 1781.[56] It began, as per its title, with a staging of Daniel Defoe's *Robinson Crusoe*, using the popular conventions of a beautifully painted set and a battle with "savages," including the "rescue and seemingly benevolent enslavement" of Friday. The second act, which takes place in Spain after Crusoe and Friday have arrived there, is a traditional British *Harlequinade*, in which Friday assumes the role of Harlequin: like *The Padlock* of 1768, the central character of this work is the comic black slave. At the conclusion of the second act, "after many fanciful distresses, and the usual pantomimical revolutions," Harlequin wins "the hand of Columbine," and "Shepherds and Shepherdesses" conclude the "Pantomime... with a grand Bower Dance."[57] (Half-price admission for the second act meant that more people probably saw the Harlequinade than saw the complete work.[58])

British pantomime was a popular eighteenth-century Christmas entertainment in the villancico vein, featuring singing, dancing, and raucous and racy antics.[59] John Rich, a celebrated mime, developed the Harlequinade out of the continental *commedia dell'arte* tradition beginning in 1717 with a series of interludes miming the comic courtship of *commedia* characters Harlequin and Columbine, a servant girl.[60] Harlequin, who since his inception in sixteenth-century Italy had worn a black mask, turned a representational corner on the English stage in 1759, when David Garrick, who would produce *The Padlock* nine years later, referred to Harlequin as "that Blackamoor man."[61] This, writes John O'Brien in *Harlequin Britain*, is the "first explicit description from within a pantomime itself that would identify Harlequin as an African," and it "positions Harlequin as the ethnographic Other against which Britishness can be defined."

The perception of Harlequin as black was widespread by the late-eighteenth century, as recorded, for example, by a French nobleman serving with Lafayette's army in the American Revolution. Coming upon a group of "Negro sentinels, soldiers of the revolutionary forces" in Rhode Island, the nobleman wrote in his diary that they looked exactly like the black Harlequins of the theater.[62] Like the pastor bobo, and like "Jim Crow," Harlequin spoke in a "hill-billy" dialect. Similarly, Friday, as described by Laurence Hutton in his *Curiosities of the American Stage* (1891), appeared "in coffee-colored tights and blackened face."[63] This "blackface clown in coffee-colored fleshings," dance historian Lincoln Kirstein later wrote, sired the "first great... indigenous stage type to stand in history beside Italian Scaramouche, French Pierrot, or English Harlequin:" "Jim Crow."[64]

Sheridan's 1781 *Robinson Crusoe or Harlequin Friday*, in which Friday in the first act was presumably played in blackface and Friday as Harlequin in the second act was played with Harlequin's black mask *over* blackface, thus maps, performance theorist Elizabeth Maddock Dillon argues, "the black-masked figure of Harlequin onto the native figure of Friday," offering a glimpse into a remarkably fluid and transitional representation of race (see Figure 4.5).[65] Dillon credits Sheridan himself with being the first author "to make Harlequin *racially* black." At the end of the eighteenth century, in works such as *Harlequin Mungo; Or, Peep into the Tower* (1787), the New World's re-imagination of

Cervantes's black slave Luis as Mungo shifted into these blackface-within-blackface, European-within-colonial representations.[66]

By 1783, dance historian Lillian Moore recounts, the Harlequinade, flavored by Charles Dibdin's blackface Mungo in *The Padlock* of fifteen years earlier, had reached American shores: "The Old American Company...announced, for September 1, its first Harlequinade...patterned after Dibdin's pantomime."[67] On September 22, 1785, John Durang, whom Moore calls "The First American Dancer," danced a " 'grotesque Necromantic Dance,' introduced into the pantomime *The Witches, or Harlequin in the Moon*." Sheridan's *Robinson Crusoe and Harlequin Friday* "was seen at the John Street Theatre, New York" on January 11, 1786.[68] By 1787 this piece had arrived in Philadelphia, and on March 20, 1789, Durang played the Harlequin Friday role for the first time.[69]

In colonial America, Lynn Brooks writes in her book on John Durang, "the spectacle component of these pantomimes, including transformation scenes and magic tricks, was essential to their success"; such "scenic effects pushed forward the sets, machines, and lighting technologies of the day."[70] These cutting-edge stage devices, in which "scenes transformed instantly, as if by magic, from one setting to another," and "characters flew on and off through grooves on the stage, as well as up and down through flies, cloud machines, and traps" would have been utilized in both acts of *Robinson Crusoe or Harlequin Friday*. In the first act, "natural phenomena—the heavens, seas, and fires"—might appear, while in the second act, as Harlequin magically metamorphosed his appearance to rendezvous with his beloved Columbine, "cutout figures might serve as character doubles during transformations, just as ingenious costume designs."

FIGURE 4.3 "Arlequin," by A. Manceau. In *Masques et bouffons : (comédie italienne)* / *texte et dessins par Maurice Sand ; gravures par A. Manceau ; préface par George Sand* (Paris: Michel Levy Freres, 1860), 80. Courtesy of The Morgan Library & Museum. PML 151757-58. Bequest of Miss Julia P. Wightman.

Citing Gregorio Lambranzi's *Neue und curieuse theatralische Tantz-Schul* (1716), Brooks provides important detail about the "enormous range of movement" that might have been employed in danced metamorphoses such as Durang's "Dwarf Metamorphosed" (in which he transformed from a "man of 3 foot to a woman of 6 foot"), or in the "Humpbacks' dance" in Lambranzi's 1716 dance manual, which Brooks uses as an illustration: "elegant posturing, dancing in baskets or with other props, splits and handstands, acrobatics and slapstick, jumping and spinning, fencing and boxing, statue-posing, climbing, and falling" (see Figure 4.4).[71]

FIGURE 4.4 | "Puricinella e Simona," by Johann Georg Puschner. In Gregorio Lambranzi, *Neue und curieuse theatralische Tantz-Schul: Teil I und II*, 1716. Jerome Robbins Dance Division, The New York Public Library. NYPL Digital Collections. Accessed December 28, 2017. https://digitalcollections.nypl.org/items/987a8b49-a7bb-8688-e040-e00a180635c6

In Charleston, South Carolina, in 1794, a "grand entertainment" concluded the second act of *Robinson Crusoe* with a "Grand Folie Despagne" (a Grand Spanish Folly), "a negroe dance, by Mr. Francisqui" (who had played Friday in the first act), and "Minuet de la Cour," a dance of the seventeenth-century French court.[72] In 1806 Charleston, in another version of the Crusoe pantomime, "Harlequin will make several leaps," will "Metamorphose...to an old woman, with the comic Dance, called FRICASSEE," and "A Corn Field will change into Cupid's Palace; with a variety of other tricks too numerous to insert."[73] "The 'Fricassee' is a traditional French country-dance that mimics a lover's quarrel and involves rhythmic stomping and slapping of one's own body parts," Dillon writes, and so "is very close to the New World African dance tradition of 'patting Juba.'"[74] Brooks adds that the "Fricassee dance," which Durang performed "throughout the 1780s," was modeled after a "French dance called *la fricassée*," "a wild bacchanal of the lower classes, performed with pantomimic elements," and drawing together "portions and tidbits excised from familiar works."[75]

In the British Harlequinade, Dillon writes, Harlequin is an "intensely physical character."[76] Harlequin not only violates the rules of dancerly decorum, but "also defies physical laws insofar as he can transform himself into other characters and other entities, including animals and even inanimate objects such as clocks or pieces of furniture, and then transform himself back again."[77] Harlequin also violates social norms. In the traditional plot of the Harlequinade, "the black-masked character of Harlequin pursues the white Columbine while Columbine's father, Pantaloon, seeks to keep the two apart." Because of his magical capacity for self-transformation, his remarkable non-fixedness or mutability of self, Harlequin unfailingly manages to elude Pantaloon and to rendezvous with his lover (see Figure 4.5).[78]

The "happy ending" of *Robinson Crusoe or Harlequin Friday* echoes Cervantes's *El celoso extremeño* (1613), in which the old man, learning of Leonora's love for a man her own age, dies of shame for what he has done to her; in Cervantes, the repentant Leonora enters a convent, but in *The Padlock*, love more unequivocally wins the day, with Don Diego giving his blessing to the young couple.[79] Elisabeth Le Guin makes the key observation that in the eighteenth-century "web of influence" entwining England's *The Padlock* with contemporaneous Spanish tonadillas such as Luis Misón's *Tonadilla de los Negros* (1761) and, in France, Pierre-Augustin Caron de Beaumarchais's *Figaro* plays (1775, 1784)—soon transported to Italy to become Austrian composer Wolfgang Amadeus Mozart's *Le nozze di Figaro* (1786) and Italian composer Gioachino Rossini's *Il barbiere di Siviglia* (1813)—the success of the romance depends on the hero's "clever machinations" to disguise and transform himself.[80] Performance is central to this process: the Enlightenment's egalitarianism, in which social standing is supposedly assessed on merit and not birth, provides the skeletal structure for all of these dramas of humanist individuation and self-actualization.

FIGURE 4.5 *Harlequin and Columbine*, by Jean-Baptiste Pater. Oil on panel, ca. 1721–36. Courtesy of El Paso Museum of Art.

Indeed, throughout the black Atlantic, writes David Worrall in *Race, Ethnicity, and the Drama of the Popular Enlightenment*, the role of Harlequin needed "an extraordinarily agile dancer and tumbler" capable of "quick, quasi-balletic turns, leaps and gymnastic tricks."[81] This is consistent with Tomko's notes about the "large-scale caprioles" used in representing "gluttony and excess" in the Italian *grotteschi* tradition; it is also consistent with Harris-Warrick and Marsh's characterization of the forward and backward jumps used to portray drunkenness at the French court as "Harlequin jumps."[82]

In Spain, the pastor bobo's transformative epiphany, I have argued in Chapter 1, was danced with the virtuosic *puntapiés*, or jumped kicks, of mid-seventeenth-century aristocratic schools, while his unredeemed confusion was represented with jumps and loud footwork. *Commedia* characters on the Spanish stage were danced with the same vocabulary. For example, in Lope de Vega's *El hijo pródigo* (The Prodigal Son, 1604) the character *Juego* (Gambling, a sin) is a *Zan* from the *commedia* tradition (*Zanni*, zany, a bumpkin servant, whom Lope also calls Harlequin).[83] Like Harlequin, Lope's Juego is dressed in a patchwork costume, speaks with jumbled and equivocally malicious language, "dances in Italian fashion" (which is to say in a foreign style), and is known as a *gran volteador*—a great jumper.[84]

Despite the fact that they are both servant characters, the eighteenth-century enactment of black Harlequin winning the hand of white Columbine was, in North American slave society, an absurdity. Accordingly, in the many reworkings of Sheridan's *Robinson Crusoe or Harlequin Friday* on the early-American stage, Dillon argues, "a gap opens between the novel's assertion of Friday's desire to be a slave for life" and his second act transformation into Harlequin.[85] Harlequin's protean and therefore essentially human and modern nature thus lays down an incongruent and unstable subtext to the blackface characters of nineteenth-century minstrelsy. Standing "at the intersection of slave culture and earlier blackface stage characters such as Harlequin," Eric Lott writes, "Jim Crow" inherits "a highly uncertain status" from an "already ambiguous stage tradition."[86]

The suspense and delight generated by these characters arises from their uncanny and virtuosic mutability, keeping audiences wondering where, and in what form, they will appear next. But Harlequin's indeterminacy, as we have seen in Spanish figures such as the diablo cojuelo, made him, as Pierre Louis Duchartre writes of *The Italian Comedy*, "both disturbing and alluring," suggesting "something savage and fiendish"—"the potentialities latent in the mask of Harlequin are various and without end."[87] Despite its mercilessly dogmatic emphasis on Blackness as a fixed and permanent state of abjection, George F. Rehin argues in his article on "Continuity and Convergence in Blackface Clowning," the blackface figure on nineteenth-century U.S. stages became "as protean a character as Harlequin."[88]

How could a broken down and thoroughly wretched figure inspire such anxiety and foreboding? Lott reproduces an extended and highly disturbing quote from an 1867 issue of the *Atlantic Monthly* on "T. D. Rice's first blackface performance in Pittsburgh around 1830," which shows how attuned Rice's "Jim Crow" act was to white fears of what Frederick Douglass called the coming "storm, the whirlwind, and the earthquake."[89]

The tale of Rice's stellar performing career began with theft: he stole the ragged clothes he used as a costume for his first blackface performance from a black stevedore snidely called "Cuff." With this break-through travesty, Rice hit the big time. The 1867 article captures the blend of apprehension and desire with which white society viewed black men, whose labor, as discussed in Chapter 3, made their lives possible. "Cuff" is "an exquisite specimen of his sort,—who won a precarious subsistence by letting his open mouth as a mark for boys to pitch pennies into." The performance climaxed when the naked Cuff, "driven to desperation, and forgetful in the emergency of every sense of propriety" (that is, the "proper" order of things in this context was that the enslaved man *had* no property, and therefore no propriety) interrupted the performance by rushing onstage to reclaim his clothing. The "fascination with Cuff's nakedness," Lott writes, became a theatrical device entailing both Cuff's "bodily presence in the show and the titillating threat that he may return to demand his stolen capital."[90] Lott's analysis of the invention of "Jim Crow" as a conjugation of *Love and Theft*, fear and desire, revealing the black man's body while simultaneously hiding his power within a representation of weakness and infirmity, offers us insight into, in Saidiya Hartman's words, the "terror perpetrated under the rubric of pleasure, paternalism, and property" that underlies such representations of race.[91]

The colonizer's sense of precariousness and vulnerability animates derisive performances of the black body in comic characters such as "Mungo" (1768), "Harlequin Friday" (1781), and "Jim Crow" (1820s and 30s), as it does earlier representations of the colonial relation, such as Defoe's *Robinson Crusoe* (1719). Elizabeth Maddock Dillon uses the inescapable referent for all modern shipwreck tales, Shakespeare's *The Tempest* (1611), to argue that the violence and dehumanization visited upon black people, whose labor materialized the world of white domination, nonetheless reflected terror back to the perpetrators of these evils. The blasphemous curse, cloaked in nonsense, imparts to these figures an enthralling yet terrifying body power.[92]

Dillon thus reads *The Tempest* as a script concerning the dilemmas of colonialism.[93] The character Caliban, born of a witch and native to the island where the other characters have been shipwrecked, is a "slave" who remembers the gluttonous Harlequin and pastor bobo in opening his speech by saying (even before he reminds Prospero that "This island's mine") "I must eat my dinner."[94] Like pastor bobo and Harlequin, Caliban, whom Shakespeare calls a grotesque "mooncalf" (malformed abortive fetus, or a fool), does not speak properly: he "gabble[s] like a thing most brutish."[95]

In marked contrast to contemporaneous Spanish dramatizations of the pastor bobo, however, Caliban overtly rejects his indoctrination in English as he rejects and works against Prospero's enslavement of him. He says to Prospero, "You taught me language; and my profit on it is, I know how to curse. The red plague rid you for learning me your language!" Caliban's curse, argues Dillon, has "a certain embodied, physical quality to it that is associated with the ability to make something happen—to perform something—in the world."[96] Dillon sees Caliban's curse as "obscene (non)language"—Caliban scorns the language imposed by the foreign invaders of his island in a gesture of disruption and resistance. Citing Fred Moten, Dillon considers the power in nonsense—a rejection of the "sense" imposed by foreign invaders—of both sound and body.

The power of such equivocal nonsense lies precisely, Benjamin Liu argues, in "the invective force of an underlying curse," which both "attenuates and suppresses" its intentionality.[97] "Were the joke to step out of its special zone of language games," Liu writes, "it would no longer be a joke." Following this representational logic illuminates what Houston Baker Jr. calls the "deforma-tion of mastery" within blackface's equivocations of speech and of body. The brokenness of Jim Crow's body is nonsense, belying the manifest strength upon which white society relied completely for slave labor, and consequently feared existentially. The antics of nineteenth-century blackface minstrelsy, like the tendentious joke, conceal behind their "playfulness a cruel will to injure"— that is, whites terrorizing blacks—but does their manic intensity not hint at a black curse too, a terrifying implicit threat of violent resistance to white subjugation?

As the blackface clown moves into the realm of the nineteenth-century circus, the bumbling, simple-minded, "light-hearted" appearance of the bobo is obviously contradicted by his "death-defying" feats of patent strength, dis-cipline, and control. Writing about Charleston, South Carolina, where blacks outnumbered whites four to one in 1780, Dillon quotes a passage from one Josiah Quincy Jr.'s 1773 journal, in which Quincy excoriates slave owners who callously enslave their own children, while owning their mothers as chattel:[98]

> The American or European White man begets his likeness with much indiffer-ence and . . . sees his progeny in bondage and misery, and makes not one effort to redeem his own blood. Choice food for satire—wide field for burlesque—and noble game for wit! Unless the enkindled blood inflame resentment, wrath and rage, and vent itself in execrations.[99]

It seems useful to bring bell hooks's voice in to comment on this passage. "The young black male body," she writes, epitomizes both a "promise of wildness, of unlimited physical prowess," and also of the fecundity of "unbri-dled eroticism."[100] This ephebic "black body" was most valuable; it was the "most 'desired' body for its labor in slavery." In blackface minstrelsy this imagined body, which Saidiya Hartman characterizes as "represented most graphically as the body in pain," is conjugated with its flip side, the body of the "light-hearted slave" with no thought or desire for rebellion against his shack-les; Hartman calls this a "promiscuous coexistence of song and shackle in the spectacle of the coffle."[101] "Two possibilities," Dillon argues, quoting Quincy, "may eventuate from the intensity of this contradiction—'burlesque,'" or else "'enkindled blood . . . wrath, and rage'—namely, revolutionary violence."[102] In the manifest impact of "Jim Crow's" bodily equivocations on what Dillon usefully terms the "performative commons" of the Atlantic world, we sense the uncanny power, the magical ambiguity, and the sheer eruptive force of the blasphemous curse. Herein lie the "pleasure in terror" and "terror in pleasure" behind not only the blackface grimace but also behind the power animating "Jim Crow's" broken body.[103]

Flamenco inherits the body power of this implicit curse, I would argue, from the equivocal confusion and bulla, the jumps, noisy footwork, and lascivious innuendo, of the Spanish bobo. The Spanish Roma, known as Gypsies for their fifteenth-century self-mythologization as Egyptians penitent for having forged the nails that crucified Christ, whether as "sorceresses" or jaques or "beggars," whether fixing the audience in their fascinating and transgressive gaze or casting the "evil eye," performing as fortune-tellers or as flamencos, have always been willing to exploit their own negative image.[104] As the verse says:

| *se vale de su talento* | It takes talent |
| *pa' engañar a las castellanas*[105] | To deceive the Castilian women |

FIGURE 4.6 "John Smith in Ecstasy." In Edward Harper, and John N. Smith, "Jim Along Josey" (1840). Connecticut College Historic Sheet Music Collection, 775. digitalcommons. conncoll.edu/sheetmusic/775

"Jim Crow" Jumps!

Dance historian Marian Hannah Winter characterizes T. D. Rice's "Jump Jim Crow" step as a blend of jig and shuffle, "with the jump coming from a jig, and the arm and shoulder movements from a shuffle."[106] Jazz dance historians Marshall and Jean Stearns concur, quoting an 1840 review of Rice's performance which remarks on "such a twitching up of the arm and shoulder."[107] They observe that this upward twitching of the arm and shoulder jives with Edmon Conner's 1881 description of the "Jim Crow" character as "deformed, the right shoulder being drawn high up," thus indicating, they argue, the "shoulder movements of the Shuffle" and perhaps implying the shuffle's "cramped footwork" as well.

According to the Stearns, the shuffle was punctuated by the jump in Rice's "Jim Crow" act. "The jump comes, as Conner says, and as the lyrics indicate, at the end of the stanza: 'I jump Jim Crow!'" And yet "the earlier phrase 'jis so' simply calls attention to the all-important style—the cramped yet rhythmic circling *before* the jump, which is a syncopated hop in the flat-footed Shuffle manner."[108] Citing Thomas W. Talley's 1922 *Negro Folk Rhymes*, the Stearns write, "the recurring hop or jump of the title is preceded by a variety of maneuvers."[109]

> *Now fall upon yō' knees*
> *Jump up an' bow low... etc.*
> *Put yō' hands upon yō' hips*
> *Bow low to yō' beau... etc.*

John F. Szwed and Morton Marks, describing the Afro-American transformation of European set dances, quote jazz pianist and composer James P. Johnson's recollections of similar calls or instructions in the country and set dances of his youth in Virginia and South Carolina. Johnson calls these country dances "shoutings," referring to the Africanist *ring shout* of black churches in the North American Southeast. This shuffling dance, Johnson points out, flowed between overlapping sacred and secular dance practices within the black community, in a manner reminiscent of the footwork dances of the Spanish-speaking colonial world discussed in Chapter 2. Not only did seminal black artists such as Johnson draw upon their own traditions in inventing jazz, but white performers incorporated parodies of the ring shout in the "walk-arounds" of blackface minstrelsy.[110]

Charles Dickens's 1842 description of a dancer, often identified as the influential William Henry Lane "Master Juba," at Almack's in New York's Five Points neighborhood, features the shuffle in describing this dancer's dizzying foot and legwork:[111]

> Single shuffle, double shuffle, cut and cross-cut; snapping his fingers, rolling
> his eyes, turning in his knees, presenting the backs of his legs in front, spinning

about on his toes and heels like nothing but the man's fingers on the tambourine; dancing with two left legs, two right legs, two wooden legs, two wire legs, two spring legs—all sorts of legs and no legs—what is this to him? And in what walk of life, or dance of life, does man ever get such stimulating applause as thunders about him, when, having danced his partner off her feet, and himself too, he finishes by leaping gloriously on the bar-counter, and calling for something to drink, with the chuckle of a million of counterfeit Jim Crows, in one inimitable sound!

An 1845 *New York Herald* article on Juba's performances at another establishment in the infamous New York neighborhood highlights the sly parody of Lane's dance "maneuvers."[112] Lane would "imitate all the dancers of the day and their special steps," and the show would end with a "comic 'walk-around,' " in which "the lean, the fat, the tall, the short, the hunchbacked, and the wooden-legged, all mixed in." These venues were sites where the purposeful "dishevelment" of black dance ideas could be imitated, appropriated, and circulated broadly on the minstrel stage, as in the case of Dave Reed (1830–1906) who, the *Herald* writes, "learned his celebrated 'stiff' leg steps" from a "one-legged performer there, whose second leg was a wooden one."[113] Yet, to cite Jayna Brown, in the "guileful ruse," the "multi-signifying practices of dissemblance" of these danced parodies, we perceive the power of black mastery—not only in virtuosic dance but, more importantly, mastery of the game of signification which, writes Houston Baker Jr., "conceals, disguises, floats like a trickster butterfly in order to sting like a bee," and is "always, also, a release from BEING POSSESSED."[114]

Tap dance historian Constance Valis Hill defines the shuffle as an "African-derived" step "in which the ball or full foot brushes or scrapes the floor."[115] According to Hans Nathan, the "double shuffle" was "originally, no doubt, some kind of repeated brush with the foot."[116] In a frontier dance in Tennessee in the 1830s, this step "was associated with 'knocking it off,' which implies noisy foot work." Nathan goes on to quote several other nineteenth-century sources in which the shuffle is associated with both sonorous footwork and with jumping, such as the 1834 *Sketches and Eccentricities of Col. David Crockett* in which the double shuffle is associated with "heel and toe," an 1864 manual on *Jig and Clog Dancing*, which describes a shuffle as "spring up with both feet; strike with the ball of the left foot, and at the same time slide the right foot forward and back without raising it from the floor," and an 1874 manual in which the dancer is instructed to imagine two V-shaped diagrams on the floor, "place the heels on the angles of the diagram and then with both feet 'tap' " first one side of the "V" and then the other.[117] Flamenco dancers will note the similarity between the shuffle and a common word for footwork in Spain: *escobilla* (little broom), a reference to the sounded in-and-out brushes with the ball of the foot used in many steps.

FIGURE 4.7 "Detail from a playbill from the Bryant's Minstrels, depicting a 'challenge dance.'" January 24, 1859. In Hans Nathan, *Dan Emmett and the Rise of Early Negro Minstrelsy* (Norman: University of Oklahoma Press, 1962), 96.

In addition to "Jim Crow's" shuffle, "Jim Crow's" jig also suggests some intriguing correspondences with Spanish dance. John Durang was well known for his hornpipe, "an acknowledged ancestor" of tap dance.[118] In seventeenth- and eighteenth-century England, "hornpipe" referred to any simple "step dance," that is, a dance of sonorous footwork.[119] The hornpipe became a staple in London theaters by the 1760s; by the nineteenth century, professional dancers embellished the hornpipe using steps and techniques from ballet. Durang gained notoriety with feats of dexterous footwork, such as dancing in the character of a shepherd on a tightrope; he also danced a "Hornpipe on 13 Eggs, blindfolded, without breaking one."[120]

Durang's hornpipe was published by his son Charles in 1850 as the "Sailor's Hornpipe—Old Style."[121] Moore identifies many of the steps listed in this transcription as preserved in the tap vocabulary of today, such as "double shuffle," "pigeon wing," and "heel and toe haul."[122]

Nathan describes the pigeon wing: "[T]he dancer jumped up and kicked his legs together in mid-air—sometimes, more specifically, his heels or his ankles."[123] *Ailes de pigeon*, or "French, pigeon wings," are defined in *The Oxford Dictionary of Dance* as "a particularly demanding ballet step" in which the dancer "throws the left leg up, springing off the right which rises to beat beneath the left calf," changing and beating the legs twice before landing "on the right foot, with the left leg stretched out into the air."[124] The *Dictionary* also lists a variant on the name of this step: "pistolet."

Historic dance expert Thomas Baird points out that Magri's *pistoletta a terra* (1779) is similar to the French *ailes de pigeon*.[125] Magri's *pistoletta*

PISTOLEES E LAS SEGUIDILLAS BOLERAS

FIGURE 4.8 *Pistolees de las seguidillas boleras*. Marcos Téllez Villar. Ca. 1790, estampa aguafuerte y buril. Biblioteca Nacional de España.

is a very brilliant step, suited to every kind of *Ballerino* and to all characters.... It is taken from fifth position... with the right foot behind; bend the
knees and detach the aforesaid foot to second in the air, then it will go to beat
on the calf of the other leg, covering ground forwards with a little light spring
done on the left, which hardly rises from the ground, and, on landing from
this, the right is carried to fifth in front.... [T]hese are the *pistolette a terra*.[126]

But this step is also strikingly similar to Esquivel's 1642 voleo, which we examined in the villano, and to the *salto albalate* from the Basque jota, both of
which involve a kick of one leg, and a jump off of the supporting leg to beat
against the leg in the air, landing first on the supporting leg. It also recalls
pistolee, *pistolet*, or *pistolea* of the Spanish bolero school, which resembles a
jeté battu derrière: in ballet, a leap with the legs beating in the air.[127] When in
early 1834 Madrid theaters were closed in the wake of the first Carlist war
(1833–40), bolero dancers Dolores Serral, Manuela Dubiñón, Francisco Font,
and Mariano Camprubí traveled to the Paris Opera to perform. Their repertoire
included a cachucha, considered to have influenced Elssler's cachucha of
1836, and their movement vocabulary included pistolets.[128]

   "At the beginning of the nineteenth century the 'pigeon wing' was a fine
point in eastern ballroom dancing, perhaps derived from the classical *entre-
chat*," Nathan writes, but "minstrels made an acrobatic fling out of it."[129] This
process is recorded in the 1830s song, called (in Black Talk) "Sich a Gitting
Up Stairs," which lists a set of footwork techniques such as striking heels and
toes, a brushing or shuffling actions, a villano-like (or patting juba-like) slap
of the foot, and the pigeon wing:[130]

> Trike de toe an heel—cut de pigeon wing,
> Scratch gravel, slap de foot—dat's just de ting.

   In the United States, the essential narrative funding Spanish imperialism's
ideas about slavery—that, despite black lineage, there might exist the possibility of redemption through Christ—was stripped away in favor of the racist
ideology that leaves "Jim Crow," as was demanded by white slave society,
permanently broken, an existentially "happy slave."[131] "Jim Crow's" deformed
and broken body, "light-heartedly" unconcerned with the ravages of violence
his body displays, speaks volumes, then, confounding both the inevitability
and "morality" of slavery which this character purports to support and also, to
return to the Quevedo quote which opens this chapter, the idea that slavery
ever succeeded in silencing its victims. In the next chapter we will meet Jacinto
Padilla, "El Negro Meri," an acrobat on a tightrope between European and
American ghettoes of fictitious Blackness, whose virtuosity defied the blackface trope of the broken and muted body.[132] In El Negro Meri's acrobatic
jumps, to recall the words of Frederick Douglass, we perceive a body full of
power—a body of fire and thunder, storm and earthquake.

5 | Tilting across the Racial Divide

JACINTO PADILLA "EL NEGRO MERI"
AND THE FLAMENCO CLOWN

Not being violent enough could cost me my body.

Being too violent could cost me my body.

...I felt in this a cosmic injustice, a profound cruelty, which infused an abiding,
irrepressible desire to unshackle my body and achieve the velocity of escape.

—*Ta-Nehisi Coates*, Between the World and Me, *28, 21*

W HEN PROFESSOR KIKO MORA of the University of Alicante asked me to collaborate with him on an article about the two short films of Spanish dance shot by Auguste and Louis Lumière at the Exposition Universelle of 1900 in Paris, I was immersed in writing about the eighteenth century.[1] But I was enticed by the fascinating bits of research Mora kept emailing me and so, somewhat reluctantly, I agreed. The enormous discovery that emerged from that research forms the basis for this chapter.

I knew, notwithstanding Thomas Edison's film of Carmen Dauset Moreno "La Carmencita" (1894), Robert W. Paul's "Andalusian dance" (1896), and the twelve dance films shot in 1898 Sevilla by the Lumière brothers, all recording what could broadly be termed "classical Spanish dance," that the Lumière films shot in 1900 were extremely significant.[2] One of the two is the earliest extant film of flamenco dance: a *cuadro* or performing ensemble consisting of singer, guitar, *palmas* or clapping percussion, and dancers. I had spent two years studying and reconstructing the 1917 footage of Juana and María Vargas "Las Macarronas" (which we will examine presently), and I was intrigued to compare that with this earlier footage. Recent research had identified José Otero Aranda, the renowned Sevilla maestro whose essential 1912 dance treatise, *Tratado de Bailes de Sociedad* we have touched upon in Chapter 2, as the

FIGURE 5.1 "Danse Espagnole de la Feria Sevillanos [*sic*]," Vue no. 1123, screen shot, 1900. Left to right: José Fernández, wearing a *traje de la estudiantina* ("student's costume," a reference to the groups of Spanish students who from the fourteenth century raised money to pay their tuition as street musicians and who, by the turn of the twentieth century, were professionals touring internationally); Jacinto Padilla, "El Negro Meri," mid-jump; an unidentified woman seated; guitarist Eduardo Salmerón Clemente (behind Reguera); Anita Reguera, "Anita de la Feria," dancing; another unidentified woman and man, seated. Filmed at the Exposition Universelle in Paris by the frères Lumière between July 1 and July 8, 1900. © Institut Lumière.

male dancer in the flamenco film segment.[3] But as we began our collaboration, Mora insisted that it could not be Otero dancing: the dancer was a black man, he asserted. I resisted, noting that the dancer in the Lumière film was costumed as Otero often was in photographs and also in the 1898 films, in which he *does* appear.[4] I assumed that the angle of the sun on his face simply made the dancer's coloring seem darker. Not until Mora had amassed firm documentation that Otero was not in Paris at this time, but Jacinto Padilla, "El Negro Meri" was, and that this "celebrated mulato"—unremembered in the flamenco community and by all but a handful of flamenco historians—was performing at the Feria restaurant in the Spanish Pavilion when the Lumière brothers filmed "Danse espagnole de la Feria," was I able look at the film and see clearly that Mora was right.[5] The first male flamenco dancer ever filmed was a black man. Which raises the question, how could I—how could *we*—not have seen this in the first place?

Tightropes and Wild Horses: The Dance of the Blackface Clown

In 1792, John Durang danced in the chorus of Alexander Placide and his wife's debut performance in New York.[6] The Placides, trained in "ballet, acrobatics, tumbling, and dancing on the tightrope," were refugees from St. Domingue (as Haiti was called before the 1791 revolution) who had settled in Charleston, South Carolina, and formed a company. Lillian Moore attributes Durang's "learning to dance on the tightrope and slack wire...which was to serve him well in his later circus days" to this "brief association with the accomplished Placides." Also in 1792, a Scotsman, John B. Ricketts, opened a circus and riding school in Philadelphia, and soon began producing pantomimes and farces at the Chestnut Street Theatre; Durang would join him in 1796.[7] This sort of crossover between dance and circus was going on in Spain as well. For example, Roxo de Flores's 1793 dance treatise includes a short chapter on "Rope Dances," which he says are just like the *Volatines* (tight-rope acrobats) of the day, "because they were danced on a slack rope and on a tight rope."[8] And in his satirical treatise on the bolero academies in 1794–1795 Madrid, Rodríguez Calderón describes students practicing caprioles with ropes.[9] Like Durang, "Monsieur Placide also danced the hornpipe, but on a rope, suspended high in the air!"[10]

Lynn Brooks notes that "rope dancing and acrobatics" were related to the "circus skills of clowning and equestrianism."[11] She describes the appeal of brilliant equestrian feats combined with burlesque humor, as in the widely-performed act *Billy Button, or the Tailor's Ride to Brentford* (or *to New York* in American shows). In this act, "Clown as tailor faced an untamable beast that he could barely mount"; then, once he had finally gotten on, "he went through contortions...to get the horse moving, and then to stay on the horse as it galloped out of control."

The equestrian clowns of this period slipped toward blackface in a manner similar to the way the black-masked Harlequin became Harlequin Friday in the late-eighteenth-century United States. For example, in 1795 London, Benjamin Handy's equestrian circus "featured a horserider billed as 'The Famous African.'"[12] Early blackface performers in the United States, such as Sam Tatnall and Barney Burns, sang "negro songs" while riding horses in acrobatic and comic equestrian acts in the sawdust ring.[13] By 1810, singing and dancing blackface clowns were common in the dance halls and circuses of New Orleans.[14] As with ballet in the early United States, blackface impersonation was somewhat impressionistic: blackface players "simply performed jigs and clogs of Irish or English origin to popular songs with topical allusions to Negroes in the lyrics."

The stars of blackface minstrelsy performed on theater stages and in circus rings with equal enthusiasm. Before he broke through as "Jim Crow,"

T. D. Rice, as we have noted, performed as a supernumerary in *Bombastes Furioso* at New York's Park Theatre, and in 1828–1829 in Cincinnati, Rice was performing "little negro bits" as a "light comedian" who "could sing a song, tell a story, dance a hornpipe."[15] George Nichols, who invented the popular black-face character "Zip Coon," a ridiculous urban dandy, was a clown for "Purdy Brown's Theatre and Circus of the South and West."[16] Nichols is said to have sung as Zip Coon "first in whiteface, then in Negro make-up."[17] And before Dan Emmett (1815–1904) formed the first blackface minstrel troupe, the Virginia Minstrels, in the early 1840s, he "debuted as a banjo player and singer in the circus ring, undoubtedly in blackface."[18] Hans Nathan quotes Emmett: "the first negro song that I wrote—twas written...for Mr. Frank Whitaker (equestrian and negro singer) about the year 1838."[19] Emmett next worked with Raymond and Waring's Circus, and, in 1842, in Spalding's North American Circus, along-side "200 Persons and Horses."[20] The Virginia Minstrels also included a comic equestrian scene in their act: "'Dan Tucker on Horseback,' with Pelham as a Negro riding master, Brower as a Negro clown, and an equestrian"; this number was introduced in the Great Olympic Circus in New York in 1843.[21]

Dan Emmett and the Virginia Minstrels, an ensemble that played fiddle, bones, banjo, and tambourine—the African instruments played on slave plan-tations—left the United States on April 21, 1843, on the packet ship *New York*, headed for Liverpool.[22] In mid-nineteenth-century Britain, Nathan writes, the music of blackface minstrelsy "made its way into every walk of life," performed in circuses and on both urban and rural stages, and "published in inexpensive sheet editions for voice and piano." "The minstrel guise was soon ubiquitous, familiar, and popular, helped by street musicians who blacked-up, learned minstrel jokes and routines, and earned their bread and beer by playing the 'n****r melodies' of the day as introduced by professional minstrels on the stage."[23]

The same was true in Spain. In his article on the Cuban habanera in nineteenth-century Spanish zarzuela, musicologist Víctor Sánchez Sánchez cites an 1860 letter to Francisco Asenjo Barbieri, musicologist, composer, and author of the 1859 *Entre mi mujer y el negro* discussed in Chapter 3. The letter describes a tango or *habanera* (used synonymously) performed at Madrid's Teatro de la Zarzuela—sung and danced "in blackface, of course."[24]

London audiences in 1843 heard in the "Ethiopian concerts" of the Virginia Minstrels "the aboriginal airs of the interior of Africa, modernized if not humanized in the slave states of the Union, and adapted to ears polite."[25] These interpolations "upon the Italian, German, and English schools of composition" were thought to possess "at least the merit of originality...an evening's relaxation, a hearty laugh and matter for speculation how certain strange feats are performed."

Of course, we have been tracking how U.S. blackface minstrelsy had indeed been shaped by colonial-era aspirations toward European culture. Yet these

readings of American performance as savage and comically inept approxima-
tions of European culture, whose entertainment value lay precisely in their
difference, raise questions about how we might interpret the correspondences
in performance conventions between emerging U.S. blackface minstrelsy and
its contemporary, flamenco. For example, another member of the Virginia
Minstrels, Frank Brower (1823–74), already known as a blackface dancer
"imitating the typical jumps and leaps of old Negroes" introduced "bone
playing" in blackface in 1841.[26]

Nathan observes that though Brower's use of bones may have been novel on
the minstrel stage, bones have a European history. Citing a passage from
Shakespeare's *A Midsummer Night's Dream*, Nathan contends that this instrument was "in use among the English peasants of the sixteenth century."[27] That
may be, but the most widely acknowledged European correlates to bones are
of course Spanish castanets. We have already seen in Chapter 1 that Domingo
González's *Villano Cavallero por lo Vaxo* (ca. 1650) included castanets; as we
have seen also in the morisca, noisy villagers' dances using castanets, footwork, bells, and tambourines performed the bobo's ethno-religious confusion.
Cotarelo lists castanets as characterizing the "obscene" zarabandas and chaconas imported to Spain from the Americas in the sixteenth century, and thence
to Europe.[28] And it has always struck me, as "the four Virginia Minstrels sat on
the stage in a semicircle, partly turned to the audience, partly to each other to
ensure rhythmic co-ordination," and as the characters "Tambo" and "Bones"
played percussion at either end, that flamenco was (and still is) staged in an
identical manner.[29]

British audiences, like Spanish audiences, saw American performance as
exotic, and colored with titillating notions of guilelessness, uninhibitedness,
and freedom from social constraint that by the beginning of the twentieth century would slide toward jazz. But earlier, at mid-century, the interest in "authenticity" would create an opening for artists of color, previously excluded
from the theater stage. Thus, for example, William Henry Lane traveled to
London in 1848 as the only black member of a blackface minstrel troupe.[30]
Theater historian Stephen Johnson writes, "Juba is habitually advertised
and reviewed separately from the rest of the troupe....He is praised for his
authenticity, for *being* black."[31] Johnson analyzes some of the very disturbing
correlations between European interest in "authentic" black American performance and the racist pseudo-science of the day. Framing the "manic movements and outrageous freedom of expression" of blackface minstrelsy as "the
mid-nineteenth-century quintessence of the body 'out of control,'" Johnson
theorizes the anatomical museums of the nineteenth century as "displays of
the body 'punished,'" "the body under *extreme* control."[32] Johnson sees these
museums as minstrelsy's polar opposite—across a spectrum of popular
performance which included freak shows and circuses. Nonetheless, and
despite their shared aesthetic and socio-economic basis in slavery and colonial

expropriation, in the cracks between European and American audiences black artists like Lane and, as we will presently see, Jacinto Padilla "El Negro Meri" found a world where they could create a new vision of modern performance.

Jacinto Padilla, "El Negro Meri"

El Mulato Méric, that breed of universal panacea, who does the *Salto de la batalla* [a breathtaking jump over various circus lads holding up rifles with bayonets] with the same skill as that with which he stabs a bull with a pair of *banderillas*, masters and trains a horse, directs the show, or sings some seguidillas.

Ecos de la Juventud, *Málaga, June 17, 1877*

The two silent motion pictures, both titled "Danse Espagnole de la Feria," filmed by the Lumière brothers between July 1 and July 8, 1900, total just over a minute in length (the subtitles are reversed in the Lumière catalog: 1123 should be "Quadro Flamenco," while 1124 should be "Sevillanos" [*sic*]).[33] Without a doubt, the importance of this footage rests in the fact that the first clip is the earliest extant motion picture of a flamenco *cuadro* or performing group, explicitly contrasted here, as in the filmographic record which precedes it, to the dances of the escuela bolera, the classical and academic school of Spanish dance.[34]

Both clips, whose titles would seem to indicate that the dancers are performers from the fashionable La Feria Restaurant in the basement of the exposition's Spanish Pavilion on the Rue des Nations, were filmed on the same smooth outdoor platform on a terrace of the Palace of Horticulture, overlooking the Seine.[35] In the flamenco clip (1123), seated in a semicircle are a guitarist, Eduardo Salmerón Clemente, Jacinto Padilla, "El Negro Meri," who in the flamenco manner both sings and dances, and two men

EL MULATO MERI

FIGURE 5.2 "El Mulato Meri." Photograph. In *Sol y Sombra* año 1, no. 37 (December 30, 1897), 9. Courtesy of the Biblioteca Digital de Castilla y León.

and two women dressed in theatrical costumes; these seated performers play *palmas*, flamenco handclaps that provide percussive musical accompaniment. One seated woman, like the female dancer, Anita Reguera, "Anita de la Feria," wears a typical late-nineteenth-century dance costume: a long dress, wrapped in a Manila shawl, her hair adorned with flowers.[36] One of the two *palmeros* (men playing palmas), José Fernández, who directs the string ensemble in the second clip, wears a *traje de la estudiantina* ("student's costume," the dress of Spanish student groups who from the fourteenth century raised money to pay their tuition as street musicians, and who, by the turn of the twentieth century were professionals touring internationally), while the other man, along with Padilla, Salmerón, and the second seated woman, wears the tight-fitting high-waisted pants and short jacket (*traje corto*) characteristically worn by male flamenco dancers from the later-nineteenth through the later-twentieth centuries.[37]

The rhythm they are dancing in the flamenco clip is what we now call *bulerías*—the $\frac{6}{8}$ rhythm of much traditional Andalusian music. The seated dancers play palmas in the manner of a flamenco cuadro from the cafés cantantes. (Padilla doesn't play palmas as he sings, but marks rhythm on the edge of his chair with a small bamboo stick.)[38] Today, professionals even from outside of Andalucía are expected to have mastered this very complex percussion system, and we certainly know this to be true of the many well-rounded dancers trained in Sevilla academies such as that of maestro Otero.[39] And yet it is clear that the dancers playing palmas in this clip are uneven in their musicianship. José Fernández, at the far left of the screen, is by far the most articulate and active palmero, marking all the beats rather than just the accents, shifting forward in his chair to better work with the dancers. Judging from the patterns he plays and from his clapping technique, his unidentified counterpart on the far right of the screen is likewise a competent musician. But aside from these "end men," Padilla, and Salmerón, the two seated women, while clearly at ease with the rhythmic and musical structure unfolding before them, are just as clearly—evidenced by their clapping technique and the patterns they play— not playing palmas for strong musical support. Both women (even though only one is dressed *en travesti*) sit back in their chairs with knees open wide; this is uncharacteristic of flamenco cuadros, in which, as Reguera does before rising at the beginning of the clip, dancers must perch at the edge of their chairs in order to stand readily and gracefully.

Anita Reguera is the only performer in both clips. She wears the same costume (with the exception of castanets tied with long ribbons worn in the classical clip) in both. She wears the large shawl folded in half as a triangle, fringes wafting over her shoulders and hanging down her back; she is modestly covered, and yet the shawl serves to delineate the curves of her body, as the movement of its fringes extends the lines of her motion. She wears white shoes with a single strap and a small heel; her dark wavy hair is parted in the center and gathered up in the back of her head. In addition to the flowers in her hair, she wears a floral corsage anchoring the shawl upon her chest.

She dances in a style—the inward circling arm gesture, for example, signaling a *llamada* or call—easily recognizable to flamenco dancers of today. The clip seems to be choreographically structured around a single verse. We enter the scene in the middle of the action: the palmeros are clapping, the guitarist is playing, the singer is singing, and Reguera, nodding to an invisible cue from off-camera, begins to dance alone. The rhythm of her llamada is easily recognizable. I've been taught that it is "old fashioned," and we will see in the next chapter that Macarrona also performs it: instead of accenting 1–2–3 in flamenco counts, the dancer hits 12 — & 2–3–4–5. This is followed by three steps backward articulating toe and heel and punctuated by two stamps (a very traditional element of a flamenco llamadas which will be easily recognizable to flamenco dancers as *tico-tico-tico-pam-pam*). She follows this with two light stamps and a little pull upward of the body, a *pellizco* (also a common traditional step, also used by Macarrona in 1917), on flamenco counts 1, 2, and 4, and she ties off the phrase with a little turn. Reguera does two *marcajes* (marking steps), both of which the Macarronas do, and both commonly used today: first, sitting into one hip while extending the other foot, with lifted posture and circling arms, and second alternating feet from right to left and left to right, elbows beautifully lifted, and hips reflecting each footfall, moving quickly and lightly side to side. The continuities in costume and movement between Reguera's performance in the two clips serve to highlight subtle stylistic differences between flamenco and classical Spanish dance in 1900: in the flamenco clip Reguera holds her body slightly more upright, lifting through the back and through the back of the neck, with a subtle shiver forward to mark an accent, but she bends in the waist only once, when Padilla crosses behind her.[40]

The male dancer of the second clip, Virgilio Arriaza, son of bolero maestro Domingo Arriaza and brother of New York émigré Aurora Arriaza, with whom he performed in Belasco's *Rose of the Rancho* in 1906 New York, is tall, slim, elegantly-coiffed and mustachioed.[41] He plays castanets and performs intricate beats and foot patterns while keeping his body controlled and upright, often inclining in a gallant diagonal toward his partner in the manner of ballet.

Padilla's dance clearly has a different technical basis: *pitos* (finger snaps) replace the castanets, he carries his arms overhead in the manner of a *banderillero* (more on that in a moment), and his jumps and pellizcos are propelled from not only deep bends in the knee, but also at the hip, the torso inclining forward in the flamenco manner. At about 00:00:19:10, when we see him forcefully exhale into a syllable, we are clearly at the beginning of a phrase or line of the verse; in light of the duration of song that has preceded this moment, and in light of the length of this phrase (four measures of six) and the way it is danced, I surmise that it is a repeat or an estribillo, a tag. It is at this moment when we see Meri's spectacular jump. Because of its impressive virtuosity, perhaps this jump has led to the erroneous assumption that the dancer was Maestro Otero. Now that we know the identity of the dancer, it provides important insight into both El Negro Meri's reputation as an artist and into the tightly enmeshed worlds of circus, bullfighting, and flamenco in 1900 (see Figure 5.1).[42]

Padilla sings the repeat, which should be four measures of six, and Reguera responds with a llamada at the beginning of the next measure of $\frac{6}{8}$. Padilla answers with a spring from his chair on the fifth beat of the third measure of $\frac{6}{8}$ ("4" in flamenco counts), landing—literally jumping on—the first beat of the fourth and last $\frac{6}{8}$ measure in the sung phrase.[43] Despite his slight paunch, and the fact that he is obviously not a young man, the intensity, held tension, dynamism, weight, and sheer power of his movement contrast markedly to hers. He springs up and lands precisely on the beat, and marks both the beat and counter-beat, that is, sixteenth notes, with pitos, for the entire duration of his dance. His landing is a llamada, which he fills in by moving toward and retreating away from his partner with the *tico-tico* step. He finishes this four-measure segment with a taurine pantomime, preparing to jump with rhythmic, sideways traveling stomps, pulling legs together and body upward into the air, arms overhead, with hands and gaze directed downward and toward his partner, as if he were a *banderillero* (the bullfighters who run and stick spikes into the bull's neck) and she a bull. Padilla lands this second jump with a spectacular running preparation, changing places with his partner with an acrobatic turn in the air. He lands the third jump on the closing beat of the measure (the flamenco "10") with another banderillero gesture, and with improvisational wit bounces out of the landing, extending it musically into a new measure, and in gesture into a sassy hip wag, looking coquettishly over his shoulder in a campy allusion to femininity.

Who was Jacinto Padilla "El Negro Meri," and why does he appear in this film (see Figure 5.2)? Mora has documented the proximate motivation for Padilla's appearance in the Lumière film: he was performing at the Feria restaurant in the Spanish Pavilion. And how did he come to be performing there? Mora cites two articles by Spanish journalist Santiago Romo-Jara describing Padilla as a "notable mulato artist," "the celebrated guitarist Meric, who accompanies, gives *jaleos* (shouts *¡Ole!*), sings and dances for himself as he did in his prime."[44]

In his article on "A Picturesque Personality of Nineteenth Century Flamenco: El Negro Meri," Eusebio Rioja notes that Padilla is little known or remarked upon today.[45] Fernando el de Triana's 1935 *Arte y artistas flamencos* does not mention him. However, in their 1988 *Diccionario enciclopédico*, José Blas Vega and Manuel Ríos Ruiz do:

MERIC, EL. Nineteenth century. Flamenco singer. Of mulato race. In 1874 and 1875, he was part of the company of the Circo Madrid, touring Andalucía.

He was sometimes announced as "the famous negro." He performed soleares, siguiriyas, tangos, and other *festero* (fiesta) styles, given that his repertoire was very broad.[46]

He has been practically forgotten, but in the last decades of the nineteenth century Padilla's reputation in the flamenco world was so widespread and so long-standing that, as José Cruz Gutiérrez documents in his book on flamenco in Córdoba from 1866–1900, "El Mulato Meric," already known as an equestrian clown, was the first flamenco artist mentioned in the Córdoba press: on May 24, 1873, the *Diario de Córdoba* wrote that "the popular and likeable flamenco mulato Meric...will sing and dance *a lo flamenco*"—in the flamenco style.[47]

As Blas Vega and Ríos Ruiz indicate, the performers in this signal event were the Equestrian and Gymnastic Company of the Circus of Madrid, and the venue was Córdoba's Circus of Santa Clara. Six months earlier, in September of 1872, El Negro Meri performed in Málaga, at Rafael Díaz's Summer Equestrian Circus.[48] The periodical *El Avisador Malagueño* published several items about "benefit" performances "for the acclaimed artist Meric," a *"simpático joven"* (charming young man), also billed as the *"AMERICANO MERIT."*[49] Ignoring the new variation in spelling Padilla's nickname, we learn here that the performer in the 1872 circus was a youth. We also learn that he was "American," which in the parlance of the day might mean Afro-Cuban.[50] Two days later, the Málaga paper described a "notable point" in the previous night's performance: "the beneficiary Meric...did very risky exercises on a horse, which justifiably and deservedly caught the attention of the large circus audience, who applauded him extraordinarily."[51] In Córdoba, Meri's flamenco number alternated with child star Billy Kenebel, *"El Hijo del Aire"* (The Son of the Air), a *saltador malabar* (acrobatic juggler), and his donkey "Rigoletto," who also jumped.[52] Padilla was still performing with Díaz's equestrian circus, "so beloved by Málaga audiences," during the summer of 1874, when he was billed with "the principal artist of the Universe, MLLE. SPELTERINI, the very same who competed against Mr. Bondiu on a tightrope across Niagara Falls, where the said artist was the winner."[53]

In Spain, the equestrian circuses of the nineteenth century often became *mojigangas*, parodies performed as interludes, a sort of "halftime entertainment" at the bullfight, not unlike rodeo clowns in the United States today, who continue the equestrian acts of blackface minstrelsy.[54] In the memoir of his 1862 Spanish tour, Davillier describes one such act in Sevilla. "The Andalusians have a special disdain" for blacks, he writes.[55] He describes the performers' entrance, "dancing the *Sopimpa*, a negro step, the orchestra marking its jerky movements," before performing "other dances of their country, such as the *cucullé* and the *tango americano*"—the American tango. Davillier continues,

> It was in vain that the placards announced them as subjects of the King of Congo, King Fulani, and other fictitious princes: the public would not consider them in a

serious light. They had arrayed them in the most grotesque costumes, their crown of feathers recalling…the sham savages exhibited in tents at fairs. The negroes, five in number, sat down without the slightest compunction, upon some straw chairs placed a few paces from the door which would admit the second bull, and holding in their hands their lances [*banderillas*, the metal spikes with which banderilleros stab the bull's shoulders, to lower his head in preparation for the matador's solo combat with the weakened and enraged animal].

The door opened, and the bull fell upon the negroes who barred his advance. They held their ground, and the unhappy wretches did not quit their post till they had employed their lances. Then came a farce which excited the hilarity of the people to the highest degree. The negroes, lifted like feathers by the infuriated animal, flew in the air *pell-mell*, accompanied by the chairs; but directly they fell to the ground, they hastened to roll themselves up in balls, and they remained thus coiled, without making the slightest movement, as they well knew that bulls prefer to attack objects in motion; nevertheless, some of them received terrible scars, much to the delight of the spectators.

As disturbing as this description is, its detail makes it a valuable document in understanding Padilla's performance vocabulary, because, while he fought bulls all over Spain in the 1870s and 1880s, he also performed in spectacles very like this one, in which he performed bullfighting, comedy, and flamenco in the same show.[56] In 1877 we find Padilla in Málaga performing both as a banderillero and in a *corrida bufa* (comic bullfight):

Despite what was advertised, El Mulato Meric presented himself before the president asking permission to place the banderillas, but the president denied this request with just cause, this determination raising such a clamor among the audience who were determined to see the agile black man fight, and although we did not see the authority give a sign of his consent, [Padilla] took up the sticks [the banderillas].[57]

Rioja even cites a novel, *El Tobalo, baratero* by Manuel Martínez Barrionuevo, published in 1887, but set in about 1880, describing a gambling den in which a black *baratero* (gangster) named "Meri" extorted a share of gamblers' winnings by using his skill with the knife. Rioja writes,

El Negro Meri had worked in the circus, not only singing *por lo flamenco*, but also as an acrobat and an illusionist. He had also worked as a horse trainer, a bullfighter, and shining shoes. He spoke various languages, and he sang and played the guitar. How could he be lacking a flamenco dimension?[58]

In 1877 Padilla also continued his long association with the equestrian circus of Don Rafael Díaz in Málaga and was indeed celebrated by Málaga audiences; in fact, as documented in the epigraph from 1877 which opens this section, he had added directing to his skills.[59]

On January 1 and 6, 1882, Padilla directed and performed in a grand *circo taurino*, a bullfight circus combining "pantomime, gymnastics, and bulls' horns" at the Plaza de Toros de Madrid.[60] The opening act was a pantomime titled *Los bandidos de Sierra Morena* (The Bandits of Sierra Morena). A group of bandits detain a carriage in which travel an Englishman, his wife, and a male servant. The bandits steal their effects and, after releasing the travelers, celebrate their deed by singing and dancing—El Meri was the singer. The *Boletín de Loterias y Toros* wrote, "The idea of giving a concert of *cante flamenco* (flamenco song) in the middle of a bullring is like letting a calf run loose on the stage of the [Teatro] Eslava."[61] This performance culminated in a pitched battle between the bandits and a group of rural police trying to arrest them, with the bandits emerging victorious. The second act of this spectacle featured Hercules Arvelini, who held a slab of granite upon his chest until a gang of wise monkeys broke it apart with hammers. "The audience... exclaimed, 'Enough!' with each hammer strike," wrote a critic: "It really could not be witnessed calmly."[62] El Meri was featured as a bullfighter in the third act of the spectacle.[63] The description in the *Boletín de Loterias y Toros* of Padilla's performance as a banderillero is remarkably similar to that of the black banderilleros of Davillier's account, sitting in the ring in cane chairs, standing their ground until the bull attacks:

> The mulato asked for a chair; he sat close to the beast and when it charged Mery **breaks out** [*quiebra*], letting the animal get too close for comfort, and so he only stuck it with one banderilla....We suggest to the mulato that he suppress his wiggling and arrogant contortions [*contoneos y desplantes*].[64]

Might Padilla's manner of "breaking out" from the chair in the mojiganga of 1882 be what we see in his jump from the chair in the Lumière film? Might his contoneos and desplantes afterward be what we see in his burlesque wiggling after the third jump?

In fact, it is an 1877 bullfight poster unearthed by Mora which provides us with Padilla's name, as well as his birthplace: Algeciras, in the province of Cádiz, Spain's major Atlantic port, near the southernmost tip of the peninsula.[65] Which is to say that this Spaniard, a youth in 1872, because he would have been born after 1837, was probably born a free man. And yet there are some indications, as seen above, that El Meri was Cuban.[66]

A search in the digitized periodicals at the Biblioteca Nacional de España (BNE) confirms Meri's notoriety as an equestrian circus performer, as a bullfighter, and in "the flamenco *canto* and dance in which Señor Meric so distinguishes himself," especially between about 1877 and 1888.[67] But there is another Meric, a "grotesque clown," who shows up even more frequently at the BNE, especially in the years 1847–1848. For example, on June 2, 1847, this Señor Meric appeared in *Intermedios* or intermission acts at the Circo de Madrid under the direction of Mr. Paul as a "*clow* [sic] *grotesco español.*"[68] On July 27 *El Clamor Público*, in an item on the Circo de Madrid wrote,

> Tomorrow Tuesday the 28th for the first time *the great extraordinary double jump or in other words two turns in the air* by Señor Meric, *clown grotesco español*: this new exercise has never been seen in this city and it is the most extraordinary [trick] that one can imagine: until now the maestros of jumping had been limited no matter how hard they worked to being able to perform one turn in the air with a springboard made for this purpose [*dandole una impulsion arreglada al efecto*], and despite their many efforts to do more than one turn; but Señor Meric with diligent and dangerous rehearsal has achieved this feat, taking an extraordinary impetus, to make his body turn twice in the air, before touching the ground.[69]

Jacinto Padilla is a mature man in the 1900 film, but he is not in his 70s. He was described in the 1870s press as a young man, and so I believe he could not have been the "Sr. Meric," a "grotesque clown"—I surmise the term grotesque here is used in the sense of the Italian *grottesco* or the French *comique* dancer, an athletic jumper—who performed bareback clowning, bottle balancing, and the "extraordinary and dangerous double somersault," with "two complete revolutions in the air" at the Madrid Circus in 1847.[70]

Unlike Padilla, billed as "El Negro Meri" and "El Mulato Meri," I find no mention in the press that this earlier artist, billed expressly as "Spanish," was either black or Cuban.[71] Nevertheless, my hypothesis, based on the flamenco custom of passing nicknames as artistic lineages within families, is that this "Sr. Meric" may have been Padilla's father. Like Sr. Meric from the 1847 Madrid circus, Padilla performed as an acrobatic clown in the equestrian circus. He may have even gotten his start through an associate of Sr. Meric: Sr. Díaz, who directed the equestrian circus where Padilla frequently performed from 1872–1877, had performed as a *clown grotesco español* alongside Sr. Meric in the Madrid circus in 1847–1848.[72] And we will presently examine clues that "Sr. Meric" *père* may indeed have been "American."

Gerhard Steingress unearths several items on the "famous mulato Meric," which provide important documentation not only about flamenco's evolution in this circus context, but also hints as to Meri's significant contributions to the development of flamenco song.[73] Steingress cites this November 27, 1874, item about Díaz's circus, in the Jerez periodical *El Guadalete*:

> Plaza de Toros.—Next Sunday a new and great spectacle presented by the accredited company of Sr. Diaz. Madam Colmar with her extremely dangerous exercises on the *velocipede* [an early form of bicycle].... The famous mulato MERIC, although not completely recovered from his painful infirmity, and dedicated to many aficionados, WILL SING *POR LO FLAMENCO*. Said mulato is worth listening to, according to those who understand [flamenco].[74]

Recall that the previous year, 1873, in the first mention of flamenco in Córdoba, "the popular and likeable flamenco mulato Meric" had sung and danced *a lo flamenco*—in the flamenco style.[75] On January 15, 1875, *El Guadalete* wrote:

> Tomorrow at the popular circus of Sr. Díaz we will have an exceptional and truly uproarious special performance. The most difficult exercises, among them some novelties, the most extravagant and funny clown scenes, and above all the unique performances of the celebrated mulato Meric, the beneficiary of the spectacle, will doubtless attract an enormous audience. Meric plans to outdo himself, if the reader will excuse the phrase, because whatever we have known about him up until this moment will be overshadowed by what he proposes to do tomorrow. This we have from well-placed sources. A great occasion, thus, for those who enjoy strong emotions and for those fascinated by the typical flamenco songs, in which Meric so greatly excels.[76]

It is fascinating to note that the circus is characterized as a place of strong emotions, from the high wire to the improvisational and emotional high wire of flamenco. Another item in the same issue of *El Guadalete* lists Meric's flamenco repertoire. These two items seem to indicate that El Meri, already "celebrated" as a circus performer, was, in 1873–75, adding flamenco as a new element in his performance toolbox. The articles make clear here that he was equally capable of singing the deepest (*jondo*) song forms as of singing and dancing comic and festive forms such as bulerías (as in the 1900 Lumière film) and tangos:

> Circo de Madrid of Don Rafael Diaz Located in the Plaza de la Revolución— Tomorrow, Saturday, there will be a benefit performance by the celebrated mulato Meric. This can really be called a grand performance, as the beneficiary will dance, play the guitar, and sing *por Soledá*, Seguidillas, and the tanguito called GANGÚ GANGÚ, that is, he will sing...!!! ¡¡¡*La Mar!!!* [The entire ocean!!!] with its boats, its fish, etc. etc.[77]

Although it is true that El Negro Meri has been largely lost to flamenco history, there are suggestions that his singing has left its mark on the flamenco repertoire. In Rafael Marín y Reus's *Método para guitarra* (1902), the first published flamenco guitar method, Marín mentions a *macho*, or ending verse, in a flamenco form called *jabera*, rarely sung today but popular in the late-nineteenth century, called *Rondeñas del Negro*.[78] José Blas Vega, writing on the *Cafés cantantes de Sevilla*, documents this form being sung in 1867 in the Salon del Recreo, a dance academy which had begun marketing "Grand Andalusian Fiestas" to local as well as tourist audiences.[79] The legendary singer Silverio Franconetti would take this locale over in 1870, founding the Café Silverio, one of the seminal stages upon which flamenco would be born. José Manuel Gamboa, in his *Historia del flamenco*, adds that this song was recorded, titled *Jabera del Negro*, accompanied by the guitar of Ramón

Montoya, in the 1920s.[80] Gamboa wonders whether the author of this ending verse, "El Negro," might be a member of the illustrious branch of the Amaya family known as the Negros de Ronda, from the Serranía de Ronda, the hills between Málaga and Cádiz. This illustrious Roma lineage includes María "La Andonda," whom flamenco scholar Loren Chuse describes as the first woman flamenco singer and a legendary creator of *soleá*, and the Peñas of Lebrija and Utrera.[81] Be that as it may, the *jabera del Negro* was part of Silverio's repertoire by the 1870s, the period during which Padilla was making a name for himself singing *por lo flamenco*.[82]

There may be more evidence suggesting Padilla's impact on flamenco song. Flamenco scholar Ramón Soler Díaz observes that the noted Gitano singer from Málaga, Rafael Flores Nieto, "El Piyayo" (1864–1940) had fought in the Cuban War of Independence (1895–1898), where he would have learned Cuban songs.[83] However, in his book on flamenco singer Antonio "El Chaqueta," Soler quotes singer Carlos Alba, who said that El Piyayo took his well-known style of tangos from El Negro Meri: "El Piyayo took that *cante* from El Negro Meric," Alba says.[84] The tangos del Piyayo "are not *tanguillos* [a form associated with Cádiz whose rhythm is a cross between $\frac{4}{4}$ and $\frac{6}{8}$], nor are they *tangos de Málaga* [tangos from Málaga]. They are *cantes del Piyayo* [Piyayo's songs] and they go a bit in the rhythm of tangos, but actually they are *guajiras*" (a form in $\frac{6}{8} - \frac{3}{4}$ associated with Cuba). Soler explains that the tangos del Piyayo are *décimas* (poems of ten eight-syllable lines), "which is the prosody of guajiras"—legendary flamenco singer Antonio Mairena, recording "Tangos de Málaga" for the Columbia label in 1958, made the cantes of El Piyayo into tangos, which are a straight $\frac{4}{4}$ form.[85]

Soler makes the fascinating observation that "at least seven verses by the Cuban poet" Juan Cristóbal Nápoles Fajardo (1829–61), who wrote under the pseudonym "El Cucalambé," have been "incorporated into flamenco guajiras and cantes del Piyayo."[86] One example is the widely known flamenco verse quoted above:

allí merca tela por metros	Over there they buy cloth by the meter
luego las vende por varas,	And sell it by the vara (a measure of length),
se vale de su talento	It takes talent
pa' engañar a las castellanas	To deceive the Castilian women

Further, Rioja cites Málaga flamenco aficionado Pepe Luque Navajas (b. 1930), who adds that El Piyayo took these well-known verses from El Negro Meri:[87]

Si tu boquita fuera	If your little mouth
aceituna verde,	Were a green olive,
toíta la noche estuviera	All night long I'd be
que muele, que muele.	pressing it, pressing it.

Si tu boquita fuera	If your little mouth were
caña de azúcar,	Made of sugar cane,
toíta la noche estuviera	All night long I'd be
que chupa, que chupa,	Sucking and sucking,
que chupa, que chupa,	Sucking and sucking,
que chupa, que chupa	Sucking and sucking

Recall, if you will, that this is the verse of *El tango americano*, the *Sa pi tu sé* or *zapitusé*, sung by Pardo and Guerrero at Madrid's Teatro de la Cruz in 1848—while Sr. Meric *père* was active in Madrid.[88] I think, in light of the flamenco custom of passing down performative inheritance (in the form of verses, songs, movement ideas, and the like), that it is possible that Padilla inherited some of his outstanding flamenco songs from his father. Either way, the identification of these songs with both Cuban verses and with El Negro Meri hints at a possible Cuban connection. Which in turn may hint at a personal story in Jacinto Padilla's life.

Kiko Mora has documented that Padilla was in Paris over a decade before he danced in the Lumière film, during the 1889 Exposition Universelle in Paris; as we will examine presently, Juana Vargas "La Macarrona" was also there. Padilla was performing as a "comic toreador" in the Spanish dance company at the Cirque d'Hiver.[89] And there are hints that while in Paris he may have established a close relationship with another black Cuban clown, the famous "Chocolat" (see Figure 5.3). Rafael "Chocolat" was born enslaved in Cuba around 1865, and therefore had no last name from birth.[90] He was raised in the slums of Havana, and when still a child was sold to a Spanish businessman who took him to labor in northern Spain. He escaped as a teenager, and eventually made his way to Bilbao where he met Tony Grice, an English clown, who hired him as an assistant and domestic servant, eventually incorporating Chocolat as a stuntman into his acts. Writing on Trinidad Huertas "La Cuenca" in 1880s Paris, flamenco historian Ángeles Cruzado says Grice had been performing comic bullfight parodies in Barcelona and Madrid before arriving with Chocolat in Paris in October 1886.[91] Cruzado provides a curious detail from Grice's 1892 obituary: Grice had married the "daughter of the noted circus impresario, Sr. Díaz," who had performed as a *clown grotesco español* alongside Meric *père* in the Madrid circus in 1847–48, and who directed the equestrian circus where Padilla frequently performed from 1872–77; Grice had died in Andalucía.[92]

In 1886 Paris Grice and Chocolat performed with Joseph Oller's New Circus, and in 1887 Chocolat, Grice, and British clown George Foottit, with whom Chocolat later formed a famous duo, all performed in.a show at Nouveau Cirque called *La feria de Sevilla*, which featured comic bullfighters and two important late-nineteenth century Spanish dancers: Trinidad Huertas, "La Cuenca" and Carmen Dauset Moreno, "Carmencita."[93] Performing in the

FIGURE 5.3 "Chocolat Dansant," by Henri de Toulouse-Lautrec. Print. 1896. Courtesy of the Metropolitan Museum of Art, The Elisha Whittelsey Collection, The Elisha Whittelsey Fund, 1962.

emptied swimming pool at the Nouveau Cirque, the bulls were played by two clowns (one in back and one in front), and the *picadors* (the bullfighters who stab the bull with lances from horseback) rode cardboard horses: "One of them," writes Cruzado, "is Chocolat" (see Figures 5.4 and 5.5).[94] In 1889, *La feria de Sevilla* was reprised at the Nouveau Cirque, and in this production, which also included equestrian and acrobatic numbers, Chocolat has replaced Grice, and Meri is now listed in the cast of comic bullfighters.[95]

Thus we know that these two contemporaries, black clowns with roots in Cuba, knew each other and worked together, at least in 1889. Chocolat, in the duo Foottit and Chocolat, would go on to great celebrity in France.

FIGURE 5.4 *Mlle Carmencita, Mlle Cuenca, Le clown Tony Grice, "Le Théatre Illustré — La 'Ferie de Sevilla' au Nouveau Cirque, Spectacle réglé par M. Agoust (Dessin de M. Adrien Marie)."* In *Le Monde illustré* (April 30, 1887), 289. Courtesy of the Bibliothèque nationale de France.

FIGURE 5.5 Detail of Figure 5.4: Grice in whiteface and possibly Chocolat as picador.

The Lumière brothers made several films of Foottit and Chocolat in 1900.[96] In 1902 the duo performed in the Nouveau Cirque show *Joyeux Nègres*, which introduced the cakewalk to continental Europe.[97] In another example of white consumption of Blackness at the dawn of the twentieth century, Chocolat was even featured in an ad campaign for Pihan chocolates.[98]

As a person of fame and stature in French society, Chocolat, whose given name was Rafael, adopted several last names. On one occasion, when asked his last name, he responded Rafael "Patodos," Rafael for everyone. His death certificate, however, reveals that his (adopted) last name was Padilla.[99] Chocolat's biographer Gérard Noriel says that the last name "Padilla" may have been adopted as an homage to the "wife of his former Spanish teacher," raising the fascinating possibility that the coincidence is no coincidence at all. Rafael Padilla "Chocolat" and Jacinto Padilla "El Negro Meri" certainly had every reason to form a close alliance—even kinship—and, for Chocolat, to take the name of a brother who had never been enslaved might have been a powerful statement, even if he never publicized it.

While this is, of course, conjecture, it is a fact that the first male flamenco dancer to be filmed was a black circus performer. This speaks volumes not only, as Eusebio Rioja and Cruz Gutierrez have observed, about the interpenetrated worlds of flamenco and circus in flamenco's formative years, but also about the ways in which this circus world was part of the conceptualizations of flamenco as it was incorporated into the elite cultural sphere of modernist art and literature.

Zapateado, footwork, and acrobatic jumping, which we have been tracing as Spanish representations of transgressive yet potentially transcendent Blackness, circulated for centuries through the black Atlantic. They were reinterpreted and reabsorbed in Spain again and again, in both religious and secular settings. We see this in the mid-seventeenth-century villanos that figured redemption, in the exotic eighteenth-century guarachas that figured the riches of the past, in the tangos performed "Dressed as Another" in 1848 Madrid, as in the bullfight parodies that brought Padilla and Chocolat together in turn-of-the-century France.

As I have argued in relation to Spain's encounter with the African American cakewalk at the dawn of the twentieth century, "[F]ootwork also seems to reference the essential rhythmicity that was so emblematic of the Primitive for Modernists."[100] Hispanist Antonio Rivas Bonillo, writing on proto-surrealist Ramón Gómez de la Serna's essay on clowns, says that Gómez de la Serna, "convinced that life is a grotesquerie," saw the circus as the place where "the grotesque harmonizes and becomes artistic expression"; the circus creates a "state of innocence" in which the viewer can be "submerged," but which nonetheless evokes a "feeling of melancholy" as we remember this innocence as bygone, lost in the past.[101] And yet for free black men like Padilla and Chocolat there can have been neither nostalgia for the "cheerful genuflections" of

"Jim Crow," nor for the melodrama of *Uncle Tom's Cabin*. Powerfully coiled, shaking off racist theatrical tropes with sly irony and physical mastery, these black clowns spring toward the twentieth century.

We should pause here to wonder over the politics of the fact that, in 1900, the Lumière brothers chose a black man as the epitome of male flamenco dance, opening a chasm between French perception of Spain and Spanish views of themselves so great that this gesture went unseen for over a century.[102] French taste in Spanish representation reveals both political and aesthetic fissures between the two nations. As we saw in the 1866 polemic in the Spanish press around Francisco Arderius's *Bufos Madrileños*, France and Spain were equally haunted and terrified, as Antonio J. Pradel says in his article on flamenco's "bastard origins," by the specter of Blackness.[103] Relations between Spain and France, fraught dynastic rivalries dating to the *ancien régime*, had taken a bloody turn with the Napoleonic invasions of 1808–1814. El Meri was a black man "playing in the field of racialized fantasy" between two white colonial powers. What doubled messages was he telegraphing from the interstices of this representational battlefield?

El Meri, as we have seen, had an important, albeit almost completely forgotten, impact on flamenco song, but in the Lumière film Padilla does almost no zapateado. Nonetheless, it is impossible from today's perspective to watch Meri's spectacular jumps without seeing how they foreshadow the signature jumps of Antonio Montoya Flores "El Farruco," one of the greatest male flamenco dancers of the twentieth century. *Farruco* translates as insolent, arrogant—ready for a fight. A wild and haughty valor, like a bullfighter brushing against death in the ring, characterizes Farruco's influential style—a fundamental reference for male flamenco dancers today—of jumping and twisting in the air with great strength, throwing his weight dangerously off-kilter only to recover in the nick of time with casual sure-footedness.[104] And it is interesting to note here that Farruco was a Gitano from Triana, a place historically populated by angry and dangerously free black men.[105]

6 | *Jaleo de Jerez* and *Tumulte Noir*

JUANA VARGAS "LA MACARRONA" AT THE EXPOSITION UNIVERSELLE, PARIS, 1889

She rose from her chair with the majestic dignity of a Queen of Sheba.
Arrogantly. Magnificently. She raises her arms over her head as if to bless the
world…grave, liturgical, she parts her unpainted lips and shows her teeth,
reddish like those of a wolf, tinged with blood…She is like a peacock, white,
magnificent and proud. Over her face the color of smoke-stained ivory, the
aggressive and dirty whites of her eyes, and in her black and matte hair faints a
carnation which falls, defeated by the shivers of the final *redoble* (stamps) of
those marvelous feet wearing carmine slippers, as if there were a pool of blood
at her feet. The audience is silent and eager, with almost religious fervor, while
the feet of La Macarrona measure out her dance. The chords of the guitar now
have an appalling quality. Because La Macarrona dances to the rhythm of her
barbaric heelwork…[she] transfigures herself. Her black face, harsh, with dirty
skin, crossed by fugitive shadows, from within which her eyes and teeth strike
like lightning, is illuminated by the harmonious line of her body. The beauty of
her bodyline is so great that the ugliness of her face is swept aside.

—*Pablillos de Valladolid, on Juana Vargas, "La Macarrona," 1914*

JUANA VARGAS "LA MACARRONA" (1870–1947) was a leading light of
flamenco dance—of the "broken dance of the Gitanos"—as it aspired to the
international stage.[1] In contrast to Jacinto Padilla, "El Negro Meri," long forgotten and virtually erased from history, La Macarrona is revered as one of the
greatest dancers of flamenco's formative period in the late-nineteenth-century
cafés cantantes. The French stage—the French audience—plays a fascinating
role in this rise, and in the careers of both artists. Macarrona's performance
at the 1889 Exposition Universelle in Paris took place at the dawn of her
career. It was one of the first sallies of emerging flamenco artists, and in
particular of a Roma performer, onto the international stage. In many ways,

FIGURE 6.1 "Juana Vargas, 'La Macarrona.'" Photograph, ca. 1889. In Fernando Rodríguez Gómez, "Fernando el de Triana," *Arte y artistas flamencos* (Madrid: Editoriales Andaluzas Unidas, S.A., [1935] 1986), 72. Courtesy of the Ateneo de Córdoba.

it represents a point of articulation in the developing language of flamenco presentation.

Macarrona's performances at the Exposition reveal folklore caught in transition: a moment in which flamenco wavered between Herderian *volkgeist*, orientalist eroticism, and a dawning modernism, heralding the Jazz Age. Flamenco's representation of the Gitano embraces a complex history of power and identity negotiations in Spain; it vibrates with love and desire, confusion and equivocation, the longing for self-determination and redemption, and the terror of slavery, and damnation. How did Macarrona's performances at that world's fair, and the reception of that performance both inside and outside of Spain, manifest these dilemmas? We have tracked the *neglita jitana huachi*, an image paradoxically folding Spanish nostalgia for lost empire and assertion of its unique European identity, its Whiteness, into the image of national self as dark-skinned Other. The thickly knotted web of analogies entangling Moorish (African) Spain and the Gitano in the romantic imaginary is here entwined with modernism's representations of Blackness at the dawn of the twentieth century: as Jayna Brown says, "Performing race had everything to do with articulating the modern world."[2] Macarrona's dance was an alloy of images representing exoticized, Gypsified Spain (and played in an ironic register), with the gestures and sounds of living cultural traditions, and the imperious grandeur of Roma artists whose performance was imitated and appropriated, but who themselves were largely excluded from the international stage until well into the twentieth century.[3]

Though Spain was a much more familiar exotic than the various African groups also performing at the 1889 Exposition Universelle, Macarrona's dance was received as a "bestial," butt-out reversal of belly dance, indicating the destabilization of the tropes of orientalism in 1889, foreshadowing the advent of the cakewalk in continental Europe in 1902, as well as the impact of African art on Henri Matisse and Pablo Picasso soon thereafter. There was a weird synergy between French audiences, who—as we saw in the Lumière brothers' choice not to distinguish between black and white Spaniards—"Blackened" Spain, and Spanish audiences, who—as is evidenced by Jacinto Padilla's erasure from flamenco history—resisted this "put-down." The linkage of flamenco to Africanist "primitivism" ironically impelled Spain toward embracing flamenco in rebuttal to cultural imports from the ascendant Americas.[4] The critical response to Macarrona at the 1889 fair, coupled with a close examination of her dance, reveals some of the transactions by which a foregrounding of the Blackness already implicit in orientalism planted flamenco dance into the iconography of modernism.

Preparing *Tricorne*: July 1917

In the spring of 1916, with World War I raging, Ballets Russes director Serge Diaghilev accepted an invitation from Spain's Alfonso XIII to bring his company to Madrid's Teatro Real.[5] There, principal dancer and choreographer Léonide Massine encountered flamenco. Massine, whose choreography was of central importance to Diaghilev's radical modernization of ballet during this seminal period, recalled in his memoir:

> Once we were firmly established in Madrid I began to spend my free evenings in the local cafes, watching the *flamenco* dancers. I was fascinated by their instinctive sense of rhythm, their natural elegance, and the intensity of their movements. They seemed to combine perfect physical control with flawless timing and innate dignity, something I had never seen before in any native folk-dancing.[6]

That year, Massine and Diaghilev met composer Manuel de Falla and flamenco dancer Félix Fernández García, "El Loco," who became their guides on several tours through Spain.[7] Falla was from Granada and already interested in flamenco: like his friend, the much-younger poet Federico García Lorca, he was

FIGURE 6.2 "Spanish dancers," screen shot, 1917. Adults, left to right: María Vargas, "La Macarrona" (seated); Juana Vargas, "La Macarrona," dancing alegrías; Baltasar Mate, "Mate Sin Pies." Filmed by Léonide Massine in Sevilla in July 1917 in preparation for *Tricorne (The Three-Cornered Hat,* 1919). Courtesy of the Jerome Robbins Dance Division, The New York Public Library for the Performing Arts, and of Tatiana Massine Weinbaum, Theo Massine, and Lorca Massine.

part of a modernist circle seeking to reenvision and reclaim flamenco from the hostility it had faced amongst Spain's educated classes at the turn of the twentieth century.[8] Both Lorca and Falla, who together organized the first Festival of *Cante Jondo* (Deep Song) in Granada in 1922, used flamenco and the figure of the Gitano (in a conceptual move similar to modernism's jazzed mimicry of Blackness) as a portal into a deeply intuitive approach to making art. They sought, as Lorca scholar Christopher Maurer says, to "[put] aside the 'riddle of metaphor' and search instead for images resistant to rational analysis."[9]

In 1914–1915, Falla composed his first flamenco ballet, *El amor brujo* (Love the Magician)—a *gitanería* (performance of Gitanoness) by the revered Roma singer-dancer, Pastora Imperio. *El amor brujo* was conceived as a means to present flamenco on a wider stage than those of the *cafés cantantes.*[10] Similar to the *cafés chantant* of Belle Époque France, and the music halls of Britain and the United States, the Spanish *cafés cantantes* were performance venues catering to newly affluent, often working class, urban audiences.[11] Flamenco had been born on these stages in the second half of the nineteenth century, but at the turn of the twentieth century these venues struggled to compete with the influx of new entertainment such as vaudeville, film, and jazz.

Describing the winter of 1916–1917, which he spent in Rome creating his futurist ballet *Parade*, Massine wrote, "Our studio in the Piazza Venezia in Rome was the meeting place for an ever-widening circle of artists," including painter Pablo Picasso, poet Jean Cocteau, and composer Eric Satie.[12] "Cubism was at its height," and Satie's music was a "subtle synthesis of jazz and ragtime." "Picasso...was at that time trying to transpose and simplify nature in much the same way as primitive African sculptors," Massine continued, "dissolving surface barriers and clearing away sentimental layers of association."[13]

Against the background of this modernist impulse, as Falla and Lorca did, Massine went looking for "authenticity."[14] Back in Spain in the spring and summer of 1917, following the premiere of Falla's pantomime *El corregidor y la molinera* in Madrid, Diaghilev and Massine decided to adapt Falla's piece for the Ballets Russes. The resulting ballet, which straddled the polarities between the avant-garde's appropriation of traditional forms and that of its romantic forebears, premiered July 22, 1919, at London's Alhambra Theatre. Titled *The Three-Cornered Hat* (in Spanish, *El Sombrero de tres picos*, in French, *Tricorne*), the ballet, recalling the riots ensuing from Esquilache's 1766 attempt to force Spaniards to wear the French-styled three-cornered hat, pits a corrupt government official against a villano-like miller and his wife. With sets and costumes by Picasso and libretto, as for *El Amor Brujo*, by Gregorio Martínez Sierra, the ballet ends with the evil Magistrate, a plaything like the empty-headed and lifeless puppet in Goya's *El pelele* (1791), being tossed up in the air by the Andalusian townspeople.[15]

As he had in *El amor brujo*, Falla wrote flamenco airs into his *Three-Cornered Hat*: the *Farruca del molinero*, the bulerías in the first verse of *Casadita, casadita*, and the fandango in *La danza de la molinera*.[16] Massine prepared to choreograph these flamenco forms by studying, first with Félix Fernández García, and then with Félix's teacher, José Molina.[17] In July 1917, Massine, Diaghilev, Falla, and Félix toured Zaragoza, Salamanca, Toledo, Córdoba, Granada, and Sevilla.[18] Félix was "accepted as a friend by the local dancers," Massine recounts.[19] "He was able to arrange several performances for us, and we spent many late nights listening to selected groups of singers, guitarists and dancers doing the *jota*, the *farruca*, or the *fandango*."

That July in Sevilla, Massine filmed La Macarrona with a 16-millimeter camera he had bought in Rome the previous winter (see Figures 6.2 and 6.4). He also filmed another dancer who I surmise is Juana's sister María Vargas, also nicknamed "La Macarrona" (see Figure 6.3), and Juana's partner, their cousin Antonio López Clavijo, "Ramírez."[20] To my knowledge, this spectacular footage is the only film of Macarrona's dancing, or of any of the late-nineteenth-century flamenco pantheon.[21] Along with the 1900 Lumière film discussed in Chapter 5, it is certainly one of the most important extant records of this early period of flamenco dance.[22]

The silent footage is composed of four segments: one of Ramírez dancing alone on a sunny rooftop, and three of the two women dancing and playing palmas for each other in what appears to be a family setting.[23] There are two alternating guitarists (one who plays and also sings in the first and third clips, another in the second), a man playing palmas who appears to be kneeling, and seven or eight children seated on the floor. I base my proposed identification of the second dancer as María on the fact that there were many sister duos and trios during this era, for example: Concha and Julia Borrull; Antonia, Josefa, and Milagros, "Las Coquineras"; the Peña and Aguilera sisters mentioned in

FIGURE 6.3 "Spanish dancers," screen shot, 1917. Adults, left to right: unidentified guitarist; María Vargas, "La Macarrona," doing "jazz hands" in tangos; Juana Vargas, "La Macarrona" (seated); Baltasar Mate, "Mate Sin Pies." Filmed by Léonide Massine in Sevilla in July 1917 in preparation for *Tricorne* (*The Three-Cornered Hat*, 1919). Courtesy of the Jerome Robbins Dance Division, The New York Public Library for the Performing Arts, and of Tatiana Massine Weinbaum, Theo Massine, and Lorca Massine.

the last chapter; and Salúd and Lola Rodríguez, "Las Hijas del Ciego."[24] Early in their careers, Juana and María often worked together as "Las Macarronas," for example, in 1884 at the Café el Imparcial in Madrid, and around 1893–1894 in Madrid's Café de la Marina.[25]

Although Juana's fame has eclipsed that of her sister (consequently, "La Macarrona" here refers to Juana), they are both included in Fernando el de Triana's *Arte y artistas flamencos* (1935).[26] There is another intriguing participant in these films: the man "kneeling" is Baltasar Mate, "Mate Sin Pies," a one-time bullfighter and "comic transformist," amputated below both knees (he is the person at the far right of the frame in Figure 6.3).[27] Mate later danced a grotesque garrotín (a form related to tangos), doing zapateado with his crutches, in whiteface, in Diaghilev's *Cuadro Flamenco* (1921)—a cast which also included Gabriela Clavijo, "La Gabrielita del Garrotín," a dwarf.[28]

In the first clip, Juana dances what flamencos would now call bulerías.[29] In the second segment, she dances alegrías with a train, a *bata de cola*. The third clip, which from the light on the wall behind them looks as though it was filmed later in the day, records María dancing tangos.[30]

One thing that strikes the viewer is how similar Juana and María's dance is to that of today: they dance with the same lifted and majestic posture, punctuated by deep breaks in the hips, sometimes leaning deeply back and side, sometimes forward (see Figures 6.2, 6.3, and 6.4). Juana in particular dances with tension, stretch, and sensuality in her hands and arms. The arm gestures signaling *llamadas* (calls) and *remates* (breaks) are immediately recognizable to a flamenco dancer of today. The sisters both jump, leap, turn, and do *pellizcos* (little lifts of the body), and they incorporate steps from the bolero school, such as *jerezanas, carrerillas,* panaderos, and *seasé con tres pasos por detrás* exactly as we do now.[31] When I deciphered the rhythm, I realized that the dance syntax

FIGURE 6.4 "Spanish dancers," screen shot, 1917. Adults, left to right: María Vargas, "La Macarrona" (seated); Juana Vargas, "La Macarrona," dancing alegrías; Baltasar Mate, "Mate Sin Pies." Filmed by Léonide Massine in Sevilla in July 1917 in preparation for *Tricorne* (*The Three-Cornered Hat*, 1919). Courtesy of the Jerome Robbins Dance Division, The New York Public Library for the Performing Arts, and of Tatiana Massine Weinbaum, Theo Massine, and Lorca Massine.

is also unchanged: the sisters were from Jerez de la Frontera, and in Juana's bulerías she calls at the halfway point in the two-measure cycle of $\frac{6}{8}$—the "6" rather than the "12" in flamenco counts—just as today's Jerez-style dancers do.

But it is María who performs the gesture that most intrigued me: in a clip that lasts only one minute and eight seconds, she trembles her open palms and fingers—"jazz hands"—twice in her tangos.[32] This hand gesture is neither part of the fundamental ornamental twirlings of fingers and wrists that today echo the sonic layer of the song's continuous melisma, nor of the emphatic hand gestures that punctuate the *cante* (song). This hand gesture is pantomimic: it is performed in quotation marks. The tradition of incorporating pantomime into dance is, as we have seen, very old in Spain, but the object of imitation here is something very new: María's gesture evokes the sonic specter of a trumpet's high brassy trill—it evokes jazz. Interestingly, alongside characteristic flamenco hand gestures referencing the movements of the bullfight, a *torero*-like thrust forward in the hips, palmas, *pitos* (finger snaps), jumps, bravura walks on the knee, and footwork, Massine also choreographed this gesture into his *Farruca del Molinero* from *The Three-Cornered Hat*.[33]

Ragtime, the forebear of jazz music, had arrived in London with John William Isham's 1897 revue *Oriental America* and in Paris with John Phillip Sousa at the 1900 Exposition Universelle. Next, cakewalk, the forerunner of many black dance forms, arrived in Paris in 1902 with the show *Joyeux Nègres*, appearing in Spain by the end of that year.[34] Having lost Cuba and the last vestiges of its American empire in 1898, Spain now faced a reversal, colonized by jazzy (as Hispanist Eva Woods Peiró says, "racy") American representations of Blackness.[35] Falla and Lorca, Massine and Diaghilev, sought to elevate and dignify flamenco as an international art form; creating an image of flamenco Spain, as British critic Edward Dent wrote in 1921, as "the ideal of a grave and passionate nobility"—in contrast to the " 'American vulgarity' that is currently degrading Northern European music."[36] Ironically, flamenco—Spain's dance of Blackness—served as a rebuttal, an essentialized and Whitened Spanish answer to the infiltration of Europe by the "vulgarities" of African American jazz.[37]

Following a script we have been tracing from the ruffian antiheroes of the sixteenth and seventeenth centuries, through eighteenth-century majismo and nineteenth-century zarzuelas such as *El Tío Caniyitas*, this resistance, this assertion of Spanish distinction, was enacted in the figure of the Gitano. As Otero writes in his 1912 *Tratado*, the "very flamenco" *tangos gitanos* (Gitano tangos) became Spain's answer to the cakewalk.[38] Recall that these tangos' immediate predecessors were Afro-Cuban tangos such as *zapitusé*, the verse which El Piyayo may have taken from El Negro Meri; nineteenth-century tangos in Spain grew out of and were implanted in the root system of Spanish representations of Blackness. Further, as in the seventeenth-century villano, and continuing in eighteenth-century dances such as chuchumbé, guaracha, and panaderos, the distinction between Black and White, equivocation and moral rectitude, confusion and redemption, was made in terms of zapateado. Thus, Otero tells us, the tangos gitanos became "charming," "agreeable," and "Andalusian," such that they "do not stray from morality" by substituting footwork for their "grotesque movements" and "indecent postures."[39] Ironically, as we see in María La Macarrona's "jazz hands," flamenco absorbed and embodied that very same danced mimicry of American Blackness.[40]

Articulating the Other: Fantasies of Spain at the Dawn of Modernism

The Gitanos are ours, the Gitanos are we.

Fernanflor, La Ilustración Ibérica, November 23, 1889

From May 6 through October 31 of 1889, Paris hosted the Exposition Universelle, the third in a series of highly successful and lucrative fairs (1867, 1878) that brought the world to Paris.[41] As Spanish novelist and essayist Emilia Pardo Bazán describes in her account of the fair, it was an unusually hot summer, and all things Spanish were the rage.[42] Composer Nikolai Rimsky-Korsakov conducted the Paris debut of his *Capriccio espagnol*, and in the audience was a fourteen-year old whose *Bolero* (1928) would become iconic: Maurice Ravel.[43] During the nearly six months of the fair, the Opéra-Comique presented Georges Bizet's *Carmen* (1875) at least once a week.[44] Rosita Mauri, the daughter of a Spanish ballet maestro, was a star at the Paris Opera (see Figure 6.5).[45] There were bullfights in the arena on the Rue Pergolese near the Bois de Boulogne, which were extensively covered in the press.[46] And grand Spanish fiestas were staged at the fair's Cirque d'Hiver, with orchestra, an

FIGURE 6.5 *Portrait of the Ballerina Rosita Mauri*, by François Comerre Léon (1850–1916). Oil on canvas. Courtesy of the Art Renewal Center.

estudiantina, and two hundred female dancers "selected from among the most beautiful Spanish types."[47] The Spanish Students—the *Estudiantina sévillane*— also performed at the *taverna* that was part of the Spanish national exhibit.[48] The Spanish pavilions took up significant space at the fair, their rounded arches, barred windows, and wooden balconies evoking Andalucía (see Figure 6.9, and Chapter 1, Figure 1.1). And the Folies Bergère, as well as the Moulin Rouge (founded that year), included Spanish dance in their line-ups of exotics. Carolina Otero, "La Belle Otero," a Spaniard known for her beauty as well as her scandalous love affairs, made her French debut at the Cirque d'Eté theater in 1889.[49]

The grand Spanish fiestas at the Cirque d'Hiver theater in 1889 were based upon a kind of spectacle long familiar to Parisian audiences. We may consider, for example, an extravaganza presented at the Hippodrome ten years earlier. With twenty thousand people in the audience, it featured seven thousand gas-lights, a model of the famous tower of Sevilla's cathedral, La Giralda, with thirty tuned bells, and a two-hundred-person orchestra.[50] The Giralda had been a minaret before the 1248 reconquest of Sevilla by Ferdinand III of Castilla; it at once evoked, like the Granada made famous by Washington Irving's *Tales of the Alhambra* (1832), romantic images of Moorish Spain and, as Ferdinand III intended, the definitive re-establishment of Christian hegemony.[51]

Rimsky-Korsakov's *Capriccio espagnol* was a virtuosic elaboration of the exotic musical stereotypes of Spanishness.[52] Like Bizet's *Carmen*, and Fanny Elssler's signature *Cachucha* (1836), these representations embroidered on the romantic dream of Spain; they were unconcerned with the "originality and 'truth' of Spanish folk music"—or dance.[53] As Théophile Gautier wrote in 1840 of the cachuchas he had seen that year in Spain:

> Spanish dances only exist in Paris, just as seashells are found only in curiosity shops, never at the seashore. O, Fanny Elssler!…even before we came to Spain, we suspected that it was you who invented the cachucha!"[54]

Edward Said, in his *Orientalism* (1978), steers us toward a deeper understanding of how mid-nineteenth-century philology (the study of the development of language), itself heavily influenced by Charles Darwin's evolutionary theory first published in his *On the Origin of Species* (1859), influenced romantic-era scholars such as Ernest Renan (an orientalist as well as a linguist), who imagined the "genius" of the primitive in the mysterious spark that engendered language.[55] Scholars like Renan thought it necessary to experience foreignness—Otherness—first hand: "to confront, almost in the manner of an audience seeing a dramatic event unfold, or a believer witnessing a revelation, the different, the strange, the distant." But these nineteenth-century investigations/confrontations were closely related to the racist theories of Renan's contemporaries such as Arthur de Gobineau, who wrote *Essai sur l'inégalité des races humaines* (1853).[56] Renan and Gobineau's shared view of the Orient, Said writes, served to reaffirm the colonial power structure: "East and West fulfill their destinies and confirm their identities in the encounter," and the "passive, seminal, feminine, even silent and supine East" is *articulated* (Said's emphasis) in the West.[57] Just as Estébanez Calderón in 1847 saw the Sevilla school as a "crucible" from which dances of the Indies emerged "distilled and dressed in Andalusian style," Renan and Gobineau saw Western reinterpretations of oriental themes as one step better than their models: dispelling "the passionate creation of primitive times" and instating "a new, and deliberate type of artificial creation."[58]

The Spanish section of the 1879 Hippodrome spectacle began with a torch march announcing a bullfight. Flamenco guitars played, men and women sang *cante flamenco*, and after a delicious *paso español* by Rosita Mauri, accompanied by a military band, there was flamenco dance: *polos*, *soleá*, *malagueñas*, and *paseos de toreros* (bullfighter promenades).[59]

Perhaps, like Quinito Valverde's Spanish musical revue, *The Land of Joy*, which premiered at New York's Park Theatre in 1917, the bullfighter promenades were danced by women *en travesti* (see Figure 6.6).[60] The following year, in 1880, Leon Sari, the director of Folies Bergère, would stage a similar spectacle

Photos White

Toreadors in Act II of "The Land of Joy" at the Park Theatre

SUNNY SPAIN DELIGHTS NEW YORK WITH DANCE AND CASTANET

PLAYERS COLLECTION

FIGURE 6.6 "Toreadors in Act II of "The Land of Joy" at the Park Theatre —Sunny Spain Delights New York with Dance and Castanet." Photograph: Photos White, 1918. In *Theatre Magazine* 27 (January 1918): 10.

at the Athenaeum, in which Trinidad Huertas "La Cuenca," performed. In this performance, La Cuenca not only danced in male drag, as a majo partnering a maja (see Chapter 5, Figure 6.4) but also in blackface: according to a review in *Le Gaulois*, between an opening, set on a beach in Málaga, and a closing, set in a salon in Sevilla, in the second act, set on a Cuban plantation, "the dancers from earlier are suddenly transformed into negroes and negresses."[61] "As they did not have a lot of time, the blackening is incomplete," the reporter continues, "but I am assured that at the premiere they will be black enough to make [lawyer, journalist, and Martinique native Victor] Cochinat blush." It is fascinating to imagine how La Cuenca, a Spanish performer known for her pantomimic abilities, and inheriting the theatrical tradition of Quevedo-esque "swimmers under the lash," "imitating the sounds and movements and hard labor of the galleys" and dancing out "torment, whipping, and...death on the gallows," might have danced this scene.[62] In the 1880 Spanish blackface performance at the Athenaeum, staged for a French audience at a time when flamenco was flourishing and Cuba was still part of the Spanish Empire, the performers rendered their impressions of the labors imposed on plantation slaves, enacting "with gestures and cries the tortures that they are sometimes subjected to."[63]

La Cuenca was known for dancing, in male costume, a "parody of the combat with a bull, from the first wielding of the cape until its death."[64] As reported acidly in the Spanish press, "The handsome youth is Mademoiselle Cuenca; she has a more than lovely body, and she will act out the favorite diversion of these Sevilla evenings; —she will fight a bull!"[65] The revealing view of a woman's hips and legs, coupled with the equally titillating representation of the brave and passionately violent domination of the brutal male animal, was the quintessence of French romanticism's dream of Spain, a "land of love intrigues, of grated windows and barred balconies, of serenades and duels, of knife thrusts and secret poisonings."[66]

From the Spanish perspective, this exoticization (what musicologist James Parakilas calls the "erasure of the grandee") rankled.[67] As Isidoro Fernández Flórez, "Fernanflor," ruefully states in the epigraph above, Spain had become the Black Moor, the exotic Gitano, in the eyes of nineteenth-century Europe. Théophile Gautier felt this frisson as he traveled south from Madrid to Granada in 1840, writing that it was "like passing suddenly from Europe to Africa."[68] Both flamenco's evolution and the complex responses it elicited in Spanish audiences reflect these larger debates. As a Spanish report on the 1880 Athenaeum spectacle complained, "for the French, all Spaniards dress as flamencos."[69]

"Reality Check"

This imagery of Spain as exoticism "distilled and dressed in the Andalusian style" continued in circulation well into the twentieth century. But at the 1889 fair it would be made to seem quaintly anachronistic, disappointingly refined— even disengaged from its subject matter—in juxtaposition to the Middle Eastern, African, and Gitano performers. "In France," Parakilas writes, "exoticism had taken a turn for the realistic."[70]

In the Paris of 1889, aristocratic and educated Emilia Pardo Bazán could not escape flamenco stereotypes. Catching a cab to an electrician's shop, the driver, noting she was Spanish, took her, with a wink, to "a suspicious-looking café, upon whose sign, in letters as big as fists, could be read the following bilingual announcement: 'Gypsy Inn. Gentlemen's Rendezvous.' "[71] It turned out that the *rendezvous* was a performance by some "Spanish flamencas, from the most dilapidated of our dives." Pardo supposed that the audience for the flamenco show offered in this inn would be only the workers of this outlying neighborhood, but, to her shock and dismay, soon flamenco was announced at the Grand Théâtre de l'Exposition: "Never was a spectacle so favored by the *crème de la crème. El Figaro* publishes daily the lists of names, each more toffee-nosed than the other." At the Grand Théâtre de l'Exposition at the Champ de Mars was a group of Andalusian Roma performers, *Les Gitanas de Grenade*. This was the debut of Juana Vargas "La Macarrona," already known at age eighteen in cafés cantantes like the Burrero and the Café de Silverio, on the international stage.

Decades earlier, as performed "national dances" were becoming flamenco in Spain, European critics, artists, and composers toured Spain (we have already mentioned the visits of Gautier in 1840, Liszt in 1844–1845, and Glinka in 1845–1847), seeking to experience its unique popular music and dance, seen as inflected with the rhythmic complexities and movement signatures of Moorish Spain. Baron Charles Davillier brought illustrator Gustave Doré with him on his 1862 visit to Spain, resulting in many widely-circulated images. Painter John Singer Sargent toured Spain in 1879, producing his well-known *El Jaleo* in 1882.[72] Liszt, Glinka, and American pianist Louis Moreau Gottschalk (who visited Spain in 1851–1852) all produced work in response to their Spanish encounters, attempting to transcribe the counter-rhythms and complex interplay of duple and triple meters of Spanish folk music.[73]

In October of 1882, in preparation for composing his orchestral rhapsody, *España*, French composer Emmanuel Chabrier went to a café cantante in Sevilla.[74] In a letter to his publishers, Chabrier wrote,

> But, my friends, you really haven't seen anything if you haven't witnessed the spectacle of two or three Andalusian women billowing their bottoms, in time both with the cries of *Anda! Anda! Anda!* and also with the eternal clapping— with a marvelous instinct they beat the $\frac{3}{4}$ in counter-rhythm…you hear them do as follows (with their hands)…it's an amalgam of the most curious rhythms. Moreover, I'm notating it all. (See Figure 6.7).[75]

Chabrier does not name the café where he saw this performance. In *Los cafés cantantes de Sevilla*, José Blas Vega calls the years from 1881 to 1900 the "Golden Age" of the cafés (he lists eleven), but the best-known cafés in 1882 Sevilla were Silverio Franconetti's Café de Silverio, and Manuel Ojeda "El Burrero's" Café del Burrero (see Figure 6.8).[76] Chabrier's description of the dancers "billowing their bottoms" alludes to a very different movement vocabulary than the balleticized techniques of the escuela bolera, as articulated by dancers on European and American stages from Fanny Elssler and Marie Guy-Stéphan to Rosita Mauri and Carmencita.

The exhibits at the 1889 fair, writes musicologist Annegret Fauser, elicited a dawning realization of the "gap between the fantasy world of musical exoticism and the actual music of the exotic Others."[77] French colonies in 1889 extended through North, West, Central, and East Africa, including Algeria, Tunisia, Ivory Coast, Mali, Senegal, Republic of Congo, and Gabon. These colonial possessions, represented in the series of expositions held in Paris, alongside Spain's increasing accessibility and popularity as a tourist destination,

FIGURE 6.7 Emmanuel Chabrier's notation of palmas from a flamenco performance in 1882 Sevilla. In "Letter to Wilhelm Enoch and Georges Costallat, 21 October 1882," Emmanuel Chabrier, *Correspondence*, ed. Roger Delage and Frans Durif with Thierry Bodin (n.p.: Klincksieck, 1994), 166–67. Courtesy of María Luisa Martínez.

FIGURE 6.8 "Café Cantante," by Emilio Beauchy y Cano. Photograph. Sevilla, ca. 1888. Café del Burrero. Seated guitarist may be Juan Breva; the dancer standing to the right of the seated woman in the center is Concha "La Carbonera."

led French audiences to develop a taste for the exotic "as an endless process of discovery, no longer as a game to be played and replayed with stereotypes."[78] The romantic vision of François-René de Chateaubriand's *Les adventures du dernier Abencérage* (written in 1810 after an 1807 visit to Granada, though not published until 1826), would give way by the end of the nineteenth century to what literary scholar and critical race theorist Lemuel Johnson calls the "dionysiac intensities" of Joseph Conrad's *Heart of Darkness* (1899).[79] For French audiences, those dionysiac intensities were embodied in the billowing bottoms that so differentiated flamenco from balletic interpretations of Spanish dance.

The Enormity of Beginning

> The exotic element... most interested me in the immense World's Fair... because of the enormity of beginning that we feel today in seeing the physiognomies of all the races who populate the planet, to learn, if it is possible, about their customs, to penetrate in their soul. To find a gathering of eight hundred human beings from the most remote climates and from the most mysterious countries; to see them eat, work, play, sing their songs, dance their dances... without having had to cross the pond in a trans-Atlantic ocean

liner, or to cross deserts, suffer mosquito bites and scares about storms and
simooms [desert winds], is a delicious plate... I know that at bottom this is
real... [but] I start to get hives when I hear some skeptical comment that all
the Turks, Moors, and Romans around here are from *Batignolles* [a Parisian
neighborhood]. To be fair, let us adopt a middle ground, and believe in the
authenticity of much of the exotic element.

Emilia Pardo Bazán, "Diversions—Strange Folks"
Letter XXIII, Paris, September 28, 1889

At the earlier 1867 and 1878 Expositions Universelles, imported "habitats"
consisted of staged *tableaux vivants* with music and dance; perhaps flamenco's
emergence on café cantante stages reflects a similar sensibility.[80] "Oriental"
dancers were among the most popular, and soon began circulating in other
Parisian venues, from boulevard theaters to the opera.[81] Representations of
oriental dance cultivated an aura of authenticity through elaborately detailed
stage sets but, as with the subsequent Spanish dance spectacles of the
Hippodrome and Athenaeum, and as recorded in Edison's 1894 footage of
Carmencita, the music and dance of orientalist spectacle "remained thoroughly
within the Western idiom."[82] In 1889, the Spanish dancer, like the oriental
dancer, was already a known exotic, well integrated into the cultural landscape
of opera, ballet, and café concert.[83]

If orientalism staged an erotic fantasy dance of an exotic Other, it also
played on another trope that would flow into primitivism: the image of the
Other as a people without history. Timeless and apart—unevolved—the exotic
was an imaginary refuge from the fierce and often catastrophically violent
jockeying for preeminence among the colonial powers of the industrial age.[84]
In *Musical Encounters at the* 1889 *Paris World's Fair*, Annegret Fauser writes,
the Orient became an "alternative space, a landscape" which could equally
"encapsulate nostalgia for a lost world or a golden age" as it could "represent
the location of forbidden erotic desires."[85] This desire to step out of time, and
into an Other body, was simultaneously congruent and at odds with the fair's
colonialist agendas, where canonical Western elaborations of exoticism vied
for audience share with the living manifestations of France's global reach.

In 1889, at the popular exposition café concerts where Egyptian dancers
and musicians performed at either end of the Rue de Caire, viewers were
caught in an uncomfortable disjuncture between the staged orientalism they
had come to know and a different, jarring reality.[86] Thus, writer and publisher
Edmond de Goncourt complained that "this Fair has no reality: it is almost as
if one were walking in the set of an oriental play." Viewers prized authenticity,
the thrill of confronting the strange actuality of foreign lands.[87] The teeming
multiplicity of the world coming to pay homage to France on a "delicious
plate" gestured toward the "enormity of beginning," as Pardo Bazán put it,
which privileged audiences, and those aspiring to privilege, perceived in this

moment of shifting political economies.[88] And yet, Fauser writes, the actual sounds "broke the sensual orientalist dream," intruding with "sonorities that seemed too loud, nasal, and 'barbaric' to Western ears."[89]

Many—though not all—of these jarring sights and sounds emanated from Africa. Pardo Bazán describes villages, and people, from Senegal, Gabon, Egypt ("olive-skinned and slender, with black eyes, very like the Gitanos of Spain"), and Nubia ("black, well-built, wooly, snub-nosed and wide-lipped.")[90] But the "barbarism" of the Other was not limited to Africa: Pardo commented also on the "cannibals of New Caledonia, who file their teeth," and the "simian aspect" of the performers from Laos and Vietnam, whose "discordant and savage screams" seemed to characterize that "horrible... hideous...monstrous...yellow race." She found relief in the dancers of the exposition's Javanese village, at whose entrance sat "three artists, consecrated to play a type of instrument that reminds one of the pipes of Pan...moist, fresh, and pastoral, the reeds remember the river in which they were born, and they sigh and sing with an aquatic sound." And she enjoyed "Señorita Fátima, from Tunis," an Algerian Jew who had arrived in Paris to perform at the fair in 1878, and had remained in Paris, performing in the Folies Bergère, during the interim.[91]

The most spectacular performance of difference at the 1889 exposition was enacted by the Moroccan Sufi brotherhood of the Aissaoua, who horrified and fascinated the Parisians with their "demonstrations of physical mortification performed to trance-inducing music."[92] Pardo Bazán described them:

> Giant negroes of I don't know what African tribe, who constitute a fanatic sect given to self-mortification and torture as a religious act in honor of the divinity. It must be that the habit of inflicting torture on themselves has hardened and habituated them to pain, or perhaps it is because of the spinning movements and magnetic steps that hypnotize them and produce local anesthesia, but the case is that the *isaguas* pinch, slice, and burn their own flesh as if they were made of wood. They swallow scorpions, lizards, cobras, embers, and knife blades as if they were sweets. They pass their tongues over red-hot irons, rub their noses in burning coals, pierce their arms with thick needles, pop their eyes out of their sockets with the tips of their thumbs...and other barbarities. All this to the sound of a strange and discordant music, with drum and small guitar, which always accelerates at the moment a new piece of mischief approaches.[93]

Although the Aissaoua were light-skinned Muslims from North Africa, their performance contrasted so absolutely with the "orientalist imaginary of the Maghreb" that, Fauser argues, they were perceived as representing "Africa's dark center," "an exotic place of subjugation of and encounter with an Other so different that race became a much more foregrounded signifier than in discussions of the Arabs."[94] The Aissaoua represented absolute alterity—yet their "barbarism," seen as an "absence of culture," sounded racial distinctions in terms of the old orientalist tropes of timelessness: primitivism cast as an unselfconscious, unevolved, Edenic state. As Pardo said, "belly dance is our flamenco dance in a larval state."[95]

The Aissaoua's performance nonetheless stood at the verge of modernism. Their hypnotic mastery over the body derived from complete surrender, plumbing the depths of trance, possession, and, ultimately, transcendent freedom; it was as powerfully erotic as it was spiritual and political. The Aissaoua reached toward the divine through mortification of the flesh, but Europeans felt this transcendent and transgressive body power also in the torso dislocations and articulately dancing hips and pelvis of both Middle Eastern and African dance—and flamenco.

Novelist François de Nion wrote in 1889:

Monstrous, lascivious, obscene Africa, a *new world*, barely known, the black world, teeming with a disquieting and robust life, the generator of a power that will one day revolutionize any exhausted societies through contact alone. This soul of Africa, that lies in the genitals... flourishes in these dislocations of the torso, and in this extreme science... to present and offer the pudenda [vulva] of a woman. The movement of the hips with their brutal jolts, this is dance *par excellence* of all of the immense triangle whose base reaches from Suez to Tétouan and whose point is the Cape.[96]

For Pardo Bazán, the difference between these "brutal jolts" of the hips and the *quebradas*, the balletic bends from the waist well known to connoisseurs of Spanish dance throughout the nineteenth century, was obvious.[97] Continuing her discussion of belly dance as a "larval" form of flamenco, she judges that, in "shaking the abdomen instead of the hips, and omitting the exceedingly salty *quiebro*, as it were, the pepper and cinnamon of this dance," belly dance "may have all the local color you'd wish for, but it has no *gracia* (charm)."[98]

Gautier's description, years before, of Fanny Elssler as "cross-bred"— Germanic in the "whiteness of her skin" and the "placidity of her forehead," Spanish in the "somewhat bold curve of her back"—adding that, "in her, two nations, two temperaments are opposed," would describe the Spanish dancers that Pardo had in mind in similar terms.[99] Spanish artists in European concert halls, James Parakilas observes, had to "fulfill international expectations of the Spanish 'type,'" (that is, "passionate"), yet "to match the manners of the concert hall, they could not be too passionate."[100] Here is the tension in romanticism between, to offer an illustrative parallel, a preference for the seashells in gift shops (i.e., constructed according to the Western canon), and the yearning to discover seashells on the seashore, to "confront" (and conquer) the Other. What James Parakilas describes as the "revolutionary" bass ostinato evoking Spanish guitars in Etienne-Nicolas Mehúl's bolero of 1806 (think of the opening of Ravel's 1928 *Bolero*), would echo in the emblematic primitivism of the opening percussive chords of Igor Stravinsky's riot-causing *Le sacre du printemps* in 1913.[101] Between those dates, in 1889, we witness Parisian audiences' attention shifting from the familiar interpretations of Spanishness in the grand spectacles at the Hippodrome, Athenaeum, and Cirque d'Hiver, to a more "authentic"—yet more foreign—brand of Spanish dance: intimate (as Spain was to France), yet far more "primitive."

The Queen of the Gypsies, *La Reina der Mundo*

Juana Vargas de las Heras, "La Macarrona," was born in the Barrio Santiago of Jerez de la Frontera on May 3, 1870.[102] She came of age in the cafés cantantes, creating a movement style and elaborating a repertoire of dances—alegrías, *tientos*, and tangos—which have impacted all flamenco dancers who followed her. In *Arte y artistas flamencos* (1935), Fernando el de Triana describes how, following a quick turn with a firm stop, "her feet are softly wrapped in the train of her bata [de cola], like a beautiful sculpture atop a delicate pedestal."[103] Of this alegrías, Macarrona said in a 1945 interview in the Spanish periodical *ABC*, "it was my first dance, and my triumph."[104] When she arrived in Paris in 1889, she was described in the French press as the "Queen of the Gypsies," a description full of irony, alluding both to Macarrona's primitivism as Roma, and that of the Spanish nation, worshiping a Gitano idol.

Juana and María, "Las Macarronas," learned to dance from their family. Their nickname derived from their forebears, Tío Juan and Tío Vicente "Macarrón," mentioned by "Demófilo" in his 1881 list of *Cantadores de flamenco* (flamenco singers).[105] The sobriquet "*Macarrón*," is tricky to translate. *Macarrón* is simply macaroni, a kind of pasta, although in the late-eighteenth century (think of the song *Yankee Doodle*) it signified effeminate foppishness. According to the *Diccionario popular de la lengua castellana* (1882), *macarrónea* is a burlesque composition in which words of various languages are confused and jumbled; *macarrónico* describes this composition's ridiculous language and lowbrow style.[106] Emilia Pardo protested the indignity of Macarrona's name, questioning why she didn't adopt the more picturesque name of the *castizo* (from *casta*, pure-blooded) Sevilla neighborhood: "What a name for a Gitana! You could just as well say *Macarena!*"[107] Yet, in addition to paying homage to her ancestors, Macarrona's sobriquet seems an apt reference to the way flamenco absorbs—and even transforms—its cultural milieu: as Jayna Brown writes, "Popular expressive forms resist purity. Expressive forms are inherently promiscuous, absorbing everything in their wake. They are contaminated from the minute they hit the air, and they refuse to be contained."[108]

Las Macarronas' father Juan Vargas, son of a *cantaor* (male flamenco singer), was a guitarist, and their mother Ramona de las Heras was a *cantaora* (female flamenco singer). In a centuries-old tradition of Roma street performance (think, for example, of Cervantes's 1613 *La gitanilla*), Macarrona began performing as a young child with her parents, passing a hat in roadside inns and country fairs.[109] In her later years, Macarrona said that all the women in her line had been dancers, which is to say that, as Juana and her sister did, they all both sang and danced. (Pineda Novo says that Macarrona would have both sung and danced in her alegrías.)[110] Of María, Fernando el de Triana said, "This good dance artist was going to be phenomenal. But just as she was gaining renown, she decided to follow the cante and left the path that, in my opinion, she should have followed, a little untended."

Flamenco scholar Daniel Pineda Novo writes that at age eight Juana debuted on the café cantante stage: "hired by the brilliant Silverio Franconetti and his business partner Frasquito 'El Manga,' with a salary of ten *reales* a night, to perform in the Sevilla Café de La Escalerilla."[111] This locale, at the intersection of Calle de Tarifa and Calle Amor de Dios, played an outsized role in flamenco's development, along with Silverio himself.[112] Originally a dance academy directed by Miguel de la Barrera in the 1840s, by the 1860s this spacious salon, reached by a narrow circular stair, had become a performance venue called the Salon del Recreo, attracting locals as well as foreign tourists. Charles Davillier and Gustave Doré recorded their visit in 1862 with a Doré engraving of bolero dancer (and Otero's teacher) Amparo Álvarez "La Campanera" (see Figure 6.9).[113]

In 1870, Silverio took over the management of the Salon Recreo. Here, at his first café, he elevated the cante to a recital form, not simply an accompaniment to dance.[114] He presented only flamenco performance, in contrast to the prevailing variety offered in other venues. Furthermore, as noted in Chapter 5, his erudite repertoire introduced new forms into the canon, such as the *jaberas del negro*. A press account from 1878, the year Macarrona performed there, provides intriguing detail about the performance at the Café de la Escalerilla. During a period in which we know that El Negro Meri was active as a flamenco artist, another performer, "*El Roteño*" (from Rota, in Cádiz) "*canta guagiras y baila a lo mulato*" (sings *guajiras*, from *guajiro*, or white Cuban, and dances in a mulato style).[115] This 1878 account hints at a greater integration of the "mulato style" in flamenco's early dance repertoire than is generally recognized; further, it suggests that perhaps there were more black flamenco artists such as El Negro Meri than we realize.

In 1880 Silverio formed a short-lived business association with Manuel Ojeda, "El Burrero," which dissolved by March of 1881, when Silverio left to found his illustrious Café de Silverio on the Calle Rosario, while El Burrero remained in the old Café de la Escalerilla.[116] The golden age of flamenco's cafés cantantes was shaped by the rivalry between these two men and their venues.

Macarrona danced in the Café de Silverio on Calle Rosario in 1886.[117] While there, as she recounted in the 1945 interview, bullfighter Luis Mazzantini's

FIGURE 6.9 *Amparo Álvarez "La Campanera,"* by Gustave Doré, 1862. In Charles Davillier and Gustave Doré, *Spain* (London: Sampson Low, Marston, Low, and Searle, 1876).

brother-in-law hired her to perform in Madrid, where she stayed for five or six months: Blas Vega places her in the Café del Romero, on Madrid's Calle Atocha, in September of 1887.[118] In 1888, the Café El Burrero moved from the ample salon with the narrow circular stair to a location on the Calle Sierpes, the same street where photographer Emilio Beauchy Cano had his studio (see Chapter 2, Figure 2.2, and Figure 6.8).[119] Fernando el de Triana recounts that the stage was so big that they even held bullfights with *"becerros de casta"* (young bulls) there.[120] Belgian poet Pierre Louÿs wrote in his diary on February 10, 1895: "I go often to the Burrero. It is the *baile de gitanos* where La Macarena [sic] was dancing when they picked her for the Exposition."[121] (Louÿs's spelling mistake is unsurprising: the French press more often than not misspelled "Macarrona," as "Maccarona," "Macarona," or "Macarena.")

In 1945, Macarrona recalled:

I returned [from Madrid] to Sevilla to dance at the Burrero on the Calle Sierpes. Word was getting out that there was a girl named La Macarrona who danced very well, and they came to hire me from Paris. Have you ever heard of the Eiffel Tower?…Well, I went, for the opening of the first Exposition.

I was seventeen. I spent three months there. My father played the guitar. I danced for the Tsar of Russia and for Isabel II, who was there. We went with a cuadro of Gitanos. They arrived first. For me it was a special trip, extraordinary. Like nothing else.[122]

The exposition had opened in early May, and Leon Sari, director of the Folies Bergère, was in charge of the program at the Théâtre de l'Exposition. But according to French music critic Arthur Pougin, his initial offerings of standard exotic fare generated a lukewarm reception:

At first we saw only spectacles of mediocre interest and doubtful originality. Among others, "La Belle Fatma, already well known to Parisians, came to sit in state in the first week of June. This...failed to satisfy the public's curiosity for more substantial fare.[123]

Pougin goes on to describe how this situation was soon rectified:

Madame Monteaux, a fanatic of the Exposition, seeing Sari's embarrassment, spoke enthusiastically to him of a curious troupe of Gitanas that, on a recent trip to Spain, she had had the opportunity to see in Granada....Sari... immediately sent an agent to investigate and to bring the troupe as soon as possible....The assurance of an unexpected fortune ultimately tipped the balance: they were offered ten francs a day, with all expenses paid, to those who usually earned just pennies (Chivo [the troupe's Captain] got fifty francs for himself and his three daughters, Soledad, Mathilda and Viva)....Five days and six nights journey!...God knows what a success!—A success that has not abated for a moment in more than four months.

The arrival of Sari's agent, Jules Grasset Cambón, was reported in the Spanish press, beginning on June 30, 1889, in *El Pais,* then on July 2 in *La Época,* on July 12 in *El Progreso,* and on July 28 in *La Correspondencia de España.* (All four articles mistakenly identify Grasset as the director of the Théâtre de l'Exposition; *El Pais* gives his full name as Jules Grasset Cambón.)[124]

The director of the Grand Theater of the Exposition of Paris, Mr. Grasset, has been in Sevilla for several days looking for Gitanos of both sexes to dance and sing in the theater of which he is the manager and impresario. It has cost him some effort, but he has finally succeeded in bringing several couples of the express race, from fifteen to twenty years of age, who will delight the Europeans attending the spectacle.[125]

If the Spanish press had greeted Mr. Grasset's interest in hiring Gitanos with a certain incredulity, Macarrona's impending arrival caused a stir in the French press. On August 1, *Le Figaro* announced that she had left Spain (the French press erroneously assume that, like the first group of performers to arrive in Paris, she was departing from Granada, rather than from Sevilla):

The Gypsy star, the idol of Andalusia, the celebrated Maccarona [sic], who had not been able to decide upon accompanying the Gitanas to Paris, has left Granada today. We await her debut at the fair next Monday or Tuesday at the Grand Théâtre de l'Exposition.[126]

On August 5, *La Lanterne* sounded the same themes:

The queen of the Gitanas—Granada is in mourning; the echoes of the Alhambra reverberate with the lamentations of noble *hidalgos* (noblemen) who lament Macarrona's departure. Madame Macarrona, *the queen of the Gitanas*, jealous of the success enjoyed by her sisters and subjects at the Grand Théâtre de l'Exposition, left Spain and is on route toward Paris. The idol of all Spain will make her debut next Monday or Tuesday...Go, lovers of strange dances, prepare for the best.[127]

Arthur Pougin described the original eleven performers from Granada. There were eight women: Soledad was the star, and her elder sisters, Mathilde and Viva, as well as Pepa, Dolores, Reyes, Lola, and Antonia.[128] There were three men: Chivo (Soledad, Mathilde, and Viva's father), Antonio, and Manuel. (The July 2 report in the Spanish periodical *La Época*, dripping with irony, gave slightly different numbers: "five gallant Gitanos and nine charming *gitanillas*," adding that the cast included the singer and celebrated beauty, *La Castañeta*.[129]) Pougin continued:

Soon afterward, a second star, la Maccarona [sic] came to join the cast, and contributed not little to the enthusiasm of the public. With her came Pichiri, a truly priceless comic, and some other dancers: Juana, Zola, Sanchez and Concepcion. I think they opened around July 10.[130]

Pepa would be featured dancing with Pichiri on the cover of the August 31 *Le Monde illustré* (see Figure 6.10).[131]

Macarrona must have made her debut on August 6. On August 7, the front page of *Le Figaro* reported, as it had been daily, on the comings and goings of the shah of Persia's visit to Paris: "At the moment the Shah entered the Grand Theater of the Exposition, La Macarrona was on stage. His majesty was very delighted by the astonishing movements of the celebrated Gitana and wanted to throw flowers and oranges by himself."[132] The following day, *La Lanterne* reported that the shah returned to see the show again:

The Shah's Day: The Shah of Persia and his first minister paid another visit to the Exposition. The Shah visited the pavilion of Brazil, and pavilion of México, and the Globe of the Earth with great and long-standing interest. Leaving the pavilion of Brazil, the Shah entered the Grand Théâtre de l'Exposition, where he attended the performance of the Gitanas. The Grand-Théâtre's new star, la *Maccarona* [sic], the queen of the Gitanas, danced before the Persian monarch, who spoke of nothing less than bringing her to Tehran.[133]

LE MONDE ILLUSTRÉ

JOURNAL HEBDOMADAIRE

ABONNEMENT POUR PARIS ET LES DÉPARTEMENTS	33ᵉ Année. — Nº 1692. — 31 Août 1889	DIRECTION ET ADMINISTRATION, 13, Q'AI VOLTAIRE

Directeur : **M. ÉDOUARD HUBERT**

EXPOSITION UNIVERSELLE. — Les gitanes de Grenade au Champ-de-Mars. — La danse du Tango.

(D'après nature, par M. Parys.)

FIGURE 6.10 *Les Gitanes de Grenade au Champ-de-Mars. La Dans du Tango. D'après nature, par M. Parys. Le Monde Illustré* (August 31, 1889) : cover. Courtesy of the Bibliothèque nationale de France.

On August 10, *Le Radical* told essentially the same story:

> His Majesty Nasser-Edin…went to the Grand Théâtre de l'Exposition to applaud La Macarrona, the new Gitana dancing star....This is not a woman but truly a serpent, said the Shah upon seeing the Queen of the Gitanas dancing before him, dances of which the almées of Tehran have no idea....[134]

Déhanchements Full of Promise

> The Flamenco dances are directly seductive. The life of the forest animal seems reproduced in the fierceness, the fitfulness, the abandon of each strange series of abrupt gesticulations. Yet these gypsy women, boldly as they play on the passions of the spectators…fling off with fiery scorn the addresses that their songs and dances court....Disdain and dislike are in the atmosphere, and never more than when the rain of silver is at its richest.
>
> Katherine Lee Bates, The New York Times, *May 14, 1899*

> Maccarona [sic] whom they call "Queen of the Gypsies"…is easily, as a dancer, the strangest creature conceivable. [She moves] like a panther, with her flexible torso, without a corset, and her *déhanchements* [squirming, wiggling, lopsided or swaying walk] full of promise.
>
> Arthur Pougin, Le théatre à l'Exposition Universelle de 1889[135]

Although, as noted by the French press, Macarrona already was known within the select circle of performers in Spain's prestigious cafés, French audiences did not notice this fact. The audience responses to the flamenco cuadro at the Théâtre de l'Exposition thus reveal shifting expectations about what the dance of a Gypsy queen should resemble. As can be seen in Figure 6.10, the stage décor of the Théâtre de l'Exposition depicted the outside of a rural inn, with whitewashed walls, laundry on the line, *búcaros* (clay jugs) for water, carafes for wine, and a shaded second-story balcony. With its depiction of street performance and fragrance of private interiors, the scene is not unlike that drawn by Doré in 1862 (see Chapter 1, Figure 1.1). Yet it contrasts completely with the decidedly bourgeois drawing room that, with one wall removed, forms the setting for the real Burrero in Sevilla (see Figure 6.8). As *Le Monde illustré* described, the "décor…is an exact replica of one of these *cuevas* (caves) carved in the rocks in the vicinity of Cádiz or the Alhambra."[136] The Théâtre de l'Exposition production set a flamenco cuadro like those of Spain's cafés cantantes in a "natural" setting: the women (as Anita Reguera would be in 1900) in Manila shawls and elegantly coifed with flowers and spit-curls, and the men dressed, as El Negro Meri would be in 1900, as Andalusian country gentlemen, in *traje corto* and *sombrero calañés*, a laborers' hat from Huelva province. Pougin wrote,

As the curtain rises, the dancers in their chairs were placed in a line across the stage, the three men in the center, the ladies on either side. The men who were not dancing played the guitar, and they were the sole orchestra in charge of the rhythmic music, accompanied in part by the castanets and in part by other women, who marked the tempo by hitting one hand against the other, and sometimes in the solemn moments, by a kind of noisy tremolo obtained with both feet.[137]

The strange music seemed to Pougin like medieval "plain-chant from the point of view of tonality, but with a lively, marked, and petulant rhythm."[138] The troupe's repertoire included tangos, fandangos, *panaderas* (possibly a misspelling of panaderos), and the *baile del novio* (dance of the bridegroom). They did five shows a day—three in the afternoon and two in the evening—with prices ranging from one to five francs—and the house was never empty.

Of Pepa, Pougin states that she was big, hearty, and "plump as a partridge, with the most beautiful arms in the world."[139] *Le Monde illustré* described her "strange and eccentric leaps."[140] Said Pougin, "she reminds us of our tall Théresa" (perhaps a reference to Fanny Elssler's sister). Mathilde seems to have adopted ideas from the contemporary Parisian dance scene: she "lifts her leg like La Goulue" (a famous can-can dancer).[141] The cover of *Le Monde illustré* depicts a tango that Pepa danced with Pichiri, "lifting her skirt in her left hand as if she were afraid she would lose it, her wrist resting on her very Andalusian rump, she does a belly-dance differently suggestive than the cold and mechanical jiggling" of the belly dancers on the Rue de Caire.

Pougin described "El Pichiri" as "an olive-skinned gentleman, dry as a match," who, "strapped in his tight trousers," performed "the most extravagant contortions of the kidneys."[142] *Le Monde illustré* commented only in passing on Macarrona's "lively fandango." But the article describes Pichiri with interest and enthusiasm:

[N]ot the least original part of the show [is] a big fellow named Picheri [*sic*], with lean and flexible legs, his body in a coquettishly tight short jacket, who with his companions attacked the dance with lightness and grace, and wriggles like the contortions of the oriental *almées*. This skinny Picheri, dancing the *dans du ventre*, is outrageous.[143]

One might read in this movement description the break forward from the hips, jacket gathered to the front to reveal and highlight the buttocks, the derisively waggling, suggestively hip-swaying walk common to men's flamenco dance in the tangos and bulerías of today (see Figure 6.10). Antonio de la Rosa, "El Pichiri," was a singer and dancer from Cádiz, who danced a bullfight pantomime in the late nineteenth century.[144] Perhaps his parody partook of the burlesque bullfight performances and equestrian clowning, the "wiggling and arrogant contortions" of performers such as El Negro Meri.[145] Pichiri is listed (along with both Macarronas) in a 1901 article in *Alrededor del Mundo* describing "celebrated flamencos."[146] Pichiri, the 1901 article says,

> [is a] *bailaor de chufla*, that is, of dances analogous to those of the blacks, tangos, etc., burlesque dances, but not so clownish and distorted as those of today, which are a mix of flamenco, *baile inglés*, and the lewd and ridiculous clownish contortions that have been imported to Spain in all the *couplet* and *danse du ventre* productions.[147]

Baile inglés is literally "English dance," but I believe the author refers to dances of the English-speaking world, including—perhaps especially—the United States.[148] The author uses the French or English spelling of "couplet" instead of the Spanish *cuplé*. Likewise, *danse du ventre* is *danza del vientre* (belly dance) in Spanish, but the author pointedly uses French. That is, Pichiri is a *bailaor de chufla*, a comic dancer performing burlesque tangos—"dances analogous to those of the blacks"—and these are set against the promiscuous "mix of flamenco, *baile inglés*," and "imported" "lewd and ridiculous clownish contortions" found in Spain's turn-of-the-century *varietés*, or vaudeville shows.[149] In contrast to the French audiences at the 1889 fair, who saw in Pichiri's wiggling hips one exotic dance (flamenco) parodying another (belly dance), Spanish audiences perceived the *tangos de negros*, imported from Cuba more than a half-century earlier, as so thoroughly nativized that they embodied a Spanish refutation of these imported performance modes.

By 1901, vaudeville threatened to put the cafés cantantes out of business; performance of the Gitano as national Other, which was both lucrative commerce and a symbolic reclaiming of past glories, was imperiled by foreign cultural impositions. This is the context in which Spanish modernists such as Lorca and Falla worked to wrest flamenco from such pandering and to elevate its indigenous aesthetics to the international stage. Pardo Bazán found it insulting that the French should grovel over flamenco artists as if they were icons of Spanish culture, but the twentieth-century avant-garde's adoption of flamenco was vested by eighteenth-century *majismo*'s resistance to the French. And the process of nativizing a black American import likewise cannot be divorced from the centuries-old practice of performing the dilemma of the bobo, the equivocating and equivocal Other, as self. The perception of tangos as "native" would focus the Spanish response to another African American dance, the cakewalk, which arrived in Spain the following year, in the rhythm of tangos. That is, Spain's response to the cakewalk of 1902 would be to adapt the old tangos de negros, which had become tangos gitanos, into new flamenco forms: *garrotín* and *farruca*.[150]

Macarrona may have been a rising star in Spain, but in Paris she had to share the limelight. Soledad, the youngest and prettiest of Chivo's three daughters (and perhaps the only unmarried one), was very popular with Parisian audiences. For example, on September 18, 1889, *La Lanterne* reported,

The administration of the Grand Théâtre de l'Exposition is pleased to announce to our readers that *Soledad*, one of the best subjects of the troupe of *Gitanas*, will resume her service that she had to suspend for two days because of a mild malaise. We are pleased to give this good news to our readers, because despite the success of la *Macarrona*, la *Pepa*, el *Pitchiri*, her public, accustomed to receiving her grace and adorable suppleness as she dances her famous *Le graciose olle andalous* with a veritable ovation, has felt the absence of la Soledad.[151]

Of these two "stars," Pougin wrote that Macarrona was Soledad's "rival, or soon her disciple"—each was announced by name, with a large placard on one side of the stage, when it was her turn to dance.[152] Soledad seems to have won audiences by blending references to the more familiar mid-nineteenth-century Spanish dance with the "savage" and exotic style of the *fils de Bohême*.[153] The dance remembered in the press is her *olle gracioso*—not a flamenco dance like fandangos or tangos, but rather, like the cachucha, drawn from the repertoire of classically-styled dances of the bolero school. Pougin described this blend: "jiggling, jumps, and movements of the rump, twiddling her hips, poses and attitudes at times strange and brutal, at times supple and feline, although with charming grace and delicious vivaciousness."[154] An article of September 3, 1889, described this dance:

> After the *tango* and the *baile del novio*, the strangely lascivious dances of Pepa and of Macarrona, behold that the Grand Théâtre de l'Exposition gives us a novelty full of charm and originality, the *gracioso olle Andalous*. One of the stars of the troupe of Gitanas, the petit Soledad executed this novel step, and we can hardly imagine anything more graceful than when, the knee dropped, she turned completely around (*elle se renverse complètement en arrière*), her rounded arms touching the stage.[155]

We have already quoted Théophile Gautier's 1845 description of this step in Elssler's cachucha: "Her swooning arms flutter about her drooping head, her body curves back, her white shoulders almost brush the floor": that is, the dancer drops to her knee and, bending at the waist, does a circular *cambré*, carrying her torso to the side, front, side, and back, arms overhead, with a bend at the waist so deep that the arms might indeed brush the stage.[156] In other words, part of Soledad's popularity with French audiences may have been precisely this movement idea from balletic renditions of Spanish dance, curiously executed, as Pougin puts it, with "training, ardour, and if I may say so ... savagery."[157]

As Emmanuel Chabrier had noted in his 1882 visit to Sevilla, Cádiz, and Granada, by the 1880s tangos were already a staple of the flamenco repertoire. The program at the 1889 exposition was replete with tangos, including forms that do not exist today, such as a *tango allegria*—perhaps this was an alegría *atangado* ($\frac{6}{8}$ alegrías done in the mode or style or perhaps the rhythm of $\frac{4}{4}$ tangos)?[158] Macarrona would have sung and danced in her alegrías; in

1904–1905 she incorporated a danced and sung tientos-tanguillos into her repertoire.[159] Whatever the rhythm, in the fascinated descriptions of all of these dancers' wigglings, squirmings, and *déhanchements*, it becomes apparent that to "tango-ize" something meant to emphasize what Chabrier called in 1882 the "billowing hips" of Andalucía, and what Rafael Marín in his 1902 guitar treatise called "contortions and . . . songs of ambiguous intention."[160]

The Grand Théâtre de l'Exposition program opened with a tango danced by Juana, whom Pougin describes as "a beautiful girl, and with a remarkable, if a little savage, physiognomy."[161] Pougin continued, describing Macarrona's sung and danced *tango allegria*,

> which is like a kind of scene: she begins by singing one or two couplets, and then a comic step, then her dance becomes tranquil and almost languorous, but she gets animated little by little, that develops with a sort of crescendo of movement that became almost contortions and finally ended with a mad fury, of extraordinary audacity and daring.[162]

After Macarrona's tangos came the "*baile del novio* by the brilliant Mathilde, that begins with a sort of pantomime scene and finishes with an animated *jaleo*" (confusion, ruckus: a popular dance in the nineteenth-century Spanish-styled ballet repertoire).[163] This piece was followed by a "*tango a quatre* by Maccarona [sic] and Pichiri, La Reyes and Dolores that would make a hypochondriac swoon. . . . there is also a *tango a cinq* with Juana, Zola, Concepcion, Dolores and the same Pichiri."[164] The program ended with a *fandango a quatre*, danced by Chivo and his three daughters, danced with "curious discipline and savage abandon."

Fauser provides a caricature by Henriot published in *Le Journal amusant* on August 17, 1889, titled "*Les Gitanas de Granade (avec leur capitain)*" containing six scenes, with captions listing the dances performed (tango, fandango, bolero, and vito). The cartoon comments wryly that the troupe is "authentic . . . too authentic," and expresses a preference for Rosita Mauri (see Figure 6.11).[165] Besides Mauri, Macarrona is the only person named in the caricature, but she is drawn with her back to the audience. With a deep break in her hips such that her upper body is nearly parallel to the floor, the viewer's attention is focused, by lines indicating motion, on Macarrona's waggling buttocks. Macarrona's name and silhouette (also emphasizing her butt-out posture) appear on a large tambourine next to her figure. The sarcastic caption beneath reads: "La Maccarona [sic]—(the opposite of *danse du ventre*, only very distinguished)" (see Figure 6.10).

Pardo saw all this *sturm und drang* as a put-on, pandering to the French audience. It is possible that she was thinking of Mathilde's can-can kicks, Soledad's dramatic backbend on one knee, or all the tangoized hip movements.

FIGURE 6.11 "Les Gitanas de Grenade (avec leur capitan)," by Henriot. *Le Journal amusant* (August 17, 1889) : 7. Courtesy of the Bibliothèque nationale de France.

> Perhaps convinced by the exhortations of the impresario that the *character* should be exaggerated and crude, the Gitanos of the Champs de Mars adopt such unseemly postures, and permit themselves such insolent movements, that it is embarrassing. Those who cheer them on compete with them in impudence, and instead of flamenco songs, they serve the public *coplillas de zarzuela* (light opera songs) from the old repertoire. The day I went, they solemnly sang, "Don't show up at the beach, etc. etc."[166]

I consider it unlikely that Macarrona's performances at the fair differed in any significant way from her performances for Spanish audiences; despite the fanciful titles given some of the pieces, the repertoire, the musical accompaniment of guitar and palmas, and, in all likelihood, the dances themselves were the same as they would have been in the Burrero the month before.[167] The distinction, then, would have been that French audiences, to Pardo's dismay, saw in Macarrona and her companions an Africanized orientalism, its unacademic authenticity imparting a gloss of modernity. As François de Nion said, "the movement of the hips with their brutal jolts…is dance *par excellence*" of Africa, "*a new world*," a "black world," a world "teeming with a disquieting and robust life, the generator of a power that will one day revolutionize any exhausted societies through contact alone."[168] "This soul of Africa, that lies in the genitals," was enacted in the déhanchements, the billowing hips of Andalusia, the *golpes de cadera* (hits with the hip), strongly punctuated hip movements as central to Macarrona's dance recorded in 1917 as they are to flamenco today.[169]

Silk and Burlap: Macarrona as Burlesque

> Idylls: LILA, dark, lively eyes, animated by flashes of lightning, her lips pulled back from fine sharp teeth that seem ready to bite, a supple waist, with lascivious *déhanchement*, like the voluptuous swaying of Macarona [sic] at the Exposition.
>
> Le Supplément, *September 16, 1897*

Although for the French, the popular performances of *Les Gitanas de Grenade* were the height of authenticity, Emilia Pardo saw them as tawdry imitations of Spain's best flamenco, as seen in its preeminent cafés:

> The dancers at the Exhibition are exceedingly ugly, ragged, cheeky, clumsy as dancers, and their voices are tinged with *aguardiente*.[170] The star of the company is La Macarrona... who dances a little better and does not lack *sandunga* [grace]; and so the spectators consider her an *houri* [in Islam, a heavenly virgin], a *Carmen*, and they're crazy for her steps and bends. The rest of the Gitanas could never get onstage over there [in Spain], nor do they in any way resemble Silverio's famous *bailadoras* and other *artists* of the finer grades of this genre, in which there is silk and there is burlap.[171]

Today it is a commonplace, as poet and flamencologist Félix Grande put it, that "in the flamenco world we all know that La Macarrona was one of the greatest *bailaoras* of all time," she was "fervently acclaimed throughout Spain and made Parisian audiences stand in ovation."[172] But for intellectuals like Pardo, in 1889, it was painfully obvious that the French conception of flamenco was with those shameless, ragged, burlap artists.

If French audiences could not or did not distinguish between the déhanchements of Soledad and of Macarrona, neither did Spain's educated classes, who saw in flamenco a reflection of their diminished standing in world affairs. As an 1891 article in the Spanish periodical *El Imparcial* put it, "What Spain has been unable to achieve with its art and with its literature: to influence the modern French spirit, attract an audience, grab its attention, deserve its esteem, is being achieved by our nation's bastard child, *flamenquismo*."[173]

Macarrona was only eighteen in 1889, at the beginning of her career, but Spain's perceptions of flamenco as lowlife performance certainly contributed to the fact that its press took little notice of her presence at the fair. José Luis Ortiz Nuevo's compilation of notices of flamenco in the nineteenth-century

Sevilla press includes several reports about the fair, including the key article from July 12, 1889, in *El Progreso* that the "director" of the Grand Théâtre de l'Exposition (Grasset) was in Sevilla looking for "Gitanos of both sexes."[174] But although in August the French press announced the arrival of the "celebrated" Macarrona, and saw her as a "star," none of the July 1889 Spanish notices that I found covering Grasset's errand in Spain mentioned Macarrona by name.[175] On the contrary, Spanish coverage universally expressed dismay that the "Spanish monomania" taking over Paris was represented not by "professional flamencos," but by "cigarette girls," "laboring women," and "an entire family," "mule and all."[176] An August 15 article in *La Ilustración española y americana* titled "Chronicles of the Exposition" includes a report on the shah of Persia's visit to the Grand Théâtre de l'Exposition, recounting the shah's comparison of Macarrona, "a new star of flamenco art," to the *almées* of Teheran in nearly identical words as the French press. But the article dwells on Rosita Mauri's flirtation with the shah, and reports extensively on the performances at the Cirque d'Hiver, concluding, "in the Grand Théâtre de l'Exposition…Nature reigns…in the Cirque d'Hiver…we caress Art."[177]

On August 8, 1889, just two days after her debut, *Le Figaro* announced that "La Maccarona [sic], the queen of the Gitanas," would dance her tangos and alegrías at the Grand Théâtre de l'Exposition, and that French soprano Jeanne Granier was simultaneously celebrating the 175th performance of her "bohemian dances, full of flavor."[178] Granier was also seen dressed as a bullfighter in a drawing inside the August 31 *Le Monde illustré* that featured Pepa and Pichiri on the cover (see Figure 6.10).[179] On November 22, among the "Varieties" notices, *La Lanterne* reported "Madame Granier appeared with a troupe of Gitanas and danced and sang flamenco with a seductive grace. She was as Gypsy and as exotic as La Macarona [sic] herself."[180] The run at the exposition had ended on October 31, 1889. Macarrona returned to Spain and, although she never enjoyed the international renown of artists like Antonia Mercé, "La Argentina," she went on to an illustrious career in the flamenco world.

In post-exposition Paris, however, Macarrona became a burlesque character.[181] On November 30, 1889, *Le Monde illustré* reported that the highlight of Granier's show was

> a parody of the dance of La Macarona [*sic*] that Mlle Jeanne Granier executed with incomparable brio. Mlle Granier is a veritable Gitana, very provocative and certainly more graceful than the *bohemienne* of the Exposition. She seizes the moment and reproduces the rhythm of Macarrona's lascivious *déhanchements* with extraordinary precision. It emphasizes the eccentricity with an almost imperceptible and deliciously characteristic exaggeration. All this with a spirit and a spiritual verve beyond anything you can imagine.[182]

On December 11, *Le Figaro* reported that Granier was studying with La Cuenca in preparation for dancing "La Macarona."[183] On December 29, *La*

Lanterne wrote, "The charming artist succeeds every afternoon with the creation of her la Macarona [sic]."[184] The inaugural issue of *La Rampe illustré* the following month featured Jeanne Granier as "la Macarona" on the cover. The accompanying article begins, "Jeanne Granier is the star of the day," and goes on to say, "La Macarona [*sic*], which is to say the Spain of folly, Spain with its pleasures and its voluptuousness, la Macarona [*sic*] which this dancer reveals to us is, in my view, a complete *arte nouveau de la danse*."[185]

Soon, Granier's impersonation of Macarrona was itself imitated: on March 15, 1890, *La Lanterne* reported that Charles Zidler, director of the Moulin Rouge, had lent one "Mlle Georgette in the role of la Macarona" to another production.[186] On March 25, *Le Radical* reported on a revue created by Ernest Blum and Raoul Toché titled *Les Miettes de l'année* in which a dancer, "aroused by the lively bolero of an Estudiantina ["Spanish student" ensemble] offers the distinguished spectacle of a woman hiking up her skirts and delivering *déhanchements de clown*, all in imitation of la Macarona [*sic*]."[187]

By 1891 there were multiple "Macarona" dancers at such places as the Moulin Rouge, and it is clear that Macarrona had entered the French imagination, through these burlesque impersonations, as a provocatively sexual figure. On May 10, 1891, the *Supplément litteraire de La Lanterne* contained a suggestive article by "Folarçon" titled "*L'enlèvement de la Sole*" ("Sole" is short for "Soledad"), which was accompanied by a front-page illustration of a watery encounter of a man and a woman in bathing suits. Upon "rescuing" the woman, the man found himself holding her in his arms:

> [upon] the contact with her supple and feminine body clinging to me with her arms around my neck, and at the sight of her torso movements that exceeded the most provocative attitudes of la Macarona [sic], I felt overwhelmed by a maddening infatuation...[188]

Even as late as 1897, as seen in the epigraph above, *Le Supplément* advertised "LILA," whose "lascivious *déhanchement*" were as provocative as the "voluptuous swaying of Macarona [sic] at the Exposition."[189] Little wonder, then, that two years after Macarrona performed her tangos at the 1889 Exposition Universelle, praise for another Spaniard performing in Paris, María "La Bonita" (Pretty María) declares that her dance cannot be compared with the "bestial Tango of the Gitanas of the Exposition."[190]

Afterword

"LILY-WHITE MAIDENS" AND "BLACK GITANOS"

The projects of "fugitive planning and black study" are mostly about reaching out to find connection; they are about making common cause with the brokenness of being, a brokenness, I would venture to say, that is also blackness.

—*Jack Halberstam*, The Undercommons

ATHERINE LEE BATES'S 1899 article in *The New York Times*, "The Gypsies of Spain," distinguishes lovely Spanish "señoritas," "lily-white maidens" whose dance is "coquetry in motion," from the dance of "black gitanos," "tawny...Ishmaels," in which "the life of the forest animal" is "reproduced in the fierceness, the fitfulness, the abandon of each strange series of abrupt gesticulations."[1] But consider this facile distinction in light of the radical disjunctures of perception activated by the stories of Jacinto Padilla, "El Negro Meri" and Juana Vargas, "La Macarrona." El Negro Meri represented Spain as Black for France, yet was erased from the flamenco record for over a century, while Macarrona was seen as "bestial" and depraved in France, yet is venerated by flamencos. Between these two flamenco artists of color, pawns, perhaps, in the culture wars of colonial superpowerdom, we perceive the dilemmas of race being negotiated with the imagined Gitana as an intermediate figure. She casts her audacious glance backward to Spain and forward into the international arena, simultaneously representing Spain's Blackness (that is, its Gitanoness) and its Whiteness (again, its Gitanoness).

A 1929 article in *Nuevo Mundo* articulates the complexities at play here. Titled "The Life of the Black in the Land of the White: In Madrid There Exists, Happy and Independent, a Black Republic; From the Gitano Faíco to Josephine Baker," it describes a Madrid cabaret and party celebrating Marcus Garvey's victory in achieving "organized solidarity among men of color"—likely relating to the upcoming convention of the Universal Negro Improvement

Association and African Communities League (UNIA-ACL), which Garvey had founded in 1914.[2] The article's author, Francisco Lucientes, describes how Francisco Mendoza Ríos, "El Faíco"—who, in response to the incursions of the cakewalk during the first decade of the twentieth century, had fashioned the flamenco farruca and garrotín out of the old tangos de negros—danced a Charleston, with the "solemn adornments of the most delicious dances of the Albaicín" (Granada's Roma neighborhood) "and the Cava" (the Roma neighborhood in Triana), to the music of a jazz band. When his dance was over, Lucientes writes, Faíco proclaimed sarcastically, "he *diznificao* el chárlestón" ("I have dignified the Charleston")—but the Black Talk of his mispronounced *dignificado* ridicules the possible dignity of both the Charleston and the speaker.

Afro-Cuban tangos were also tangos gitanos by the mid-nineteenth century, referencing, like the suggestive verses of the 1848 *zapitusé*, like Chabrier's 1882 "billowing hips" and "Andalusian derrieres," and like Pougin's 1889 "déhanchements, full of promise," the long-standing Blackness of the imagined Gitano.[3] As John Martin wrote in 1929 of Vicente Escudero (who claimed to be a "full-blooded 'gitano' "), flamenco was seen as bloodline—*raza*. "Naturalness," Martin wrote, was an "innate quality of [this] art."[4]

The 1889 fair was a theater in which European audiences could, as Emilia Pardo Bazán put it, "penetrate the soul" of the Other. This place of flamenco's soul is the place of exile, the place at the heart of Spanish identity wherein lie "the Gypsy, the black, the Jew [and] the Moor."[5] This is the place of flamenco's purposefully duplicitous roar, its nonsense, its cacophony, its irony—its *sonidos negros*. As Fred Moten writes in *The Undercommons: Fugitive Planning and Black Study* (2013), this is the place we must "inhabit and maybe even cultivate...[the] place which shows up here and now, in the sovereign's space and time, as absence, darkness, death, things which are not."[6]

Stuart Hall has theorized diaspora as a "radical homelessness," an expression of an "ethics of the self...attuned to the edges."[7] Flamencos, whose minstrelized Blackness is figured by the Spanish Roma, have always known this statelessness, have always adhered to this code.

The strange and "natural" flamenco danced by *Les Gitanas de Granade* at the Grand Théâtre de l'Exposition was a milestone on the path to the progressive "Gypsification" of flamenco, and yet in Mathilde's can-can kicks, Soledad's cachucha drop to the knee, Pichiri's Afro-Cuban-inflected *chuflas*, Macarrona's jazz hands, and Faíco's Charleston, we perceive what Jayna Brown describes as the "guileful ruse" of the black "variety performer," who plays "in the field of racialized fantasies." Brown continues,

> Popular performance is not the site to find authentic folk types or instances of racial authenticity or explicit resistance. But what these acts did do was to expose race 'typologies' as conceptual categories bound by time and place, produced out of relations of power.[8]

As flamenco legend Carmen Amaya said of the story of her family setting fire to a chest of drawers in order to grill sardines at the Waldorf Astoria in 1941, "but son, how were we to eat sardines grilled on the floor like savages? At least we would have grilled them on a stuffed cushion!"[9]

The many Macarrona impersonations, embodied not only in the French burlesque but, as flamenco became a globalized art form, by deeply respectful and knowledgeable practitioners all over the world, reveal the "desire to become," the ability to "change, become, and pass"—which Eva Woods Peiró calls "indices of the modern."[10] As Pardo Bazán said, "let us...believe in the authenticity of much of the exotic element," for what it reveals of "the enormity of beginning."[11]

NOTES

Introduction

1. Baltasar Fra Molinero, *La imagen de los negros en el teatro del Siglo de Oro* (Madrid: Siglo XXI de España, 1995), 2, 7.

2. Toni Morrison, *Playing in the Dark: Whiteness and the Literary Imagination* (Cambridge, MA: Harvard University Press, 1992), 5–6, 37.

3. Brenda Dixon Gottschild, *Digging the Africanist Presence in American Performance: Dance and Other Contexts* (Westport, CT: Greenwood Press, 1996).

4. Paul Gilroy, *The Black Atlantic: Modernity and Double Consciousness* (Cambridge, MA: Harvard University Press, 1993).

5. "Çapato," Sebastián de Covarrubias Orozco, *Tesoro de la Lengua Castellana o Española* (Madrid: Luis Sanchez, impressor del Rey N.S., 1611), 263–64.

6. Real Academia Española (RAE), "zapateador," *Diccionario de la lengua castellana en que se explica el verdadero sentido de las voces... con las phrases o modos de hablar, los proverbios o refranes y otras cosas convenientes al uso de la lengua*, vol. 6 (Madrid: Francisco del Hierro, 1739), 558, cites Miguel de Cervantes, *Don Quixote de La Mancha*, vol. 2, ch. 9.

7. Thoinot Arbeau, *Orchesography*, translation by Mary Stewart Evans, Introduction and Notes by Julia Sutton, Labanotation section by Mirielle Backer and Julia Sutton (New York: Dover Publications, Inc., 1967 [1589]), 177; Miguel Querol Gavaldá, *La música en la obra de Cervantes* (Madrid: Ed. del Centro de Estudios Cervantinos, 2005), 198; John Forrest, *The History of Morris Dancing, 1483–1750* (Cambridge: Clarke, 1999), 9, 82, 100. For an example related to this tradition in Spain today, see "Los negritos de San Blas. Zapateta y danza del pie," *YouTube*, July 21, 2013, https://www.youtube.com/watch?v=LXTvRtVwQhA.

8. Frank Flinn, "The Phenomenology of Symbol: Genesis I and II," in *Phenomenology in Practice and Theory*, ed. William S. Hamrick (Dordrecht: Springer Netherlands, 1984), 223–49.

9. David Goldenberg, "Racism, Color Symbolism, and Color Prejudice," in *The Origins of Racism in the West*, ed. Miriam Eliav-Feldon, Benjamin Isaac, and Joseph Ziegler (Cambridge: Cambridge University Press, 2013), 94–95.

10. For but one powerful example, see Jordan Peele's film *Get Out* (2017).

11. Javier Irigoyen-García, *The Spanish Arcadia: Sheep Herding, Pastoral Discourse, and Ethnicity in Early Modern Spain* (Toronto: University of Toronto Press, 2014), 70–71.

12. "Soy de la raza calé / y el mundo dicta mis leyes / Hija de padres Gitanos / y tengo sangre de reyes / en la palma de la mano" (I am of the Calé race / and the World dictates my laws / I am the daughter of Gitano parents / and the blood of kings flows / in the palm of my hand). K. Meira Goldberg, "Dancing the Image," *Border Trespasses: The Gypsy Mask and Carmen Amaya's Flamenco Dance* (doctoral dissertation, Temple University, Philadelphia, PA: 1995), xix.

13. Antonio Cairón, *Compendio de las principales reglas del baile* (Madrid: Repullés, 1820), 116.

14. See K. Meira Goldberg, "Sonidos Negros: On the Blackness of Flamenco," *Dance Chronicle* 37, no. 1 (2014): 85–113; and K. Meira Goldberg, "*Jaleo de Jerez* and *Tumulte Noir*: Primitivist Modernism and Cakewalk in Flamenco, 1902–1917," in *Flamenco on the Global Stage: Historical, Critical, and Theoretical Perspectives*, edited by K. Meira Goldberg, Ninotchka Devorah Bennahum, and Michelle Heffner Hayes (Jefferson, NC: McFarland Books, 2015), 124–42.

15. Dixon Gottschild, *Digging the Africanist Presence*, 9.

16. See Mark Franko on the "Political Erotics of Burlesque Ballet, 1624–1627" in *Dance as Text: Ideologies of the Baroque Body* (Cambridge: Cambridge University Press, 1993), 62–106.

17. Jayna Brown, *Babylon Girls: Black Women Performers and the Shaping of the Modern* (Durham, NC: Duke University Press, 2008), 6, cites Michel de Certeau, *The Practice of Everyday Life*, translated by Steven Rendall (Berkeley: University of California Press, 1984), 37; and Marvin Carlson, *Performance: A Critical Introduction* (London: Routledge, 1996), 173.

18. W. E. B. Du Bois, *The Souls of Black Folk* (New York: Vintage Books/Library of America, 1990 [1903]), 3. In addition to Gilroy, *The Black Atlantic*, and Brown, *Babylon Girls*, sources responding to the concept of "double consciousness" include Ralph Ellison, "Change the Joke and Slip the Yoke," *Partisan Review* 25 (Spring 1958): 212–22, reprinted in Ralph Ellison, *Shadow and Act* (New York: Random House, 1964), 45–59; and Frantz Fanon, *Black Skin, White Masks* (New York: Grove Press, 1967).

19. See, for example, José María Díez Borque, *Sociedad y teatro en la España de Lope de Vega* (Barcelona: Antoni Bosch, 1978), 207, cited in Antonia Martín Marcos, "El actor en la representación barroca: Verosimilitud, gesto y ademán," in *Diálogos hispánicos de Amsterdam 8/I—El teatro español a fines del siglo XVII—Historia, cultura y teatro en la España de Carlos II, vol. 3, Representaciones y fiestas*, edited by Javier Huerta Calvo, Harm den Boer, and Fermín Sierra Martínez (Amsterdam, Atlanta, Georgia: Rodipi, 1989), 764; and José María Díez Borque, *Sociología de la comedia española del siglo XVII* (Madrid: Cátedra, 1976).

20. See, for example, John Brotherton's discussion of the pastor bobo as *Hombre*, or Everyman. *The Pastor-Bobo in the Spanish Theatre, before the Time of Lope de Vega* (London: Tamesis, 1975), 60–61; also, *Literatura y música del hampa en los Siglos de Oro*, María Luisa Lobato and Alain Bègue, eds. (Madrid: Visor Libros: 2014).

21. Nicholas Spadaccini and Jenaro Taléns, *Through the Shattering Glass: Cervantes and the Self-Made World* (Minneapolis: University of Minnesota Press, 1993), xiv.

22. Françoise Cazal, "Del pastor bobo al gracioso: El pastor de Diego Sánchez de Badajoz," *Criticón*, no. 60 (1994): 9–10.

23. Ignacio Arellano, "La poesía burlesca áurea, ejercicio de lectura conceptista y apostillas al romance 'Boda de negros' de Quevedo," *Filología Románica*, vol. 5 (Madrid: Editorial Universidad Complutense, 1987–1988): 263. This practice was a common response to official censorship. See, for example, Ted Bergman, "La criminalidad como diversión pública y las jácaras entremesadas," in Lobato and Bègue, *Literatura y música del hampa*, 77–92.

24. Elisabeth Le Guin, *The Tonadilla in Performance: Lyric Comedy in Enlightenment Spain* (Berkeley: University of California Press, 2014), 154, cites Juan Manuel, Prince of Villena, "Exemplo XXXII," noting that "the *Libro de los exemplos*, or *El Conde Lucanor* (1335), a medieval Spanish collection of fables and parables, was the source for Hans Christian Andersen's allegory of 'The Emperor's New Clothes.'"

25. Benjamin Liu, *Medieval Joke Poetry: The Cantigas d'Escarnho e de Mal Dizer* (Cambridge, MA: Harvard University Press, 2004).

26. Jacques Attali, *Noise: The Political Economy of Music* (Minneapolis: University of Minnesota Press, 1985).

27. Bronwen Jean Heuer, *The Discourse of the Ruffian in Quevedo's "Jácaras"* (doctoral dissertation, State University of New York at Stony Brook, 1991), 105; cites Eugenio Asensio, *Itinerario del entremés: Desde Lope de Rueda a Quiñones de Benavente* (Madrid: Gredos, 1971), 92; and Juan Hidalgo, *Bocabulario* (1609), in Rafael Salillas, "Vocabulario de germanía," *El lenguaje: (estudio filológico, psicológico y sociológico); Con 2 vocabularios jergales* (Madrid: Suárez, 1896), 272. Also, see Emilio Cotarelo y Mori, *Colección de Entremeses, Loas, Bailes, Jácaras y Mojigangas desde fines del siglo XVI à mediados del XVIII* (Madrid: Bailly Ballière, 1911), cxciii, clxxxix.

28. Saidiya V. Hartman, *Scenes of Subjection: Terror, Slavery, and Self-Making in Nineteenth-Century America* (New York: Oxford University Press, 1997), 33.

29. See Goldberg, "Dancing the Image," *Border Trespasses*, 48–59.

30. Glenn Swiadon Martínez, "Los villancicos de negro y el teatro breve: Un primer acercamiento," in *La literatura popular impresa en España y en la América colonial. Formas & temas, géneros, funciones, difusión, historia y teoría*, edited by Pedro M. Cátedra (Salamanca: Seminario de Estudios Medievales y Renacentistas—Instituto de Historia del Libro y de la Lectura, 2006), 162.

31. Fra Molinero, "Las ideas renacentistas sobre la esclavitud," *La imagen de los negros*, 1995, 10–18.

32. See Ilona Katzew, *Casta Painting: Images of Race in Eighteenth-Century Mexico* (New Haven, CT: Yale University Press, 2004), 39–52.

33. Bartolomé de las Casas, *A Short Account of the Destruction of the Indies: Or, a Faithful Narrative of the Horrid and Unexampled Massacres, Butcheries, and All Manner of Cruelties, . . . the Time of Its First Discovery by Them* (Great Britain: Pantianos Classics, 2016), 8–10, 25.

34. Fernando Ortiz, *Cuban Counterpoint: Tobacco and Sugar* (New York: Knopf, 2013).

35. Rolando Antonio Pérez Fernández, *La música afromestiza mexicana* (Xalapa: Universidad Veracruzana, Dir. Ed, 1990), 39; Aurelia Martín Casares, "Evolution of the Origin of Slaves Sold in Spain from the Late Middle Ages till the 18th Century," in *Serfdom and Slavery in the European Economy, 11th–18th Centuries*, ed. Simonetta

Cavaciocchi and E. Schiavitù (Firenze: Firenze University Press, 2014), 429. The first New World plantation was established in 1506 on Hispaniola, present-day Haiti and Dominican Republic (José Luis Cortés López, *La esclavitud negra en la España peninsular del siglo XVI* [Salamanca: Ed. Universidad de Salamanca, 1989], 183).

36. Katzew, *Casta Painting*, 39–52; Tamar Herzog, "Beyond Race: Exclusion in Early Modern Spain and Spanish America," in *Race and Blood in the Iberian World*, edited by María Elena Martínez, David Nirenberg, and Max S. Hering Torres (Zürich, Berlin: Lit, 2012), 151–68; Irigoyen-García, *The Spanish Arcadia*, 86.

37. Max S. Hering Torres, "Purity of Blood: Problems of Interpretation," in Martínez, Nirenberg, and Hering Torres, *Race and Blood in the Iberian World*, 13; María Elena Martínez, "The Black Blood of New Spain: Limpieza de Sangre, Racial Violence, and Gendered Power in Early Colonial Mexico," *The William and Mary Quarterly* 61, no. 3 (July 2004): 479–520; and Richard Aste, *Behind Closed Doors: Art in the Spanish American Home, 1492–1898* (Brooklyn: Brooklyn Museum; New York: Monacelli Press, 2013).

38. Irigoyen-García, *The Spanish Arcadia*, 3–34.

39. I have been working on the fandango as an eighteenth-century mestizaje for some years now. It is considered in my articles "Sonidos Negros" and, with Thomas Baird and Paul Jared Newman, "Changing Places: Toward the Reconstruction of an Eighteenth Century Danced Fandango," in *Españoles, indios, africanos y gitanos. El alcance global del fandango en música, canto y baile*, edited by K. Meira Goldberg and Antoni Pizà, *Música Oral Del Sur*, no. 12 (2015): 619–56; and *The Global Reach of the Fandango in Music, Song and Dance: Spaniards, Indians, Africans and Gypsies*, edited by K. Meira Goldberg and Antoni Pizà (Castle-upon-Tyne: Cambridge Scholars Publishing, 2016), 579–621. These bilingual and all English volumes are proceedings of an international conference Antoni Pizà and I organized in 2015 at the Foundation for Iberian Music at the CUNY Graduate Center. In 2017, with Pizà and Walter Clark, I organized a second conference, *Spaniards, Natives, Africans, and Gypsies: Transatlantic Malagueñas and Zapateados in Music, Song, and Dance* at the Center for Iberian and Latin American Music at the University of California, Riverside. A volume of selected essays stemming from that conference is forthcoming (2018) from Cambridge Scholars Publishing. My research for that conference, with Anna de la Paz and Elisabet Torras Aguilera, is titled " 'The Name Might Change, but the Form Will Not:' Figuring Race and Empire from the *Villano* to the *Guaracha*." The third conference in this series will be held at the Instituto Veracruzano de la Cultura (IVEC) in Veracruz, México on April 11–13, 2019. Katzew, *Casta Painting*, 56–61; Fernando Ortiz (1881–1969) and Diana Iznaga, *Los negros curros* (La Habana: Editorial de Ciencias Sociales, 1986), xix.

40. I am here extending Judith Etzion's argument: "The Spanish Fandango from Eighteenth-Century 'Lasciviousness' to Nineteenth-Century Exoticism," *Anuario Musical*, no. 48 (1993): 229–50.

41. Elizabeth Maddock Dillon, *New World Drama: The Performative Commons in the Atlantic World, 1649–1849* (Durham, NC: Duke University Press, 2014), 156.

42. Eric Lott, "Blackface and Blackness: The Minstrel Show in American Culture," in *Inside the Minstrel Mask: Readings in Nineteenth-Century Blackface Minstrelsy*, edited by Annemarie Bean, James V. Hatch, and Brooks McNamara (Hanover, NH: Wesleyan University Press, 1996), 5. See also David Blight, *Race and Reunion: The Civil War in American Memory* (Cambridge, MA: Harvard University Press).

43. Fra Molinero, *La imagen de los negros*, 17.

44. Ta-Nehisi Coates, *Between the World and Me* (New York: Spiegel & Grau, 2015), 21.

45. Ned and Constance Sublette, *The American Slave Coast: A History of the Slave-Breeding Industry* (Chicago: Lawrence Hill Books, 2016).

46. Hartman, *Scenes of Subjection*, 7.

47. See Alberto del Campo Tejedor and Rafael Cáceres Feria, "Los Morenos Andaluces," *Historia cultural del flamenco (1546–1910): El barbero y la guitarra* (Córdoba: Almuzara, 2013), 121–39.

48. Luis Lavaur, "Teoría romántica del cante flamenco," *Revista de Ideas Estéticas*, no. 107 (July–September, 1969): 17. This is also true in the U.S.: see Dale Cockrell, *Demons of Disorder: Early Blackface Minstrels and Their World* (Cambridge: Cambridge University Press, 1997), 16: "Most urban American theaters before 1843 were...places where educated, well-off, often elite white men gathered."

49. Serafín Estébanez Calderón, illustrated by Francisco Lameyer, *Escenas andaluzas: Bizarrías de la tierra, alardes de toros, rasgos populares, cuadros de costumbres y artículos varios...* (Madrid: Balt. González, 1847), 204–205.

50. Kiko Mora, "¡Y dale con Otero!...Flamencos en la Exposición Universal de París de 1900," *Cadáver Paraíso* (blog), June 11, 2016, https://goo.gl/YCTtSJ.

51. Houston A. Baker, *Modernism and the Harlem Renaissance* (Chicago: University of Chicago Press, 1987), 15.

52. Emilia Pardo Bazán, "Diversions—Strange Folks" Letter XXIII, Paris, September 28, 1889, in *A los pies de la torre Eiffel, Obras completas* 19 (1891): http://cdigital.dgb.uanl.mx/la/1020027895/1020027895.PDF, 276–77.

53. Monday, "París, 13 de Junio" *El Imparcial*, June 15, 1891; Arthur Pougin, *Le Théatre à l'Exposition universelle de 1889, notes et descriptions, historire et souvenirs* (Paris: Librairie Fischbacher, 1890), 106.

54. Katherine Lee Bates, "The Gypsies of Spain: Gitanas Sing and Dance, Beguiling Tourists with Coquetry—The Beggars are Persistent—Young and Old Alike are Irresistible in their Clamour for Pennies—the Fair at Seville," *New York Times* (May 14, 1899), 15.

55. Walt Whitman, "One's-self I Sing," *Walt Whitman*, edited by Mark Van Doren and Malcolm Cowley (New York: Viking Press, 1974), 271.

56. Emilia Pardo Bazán, "Diversiones," 276–7.

57. Du Bois, *The Souls of Black Folk*, 3.

58. Fanon, *Black Skin, White Masks*, 90.

59. Ralph Ellison, *Invisible Man* (New York: Modern Library/Random House, 1952).

60. Ellison, "Change the Joke and Slip the Yoke," in *Shadow and Act* (1964), 47–49, 56.

61. Baker, *Modernism and the Harlem Renaissance*, 50, 56.

62. Fred Moten, *In the Break: The Aesthetics of the Black Radical Tradition* (Minneapolis: University of Minnesota Press, 2003), 255–56.

63. Moten, *In the Break*, 7, cites Edouard Glissant, *Caribbean Discourse: Selected Essays*, translated by J. Michael Dash (Charlottesville: Caraf Books/University Press of Virginia, 1989), 124–25.

64. Brown, *Babylon Girls*, 17, cites Fanon, *Black Skin, White Masks*, 252; Susan Buck-Morss, "The Flâneur, the Sandwichman and the Whore: the Politics of Loitering,"

New German Critique 39 (1986): 128; and Patricia Petro, "Perceptions of Difference: Women as Spectator and Spectacle," in *Women in the Metropolis: Gender and Modernity in Weimar Culture*, edited by Katherina Ankum (Berkeley: University of California Press, 1997), 53.

65. Faustino Núñez, *Guía comentada de música y baile preflamencos (1750–1808)* (Barcelona: Ediciones Carena, 2008), 447, note 102.

66. Gerhard Steingress, *Sociología del cante flamenco* (Jerez: Centro Andaluz del Flamenco, 1991), 198. The arguments presented here grow out of many fruitful discussions with my friends Kiko Mora and Belén Maya.

67. Isidoro Moreno Navarro, *La antigua hermandad de los negros de Sevilla: etnicidad, poder y sociedad en 600 años de historia* (Sevilla: Secr. de Publ. de la Universidad de Sevilla, 1997); Jesús Cosano Prieto, *Los invisibles. Hechos y cosas de los negros de Sevilla* (Sevilla: Aconcagua, 2017).

68. Antonio Domínguez Ortiz, *La esclavitud en Castilla en la Edad Moderna y otros estudios de marginados* (Granada: Editorial Comares, 2003 [1952]), 18–19; Alfonso Franco Silva, "La esclavitud en Sevilla en la Baja Edad Media y comienzos de la Edad Moderna," in Moreno Navarro, *La antigua hermandad de los negros de Sevilla*, 490.

69. Ruth Pike, "Sevillian Society in the Sixteenth Century: Slaves and Freedmen," *The Hispanic American Historical Review* 47, no. 3 (1967): 354–55, cites Juan de Mata Carriazo, "Negros, esclavos y extranjeros en el barrio sevillano de San Bernardo," *Archivo hispalense* 20 (1954), 123.

70. Franco Silva, "La esclavitud en Sevilla," in Moreno Navarro, *La antigua hermanadad*, 491. This strategy of subjugation was also employed in the post-bellum United States. See, for example, Hartman, *Scenes of Subjection*, 134–35.

71. Ruth Pike, "Sevillian Society in the Sixteenth Century," 356, cites Luis Zapata, "Miscelánea," in *Memorial histórico español* (Madrid, 1859), XI, 49.

72. Franco Silva, "La esclavitud en Sevilla," in Moreno Navarro, *La antigua hermandad* 489–91; Alfonso Franco Silva, *La esclavitud en Andalucía, 1450–1550* (Granada: University of Granada, 1992); see also William D. Phillips, *Slavery in Medieval and Early Modern Iberia* (Philadelphia: University of Pennsylvania Press, 2014).

73. Natalie Vodovozova, *A Contribution to the History of the Villancico de Negros* (master's thesis, University of British Columbia, 1996), 30; Pike, "Sevillian Society," 354–56. Jerónimo de Alba y Diéguez, "El Bachiller Revoltoso," in *Libro de la gitaneria de Triana de los años 1740 a 1750 que escribió el bachiller revoltoso para que no se imprimiera*, edited by Antonio Castro Carrasco (Sevilla: Coria Gráfica, S.L., 1995), 5–6. See also Navarro García, "Negros y Gitanos," in *Semillas de ébano*, 49–53; and del Campo and Cáceres, "Los Morenos Andaluces," in *Historia cultural del flamenco*, 121–39.

74. Eduardo Molina Fajardo, *El flamenco en Granada: Teoría de sus orígenes e historia* (Granada: Manuel Sánchez, 1974), 28–35. Blas Infante, *Orígenes de lo flamenco y secreto del cante jondo (1929–1933)* (Sevilla: Junta de Andalucía, Consejería de Cultura, 1980); and Manuel Barrios, *Gitanos, moriscos y cante flamenco* (Sevilla: RC Editor, 1989) both similarly argue that Ibero-Muslims found refuge and cultural survival among the Spanish Roma. Aurelia Martín Casares and Marga G. Barranco explain that most marriages were based on the "similarity of skin colour... regardless of their place of origin," whether Senegal, Angola, North Africa, or Portuguese India. "Popular Literary Depictions of Black African Weddings in Early Modern Spain," in *Sub-saharan Africa*

and Renaissance and Reformation Europe: New Findings and New Perspectives, edited by Kate J. P. Lowe; *Renaissance et Réforme* 31, no. 2 (Spring 2008): 111–12. Gretchen Williams's forthcoming doctoral dissertation *Hidden in Plain Sight: Deciphering the Code of the Calé in Sixteenth Century Spain* under Aliza Wong (Texas Tech University, 2019) promises to be a significant contribution to tracing the genealogies of Roma families in early modern Spain.

75. Richard Pym, *The Gypsies of Early Modern Spain, 1425–1783* (Basingstoke [England]: Palgrave Macmillan, 2007), 2; Antonio Zoido Naranjo, *La Ilustración contra los gitanos: antecendentes, historia y consecuencias de la Prisión General* (Sevilla: Signatura Ediciones de Andalucía, 2009), 15; del Campo and Cáceres, *Historia cultural del flamenco*, 132–33.

76. Ostalinda Maya Ovalle & Anna Mirga, "The Myth of the Spanish Model of Roma Inclusion," Open Society Foundations, August 27, 2014, https://www.opensociety-foundations.org/voices/myth-spanish-model-roma-inclusion. See also "Antigypsyism—A Reference Paper," http://antigypsyism.eu/; and "Política sobre los gitanos en la Unión Europea," *Wikipedia*, https://es.wikipedia.org/wiki/Pol%C3%ADtica_sobre_los_gitanos_en_la_Uni%C3%B3n_Europea.

77. The 1619 edict is translated in George Borrow, *The Zincali, or, An Account of the Gypsies of Spain with an Original Collection of Their Songs and Poetry, and a Copious Dictionary of Their Language* (London and New York: John Lane, 1902 [1841]), 140–41; cited in Goldberg, *Border Trespasses*, 23.

78. For considerations of such questions in relation to North American concert dance, see *The Oxford Handbook of Dance and Politics*, edited by Rebekah J. Kowal, Gerald Siegmund, and Randy Martin (New York: Oxford University Press, 2017); and Anthea Kraut, *Choreographing Copyright: Race, Gender, and Intellectual Property Rights in American Dance* (New York: Oxford University Press, 2016). For an exploration of racialized market pressures impacting flamenco's development in the early-twentieth century, see Kiko Mora and K. Meira Goldberg, "Spain in the Basement: Dance, Race, and Nation at the Paris Exposition, 1900," in *The Body, the Dance and the Text: Essays on Performance and the Margins of History*, edited by Brynn Shiovitz (Jefferson, NC: McFarland, forthcoming, 2018).

79. Enrique Baltanás, "The Fatigue of the Nation," in *Songs of the Minotaur: Hybridity and Popular Music in the Era of Globalization: A Comparative Analysis of Rebetika, Tango, Rai, Flamenco, Sardana, and English Urban Folk*, edited by Gerhard Steingress (Münster: Lit, 2002), 161–62. See also Cristina Cruces Roldán, "El flamenco y la política de patrimonio en Andalucía. Anotaciones a los registros sonoros de la Niña de los Peines," http://www.iaph.es/export/sites/default/galerias/patrimonio-cultural/imagenes/patrimonio-inmueble/atlas/documentos/ph30-130_El_flamenco_y_la_polxtica_de_patrimonio.pdf.

80. In the summer of 2017 Madrid held Flamenco Diverso, its first LGTB Flamenco Festival, headlined by singer Miguel Poveda and dancer Rocío Molina. For a discussion of some of the issues at stake in queer representations of flamenco, see Michelle Heffner Hayes, "'Somos Anti-Guapas'—Against Beauty in Contemporary Flamenco," *Flamenco: Conflicting Histories of the Dance* (Jefferson, NC: McFarland, 2009), 167–86.

81. Gonzalo Montaño Peña, *RomArchive, The Digital Archive of the Roma*. https://blog.romarchive.eu/?page_id=7768.

82. Nora Chipaumire, "Double Plus: Yinka Ese Graves + Shamar Wayne Watt," http://artsinitiative.columbia.edu/events/doubleplus-yinka-esi-graves-shamar-wayne-watt.

83. I first presented my bobo research, "Bumpkin Shepherds and *Pastor Bobo*: Noise as Social Critique in the Global Circulation of *Zapateado*," in November 2014 at the joint conference of the Congress on Research in Dance and Society of Dance History Scholars, Iowa City, IA.

84. Nicholas Jones, *Lumbe, Lumbe! Radical Performances of Habla de negros in Early Modern Spain* (University Park, PA: Penn State University Press, forthcoming). Jones cites Johnnella E. Butler and John C. Walter, *Transforming the Curriculum: Ethnic Studies and Women's Studies* (Albany: State University of New York Press, 1991) for this usage.

85. John Beusterien, in *An Eye on Race: Perspectives from Theater in Imperial Spain* (Lewisburg, PA: Bucknell University Press, 2006) uses "Black talk."

86. For a discussion of the politics of the word "Gitano," see "Some Editorial Considerations," in Goldberg, Bennahum, and Hayes, *Flamenco on the Global Stage*, 9–13.

87. Isidoro Fernández Flórez, "Fernanflor," "Seño José—Soledad—El Boyardo" *La Ilustración Ibérica*, (November 23, 1889), vol. 7 (México: Sres. Ballescá y Ca.: 1889), 738–39. Reproduced in David Pérez Merinero, "La Macarrona con Edison," October 12, 2012, http://www.papelesflamencos.com/2012/10/la-macarrona-con-edison.html.

88. Eva Woods Peiró, *White Gypsies: Race and Stardom in Spanish Musicals* (Minneapolis: University of Minnesota Press, 2012), 108.

89. Federico García Lorca, *Obras*, ed. Miguel García-Posada (Madrid: Akal, 1980), 328. See also Federico García Lorca, *In Search of Duende*, edited and translated by Christopher Maurer (New York: New Directions, 1998), 49. I am grateful to Estela Zatania for helping me articulate this reading of Lorca's term.

90. Christopher Maurer and Andres Olmedo, on Lorca's *Poet in New York*, written in New York in 1929, and citing a lecture, "Imagination, Inspiration, Evasion," given that year at Columbia University: Christopher Maurer and Andrés Soria Olmedo, curatorial statement displayed in *Back Tomorrow: Federico García Lorca/Poet in New York* (exhibition, New York Public Library, April 5–July 20, 2013).

91. Christopher Maurer and Andrés Soria Olmedo, *Back Tomorrow: Federico García Lorca/Poet in New York* (exhibition, New York Public Library, April 5–July 20, 2013, New York: New York Public Library), exhibit brochure, 7. See Barbara Fuchs, *Exotic Nation: Maurophilia and the Construction of Early Modern Spain* (Philadelphia: University of Pennsylvania Press, 2009).

Chapter 1

Note to Epigraph: Judith Etzion, "Spanish Music as Perceived in Western Music Historiography: A Case of the Black Legend?" *International Review of the Aesthetics and Sociology of Music* 29, no. 2 (1998): 102–3, cites Bourdelot-Bonnet, *Histoire de la musique et des ses effets* I, 259; this passage is also cited in Casiano Pellicer, *Tratado histórico sobre el origen y progresos de la comedia y del histrionismo en España: y con la noticia de algunos célebres comediantes y comediantas así antiguos como modernos* (Madrid: Imprenta de la Administración del Real Arbitrio de Beneficiencia, 1804), 194–95.

1. Ellison, "Change the Joke and Slip the Yoke."

2. James Pyle Wickersham Crawford, "The Pastor and Bobo in the Spanish Religious Drama of the Sixteenth Century," *The Romanic Review*, no. 2 (1911): 376–401; William S. Hendrix, *Some Native Comic Types in the Early Spanish Drama*, (doctoral dissertation, University of Chicago, 1922); Brotherton, *The Pastor-Bobo*; Warren Edminster, "Foolish Shepherds and Priestly Folly: Festive Influence in Prima Pastorum," *Medieval Perspectives* 15 (2000): 57–73; and Edwin D. Craun, *Lies, Slander, and Obscenity in Medieval English Literature: Pastoral Rhetoric and the Deviant Speaker* (Cambridge: Cambridge University Press, 1997).

3. Brotherton, *The Pastor-Bobo*, x.

4. Crawford, "The Pastor and Bobo," 380; Lynn Brooks, *The Dances of the Processions of Seville in Spain's Golden Age* (Kassel: Ed. Reichenberger, 1988), 176; Albert E. Sloman, "The Phonology of Moorish Jargon in the Works of Early Spanish Dramatists and Lope de Vega," *Modern Language Review* 44, no. 2 (April, 1949): 207.

5. Brotherton, *The Pastor-Bobo*, x; Crawford, "The Pastor and Bobo," 380.

6. Charlotte Stern, "Fray Iñigo de Mendoza and Medieval Dramatic Ritual," *Hispanic Review* 33, no. 3 (1965): 204–205.

7. Crawford, "The Pastor and Bobo," 395–96. See also Tess Knighton and Álvaro Torrente, *Devotional Music in the Iberian World, 1450–1800: The Villancico and Related Genres* (Aldershot, Hants, England: Ashgate, 2007), 43–45.

8. See Brooks, *Dances of the Processions*, and Lynn Matluck Brooks, *The Art of Dancing in Seventeenth-Century Spain: Juan de Esquivel Navarro and His World* (Lewisburg, PA: Bucknell University Press, 2003), 40–41; also Max Harris, *Aztecs, Moors, and Christians: Festivals of Reconquest in Mexico and Spain* (Austin: University of Texas Press, 2010).

9. Stern, "Iñigo," 229, cites Fray Íñigo de Mendoza, *Vita Christi* (Zamora, 1482) incunabulum facsimile (Madrid: Real Academia Española, 1953), http://www.biblioteca.org.ar/libros/130403.pdf; Knighton and Torrente, *Devotional Music*, 66–68.

10. Stern, "Iñigo," 205, cites Íñigo de Mendoza, *Vita Christi*, 147; RAE, "marrar," http://dle.rae.es/?id=OTw165C.

11. Stern, "Iñigo," 229.

12. Stern, "Iñigo," 230.

13. Carlos Clavería, "Contribución a la semántica de Belén," *Hispanic Review* 27, no. 3, *Joseph E. Gillet Memorial Volume, Part III* (July 1959): 346.

14. Linda J. Tomko, "Magri's *Grotteschi*," in *The Grotesque Dancer on the Eighteenth-Century Stage: Gennaro Magri and His World*, edited by Rebecca Harris-Warrick and Bruce A. Brown (Madison: University of Wisconsin Press, 2005), 151–72. Anna de la Paz and I presented this research at the 2017 conference on *Transatlantic Malagueñas and Zapateados*. A video of the presentation is here: Iberian Music, "K. Meira Goldberg, Anna de la Paz, Zapateados Conference, UC Riverside," *YouTube* (April 25, 2017), https://www.youtube.com/watch?v=-1zGf37ufb8&t=17s.

15. Robert Hughes, *Goya* (New York: Knopf, 2006), 182, 153. See also Noel Allende-Goitía, "The Mulatta, the Bishop, and Dances in the Cathedral: Race, Music, and Power Relations in Seventeenth-Century Puerto Rico," *Black Music Research Journal* 26, no. 2 (2006): 143.

16. Vicente Chacón Carmona, "Singing Shepherds, Discordant Devils: Music and Song in Medieval Pastoral Plays," *Medieval English Theatre*, no. 32 (2010), 66–67, cites

and translates Arnould Gréban's (ca. 1420–1471) *Le Mystère de la Passion de Notre Sauveur Jésus-Christ*, edited by Gaston Paris and Gaston Raynaud (Paris: Vieweg, 1878; reprinted Geneva: Slatkine, 1970), 3722–32.

17. Brotherton, *The Pastor-Bobo*, 17–20; Charlotte Stern, "The Coplas de Mingo Revulgo and the Early Spanish Drama," *Hispanic Review* 44, no. 4 (1976): 327, 330.

18. "[P]or ser la cosa mas humilde que ay, trayendolo debaxo del pie...Meterse en un çapato es tener miedo...çapatear a uno, castigarle, o de palabra, o de obra. Este termino se usa en la esgrima, quando uno ha dado a otro muchos golpes fracos; çapatear, baylar, dando con las palmas de las manos, en los pies, sobre los çapatos, al son de algun instrumento; y el tal se llama çapateador: çapatetas; los tales golpes en los çapatos." "Çapato," Covarrubias, *Tesoro*, 263–64.

19. RAE, "Zapateado," vol. 6 (1739), 558.

20. "El golpe, ò palmada que se da en el pié, ù zapato, brincando al mismo tiempo en señal de regocijo...Cervantes *Quixote*, Tom. 1 cap. 25: 'Luego sin mas, ni mas dió dos zapatétas en el áire.' Alfar. part. 1, lib. 1, cap. 5: 'Levantó la pierna, y en el aire dió por delante una zapatéta.'" RAE, "Zapateta," vol. 6 (1739), 559.

21. "Tiene asimismo malheridas danzas, assi de espadas, como de cascabel menudo...De zapateadores no digo nada, que un juicio los que tiene muñidos." RAE, "Zapateador," vol. 6 (1739), 558, cites Cervantes, *Quixote*, vol. 2, ch. 19. Translation: Miguel de Cervantes Saavedra, and John Ormsby, *The Ingenious Gentleman Don Quixote of La Mancha...a Translation, with Introduction and Notes by John Ormsby*, vol. 3 (London: Smith, Elder & Co., 1885), 205.

22. "1) Golpear à alguno con el zapato, 2) Por semejanza vale traher à algunos à mal traher, de obra, ù palabras, 3) En la Esgrima vale dar, ù señalar muchos golpes à su contrario sin recibir algunos, 4) Significa también acompañar al tañido, dando golpes en las manos, y dando alternativamente con ellas en los pies, los que se levantan à este fin con varias posturas, siguiendo el mismo compás. Úsanse mas frequentemente en la danza llamada el villano. Lat. Ad. numeram saltare, percusso calceo crebris palmis, 5) En la caza es dar el conejo golpes en la tierra con los pies, 6)...toparse, y alcanzarse las mulas..." RAE, "zapatear," vol. 6 (1739), 558.

23. RAE, vol. 6 (1739), 558, cites Cervantes, *Quixote*, vol. 2. ch. 62: English translation: Ormsby, *Quixote*, vol. 4, 253.

24. Cotarelo, *Entremeses*, cclxiii–v; cites Agustín de Rojas, *loa*, "Hoy que es día de alegría," cited in Margit Frenk Alatorre, *Nuevo corpus de la antigua lírica popular hispánica, Siglos XV a XVII* (México, D.F: Facultad de Filosofía y Letras, Universidad Nacional Autónoma de México, 2003), 1070–73: Agustín de Rojas, Jean Pièrre Ressot, ed., *Viaje entretenido* III (Madrid: Castalia, [1603] 1972), 378. Cotarelo also cites Luis Briceño, *Método muy facilisimo para aprender a tañer la guitarra á lo español* (Paris: Pedro Ballard, 1626); Rodrigo Caro, *Días geniales ó lúdicros, libro expósito dedicado á Don Fadrique Enrriquez Afan de Rivera* (Sevilla: Impr. de El Mercantil Sevillano, [1664] 1884), 64; and Cervantes's farce, *El rufián viudo* (1610–15), in which the jaque Escarramán pronounces: "Vaya El Villano, á lo burdo, / con la cebolla y el pan" (There goes the Villano, in his coarse manner / with the onion and the bread).

25. Cotarelo, *Entremeses*, cclxiv.

26. Cotarelo, *Entremeses*, cclxiv.

27. Ana Pelegrin Sandoval, *Juegos y poesía popular en la literatura infantil-juvenil 1750–1987* (PhD dissertation, Universidad Complutense de Madrid, 1992), http://pendientedemigracion.ucm.es/BUCM/tesis/19911996/H/3/AH3039402.pdf, page 100, on this tag in children's songs, 89–90. For more on children performing in Spanish religious celebrations, see Lynn Matluck Brooks, " 'Los Seises' in the Golden Age of Seville," *Dance Chronicle* 5, no. 2 (1982): 121–55; on malambo: Robert Farris Thompson, *Tango: The Art History of Love* (New York: Vintage Books, a Division of Random House, 2005), 92.

28. Frenk Alatorre, *Nuevo corpus*, 1072.

29. Stern, "Coplas de Mingo," 318; Brotherton, *The Pastor-Bobo*, 3, x–i.

30. Irigoyen-García, *The Spanish Arcadia*, 46–47.

31. Stern, "Coplas de Mingo," 321.

32. Stern, "Coplas de Mingo," 330.

33. Stern, "Iñigo," 204–205.

34. Cotarelo, *Entremeses*, clxxii–iii, cites "Memoria de las danzas del día de Ntra. Sra. de Agosto, deste año de 1554," and Leg. 2.°, Archivo que fué de la Obra y Fábrica de la catedral de Toledo; the 1561 fiesta is cited in José María Díez Borque, "Liturgia-fiesta-teatro: órbitas concéntricas de teatralidad en el siglo XVI," *Dicenda*, no. 6 (1987): 495, cites Ramón Perales de la Cal, *Papeles Barbieri* (Madrid: Alpuerto, 1985), 110.

35. Querol Gavaldá, *La música en la obra de Cervantes*, 198. On the morisca/moresca/morris, and *momos* (mummery), which Cotarelo relates to the origins of the entremés, see Cotarelo, *Entremeses*, lvi–iii, ccliv. Also, Ludwig Pfandl, *Cultura y costumbres del pueblo español de los siglos XVI y XVII: Introducción al estudio del Siglo de Oro* (Madrid: Visor, [1929] 1994); Forrest, *Morris Dancing*; Max Harris and Lada C. Feldman, "Blackened Faces and a Veiled Woman: the Early Korčula Moreška," *Comparative Drama* 37 (2003): 297–320; and Anthony M. Cummings, "Dance and 'The Other': The Moresca," in Barbara Grammeniati, ed., *Seventeenth-Century Ballet a Multi-Art Spectacle* (Bloomington, IN: Xlibris Corporation, 2011), 39–60.

36. Arbeau, *Orchesography*, 177.

37. Howard Mayer Brown, *Music in the French Secular Theater, 1400–1550* (Cambridge, MA: Harvard University Press, 1963), 162, cited in Cummings, "Moresca," 47.

38. Irigoyen-García, *The Spanish Arcadia*, 94.

39. Juan José Rey, *Danzas cantadas en el renacimiento español* (Madrid: SedeM, 1978), 36–37, 40–43, cites Cancionero Musical del Palacio (CMP), 282, 309; Cotarelo, *Entremeses*, clxxvi; Stern, "Iñigo," 221; Craig H. Russell, *Santiago de Murcia's "Códice Saldívar No. 4": A Treasury of Secular Guitar Music from Baroque Mexico*, vol. 1 (Urbana: University of Illinois Press, 1995), 36, cites Calderón, *Relación de una fiesta que la Universidad de Baeza celebra á la Inmaculada Concepción* (Baeza: Pedro de la Cuesta 1618), cited in Cotarelo, *Entremeses*, ccl, cclxiv; Lucas Marchante-Aragón, "The King, the Nation, and the Moor: Imperial Spectacle and the Rejection of Hybridity in *The Masque of the Expulsion of the Moriscos*," *Journal for Early Modern Cultural Studies* 8, no. 1 (2008): 111.

40. Irigoyen-García, *The Spanish Arcadia*, 5, 82.

41. Benjamin Liu, "Social Antagonisms in the Serranillas," paper presented at the conference *Sounding Communities: Music and the Three Religions in Medieval Iberia*, New York: Columbia University and CUNY Graduate Center, February 27–28, 2014,

citing serranillas by Juan Ruiz (ca. 1283–ca. 1350), the Archpriest of Hita, and Serranillas VI by Íñigo López de Mendoza, 1st Marquis of Santillana (1398–1458).

42. Liu, "Social Antagonisms in the Serranillas."

43. Irigoyen-García, *The Spanish Arcadia*, 88.

44. Liu, "Serranillas." On the suspect allegiances of Spaniards of Muslim descent, see Marchante-Aragón, "The King, the Nation, and the Moor."

45. Hendrix, *Native Comic Types*, 16–20.

46. Miguel de Cervantes Saavedra, "La ilustre fregona," in *Novelas ejemplares* (Colombia: Panamericana Editorial, [1613] 1993), 165–214.

47. Louise K. Stein, "Eros, Erato, Terpsíchore and the Hearing of Music in Early Modern Spain," *The Musical Quarterly* 82, no. 3/4, Special Issue: *Music as Heard* (Autumn–Winter, 1998): 668–70. Jordi Savall and Tembembe Ensamble Continuo recorded the Arañés "Chacona:" http://www.rtve.es/alacarta/videos/atencion-obras/jordi-savall-tembembe-ensamble-continuo-ponen-fiesta/1775440/.

48. RAE, "respingo," http://dle.rae.es/?id=WCNB91M.

49. Stein, "Eros, Erato, Terpsíchore," 668–70.

50. José Manuel Pedrosa, "Zangorromangos, bimbilindrones, chuchumbés y otros eufemismos líricos populares." *Olivar*, no. 18 (2012): 138–42. As found in music-dance names such as "tango" and "fandango," many Spanish scholars have attributed West African origin to the "-ngo" suffix. See Fernando Ortiz, "Fandango," and "Tango," *Glosario de afronegrismos: con un prólogo por Juan M. Dihigo* (Habana, 1924), 201–203, 447–48; and Juan B. Selva, "Sufijos americanos," *Thesaurus: boletín del Instituto Caro y Cuervo*, vol. 5, nos. 1–3 (1949); 192–213.

51. Irigoyen-García, *The Spanish Arcadia*, 83, 55, 57.

52. Nick Jones, "Cosmetic Ontologies, Cosmetic Subversions: Articulating Black Beauty and Humanity in Luis de Góngora's 'En la fiesta del Santísimo Sacramento,'" *Journal for Early Modern Cultural Studies* 15, no. 1 (Winter 2015): 49, note 2, quotes Israel Burshatin, "The Moor in the Text: Metaphor, Emblem, and Silence," *"Race," Writing, and Difference. Special Issue of Critical Inquiry* 12, no.1 (Autumn 1985): 113; and Georgina Dopico Black, "Ghostly Remains: Valencia, 1609," *Arizona Journal of Hispanic Cultural Studies* 7 (2003): 93.

53. Irigoyen-García, *The Spanish Arcadia*, 57.

54. Marchante-Aragón, "The King, the Nation, and the Moor," 107.

55. Irigoyen-García, *The Spanish Arcadia*, 57.

56. Marchante-Aragón, "The King, the Nation, and the Moor," 105, cites Noël Salomon, *Lo villano en el teatro del Siglo de Oro* (Madrid: Castalia, 1985), 676.

57. Cotarelo, *Entremeses*, cclxiii–v, cites Juan de Esquivel Navarro, *Discursos sobre el arte del dançado y sus excelencias y primer origen, reprobando las acciones deshonestas* [Texto impreso]/compuesto por Iuan de Esquiuel Nauarro…Impressos en Seuilla: por Iuan Gomez de Blas, 1642, f. 19, http://bdh-rd.bne.es/viewer.vm?id=0000115522&page=1. All English translations of Esquivel are from Brooks, *Esquivel: Discursos* title: 255; on *voleo*: 116–17, 150–51, Spanish: 220, 229, English: 271, 281 (ff. 19–19v); on villano: 148–51, Spanish: 232, English: 284–85 (ff. 23–4). See two reconstructions of a villano: drewdavis58, "Donaires: Villano," choreography: Ana Yepes, music: Ignacio Yepes, *YouTube* (February 4, 2009), https://www.youtube.com/watch?v=nKq_oPUQR98; and Xuriach, "Villano—Xuriach, SONEN BALADES," Music: traditional Catalan,

F. Guerau, G. Sanz, choreography: J. A. Jaque, P. Minguet, A. Romaní, dancers: Anna Romaní and Jaime Puente, *YouTube* (March 28, 2010), https://www.youtube.com/watch?time_continue=185&v=pUDu_hhU_XI.

58. "…salto…apastoradamente; de manera que se reconozca que se remedan las Mudanzas de la Aldeas." Brooks, *Esquivel*, Spanish: 232, English: 284–85 (f. 23–4).

59. RAE, "puntapié," vol. 5 (1737), 433.

60. Brooks, *Esquivel*, Spanish: 229, English: 281 (ff. 19–19v).

61. Brooks, *Esquivel*, 116.

62. Brooks, *Esquivel*, 116, Spanish: 229, English: 281 (ff. 19–19v); RAE, "volear": http://dle.rae.es/?id=c1LoXmT.

63. Brooks, *Esquivel*, 116–17, cites Fabritio Caroso, Julia Sutton, and F. Marian Walker, *Courtly Dance of the Renaissance* (New York: Dover, 1995), 119; and Cesare Negri, *Le gratie d'amore* (Forni Editore Bologna: 1602 Reprint 1969, translated into Spanish and hand-copied in Madrid in 1630 as *El Arte para aprender a danzar*), 65–67.

64. In a lecture given with Anna Romani at the Centre Nacional de la Danse, Ana Yepes comments that, though steps like *floreta* retain their basic nomenclature across Spanish, French, and Italian schools, Esquivel's *voleo* is also called *puntillazo* and *patada arriba*. Drewdavis58, "Conference sur 'La Danse du Siecle d'Or Espagnol' par Ana Yepes et Anna Romani," *YouTube*, February 2, 2015, https://www.youtube.com/watch?v=-l_s5bnOfBo, timestamp 24:00.

65. Gennaro Magri, *Theoretical and Practical Treatise on Dancing*, translated by Mary Skeaping, with Anna Ivanova and Irmgard E. Berry, edited by Irmgard E. Berry and Annalisa Fox (London: Dance Books, 1988), 159–60, cited in Harris-Warrick and Brown, *Gennaro Magri and His World*, 350.

66. Mabel Dolmetsch, *Dances of Spain and Italy from 1400 to 1600* (New York: Da Capo Press, 1975), 12, 74. On Negri, see also Margaret McGowan, *Dance in the Renaissance: European Fashion, French Obsession* (New Haven, CT: Yale University Press, 2008), 10–15. This site offered helpful practical information on these jumps: Nathan Kronenfeld (Daniele di Padola), "Cesare Negri's Salti del Fiocco," http://www3.sympatico.ca/kronenfeld/Negri/tassel-reconstruction.html.

67. Rey, *Danzas cantadas*, 23–24.

68. Dolmetsch, *Dances of Spain and Italy*, 82; Brooks, *Esquivel*, 148–49.

69. Dolmetsch, *Dances of Spain and Italy*, 82–89. For two reconstructions of Negri's *Il Villanicco*, see cpcontrapaso (Contrapasso Renaissance dance, Copenhagen), "Villanicco," *YouTube* (June 24, 2012), https://www.youtube.com/watch?v=jaKdKN4Yvss; and ilballerino, "Cesare Negri—Il Villanicco—Soubor Anello," *YouTube* (December 15, 2012), https://www.youtube.com/watch?v=xOQt3Jz_dGk.

70. Juan Antonio Jaque, José Subirá, *"Libro de danzar de Don Baltasar de Rojas Pantoja*, compuesto por el maestro Juan Antonio Jaque," *Anuario Musical*, vol. 5 (Barcelona: Consejo Superior de Investigaciones Científicos, Instituto Español de Musicología [ca. 1680] 1950): 196–97. On Baltasar de Rojas Pantoja: José Luis Barrio Moya, "La librería de Don Baltasar de Rojas Pantoja, regidor de Toledo y primer marqués de Valcerrada (1731)," *Anales Toledanos* 31 (February 14, 2014): 189–202; and Brooks, *Esquivel*, 183, cites Jane Gingell, "Dances of Seventeenth-Century Spain," in *Proceedings, Society of Dance History Scholars* (University of California, Riverside: Society of Dance History Scholars, 1991), 166–77.

71. With regard to Jaque's omission of the special villano kick to the hat, Ana Yepes notes that Jaque does include "'*patada sobre los dos pies*' (kick on two feet) instead of the kick to the hat": she wonders whether Jaque's phrase refers to the stamp before the kick to the hat (in González) plus the kick to the hat. She adds that "whether or not the kick to the hat is done in preparation for the bow" is perhaps "not very important." The kick to the hat is "a special bow for the villano, and in Jaque we do not see it fully formed." "But Jaque," Yepes notes, "gives an overview in many cases." Ana Yepes, email communication, February 10, 2017. "Cabriola...quedando en Ayre el Pie": Jaque, *Libro de danzar*," 196–97. *Floreo*: Brooks, *Esquivel*, Spanish: 228, English: 280 (f. 8).

72. Pablo Minguet é Irol, *Arte de danzar a la francesa, adornado con quarenta figuras, que enseñan el modo de hacer todos los diferentes passos de la danza del minuete, con todas sus reglas, y de conducir los brazos en cada passo: Y en quatro figuras, el modo de danzar los tres passapies. Tambien estàn escritos en solfa, para que qualquier musico los sepa tañer. Su autor Pablo Minguet e Irol...Añadido en esta tercera impression todos los passos, ó movimientos del danzar à la española...* (Madrid, P. Minguet, en su casa, [1737?] 1758), 1–36, Minguet é Irol, *Explicacion del Danzar a la Española* (appendix: 1764), 37–72 (the villano is on pp. 64–67), https://www.loc.gov/resource/musdi. 118.0?st=gallery&c=160. Pablo Minguet é Irol, *Breue tratado de los passos del danzar a la española [Texto impreso]: que oy se estilan en las seguidillas, fandango, y otros tañidos* (Madrid: Imprenta del autor, 1764), http://bdh-rd.bne.es/viewer.vm?id=0000061855 &page=1.

73. Brooks, *Esquivel*, 151; RAE, "puntillazo," http://dle.rae.es/?id=Ug5lKpU.

74. Minguet é Irol, *Explicacion*, 67.

75. Domingo González, *Escuela por lo vajo de Domingo González* (Real Academia de Bellas Artes San Fernando, signatura A/1736 (2)), 93–96 (digital page numbers), http://www.realacademiabellasartessanfernando.com/assets/docs/noveli/noveli.pdf. Brooks, *Esquivel*, on Antonio de Almenda: 44–52, cites Maurice Esses, *Dance and Instrumental Diferencias in Spain during the 17th and Early 18th Centuries*, vol. 1 (Stuyvesant, New York: Pendragon Press, 1992), 487–501; on Domingo González: Spanish: 251–52, English: 303–304 (ff. 47–8). See also María José Ruiz Mayordomo "Los maestros de danzar en la corte de los Austrias," *La Memoria de la dansa: Colloqui internacional d'historiadores de la dansa* (Barcelona, Oct. 27–30, 1994): 63–78.

76. Ana Yepes, "From the *Jácara* to the *Sarabande*," in Goldberg, Bennahum, and Hayes, *Flamenco on the Global Stage*, 67–68, 70.

77. Domingo González, *Escuela por lo vajo*, 93 (digital page number). I am grateful to Craig Russell for noting the abbreviation for *tiempo*.

78. Brooks, *Esquivel, cuatropeados*: Spanish: 224, English: 276 (f. 15); *floretas*: Spanish: 220–21, English: 271–72 (ff. 10–10v). *Campanelas sacudidas* may be *campanelas*, a hop with the gesturing leg tracing a circle in the air while shaking or beating: Brooks, *Esquivel, campanelas*: Spanish: 223, English: 273 (ff. 11v–12), *sacudidos*: Spanish: 224, English: 276 (ff. 14v–15).

79. Diana Campóo Schelotto, "The *Pavana* in the *Choregraphie figurativa, y demostrativa del Arte de Danzar, en la forma Española* by Nicolás Rodrigo Noveli (Madrid, 1708): Its Contextualization and Comparative Study with the Spanish Sources of the 17th and 18th Centuries," *Historical Dance* 4, no. 3 (2016): 2–3. Esquivel's description of the villano bow: Brooks, *Esquivel*, Spanish: 232, English: 284–85 (ff. 23–23v).

80. The Spanish word *cortesía* means "courtesy," and "curtsey," while *reverencia* means "reverence" (consider the reverence which ends a ballet class): both words here refer to a bow.

81. Discussing the villano, Brooks writes, "Minguet refers to an action called *un pino* (pine tree, upright movement) which never appears in the *Discursos*. It would make sense in the choreography to interpret this as an *elevé* action." Brooks, *Esquivel*, 151.

82. Flamenco dancers use the term *plantarse bien* today. The *planta* is a pose, it is to hold an image with the body. It is also the sole of the foot, and so can be a stamp (as in *media planta*, the metatarsal sound), and in baroque Spanish dance refers to the position of the feet. Brooks translates Esquivel's *planta* as "stance": "In discussing the *planta* (stance) [Esquivel] states, 'One must place oneself with much ease, the body very straight.'" Brooks, *Esquivel*, 86, on planta: Spanish, 231–32, English, 283–84 (ff. 22–3).

83. Liu, "Serranillas."

84. Irigoyen-García, *The Spanish Arcadia*, 86.

85. Brooks, *Esquivel*, 78.

86. Brooks, *Esquivel*, 255; Marchante-Aragón, "The King, the Nation, and the Moor," 111.

87. YouMoreTv—cultura, "Gran Jota" de "La Dolores" *YouTube*, April 4, 2014, https://www.youtube.com/watch?v=Pi8Nc4vTvgk; the final phrase of saltos de albalate and batudas begins at 5:10. For a less theatrical staging of this folkdance, see Somerondon "05 Jota de Albalate—XXV Aniversario" *YouTube*, December 26, 2008, https://www.youtube.com/watch?v=_DjlXcA_SVk.

88. Jean-Frédéric Schaub and Silvia Sebastiani, "Between Genealogy and Physicality: a Historiographical Perspective on Race in the Ancien Régime," *Graduate Faculty Philosophy Journal* 35, no. 1 (2014): 23–51; Jon Arrieta Alberdi, "La idea de España entre los vascos de la Edad Moderna," *Anales 1997–1998* (Real Sociedad Económica Valenciana de Amigos del País), 130; María Elena Martínez, *Genealogical Fictions: Limpieza de Sangre, Religion, and Gender in Colonial Mexico* (Stanford, CA: Stanford University Press, 2008), 80.

89. Albert Cohen, "Spanish National Character in the Court Ballets of J.-b. Lully," *Revista de Musicología* 16, no. 5 (1993): 2987.

90. Fra Molinero, "Las ideas renacentistas sobre la esclavitud," *La imagen de los negros*, 10–18.

91. Irigoyen-García, *The Spanish Arcadia*, 85.

92. Marchante-Aragón, "The King, the Nation, and the Moor," 123.

93. Malcolm K. Read, *Visions in Exile: The Body in Spanish Literature and Linguistics: 1500–1800* (Amsterdam: John Benjamins, 1990), ix.

94. Rainer Kleinertz, "Music Theatre in Spain," in Simon P. Keefe ed., *The Cambridge History of Eighteenth-Century Music* (Cambridge: Cambridge University Press, 2011), 413; Russell, *Santiago de Murcia*, 17.

95. Rainer Kleinertz, "Ruler-Acclamation in Spanish Opera of the 1730s," in Melania Bucciarelli, Norbert Dubowy, and Reinhard Strohm, eds., *Italian Opera in Central Europe: Vol. 1* (Berlin: BWV, Berliner Wiss.-Verl, 2006), 235.

96. Ignacio López Alemany, " 'En música italiana/y castellana en la letra': El camino hacia la ópera italianizante en el teatro palaciego de Felipe V," *Dieciocho* 31, no. 1 (2008):

7–22; Emilio Cotarelo y Mori, *Orígenes y establecimiento de la opera en España hasta 1800* (Madrid: Tip. de la "Revista de arch., bibl., y museos," 1917), 7–24; W. N. Hargreaves-Mawdsley, *Spain Under the Bourbons, 1700–1833: A Collection of Documents, Edited and Translated with a Critical Introduction* (Columbia, South Carolina: University of South Carolina Press, 1973), xxii; Kathleen Kuzmick Hansell, "Eighteenth-Century Italian Theatrical Ballet: The Triumph of the *Grotteschi*," in Harris-Warrick and Brown, *The Grotesque Dancer on the Eighteenth-Century Stage*, 15–32; Michael F. Robinson, *Naples and Neapolitan Opera* (Oxford: Clarendon P, 1972).

97. Kleinertz, "Music Theatre in Spain," 407, 411.

98. Diana Campóo Schelotto, "Danza y educación nobiliaria en el siglo XVIII: El *Método* de la escuela de baile en el Real Seminario de Nobles de Madrid," *Ars Bilduma* (2015): 161; Russell, *Murcia*, 20, cites Aurelio Capmany, "El baile y la danza," in Francesch Carreras y Candi, *Folklore y costumbres de España: II* (Barcelona: Casa Editorial Alberto Martin, 1931), 354.

99. Zoido, *La ilustración contra los gitanos*, 12.

100. Rocío Plaza Orellana, *Los caminos de Andalucía: Memorias de los viajeros del siglo XVIII* (Sevilla: Universidad de Sevilla, 2008).

101. Etzion, "Spanish Music," 102–103; and Etzion, "The Spanish Fandango," 229; Julián Zugasti, *El bandolerismo: Estudio social y memorias históricas* (Madrid: Impr. de T. Fortanet, 1876); Casanova, *History of My Life*, vols. 9 and 10, 317, 321, cited in Baird, Goldberg, and Newman, "Changing Places, : Toward the Reconstruction of an Eighteenth Century Danced Fandango," in *Españoles, indios, africanos y gitanos. El alcance global del fandango en música, canto y baile*, edited by K. Meira Goldberg and Antoni Pizà, *Música Oral Del Sur*, no. 12 (2015): 631–32; (2016): 582–83; On the Conde de Aranda's 1767 lifting of the prohibition against public masked balls, see Clara Rico Osés, "De las ceremonias de los bailes: política, identidad y representaciones a través del baile español del siglo XVIII," *Bulletin hispanique* 114, no. 2 (2012), 654.

102. Immanuel Kant, "On National Characteristics, so Far as They Depend upon the Distinct Feeling of the Beautiful and Sublime," in *Race and the Enlightenment*, edited by Emmanuel Chukwudi Eze (Malden, MA, and Oxford: Blackwell Publishers, 1997), 51; Zoido, *La Ilustración contra los gitanos*, 16–17.

103. Zoido, *La Ilustración contra los gitanos*, 15.

104. Zoido, *La Ilustración contra los gitanos*, 15.

105. For example, between 1650 and 1750 Cádiz eclipsed Sevilla as the principal "commercial emporium" for slaves. Antonio Rumeu de Armas, *España en el África Atlántica* (Madrid: Consejo Superior de Investigaciones Científicas. Instituto de Estudios Africanos, 1956), 163; Antonio Zoido Naranjo, "Prologue," in Rocío Plaza Orellana, *El flamenco y los románticos: Un viaje entre el mito y la realidad* (Sevilla: Bienal de Arte Flamenco, 1999), 19, 23; Martín Casares, "Origin of Slaves," 418; Pablo Antón Solé, *Los villancicos de la Catedral de Cádiz* (Cádiz: Universidad de Cádiz, Servicio de Publicaciones, 1986), 117.

106. Rebecca Haidt, "Los Majos, el 'españolísimo gremio' del teatro popular dieciochesco: sobre casticismo, inestabilidad y abyección," *Cuadernos de Historia Moderna, Anejo X: Los extranjeros y la Nación en España y la América española* (Madrid: Universidad Complutense, 2011): 158, 169.

107. Baird, Goldberg and Newman, "Changing Places" (2015): 632; (2016): 583.

108. "Reglamentos para el baile de mascaras de Sevilla," 1768, Sevilla, Archivo Municipal. Sección del Conde del Águila, t. 62 (núm. 61), Simancas, Archivo General, Gracia y Justicia, leg. 979, published as an appendix in Francisco Aguilar Piñal, *Sevilla y el Teatro en el siglo XVIII* (Oviedo: Universidad de Oviedo, 1974), 261–65, cited in Plaza Orellana, *El flamenco y los románticos*, 748. See also Susannah Worth, "The Development of the Image, 1759–1808," *Andalusian Dress and the Andalusian Image of Spain, 1759–1936* (doctoral dissertation, Ohio State University, 1990), 44–56.

109. Richard Bright, *Travels from Vienna Through Lower Hungary: With Some Remarks on the State of Vienna During the Congress, in the Year 1814* (Edinburgh: Printed for A. Constable, 1818), lxxvi, cited in Worth, *Andalusian Dress*, 71.

110. Del Campo Tejedor and Cáceres Feria address this idea in their chapter "Lo castizo y lo mestizo: Andaluz, gitano, negro y moro—Andalucización de España," *Historia cultural del flamenco*, 315–36. See also Barbara Fuchs, *Exotic Nation: Maurophilia and the Construction of Early Modern Spain* (Philadelphia: University of Pennsylvania Press, 2009).

111. Frida Weber de Kurlat, *El tipo del negro en el teatro de Lope de Vega: Tradición y creación* (Nimega: Asociación Internacional de Hispanistas, Instituto Español de la Universidad de Nimega, 1967), 697–98.

112. Julio Caro Baroja, "Los majos," in *Temas castizos* (Madrid, Ediciones Istmo, 1980), 77, cited in Haidt, "Los Majos," 160.

113. D. Ramón de Mesonero Romanos, *El antiguo Madrid, paseos históricos-anecdóticos por las calles y casas de esta villa* (Madrid: Don F. de P. Mellado, 1861), 188–89; Ramón de la Cruz, *Manolo*, in Emilio Cotarelo y Mori, *Sainetes de Don Ramón de la Cruz en su mayoría inéditos*, vol. 2 (Madrid, Bailly-Bailliere, 1915–1928), 48–55, both cited in Haidt, "Los Majos," 160, 166. See also Ramón de la Cruz, *Manolo: Tragedia para reir, ó saynete para llorar. Primera Parte* (Madrid: por Don Benito Cano…Se hallará en la Librería de Quiroga, calle de las Carretas, 1803).

114. Mesonero Romanos, *El antiguo Madrid*, 188–89.

115. Haidt, "Los Majos," 170–71, cites Wenceslao Ayguals De Izco, *María, la hija de un jornalero* (Madrid, 1846–47, 2 vols., ch. 13), 116.

116. El bachiller revoltoso's *Libro de la gitaneria de Triana de los años 1740 a 1750* must be considered in this light. I have made this argument regarding the "Competition for the Image of the Gypsy" in Goldberg, *Border Trespasses*, 144–49. Haidt, "Los Majos," 172.

117. P. Vizuete Picón, "baile," *Diccionario Enciclopedico Hispano-Americano de Literatura, Ciencias y Artes…*, vol. 3 (Barcelona: Montaner y Simón, 1888), 63–64.

118. Irigoyen-García, *The Spanish Arcadia*, 3–34.

119. Consider, for example, the casta paintings of eighteenth-century México. Katzew, *Casta Painting*.

120. Some of the texts which I have referenced in thinking about this include Liu, *Medieval Joke Poetry*; Craun, *Lies, Slander, and Obscenity*; Lobato and Bègue, *Literatura y música del hampa en los Siglos de Oro*; Maxime Chevalier, *Quevedo y su tiempo: La agudeza verbal* (Barcelona: Editorial crítica, 1992), and Nicholas Spadaccini and Jenaro Taléns, *Through the Shattering Glass: Cervantes and the Self-Made World* (Minneapolis: University of Minnesota Press, 1993).

121. See Goldberg, "Callico (The Beginning)," *Border Trespasses*, 19–106.

122. Vizuete Picón, "baile," in *Diccionario Enciclopedico Hispano-Americano*, 63–64. On the word "flamenco" as a referent for Roma, see "Some Editorial

Considerations," in Goldberg, Bennahum, and Hayes, *Flamenco on the Global Stage*, 9–13.

Chapter 2

Note to Epigraph: Alan Jones's new translation of Martí's 1712 letter from Latin to English is discussed in his article "Emergence and Transformations of the Fandango," in Goldberg and Pizà, *The Global Reach of the Fandango* (Spanish Edition 2015): 562–85; (2016): 518–35. An often-cited Spanish translation from the Latin can be found in Capmany, "El baile y la danza," 248.

1. Ángel Alloza Aparicio, José Miguel López García, and José Luis de Pablo Gafas, "Prevention and Repression: Food Supply and Public Order in Early Modern Madrid," Equipo Madrid de Estudios Históricos, Universidad Autónoma de Madrid: *Mélanges de l'École française de Rome. Italie et Méditerranée* 112, no. 2 (2000): 615–44, http://digital.casalini.it/17242142.

2. David A. Brading, *The First America: The Spanish Monarchy, Creole Patriots, and the Liberal State, 1492–1867* (Cambridge [England]: Cambridge University Press, 1991), 499, 502; Oliver W. Holmes, "José Miguel López García. El motín contra Esquilache: Crisis y protesta popular en el Madrid del Siglo XVIII," *The American Historical Review* 24, no. 5 (2009): 1538–39.

3. Campóo Schelotto, "Danza y educación nobiliaria," 167, cites Antonio Álvarez-Ossorio Alvariño, "Rango y apariencia. El decoro y la quiebra de la distinción en Castilla (ss. XVI–XVIII)," *Revista de Historia Moderna* 17 (1998–1999): 278.

4. Hughes, *Goya*, 240–41, 331–32.

5. Campóo Schelotto, "Danza y educación nobiliaria," 163–65.

6. Campóo Schelotto, "Danza y educación nobiliaria," 167, cites Plan de educación de la nobleza trabajado de orden del Rey en 1798, in Miguel Adellac González De Agüero, *Manuscritos inéditos de Jovellanos* (Gijón, L. Sangenís, 1915), 232, https://bibliotecavirtual.asturias.es/i18n/consulta/registro.cmd?id=2819. On the bolero as descended from the fandango, see Cairón, *Compendio*, 103, 110. My translation of Cairón's description of the fandango is in Baird, Goldberg, and Newman, "Changing Places" (2015): 657–59, (2016): 613.

7. Campóo Schelotto, "Danza y educación nobiliaria," 167–68, cites G. Mera, "Los ilustrados y la danza a principios del siglo XIX. Polémicas sobre la construcción de una identidad nacional frente al modelo francés," in *Coreografiar la historia europea: Cuerpo, política, identidad y género en la danza*, edited by B. Martínez del Fresno (Oviedo: Universidad de Oviedo, 2011), 173–97. A good starting place on the bolero school in English is Javier Suárez-Pajares and Xoan M. Carreira, eds., *The Origins of the Bolero School: Studies in Dance History*, vol. 4, no. 1 (New Jersey: Society of Dance History Scholars, 1993); and Marina Grut, Alberto Lorca, Ángel Pericet Carmona, Eloy Pericet, and Ivor Forbes Guest, *The Bolero School: An Illustrated History of the Bolero, the Seguidillas and the Escuela Bolera: Syllabus and Dances* (Alton, Hampshire, UK: Dance Books, 2002). See also Kiko Mora's chapter on the historiography of the Spanish *bailable*, in Goldberg, Bennahum, and Hayes, *Flamenco on the Global Stage*, 103–16.

8. Haidt, "Los Majos," 170, cites Cruz, *Manolo*, in Cotarelo, *Sainetes*, 50; and Cruz, *El muñuelo*, in Ignacio Bauer, *Sainetes* (Madrid, n.d.), 49.

9. Le Guin, *Tonadilla*, 163, quotes and translates Javier Huerta Calvo, "Comicidad y marginalidad en el sainete dieciochesco," *Scriptura* 10, no. 15 (1999): 61, https://dialnet.unirioja.es/servlet/articulo?codigo=157246.

10. Heuer, *The Discourse of the Ruffian*, iv.

11. Marie Catherine Le Jumel de Barneville d'Aulnoy, *The Ingenious and Diverting Letters of the Lady's—Travels into Spain Describing the Devotions, Nunneries, Humours, Customs, Laws, Militia, Trade, Diet, and Recreations of that People* (London: Printed for S. Crouch, 1692), 136–37.

12. Louise K. Stein, "The Origins and Character of *recitado*," *Journal of Seventeenth-Century Music* 9, no. 1 (2003), 3.3, http://sscm-jscm.org/v9/no1/stein.html#ch3.

13. Díez Borque, "Liturgia-fiesta-teatro," 487.

14. The 1479 settlement of the Castilian War of Succession granted the Canary Islands to Spain, and a monopoly on the slave trade to Portugal. Also, see Brooks, *Processions*, on Juan Antonio de Castro, a free black Sevillano who had a touring company and in 1693–1694 directed a city-sponsored processional dance called *Montezuma*: *Processions*, 186–87, 237, 265.

15. Casiano Pellicer, *Tratado histórico sobre el origen y progresos de la comedia y del histrionismo en España: y con la noticia de algunos célebres comediantes y comediantas así antiguos como modernos* (Madrid: Imprenta de la Administración del Real Arbitrio de Beneficiencia, 1804), 36–37.

16. Pellicer, *Tratado histórico*, 39.

17. Cohen, "Spanish National Character in the Court Ballets of J.-B. Lully," 2982–87. Part of the motivation for choreographing music into the production was to cover the sound of mechanical set changes: moving clouds, thrones going up and down, hatches, and the appearance or disappearance of important characters such as royalty, divinities such as the Virgin Mary, or Greek and Roman gods: Danièle Becker, "El teatro palaciego y la música en la segunda mitad del siglo XVII," in Sebastián Neumeister, ed., *Actas del IX Congreso de la Asociación Internacional de Hispanistas* (1986): 353, http://cvc.cervantes.es/literatura/aih/aih_ix.htm.

18. Díez Borque, "Liturgia-fiesta-teatro," 492, cites Diego Sánchez de Badajoz (ca. 1479–1549), "Danza de los Pecados"; Cotarelo, *Entremeses*, clxxiv–v, cites Francisco de Bances Candamo (1662–1704), *Teatro de los teatros*, unpublished and unfinished manuscript.

19. Pellicer, *Tratado histórico*, 25.

20. Cohen, "Spanish National Character," 2982, quotes Louise K. Stein, "La plática de los dioses," in Pedro Calderón de la Barca, *La Estatua de Prometeo* (Kassel, Edition Reichenberger, 1986), 13.

21. Pellicer, *Tratado histórico*, 41.

22. Becker, "El teatro palaciego," 353.

23. Cotarelo, *Entremeses*, clxxxiii. A similar process led to the "Triumph of the Grotteschi" in eighteenth-century Italy. See Kuzmick Hansell, "Eighteenth-Century Italian Theatrical Ballet," 15–32.

24. Cotarelo, *Entremeses*, clxxxiii–v; Rey, *Danzas cantadas*, 34. See Esses's chapter "The Uses of Dance in Spain," *Dance and Instrumental Diferencias*, 345–418.

25. Cotarelo, *Entremeses*, clxxxv–vi.

26. Rey, *Danzas cantadas*, 40–41; Knighton and Torrente, *Devotional Music*, 3.

27. Cotarelo, *Entremeses*, clxxxiv–v, clxxxii.

28. For a discussion of the centrality of the sung verse in flamenco dance improvisation, see Goldberg, "Sonidos Negros," 102–104.

29. Cotarelo, *Entremeses*, clxxxiii–iv, cites José Antonio González de Salas, introduction to the bailes of Quevedo, edited by Don Florencio Janer, *Obras de Quevedo*, vol. 3 (Madrid: Rivadeneyra, 1877), 367, and *Nueva idea de la tragedia antigua, o ilustración último al libro singular de Aristóteles Stagirita*, vol. 1 (Madrid: Antonio de Sancha, [1633] 1778), 173.

30. Brooks, *Esquivel*, 93, Spanish: 236, English: 288.

31. López Alemany, "En música italiana/y castellana en la letra," 12–14, 19. See also Ignacio López Alemany and John E. Varey, *El teatro palaciego en Madrid: 1707–1724; Estudio y documentos* (Woodbridge: Támesis, 2006), 27–31, 223–30.

32. "Ercules en un cavallo de fachada con dos timbales dorados midiendo en movimiento suabe y continuo el ayre y, al compás del ada, tocándolos y, de la una y otra parte, Ceto y Calais con espadas y rodelas y, de la otra, las dos arpías combatiéndose en buelo subcedido [*sic*] de suerte que los golpes llev[an] en el compás mismo que Hércules." Notes to the opening of Act II in *La hazaña mayor de Alcides* by José de Cañizares and Giacomo Facco, BNE, Mss. 155 599, fol. 21r, cited in López Alemany, " 'En música italiana/y castellana en la letra,' " 12–13.

33. Díez Borque, "Liturgia-fiesta-teatro," 491, cites Diego Pérez de Valdivia (1510–89), *Plática o lección de las mascaras, en la qual se trata, si es pecado mortal o no, el enmascararse* (Barcelona: En Barcelona por Geronymo Margarit, y a su costa, 1618).

34. Pellicer, *Tratado histórico*, 122, 124–25, cites "un Memorial á Felipe en año 1598" (Bibliot. Real: Est. M. Cód. 4I, fol. 3). For a vivid description of the outrageous yet sly responses in seventeenth-century jácaras to censorship, see Ted Bergman, "La criminalidad como diversión pública y las jácaras entremesadas," in Lobato and Bègue, *Literatura y música del hampa en los Siglos de Oro*, 78–91.

35. Directorio Franciscano, La Oración de cada día, «VÍA CRUCIS» con las Estaciones comentadas e ilustradas, http://www.franciscanos.org/oracion/viacruz00.htm.

36. Brooks, *Processions*, 53.

37. Díez Borque, "Liturgia-fiesta-teatro," 489, 492; Pellicer, *Tratado histórico*, 41.

38. Becker, "El teatro palaciego," 354. For more on Cupid's laments, see Maria Virginia Acuña, *The Spanish* Lamento: *Discourses of Love, Power, and Gender in the Musical Theatre (1696–1718)* (doctoral dissertation, University of Toronto, 2016).

39. The word "tonada" is also referenced in "tonadilla" (little tonada). Manuel Alvar, *Villancicos dieciochescos (la colección malagueña de 1734 a 1770): [editados con un estudio de] Manuel Alvar* (Málaga: Delegación de cultura excmo. ayuntamiento de Málaga, 1973), 18–19; Vodovozova, *Villancico de Negros*, 14.

40. María Cruz García de Enterría, "Literatura de cordel en tiempo de Carlos II: generos parateatrales," in Javier Huerta Calvo, Harm den Boer, and Fermín Sierra Martínez, eds., *El teatro español a fines del siglo XVII—Historia, cultura y teatro en la España de Carlos II*, vol. 1, Historia y literatura en el reinado de Carlos II (Amsterdam, Atlanta, Georgia: Rodipi, 1989): 149–50.

41. Alvar, *Villancicos dieciochescos*, 10, 26.

42. Alvar, *Villancicos dieciochescos*, 12, cites José Subirá, *La tonadilla escénica*, vol. 2 (Madrid: Tipografía de Archivos, 1928–1930), 12. See also Knighton and Torrente, *Devotional Music*, 266; and Bergman, "La criminalidad como diversión pública."

43. Ted L. L. Bergman, *The Art of Humour in the Teatro Breve and Comedias of Calderón de la Barca* (Woodbridge: Tamesis, 2003), 196–97. Escarramán was condemned to slavery in the galleys toward the end of the sixteenth century and immortalized in poet and dramatist Francisco de Quevedo's *Carta de Escarramán a la Méndez*. See Felipe Pedraza Jiménez, "De Quevedo a Cervantes: La génesis de la jácara," in *La comedia de caballerías: Actas de las XXVIII jornadas de teatro clásico de Almagro, 12, 13 y 14 de julio de 2005*, edited by Felipe Pedraza Jiménez, Elena E. Marcello, and Rafael González Cañal (Almagro: Ed. de la Univ. de Castilla–La Mancha, 2006), 77–88.

44. Cruz García de Enterría, "Literatura de cordel," 152, 144; Alvar, *Villancicos dieciochescos*, 17.

45. Cruz García de Enterría, "Literatura de cordel," 139–41, 143, 147; Alvar, *Villancicos dieciochescos*, 17.

46. Cruz García de Enterría, "Literatura de cordel," 143–44; Pellicer, *Tratado histórico*, 164; Díez Borque, "Liturgia-fiesta-teatro," 489–91; Bergman, "La criminalidad como diversión pública."

47. Pellicer, *Tratado histórico*, 102–106, 119–25; Díez Borque, "Liturgia-fiesta-teatro," 488–89, cites Jean Sentaurens, *Seville et le théâtre. De la fin du Moyen Age a la fin du XVIIe siécle*, vol. 1 (Lille: Université, 1984), 23, 29. See also Emilio Cotarelo y Mori, *Bibliografía de las controversias sobre la licitud del teatro en España* (Madrid: Revista de Archivos, Bibliotecas y Museos, 1904).

48. Alvar, *Villancicos dieciochescos*, 19, 21 quotes Subirá, *La tonadilla escénica*, vol. 1, 14, 84.

49. Alvar, *Villancicos dieciochescos*, 16–17, 54, 73.

50. Antonia Auxiliadora Bustos Rodríguez, "Divertimentos en el siglo de oro español," *Danzaratte: Revista del Conservatorio Superior de Danza de Málaga*, no. 6 (2009): 37; Manuel Dávila y Collado, *Reinado De Carlos III*, vol. 6 (Madrid: El Progreso Editorial, 1893), 440. On giants, large puppets popular in religious processions, see Brooks, *Processions*, 214.

51. Sister Mary Paulina Saint Amour, *A Study of the Villancico* (New York: AMS Press, 1969), vii; Alvar, *Villancicos dieciochescos*, 16.

52. Fernando Ortiz, *La antigua fiesta afrocubana del "Día de Reyes"* (La Habana: República de Cuba, Ministerio de Relaciones Exteriores, Departamento de Asuntos Culturales, División de Publicación, 1960); Roberto González Echevarría, *Celestina's Brood: Continuities of the Baroque in Spanish and Latin American Literatures* (Durham, NC: Duke University Press, 1993), 189–92.

53. Cruz García de Enterría, "Literatura de cordel," 150; Russell, *Murcia*, 70; Margit Frenk Alatorre and Mariana Masera, *La otra Nueva España: la palabra marginada en la colonia* (Barcelona: Azul, 2002), 43. On villancicos de negros, see Horacio Becco, *El tema del negro en cantos, bailes y villancicos de los siglos XVI y XVII* (Buenos Aires: Ollantay, 1951); Vodovozova, *Villancico de Negros*; José Julián Labrador Herraiz and Ralph A. DiFranco, "Villancicos de negros y otros testimonios al caso en manuscritos del Siglo de Oro," in *De la canción de amor medieval a las soleares: Profesor Manuel Alvar "In Memorian,"* edited by Pedro Manuel Piñero Ramírez (Sevilla: Actas del Congreso Internacional "Lyra mínima oral III" [26–28 de noviembre de 2001], 2004): 163–88; and Glenn Swiadon Martínez, *Los villancicos de negro en el siglo XVII* (doctoral dissertation, Universidad Nacional Autónoma de México 2000). For more on a particular villancico de negros, Gaspar Fernandes's *Guineo a 5: Eso rigor e repente*, written in the Cathedral of

Puebla, México between 1609–1616, see Goldberg, "Sonidos Negros," 88–91; and Robert Stevenson, "The Afro-American Musical Legacy to 1800," *Musical Quarterly* 54, no. 4 (1968): 489–97. On guineo, see Cotarelo, *Entremeses*, ccl–i; Esses, *Dance and Instrumental Diferencias*, 662–64; Russell, *Murcia*, 69–73; and Marcella Trambaioli, "Apuntes sobre el guineo o baile de negros: tipologías y funciones dramáticas," in *Actas de los Congresos de la Asociación Internacional Siglo de Oro (1987–2005)*, vol. 6, no. 2, edited by María Luisa Lobato y Francisco Domínguez Matito (2004): 1773–83.

54. María José Ruiz Mayordomo "El papel de la danza en la tonadilla escénica," in *Paisajes sonoros en el Madrid del S. 18. La tonadilla escénica: Museo de San Isidro, Madrid, mayo-julio 2003*, edited by Begoña Lolo and Andrés Amorós (Madrid: Ayuntamiento de Madrid, 2003), 61–62.

55. Díez Borque, "Liturgia-fiesta-teatro," 488, cites Louise Fothergill-Payne "Del carro al corral: la comunicación drantática en los años setenta y ochenta del siglo XVI," *Revista Canadiense de Estudios Hispánicos* 8, no. 2 (Invierno 1983), 260.

56. Swiadon Martínez, *Los villancicos de negro*, 162.

57. Glenn Swiadon Martínez, "Los personajes del villancico de negro en su entorno social (siglo XVII)," in *Actas del XV Congreso de la Asociación Internacional de Hispanistas "Las dos orillas,"* vol. 1, edited by Beatriz Mariscal and María Teresa Miaja de la Peña (Monterrey, México: [del 19 al 24 de julio de 2004], 2007): 595.

58. Swiadon Martínez, "Los personajes del villancico de negro," 601, cites "Villancicos que se cantaron en la S. I. Metropolitana de Méjico en honor de María Santísima, Madre de Dios, en su Asunción triunfante, y se imprimieron en el año de 1685," in *Sor Juana Inés de la Cruz. Obras completas, vol. 2, Villancicos y letras sacras*, edited by Alfonso Méndez Plancarte (México, Fondo de Cultura Económica, 1994), 97.

59. Pellicer, *Tratado histórico*, 25. See also Sir D. Brewster, "Drama," *The Edinburgh Encyclopaedia*, vol. 7 (Philadelphia: J. and E. Parker, 1832), 709–10; and Antonia Martín Marcos, "El actor en la presentación barroca: verosimilitud, gesto y ademán," in *Diálogos hispánicos de Amsterdam 8/I—El teatro español a fines del siglo XVII—Historia, cultura y teatro en la España de Carlos II, vol. 3, Representaciones y fiestas*, edited by Javier Huerta Calvo, Harm den Boer, and Fermín Sierra Martínez (Amsterdam, Atlanta, Georgia: Rodipi, 1989): 763–64.

60. Juan de Zabaleta, *El día de fiesta por la mañana y por la tarde: con una advertencia preliminar* (Barcelona: Daniel Cortezo y Ca., 1885), 155–56, cited in Martín Marcos, "El actor en la representación barroca," 765.

61. Cotarelo, *Entremeses*, cxc, cites Cotarelo, *Controversias*, 218.

62. RAE, "Marica," http://dle.rae.es/?id=OPMBIVV.

63. Cotarelo, *Entremeses*, cxci.

64. Padre Juan de Mariana, "Del baile y cantar llamado zarabanda," *Obras del Padre Juan de Mariana: Historia de España, tratado contra los juegos públicos*, vol. 2 (ca. 1601; rpt. Madrid: M. Rivadeneyra, 1854), 432–34. The original work is available online: BNE Mss/5735, ff. 55–8 (61–4 digital page numbers) http://bdh-rd.bne.es/viewer. vm?id=0000080960&page=1; cited in Goldberg, "Sonidos Negros," 90–91.

65. Ana Yepes, "From the *Jácara* to the *Sarabande*," in Goldberg, Bennahum, and Hayes, *Flamenco on the Global Stage*, 59, 68–69, cites Cotarelo, *Entremeses*, cl; and Jaque and Subirá, "*Libro de danzar*," 194, 198.

66. Yepes, "*Jácara*," 68–69, cites González, *Escuela por lo vajo*, fol. 44–5 (pdf 98); and Frenk Alatorre, *Nuevo corpus*, 803: Frenk's sources are Quiñones de Benavente, *El*

Amolador, in BNM, ms. 14851, fol. 11, and *Entremeses nuevos* (Alcalá, 1643). Luis Quiñones de Benavente, *El Amolador* (Madrid, 1643), Biblioteca Nacional de España, Ms. 14851, is available online: http://bdh-rd.bne.es/viewer.vm?id=0000214150&page=1, digital page numbers 17–20. Benavente's *Amolador* is also cited in Cotarelo, *Entremeses*, clxxix.

67. Rodrigo Noveli, *Chorégraphie figurativa y demostrativa del arte de danzar en la forma española* (MS. Madrid, 1708), http://www.realacademiabellasartessanfernando. com/assets/docs/noveli/noveli.pdf. f. 24 (pdf 55); Bergman, *The Art of Humour*, 196–97.

68. Yepes, "Jácara," 59, cites Bartolomé Ferriol y Boxeraus, Joseph Testore, and Santiago Perez Junquera, *Reglas útiles para los aficionados a danzar...* (Capoa: A costa de Joseph Testore, mercador de libros, à la Calle Nueva, 1745), 47 (pdf 270). For Yepes's discussion and demonstration of the amolador, see drewdavis58, "Conference sur 'La Danse du Siecle d'Or Espagnol' par Ana Yepes et Anna Romani," *YouTube*, Feb. 2, 2015, https://www.youtube.com/watch?v=-l_s5bnOfBo, 46:58 - 52:00.

69. Brooks, *Processions*, 35–37, cites Capmany, "El baile y la danza," 69–74; Yepes, "Jácara," 67–68.

70. Heuer, *The Discourse of the Ruffian*, 104–105, cites Asensio y Quevedo, *Itinerario del entremés*, 92, and Juan Hidalgo's 1609 *Bocabulario*, in Salillas, "Vocabulario de germanía," 272; RAE, "baile" http://dle.rae.es/?id=4nROyIQl4nRicRY. See also Esses, *Dance and Instrumental Diferencias*, 347–48.

71. Heuer, *The Discourse of the Ruffian*, 105, cites Francisco de Quevedo, *Cortes de los Bailes*, in Francisco de Quevedo, *Poësias de Don Francisco de Quevedo Villegas...* (en Bruselas: Francisco Foppens, 1661), 244–46, https://play.google.com/books/reader?id=O_VFAAAAcAAJ&printsec=frontcover&output=reader&hl=en&pg=GBS.PA244. See also Francisco Sáez-Raposo, "Entre danzas antiguas y bailes nuevos: la huella de Francisco de Quevedo en la evolución del baile dramático," *La Perinola. Revista de Investigación Quevediana*, no. 17 (2013): 179–200.

72. Heuer, *The Discourse of the Ruffian*, 10.

73. Heuer, *The Discourse of the Ruffian*, 106–107.

74. Heuer states that Quevedo (*Poësias*, 246–48) uses this play on words in, for example, *Las sacadoras*, which "instructs women to take from men." Heuer, *The Discourse of the Ruffian*, 110; Cotarelo, *Entremeses*, clxxxix. RAE, "salto" (jump) is "pillaje" (plunder): http://dle.rae.es/?id=X79BxUq.

75. Heuer, *The Discourse of the Ruffian*, 106–107, cites Quevedo, *Los nadadores*, in *Poësias*, 248–50.

76. Cotarelo, *Entremeses*, clxxxix; on baile de Juan Redondo, cclii. Quevedo, *Poësias, Los galeotes*, 239–41.

77. In Esquivel, "*natural*" (natural) relates to style, "ease of bearing." An "open fourth position" of the feet used in a gentlemanly bow, "*planta natural,*" writes Brooks, is a "posture" or "stance" "documented in texts of manners and deportment." "*Naturales,*" she adds, are also a "movement of the sword downward from a raised position," among the "five Movements in Dancing, the same as in Arms": the comparison between dancing and fencing flows from Esquivel's "mission to raise the status of dance by linking it to the art of the sword." Brooks, *Esquivel*, on "ease of bearing": 91, on "bodily comportment": 85–89, Spanish: 231, English: 283 (ff. 21–21v); on Esquivel's five movements: 95–97, Spanish: 220, English: 271 (f. 9v). A "*pase natural*" is a cape movement in bullfighting, similarly referencing coolness and grace under pressure. On *pase natural*: Barnaby Conrad, *Encyclopedia of Bullfighting* (Boston: Houghton Mifflin, 1961), 168.

78. Cotarelo, *Entremeses*, clxxxix.

79. Cotarelo, *Entremeses*, cxcii–cxciii; see also Pedraza Jiménez, "La génesis de la jácara."

80. On El Mellado, see Elena Di Pinto, "El mundo del hampa en el siglo XVII y su reflejo en la jácara: ¿realidad o ficción literaria?" in Lobato and Bègue, *Literatura y música del hampa en los Siglos de Oro*, 195–217.

81. Bergman, *The Art of Humour*, 196–97, cites Pedro Herrera Puga and José Cepeda Adán, *Sociedad y delincuencia en el Siglo De Oro* (Madrid: La Editorial Católica, 1974), 255–68; Pedro Calderón de la Barca, (1600–1681), edición, introducción y notas de Evangelina Rodríguez y Antonio Tordera, "Jácara del Mellado" (Alicante: Biblioteca Virtual Miguel de Cervantes, 2000), http://www.cervantesvirtual.com/obra/jacara-del-mellado--o/.

82. Heuer, *The Discourse of the Ruffian*, 67.

83. Pellicer quotes Padre Mariana on the role of Magdalena in the *Comedias de Santos*, which gave a veneer of respectability to the theater. *Tratado histórico*, 122, 124–25.

84. Heuer, *The Discourse of the Ruffian*, 128, quotes Javier Herrero, "Renaissance Poverty and Lazarillo's Family: The Birth of the Picaresque Genre," *PMLA* 94 (1979): 883–84.

85. Bergman, *The Art of Humour*, 196–97. On the jácara as moral lesson: Heuer, *The Discourse of the Ruffian*, 118–19.

86. Cotarelo, *Entremeses*, cxcii–iii.

87. Stevenson, "The Afro-American Musical Legacy," 489, cites Jean-Baptiste Labat, *Nouveau Voyage aux isles de l'Amdrique* (Paris, 1722), vol. 4, 154; and "calenda," Covarrubias, *Tesoro*, (Barcelona, 1943), 269.

88. "Calenda," Covarrubias, *Tesoro*, 175, 510.

89. Knighton and Torrente, *Devotional Music*, 106–107.

90. Stevenson, "The Afro-American Musical Legacy," 488, cites Labat, *Nouveau Voyage*, 154. For more on the calenda as an Afro-Caribbean dance, see Yvonne Daniel, *Caribbean and Atlantic Diaspora Dance: Igniting Citizenship* (Urbana: University of Illinois Press, 2011).

91. Julian Gerstin, "Tangled Roots: Kalenda and Other Neo-African Dances in the Circum-Caribbean," *New West Indian Guide/Nieuwe West-Indische Gids* 78, no. 1/2 (2004), 7, translates and cites Jean Baptiste Labat, *Nouveaux voyages aux isles de l'Amérique, 1693–1705* (Fort-de-France: Editions des Horizons caraïbes, [1722], 1972), 401–403. Part of this passage is in Alejo Carpentier, Timothy Brennan, and Alan West-Durán, *Music in Cuba* (Minneapolis: University of Minnesota Press, 2001), 100–101.

92. Yvonne Daniel, *Rumba: Dance and Social Change in Contemporary Cuba* (Bloomington: Indiana University Press, 1995), 4.

93. José López Pinillos, " 'La Perla Negra,' Gente graciosa y gente rara," Madrid, Pueyo ([1917] 1920), 202, cited in Kiko Mora, "La representación contra-hegemónica de la negritud: La Perla Negra, entre la rumba y la danza moderna (1913–1928)," *Sinfonía Virtual* 32 (Invierno 2017), 1–36.

94. "Bèlè, Mabélo a folk dance from Martinique. An African fertility dance, commonly danced during the evening of a full moon," Iagoyave, "Martinique—Bèlè—Mabélo," *YouTube*, https://www.youtube.com/watch?v=UtG2uLDEUUI. Thanks to Kevin Jones for this reference. On batuque, Kariamu Welsh-Asante, *African Dance: An Artistic, Historical,*

and Philosophical Inquiry (Trenton, NJ: Africa World Press, 1998), 82–86; on ombligada, Thompson, *Tango*, 97; on rumba, Janheinz Jahn, *Muntu: African Culture and the Western World* (New York: Grove Weidenfeld, [1961] 1990), 78–90; Ned Sublette, *Cuba and Its Music: From the First Drums to the Mambo* (Chicago, Ill: Chicago Review Press, 2004), 271; and Daniel, *Rumba*, 69. On resbalosa: Carpentier, *Music in Cuba*, 101–103, cites Max Radiguet, *Souvenirs de L'amérique Espagnole: Chili, Pérou, Brésil* (Charleston, SC: BiblioLife, [1874] 2009), 60; translation of this work into Spanish: Max Radiguet, *Lima y la sociedad peruana: Colección de clásicos de la literatura europea "carrascalejo de la jara,"* e-Libro (2004) https://elbaile.com.ar/2016/11/08/lima-y-la-sociedad-peruana/. On cumbé: Antonio García de León Griego, *El mar de los deseos: el Caribe hispano musical historia y contrapunto* (Coyoacán, México y Buenos Aires Argentina: Siglo Veintiuno Editores, S.A. de C.V., 2002), 170. On currulao and joropo: Nubia Flórez Forero, "Zapateado dances in Colombia and their imaginarium of seduction," in *Spaniards, Natives, Africans, and Roma: Transatlantic Malagueñas and Zapateados in Music, Song, and Dance*, edited by K. Meira Goldberg, Walter Clark, and Antoni Pizà (Castle upon Tyne: Cambridge Scholars Publishing, forthcoming 2018). Fernando Ortiz also mentions cumbia as an obscene dance of Panamá: *Los instrumentos de la música afrocubana*, vol. 2 (Habana: Publicaciones de la Dirección de Cultura del Ministerio de Educación, 1952), 198. Gerstin, "Tangled Roots," lists and discusses many manifestations of vacunao dances in the Americas.

95. "Cumbé," RAE, vol. 2 (1729), 700.

96. Russell, *Murcia*, 71.

97. Frenk Alatorre and Masera, *La otra Nueva España*, 44.

98. Cotarelo (*Entremeses*, ccl) gives this verse in the ca. 1670 *Mojiganga de la gitanada*: *gitanada*, from *gitana*, means swindle, somewhat like the racial slur "gyp," from the word "gypsy."

99. Di Pinto, "El mundo del hampa," 199.

100. Donald Posner, "Jacques Callot and the Dances Called Sfessania" *The Art Bulletin* 59, no. 2 (June 1977): 205–207. Posner cites a poem by Giovan Battista Del Tufo. *"Cucurucucu," "cu(u),"* and *"guuú, guuú"* may also be wordplays on *"culo"* (ass), explains Karen Taylor, citing Pierre Bec on *"culada* (asshole) and *culavis* (probably 'coup de cul' ... 'butt blow' or 'buttscrew' ... Walther von Wartburg's *FEW* [Französisches etymolgisches Wörterbuch] has almost twenty pages of *culus* derivatives." Karen Taylor, *Gender Transgressions: Crossing the Normative Barrier in Old French Literature* (Routledge, 2015), 34, cites Pierre Bec, *Burlesque Et Obscenite Chez Les Troubadours: Pour Une Approche Du Contre-Texte Medieval* (Paris: Stock, 1984), 136–37, 163; and Antonio Tello, *Gran diccionario erótico: De voces de España e hispanoamérica* (Madrid: Ed. Temas de Hoy, 1992), 135–36.

101. "Si escribes comedias y eres poeta sabrás guineo en volviendo las RR LL, y al contrario: como Francisco, Flancisco: primo, plimo." Stevenson, "The Afro-American Musical Legacy," 486, cites Francisco de Quevedo y Villagas, *Obras completas*, edited by Felicidad Buendia (Madrid, 1966 [6th ed.]), vol. 1, 114. On Sor Juana: Vodovozova, *Villancico de Negros*, 104.

102. Cotarelo, *Entremeses*, ccxx, cclxxxviii; Russell, *Murcia*, 72–3.

103. Martín Casares and Barranco, "Black African Weddings," 113, cite Francisco de Avellaneda, *Bayle entremesado de negros* (Madrid: Andrés García de la Iglesia, 1663 [BNE: R. 6355]), 67–70.

104. Martín Casares and Barranco, "Black African Weddings," 109, 114–17, cite *Nueva relación y curioso romance, en que se refiere la celebridad, galanteo y acaso de una boda de Negros* (BNE: VE/1348/15).

105. Brenda Dixon Gottschild, *The Black Dancing Body: A Geography from Coon to Cool* (New York: Palgrave Macmillan, 2003), 7.

106. Baird, Goldberg, and Newman, "Changing Places," (2015): 636, (2016): 587–88. Translating the movement of the thighs as "twitching," Alan Jones makes the very significant observation that "the 'stamping' found in some translations appears in fact to be some kind of throbbing or twitching movement originating in the thighs." Jones, "Fandango," (2015): 564–65, and (2016): 520–21.

107. Ned Sublette, *The World That Made New Orleans: From Spanish Silver to Congo Square* (Chicago: Lawrence Hill Books, 2008), 188, translates M. L. E. Moreau de St. Méry, *Danse. Article extrait d'un ouvrage* (Philadelphia: Imprimé par l'Auteur, 1796) 51–53. See also: Claudia Jeschke with Robert Atwood, "Hispanomania in Nineteenth-Century Dance Theory and Choreography" in Goldberg, Bennahum and Hayes, *Flamenco on the Global Stage*, 98, which cites Médéric Louis Élie Moreau de Saint-Méry, *De la danse* (Parma: Bodoni, 1803), 50–61.

108. Cairón, *Compendio*, 116.

109. Sublette, *New Orleans*, 188–89.

110. Ortiz, "Cumbé," *Glosario de afronegrismos*, 154–55.

111. W. H. Bentley, *Dictionary and Grammar of the Kongo Language, As Spoken at San Salvador, the Ancient Capital of the Old Kongo Empire, West Afrika [and Appendix] Compiled and Prepared for the Baptist Mission on the Kongo River, West Africa* (London: Baptist Missionary Society, and Trübner & Co, 1887), *kumba, kumbu*: 312; *kemba*: 95, 169, 293; *kembela*: 23, 76, 94, 164, 194, 293; *nkumbi*: 385, cited in Ortiz, "Cumbé," *Glosario de afronegrismos*, 154–55.

112. On *nkumba*: Ortiz, *Los instrumentos de la música afrocubana*, vol. 2, 198.

113. For an overview of the ethnic origins of Africans enslaved on the Iberian Peninsula, see Martín Casares, "Origin of Slaves."

114. Stevenson, "The Afro-American Musical Legacy," 488, cites Labat, *Nouveau Voyage*, 154.

115. Thompson, *Tango*, 64. See also Maureen Warner-Lewis, *Central Africa in the Caribbean: Transcending Time, Transforming Cultures* (Kingston: Univ. of the West Indies Press, 2003), 309.

116. Gabriel Saldívar, with Elena Osorio Bolio, *Historia de la música en México (Épocas precortesiana y colonial) [with Musical Notes]* (México, 1934), 224–26.

117. Magali M. Carrera, *Imagining Identity in New Spain: Race, Lineage, and the Colonial Body in Portraiture and Casta Paintings* (Austin: University of Texas Press, 2003), 27.

118. Saldívar, *Historia de la música en México,* 226; Georges Baudot and María A. Méndez, "El Chuchumbé, Un Son Jácarandoso Del México Virreinal," *Cahiers Du Monde Hispanique Et Luso-Brésilien*, no. 48 (1987): 165.

119. Saldívar, *Historia de la música en México,* 226–27; Baudot and Méndez, "El Chuchumbé," 165, cite *Archivo General de la Nación (México), Inquisición*, vol. 1052, fols. 298r; Elena Deanda-Camacho, " 'El chuchumbé te he de soplar:' Sobre obscenidad, censura y memoria oral en el primer 'son de la tierra' novohispano," *Mester* 36, no. 1

(2007), 56, cites "La denuncia, las circulares administrativas, los testimonios y las ratificaciones se encuentran en el mismo expediente," *Inquisición*, vol. 1052, exp. 20., ff. 292–98.

120. Deanda-Camacho, "El chuchumbé," 55, cites *Inquisición*, vol. 1052, exp. 20, fojas 292–95; Deanda notes that all the verses cited in her work come from the denunciation against the "Chuchumbé" in Inquisition records cited above, ff. 294, 294v, and 295.

121. Le Guin, *Tonadilla*, 140.

122. Ortiz and Iznaga, *Los negros curros*, xix.

123. Pérez Fernández, *La música afromestiza mexicana*, 54–55.

124. Ortiz and Iznaga, *Los negros curros*, 54–55.

125. Deanda-Camacho, "El chuchumbé," 57–58, cites Gonzalo Aguirre Beltrán, *La población negra de México: Estudio etnohistórico* (México: FCE, 1989) in using the term "afromestizos" to distinguish groups of African lineage from "indomestizos" or those of Native American lineage. Deanda adds that "During the seventeenth century African communities enjoyed great liberty in comparison with other colonial domains. Cimarrones [escaped slaves] established *quilombos*, *palenques*, and *mocambos* [hideouts, hidden settlements] with names [making reference to African peoples] such as Mandinga, Matamba and Yanga." On this topic, Deanda cites Alfredo Delgado Calderón, "Los negros del sur," *Son del sur 1* (1995): 27–32; Octaviano Corro Ramos, *Cimarrones en Veracruz y la fundación de Amapa* (Veracruz: Citlaltépetl, 1974); and Patrick Carroll, *Blacks in Colonial Veracruz: Race, Ethnicity, and Regional Development* (Austin: University of Texas Press, 1991).

126. Deanda-Camacho, "El chuchumbé," 59–60, 66.

127. See Russell, *Murcia*, 69–77 on "Cumbées;" and José Antonio Robles Cahero "La memoria del cuerpo y transmisión cultural: las danzas populares en el siglo XVIII novohispano," *Heterofonía*, no. 85 (April–June 1984): 29.

128. Baudot and Méndez, "El Chuchumbé," 55.

129. José Otero Aranda, *Tratado de Bailes de Sociedad, regionales españoles, especialmente andaluces, con su historia y modo de ejecutarlos* (Seville: Tip. de la Guía Oficial, Lista núm. 1, 1912), 198–211.

130. Georges Baudot and María Águeda Méndez, *Amores prohibidos: la palabra condenada en el México de los Virreyes: Antología de coplas y versos censurados por la Inquisición de México* (México: Siglo Veintiuno, 1997), 51–57; Alejandro Martínez de la Rosa, "Censura de la Inquisición: 231 años de un son mexicano," *Antropología: Boletín Oficial del Instituto Nacional de Antropología e Historia*, no. 91 (2011), 22–26, https://revistas.inah.gob.mx/index.php/antropologia/article/view/2739/2641, cites *La danza en México. Visiones de cinco siglos. Volumen II: Antología: Cinco siglos de crónicas, crítica y documentos (1521–2002)*, edited by Maya Ramos Smith y Patricia Cardona Lang (México, Conaculta/Escenología, 2002), 111–17.

131. Hemispheric Institute, "Cuaderno/censura/danza: Los panaderos, Archivo General de la Nación," *Inquisición*, vol. 1178, exp. 2, ff. 24–36r. "Celaya año de 1779. Expediente formado con motivo del canto y Vayle, que llaman de los Panaderos," http://www.hemisphericinstitute.org/cuaderno/censura/html/danza/panaderos.htm.

132. Translation: Juan Pedro Viqueira Albán, Sonya Lipsett-Rivera, and Ayala S. Rivera, *Propriety and Permissiveness in Bourbon Mexico* (Wilmington, DE: Scholarly

Resources, 2004), 125; on persecuted dances, the authors cite Pablo González Casanova, *La literatura perseguida por la Inquisición*, (México: Ed. Contenido, 1992), 74.

133. Otero, *Tratado de Bailes*, 198–99, 201, 207; on panaderos as from Cádiz: Grut, et al., *The Bolero School*, 121; Grut also notates this dance: 353–57.

134. Otero, *Tratado de Bailes*, 207.

135. Goldberg, "Sonidos Negros," 96–98; Baird, Goldberg and Newman, "Changing Places," (2015): 636–67; (2016): 587–89.

136. The following sources are included in José Luis Navarro García's appendix on the Fandango: *Semillas de ébano: El elemento negro y afroamericano en el baile flamenco* (Sevilla: Portada Editorial, S. L., 1998), 199–216. Giuseppe Baretti, "Letter XXXVII, Elvas, Sept. 22, 1760, in the morning," *A Journey from London to Genoa: Through England, Portugal, Spain, and France*, vol. 2 (London: Printed for T. Davies..., and L. Davis, 1770), 48–50.

137. Hugh Thomas, *Beaumarchais in Seville: An Intermezzo* (New Haven, CT: Yale University Press, 2006), 120–21.

138. Jean F. Bourgoing, *Modern State of Spain...Translated from the Last Paris Edition of 1807...to Which Are Added, Essays on Spain by M. Peyron, and the Book of Post Roads. With...Atlas of Plates* (London: John Stockdale, 1808), 300–301, cited in Lou Charnon-Deutsch, "Like Salamanders in a Flame: The Fandango and Foreign Travellers to Spain," in Goldberg and Pizà, *Global Reach of the Fandango* (Spanish Edition 2015): 586–603; (2016): 536–52.

139. Étienne F. Lantier, *Oeuvres Complètes de E.f. de Lantier* (Paris: Bertrand, 1836), 253.

140. Marcellus Vittucci, "Matteo," with Carola Goya, *The Language of Spanish Dance* (Norman: University of Oklahoma Press, 1990), 142, 165.

141. I have argued that the pasada both structures the fandango syntactically and dances its sexy chase in Baird, Goldberg, and Newman, "Changing Places."

142. Otero, *Tratado*, 207.

143. Jeschke with Atwood, "Hispanomania," 98, cites Moreau de Saint-Méry, *De la danse*, 55.

144. Carpentier, *Music in Cuba*, 100–101.

145. Alejo Carpentier, *La música en Cuba* (México: Fondo de Cultura Económica, 1946), 66.

146. Quiñones de Benavente, *Entremés famoso: Don Gaiferos*, in *Entremeses nuevos* (Alcalá 1643), cited and reproduced in Cotarelo, *Entremeses*, ccxxx, 611–13.

147. Claudia Jeschke, Gabi Vettermann, and Nicole Haitzinger, *Les Choses Espagnoles: Research into the Hispanomania of 19th Century Dance* (Múnchen: epodium, 2009), 48–49.

148. Blasis and Barton, *Notes upon Dancing*, 24–25, cited in Jeschke, Vettermann, and Haitzinger, *Les Choses Espagnoles*, 40–41.

149. Campóo Schelotto, "Danza y educación nobiliaria," 165, cites Archivo Histórico Nacional, Universidades, 676, exp.1.

150. Juan Jacinto Rodríguez Calderón, *La bolerología o quadro de las escuelas del baile bolero, tales cuales eran en 1794 y 1795 en la corte de España* (Philadelphia: Zacarias Poulson, [1807] 1993), 4, 8, 17, 22, iv.

151. "Los bailes populares y truanescos que se introdujeron en los teatros y cundieron en el pueblo fueron muchos. Tales eran...'el Guineo, la Perra Mora, el Guiriguirigay...el villano o las zapatetas...el canario, o el zapateado.'" Pellicer, *Tratado histórico*, 126. Pellicer's list is in quotes, citing Caro, *Días geniales*, 64. This passage is cited often: in Russell, *Murcia*, 36; Cecilio de Roda, *Los instrumentos músicos y las danzas. Las canciones. Conferencias dadas en el Ateneo de Madrid, los días 1 y 13 de mayo de 1905 con ocasión del tercer centenario de el Ingenioso hidalgo don Quijote de la Mancha* (Madrid: B. Rodríguez, 1905), 25; and Weber de Kurlat, "El tipo del negro," 701.

152. Cairón, *Compendio*, 116, 114.

153. "danza haciendo castañetas, zapatetas y cabriolas, como en el villano." Caro, *Días geniales*, 200. Exekiel 25:6–7, New International Version.

154. Cotarelo, *Entremeses*, ccxxx, 611–13.

155. María José Ruiz Mayordomo, "Danza impresa durante el siglo XVIII en España: ¿inversión o bien de consumo?" in *Imprenta y edición musical en España (SS. XVIII–XX)*, edited by Begoña Lolo and Carlos José Gosálvez Lara (Madrid: Universidad Autónoma de Madrid, Ministerio de Economía y Competitividad, 2012), 132. For more on Minguet, see Esses, *Dance and Instrumental Diferencias*; and Clara Rico Osés, "French Dance in Eighteenth-Century Spain," *Dance Chronicle* 35, no. 2 (2012): 133–72.

156. Jones, "Fandango," (2015): 557; (2016): 522.

157. "...texidos y enlaces de pies." Felipe Roxo de Flores, *Tratado de recreacion instructiva sobre la danza: su invencion y diferencias* (Madrid: En la Imprenta Real, 1793), 101–102.

158. Cotarelo, *Entremeses*, clxxxi; Querol, *La música en la obra de Cervantes*, 152–53, citing Cervantes, "La gitanilla."

159. Shirley Spackman Wynne, *The Charms of Complaisance: The Dance in England in the Early Eighteenth Century* (doctoral dissertation, Ohio State University, 1967), 115; RAE, "polvo," http://dle.rae.es/?id=TbjKOoT.

160. Cotarelo, *Entremeses*, lxvii, clxxvii–ix, cclvii–viii, cclxviii, cites Salas Barbadillo's 1615 chapter *Curioso y sabio Alejandro* from the *Vida del tramoyero ridiculo*; and Padre Fray Juan de la Cerda in his *Vida política de todos los estados de mujeres* (Alcalá, 1499, 468).

161. Noveli, *Chorégraphie figurativa*, 135, f. 62.

162. "El villano: Baile que se acompaña su tañido dando golpes con las manos, y dándose alternativamente con ellas en los pies, y algunas veces en el suelo: se hacen varias posturas corriendo á un lado y á otro, y algunas veces sentándose en el suelo se elevan los pies haciendo una especie de patalatilla: este baile es propio de los labradores de las aldeas; razón porque se llamó villano." Cairón, *Compendio*, 123. RAE gives "pataleta" as a convulsion, especially when it's faked, or anger: http://dle.rae.es/?id=S7g9OGL.

163. Fra Molinero, *La imagen de los negros*, 2–17.

164. Irigoyen-García, *The Spanish Arcadia*, 29, cites Étienne Balibar and Immanuel M. Wallerstein, *Race, Nation, Class: Ambiguous Identities* (London [England]: Routledge, Chapman & Hall, 1991), 57–58.

165. Irigoyen-García, *The Spanish Arcadia*, 25.

166. See James Carroll, *Constantine's Sword: The Church and the Jews; A History* (Boston: Houghton Mifflin, 2002).

167. Casas, *Destruction of the Indies*. On Aristotle's "natural slave": Eze, *Race and the Enlightenment*, 4.

168. Basilio Sebastián Castellanos de Losada, Félix de Azara, and Agustín de Azara, *Glorias de Azara en el siglo XIX. Acta de la solemne inauguracion del monumento erigido en Barbuñales de Aragón, El 27 de noviembre de 1850, Al célebre diplomático...Don José Nicolás de Azara y Perera, Primer Marqués de Nibbiano, por Don Agustín de Azara, Tercer Marqués del Mismo Titulo...Corona (poético-Musical) que los poetas, orientalistas, hombres políticos, y artistas españoles, consagran al espresado señor. Obra escrita en parte y dirigida en lo demás por Don B.S. Castellanos de Losada* (Madrid, 1852), 888.

169. Estébanez Calderón, *Escenas Andaluzas*, 204–205.

170. Gaspar Úbeda y Castelló, "Villancico IX," *Letras de los villancicos, que se cantaron en la Iglesia Cathedral de Cadiz, en la kalenda, noche, y dias del nacimiento de N. Sr. Iesu-Christo este año de 1709* (1709), BNE R/34199/40, http://bdh-rd.bne.es/viewer.vm?id=0000060845&page=1.

171. "Monicongo" refers to an African place of origin: "Congo" or "Kongo": John M. Lipski, *A History of Afro-Hispanic Language: Five Centuries, Five Continents* (Cambridge [u.a.: Cambridge University Press, 2010), 41. But "monicongo" also may mean a scrawl, a ridiculous figure such as a puppet or a scarecrow placed somewhere to be mocked: Alfredo Edgardo Alvarez Ahumada, "monicongo," *Diccionario abierto de español*, http://www.significadode.org/monicongo.htm.

172. RAE, "jeta," http://dle.rae.es/?id=MRPSufz|MRQv4Hx.

173. For a discussion of the politics of the word "flamenco," see Goldberg, Bennahum, and Hayes, *Flamenco on the Global Stage*, 9–13. On Arará in eighteenth-century Spanish literature: Arturo Morgado García, "Guerra y esclavitud en el Cádiz de la modernidad," in Aurelia Martín Casares and Marga García Barranco, eds., *La esclavitud negroafricana en la historia de España siglos XVI y XVII* (Granada: Editorial Comares, S. L., 2010), 69; Swiadon Martínez, "Los personajes del villancico de negro," 603.

174. Henry Kamen, *Spain, 1469–1714: A Society of Conflict* (London: Routledge, 2005), 276–96.

175. The Spanish verb *compasar*, and the noun *compás*—English cognates are "encompass" and "compass"—mean "measure," in the sense of size or geography, as a musical measure, and also in the sense of measured or regulated behavior. RAE, "compás," http://dle.rae.es/?id=9zfD9l8. I am grateful to Kiko Mora and Nick Jones for help with this translation.

176. Goldberg, *Border Trespasses*, 163.

177. Katzew, *Casta Painting*, 44.

178. Antonio Rosales, *La jitanilla en el coliseo* (1776), in Subirá, *La tonadilla escénica*, vol. 3, 65–66, cited in Ricardo de la Fuente, "El personaje negro en la tonadilla escénica del siglo XVIII" *Revista de Folklore* vol. 4B, no. 48 (1984): 190–96, http://www.cervantesvirtual.com/obra-visor/el-personaje-del-negro-en-la-tonadilla-escenica-del-siglo-xviii/html/. On sneeze as a "customary sidewalk jeer," see Pike, "Sevillian Society," 357. On *axé*, Robert Farris Thompson, *Flash of the Spirit: African and Afro-American Art and Philosophy* (New York: Vintage Books, 1984), 5–9. On African retentions in these nonsense syllables, see Vodovozova, *Villancico de Negros*, 103–105.

179. Luis Misón, *Tonadilla de los negros* (1761), Musical score, http://www.memoriademadrid.es/buscador.php?accion=VerFicha&id=20810&num_id=1&

num_total=244&voto=5, "neglita gitana huachi": 3, 5, "vaylan con taconeo": 26. In Subirá, *La tonadilla escénica*, vol. 3 (Madrid: Tipografía de Archivos, 1928–1930), 109–10. Cited in de la Fuente Ballesteros, "El personaje negro en la tonadilla escénica del siglo XVIII," 190–96. http://www.cervantesvirtual.com/obra-visor/el-personaje-del-negro-en-la-tonadilla-escenica-del-siglo-xviii/html/.

180. RAE, "guacho/a/huacho/a," http://dle.rae.es/?id=JcowZHs. On Spanish *huacho*, and Quechua *huaccha* or *huacchu*, illegitimate child, orphan, or bastard: Diccionario etimológico español en línea, " 'huaso' o 'guaso,' " http://etimologias.dechile.net/?huaso. On Quechua *wakchu*, orphan: Glosbe, *Quechua-English Dictionary*, "wakchu," https://glosbe.com/qu/en/wakchu.

181. Ortiz, "Guaricha," *Glosario de afronegrismos*, 235–36, cites Manuel de Toro y Gispert Pequeño, *Larrouse ilustrado* (1919), and Manuel Gómez de la Maza, "Etimología correspondencia filológica de los supuestos nombres indocubanos de plantas y productos" (inédito); RAE, "guaricha," http://dle.rae.es/?id=JkR5l3F.

182. Ortiz, *Los instrumentos de la música afrocubana*, vol. 1, 132.

183. Pellicer, *Tratado histórico*, 138, cites Juan de Mariana, "Del baile y cantar llamado zarabanda," *Obras*, 432–34.

184. Roxo de Flores, *Tratado*, 101–102, 121.

185. Cairón, *Compendio*, 116, 114.

186. Cotarelo, *Entremeses*, cclxv, cites RAE, "zapateado," and Caro, *Días geniales*, 64.

187. The canario is also in Michael Praetorius's compendium of dance music (1612). Caroso, Sutton, and Walker, *Courtly Dance of the Renaissance*, 44–45, 110–11; Arbeau, *Orchesography*, 179–81; Cesare Negri, Rovere G. M. Della, and Leone Pallavicini, *Nuove Inventioni Di Balli:…* (Milano: G. Bordone, 1604), 198–202, https://www.loc.gov/search/?fa=segmentof:musdi.121.0/&q=Cesare+Negri+Rovere+Della+Leone+Pallavicini+Nuove+Inventioni+Di+Balli&st=gallery. See film of a canario step (Renaissance): reconstructed by Elizabeth Aldrich, Cheryl Stafford, dancer; Susan Manus, violin, music: canario from "Adda Felice" from *Nuove inventioni di balli*, based on descriptions found in Caroso, *Nobiltà di dame* (#199], sequito spezatto schischiato, p. 33; and Negri, *Nuove inventioni di balli*, (#121), sequito battuto al canario, p. 109, https://www.loc.gov/item/musdivid.035/. For a discussion of correspondences between the canario and flamenco footwork, see Goldberg, *Border Trespasses*, 92–93.

188. Ortiz, *Los instrumentos*, vol. 1, 132, cites Julio Ayllón Morgan, *Romancero Cubano (los De Abajo)* (La Habana, Cuba: Editorial Rebeldía estudiantil, 1946).

189. I am grateful to Raúl Fernández for help with this translation.

190. Ortiz, *Los instrumentos*, vol. 1, 132.

191. Fernando Ortiz, *Los factores humanos de la cubanidad* (Habana: Impreso por Molina y cia, 1940), translated and discussed in João Felipe Gonçalves and Gregory Duff Morton, "The ajiaco in Cuba and beyond: Translator's Preface to 'The human factors of cubanidad' by Fernando Ortiz," *HAU—Journal of Ethnographic Theory* 4, no. 3 (2014), 13, 24, https://www.haujournal.org/index.php/hau/article/view/hau4.3.031/1723.

192. Stevenson, "The Afro-American Musical Legacy," 496–97.

193. Ortiz, *Los instrumentos*, vol. 1, 133–34.

194. Ortiz, *Los instrumentos*, vol. 1, 133–34.

195. Ortiz, *Los instrumentos*, vol. 1, 133–34.

196. Ruiz Mayordomo, "El papel de la danza," 67; Arcadio Larrea Palacín, *El flamenco en su raíz* (Sevilla: Signatura, [1974] 2006), 70.

197. RAE, "guacharo," http://dle.rae.es/?id=JbloGVr; RAE, "esguachar/esguazar," http://dle.rae.es/?id=GQTKo2A.

198. Ruiz Mayordomo, "El papel de la danza," 67.

199. Estébanez Calderón, *Escenas andaluzas*, 204–205.

200. Goldberg, "*Jaleo de Jerez* and *Tumulte Noir*," 136–37.

201. Hughes, *Goya*, 383.

202. Pedraza Jiménez, "La génesis de la jácara," 80–81, 85.

203. Brown, *Babylon Girls*, 6. I have made this argument regarding the Spanish Roma in "The Use of the Ambivalent Image," in Goldberg, *Border Trespasses*, 35–42.

204. Henry Swinburne, *Travels through Spain, in the Years 1775 and 1776* (Dublin: Printed for S. Price, R. Cross, J. Williams [and 8 others], 1779), 353–54.

205. Alba y Diéguez, *Libro de la gitaneria*, 3–4, 21.

206. Roxo de Flores, *Tratado*, 101–102.

207. Rodríguez Calderón, *Bolerología*, 4, 8, 17, 22; Campóo Schelotto, "Danza y educación nobiliaria," 165.

208. "Baile gitano. El Zapateado: 15 Dec. 1806. Función a beneficio del barba. Por primera en un folleto conservado con esta especificación del baile gitano," cited in Plaza Orellana, *El flamenco y los románticos*, 722.

209. Théophile Gautier and Ivor F. Guest, "Théophile Gautier on Spanish Dancing," *Dance Chronicle* 10, no. 1 (1987): 94. According to Judith Chazin-Bennahum, the ballet is by Auber, costumes by Lecomte. Judith Chazin-Bennahum, *The Lure of Perfection: Fashion and Ballet, 1780–1830* (New York: Routledge, 2005), 197, fig. 66.

210. Sublette, *Cuba and Its Music*, 238, cites Argeliers León, *Del canto y el tiempo* (La Habana: Letras cubanas, 1984), 25.

211. Victoria Eli Rodríguez and María de los Ángeles Alfonso Rodríguez, "Tangos, habaneras y guarachas en la zarzuela española del siglo XIX," *La música entre Cuba y España: Tradición e innovación* (Madrid: Fundación Autor, 1999), 35–36.

212. Ortiz, *Los instrumentos*, 136–37, cites William C. Farabee, *The Central Caribs* (Philadelphia: University Museum, 1924), 233; and Nicolas Slonimsky, *Music of Latin America* (New York: Thomas Y. Crowell Company, 1946).

213. Ortiz, *Los instrumentos*, 136–37.

214. For a powerful portrait of such customs in México today, see Raquel Paraíso, "Re-Contextualizing Traditions and the Construction of Social Identities through Music and Dance: A Fandango in Huetamo, Michoacán," in Goldberg and Pizà, *The Global Reach of the Fandango* (Spanish Edition 2015): 435–51; (2016): 396–417. Paraíso's short film, "The Planting of the Tabla" may be viewed here: https://vimeo.com/133244148.

215. Saldívar, *Historia de la música en México*, 224, cited in Baudot and Méndez, "El Chuchumbé," 164.

216. Stevenson, "The Afro-American Musical Legacy," 496–97; Ortiz and Iznaga, *Los negros curros*, ix.

217. Enrique Guerrero, "Convidando está la Noche" ~ "Ay que me abraso" (Juguete a 4 y Guaracha) de Juan García de Céspedes (1619–1678), *YouTube*, https://www.youtube.com/watch?v=kXw8JZ3dYNM.

218. Goldberg, "Sonidos Negros," 98.

Chapter 3

1. See José Blas Vega, *Los cafés cantantes de Sevilla* (Madrid: Cinterco, 1987), and *Los cafés cantantes de Madrid: (1846–1936)* (Madrid: Ediciones Guillermo Blázquez, 2006). Also, Etzion, "Spanish Music," 110; Zoido, *La Ilustración contra los gitanos*, 201. Goldberg, "'El Firmamento' (Flamenco Society 1780–1913)," in *Border Trespasses*, 107–61, contains an earlier version of these arguments.

2. Federico Olmedo, "Canciones populares de la guerra de la independencia española," *La Ilustración Española y Americana*, vol. 32 (Madrid: August 30, 1908): 129–32, http://bdh.bne.es/bnesearch/detalle/0001216331

3. María Mercedes Romero Peña, *El teatro en Madrid a principios del siglo XIX (1808–1814), en especial el de la guerra de la independencia* (doctoral dissertation, Universidad Complutense de Madrid, 2006), 775.

4. Mora, "*Bailable Español*," in Goldberg, Bennahum, and Hayes, *Flamenco on the Global Stage*, 106; Romero Peña, *El teatro en Madrid*, 781–82.

5. Luis Lavaur, "Teoría romántica del cante flamenco," *Revista de Ideas Estéticas* (July–September, 1969): 7. This is one of a series of articles Lavaur wrote beginning in 1968, published in book form as *Teoría romántica del cante flamenco* (Madrid: Editora Nacional, 1976). See also José Subirá's discussion on the polemic regarding ancient Spanish seguidillas sung to guitar accompaniment versus popular imitations of Italian opera at the turn of the nineteenth century, in *La tonadilla escénica*, vol. 2, 218–20.

6. Lavaur, "Teoría romántica," 5, 8. For more on the migrations and permutations of Italian opera and Italian performers in eighteenth-century Spain, see Cotarelo, *Orígenes y establecimiento de la opera en España. hasta 1800* (Madrid: Tip. de la "Revista de arch., bibl., y museos," 1917).

7. Carlos III banned the *auto da fé* as "indecorous" in 1765. Kant, "On National Characteristics," in *Race and the Enlightenment*, edited by Emmanuel Chukwudi Eze (Malden, MA: Blackwell Publishers, 1997), 51.

8. Dominique Dufour de Pradt, *Mémoires historiques sur la révolution d'Espagne* (Paris: Rosa [etc.], 1816), 168, cited and translated in, Kalabeul, "The True Origins of 'Africa Begins at the Pyrenees,'" *London's Singing Organ Grinder* blog, February 5, 2010, http://oreneta.com/kalebeul/2010/05/02/the-true-origins-of-africa-begins-at-the-pyrenees/. Cited in Goldberg, "Sonidos Negros," 93.

9. Parakilas, "How Spain Got a Soul," 138–39.

10. Gerhard Steingress, "La Aparición del Cante Flamenco en el Teatro Jerezano del Siglo XIX," in *Dos Siglos de Flamenco: Actas de la Conferencia Internacional. Jerez 21–25 junio, 1988* (Jerez de la Frontera: Fundación Andaluza de Flamenco, 1989), 351. See also Ballesteros, "El personaje negro," *Revista de Folklore* 4B, no. 48 (1984): 190–96, http://www.cervantesvirtual.com/obra-visor/el-personaje-del-negro-en-la-tonadilla-escenica-del-siglo-xviii/html/; Ballesteros, "El moro en la tonadilla escénica," *Revista de Folklore* 5A, no. 49 (1985): 32–36, http://www.cervantesvirtual.com/obra/revista-de-folklore-125/; and Ballesteros, "Los gitanos en la tonadilla escénica," *Revista de Folklore* 4A, no. 40 (1984): 122–26, http://www.cervantesvirtual.com/obra/revista-de-folklore-13/.

11. Lavaur, "Teoría romántica," 14. "The first duty in life is to be as artificial as possible," Wilde famously writes in *Phrases and Philosophies for the Use of the Young* (1894). Oscar Wilde, *The Plays of Oscar Wilde* (Ware: Wordsworth, 2000), xv.

12. Washington Irving, *The Alhambra: a Series of Tales and Sketches of the Moors and Spaniards* (Philadelphia: Carey, Lea & Blanchard, 1837); Prosper Mérimée, *Carmen* (Paris: M. Lévy frères, 1846); Théophile Gautier, *A Romantic in Spain*, translated by Catherine Allison Phillips (New York: Interlink Books, [1926] 2001); Reynaldo Fernández Manzano, "La Granada de Glinka (1845–1846)," *Los papeles españoles de Glinka* (Madrid: Consejería de Educación y Cultura, Comunidad de Madrid, 1996), 19–24; Jean-Charles Davillier and John Thomson, translation, *Spain, by the Baron Ch. Davillier, illustrated by Gustave Doré...* (London: S. Low, Marston, Low and Searle, 1876), 186–89.

13. María Elena Sánchez Ortega, "Evolucion y contexto historico de los gitanos españoles," in *Entre la marginación y el racismo: Reflexiones sobre la vida de los gitanos*, edited by Teresa San Román (Madrid: Alianza Editorial S.A., 1986), 45–46.

14. Borrow, *Zincali*, 15.

15. Diana Taylor, *The Archive and the Repertoire: Performing Cultural Memory in the Americas* (Durham, NC: Duke University Press, 2003), 20; Misón, *Tonadilla de los Negros*. Cristina Cruces Roldán's concepts of flamenco *de uso*, everyday flamenco, and *de cambio*, or commercial flamenco, are useful here. See Cristina Cruces Roldán, *Más allá de la música (II). Antropología y flamenco: Identidad, género y trabajo* (Sevilla: Signatura, 2003).

16. Lavaur, "Teoría romántica," 20.

17. On Rice: Art and Picture Collection, The New York Public Library, "T. D. Rice as the Original 'Jim Crow'; James Roberts in the Song 'Massa George Washington and Massa Lafayette,'" *The New York Public Library Digital Collections* (1889), http://digitalcollections.nypl.org/items/510d47e0-fc18-a3d9-e040-e00a18064a99; on Blakely and Signora Ferreiro: Laurence Hutton, *Curiosities of the American Stage* (New York: Harper & Brothers, 1891), 122–23.

18. Rocío Plaza Orellana, "Spanish Dance in Europe: From the Late Eighteenth Century to its Consolidation on the European Stage," in Goldberg, Bennahum, and Hayes, *Flamenco on the Global Stage*, 71–80.

19. Antonio Cairón, *El encuentro feliz o Los americanos o La espada del mago* (1818), Biblioteca Histórica Municipal de Madrid (BHM) MUS 605–7, http://catalogos.munimadrid.es/cgi-bin/historica/O7709/ID22f2cd2e/NT1.

20. Plaza Orellana, "Spanish Dance in Europe," 71–80; Harris-Warrick and Brown, *The Grotesque Dancer*; María José Ruiz Mayordomo and Aurèlia Pessarrodona, "Choreological Gestures in Iberian Music of the Second Half of the Eighteenth Century: A Proposal for Historically Informed Performance of the Fandango," in Goldberg and Pizà, *The Global Reach of the Fandango in Music* (Spanish Edition 2015): 666–719; (2016): 622–67.

21. Castellanos de Losada, *Glorias de Azara en el siglo XIX. Acta de la solemne inauguracion del monumento erigido en Barbuñales de Aragón, El 27 de noviembre de 1850, Al célebre diplomático... Don José Nicolás de Azara y Perera, Primer Marqués de Nibbiano, por Don Agustín de Azara, Tercer Marqués del Mismo Titulo... Corona (poético-Musical) que los poetas, orientalistas, hombres políticos, y artistas españoles, consagran al espresado señor. Obra escrita en parte y dirigida en lo demás por Don B.S. Castellanos de Losada* (Madrid, 1852), 865–66.

22. "Teatros," *Diario de Madrid*, no. 120 (May 1, 1818), 582; "Teatros," *Diario de Madrid* no. 183 (July 3, 1818), 4; cited in Núñez, *Guía*, 97.

23. See José Luis Ortiz Nuevo y Faustino Núñez, *La rabia del placer: El nacimiento cubano del tango y su desembarco en España (1823–1923)* (Sevilla: Diputación de Sevilla, Área de Cultura y Ecología, 1999).

24. On the circulation of U.S. blackface minstrelsy in Europe, see Hans Nathan, "Negro Impersonation in Eighteenth Century England," *Notes, Second Series* 2, no. 4 (September 1945), 245–54; Hans Nathan, *Dan Emmett and the Rise of Early Negro Minstrelsy* (Norman: University of Oklahoma Press, 1962); Thomas L. Riis, "The Experience and Impact of Black Entertainers in England, 1895–1920," *American Music* 4, no. 1, *British-American Musical Interactions* (Spring 1986): 50–58; Rainer E. Lotz, "The 'Louisiana Troupes' in Europe," *The Black Perspective in Music* 11, no. 2 (Autumn 1983): 133–42; and Stephen Johnson, "Juba's Dance: An Assessment of newly acquired documentation," *Proceedings of the Twenty-Sixth Annual Conference, University of Limerick, Limerick, Ireland, 26–29 June, 2003* (United States: Society of Dance History Scholars, 2003), http://www.utm.utoronto.ca/~w3minstr/featured/pdfs/JubasDance.pdf.

25. Following her 1840–1842 tour of the United States, Elssler's cachucha was performed by Christy's Minstrels in 1847, the Virginia Serenaders in 1849, and White's Serenaders in 1853. William J. Mahar, *Behind the Burnt Cork Mask: Early Blackface Minstrelsy and Antebellum American Popular Culture* (Urbana: University of Illinois Press, 1999), 9, 56, 370. On Elssler's visit to the US: Ninotchka Bennahum, "Early Spanish Dancers on the New York Stage," in *100 Years of Flamenco in New York City* by Ninotchka Devorah Bennahum and K. Meira Goldberg (New York: New York Public Library for the Performing Arts, 2013), 27–57.

26. Ortiz, *Los instrumentos*, vol. 1, 133–34.

27. Sublette, *Cuba and Its Music*, 171–72, cites José Luciano Franco, "The slave trade in the Caribbean and Latin America," in *The African Slave Trade from the fifteenth to the nineteenth century* (Paris: UNESCO, 1979), 96, 238–39; José Luis Ortiz Nuevo, *Tremendo Asombro* (Sevilla: Libros con Duende, S.A., 2012), 81, cites *El Regañón*, February 23, 1800. For an examination of Spain's uptake of the early-twentieth century cakewalk in terms of the flamenco tango, see Goldberg, "*Jaleo de Jerez* and *Tumulte Noir.*"

28. Vodovozova, *Villancico de negros*, 27; Alfonso Franco Silva, *La esclavitud en Andalucía, 1450–1550* (Granada: University of Granada, 1992), 47–48.

29. Domínguez Ortiz, *La esclavitud*, 37, 39; Rumeu de Armas, *España en el África atlántica*, 163.

30. Aurelia Martín Casares and Marga García Barranco, "Legislation on Free Soil in Nineteenth-Century Spain: The Case of the Slave Rufino and Its Consequences (1858–1879)," *Slavery & Abolition* 32, no. 3 (2011): 461–76; and Martín Casares, "Evolution of the Origin of Slaves," 415.

31. Meyer Weinberg, *A Short History of American Capitalism* (New History Press, 2002), 41, cites Russell R. Menard, "Economic and Social Development of the South," in *The Cambridge Economic History of the United States*, vol. 1: The Colonial Era, edited by Stanley L. Engerman and Robert E. Gallman (Cambridge University Press, 1996).

32. Ta-Nehisi Coates, "Slavery Made America: The Case for Reparations, a Narrative Bibliography," *The Atlantic* (June 24, 2014), https://www.theatlantic.com/business/archive/2014/06/slavery-made-america/373288/. Cites David Blight, HIST 119: THE CIVIL WAR AND RECONSTRUCTION ERA, 1845–1877, *Open Yale Courses*, http://oyc.yale.edu/history/hist-119, and Roger Ransom, "Economics of the Civil War," *EH.Net*

Encyclopedia, edited by Robert Whaples (August 24, 2001), http://eh.net/encyclopedia/the-economics-of-the-civil-war/.

33. Eric Lott, *Love and Theft: Blackface Minstrelsy and the American Working Class* (New York: Oxford University Press, 1993), 17.

34. Lott, *Love and Theft*, 29, on "blackface-on-black violence," cites Susan G. Davis, "'Making Night Hideous': Christmas Revelry and Public Order in Nineteenth-Century Philadelphia," *American Quarterly* 34, no. 2 (1982): 185–99.

35. On "white egalitarianism:" Lott, *Love and Theft*, 29, cites Alexander Saxton, *The Rise and Fall of the White Republic: Class Politics and Mass Culture in Nineteenth-Century America* (London: Verso, 1990). On legislative and procedural efforts to "foster the contempt of whites for blacks and Indians," for example, in 1682, the Commonwealth of Virginia "declared Indians and Africans were declared to be the only persons subject to enslavement." Weinberg, *A Short History of American Capitalism*, cites Edmund S. Morgan, *American Slavery, American Freedom: The Ordeal of Colonial Virginia* (New York: W. W. Norton & Company Inc., 2003).

36. Lott, "Blackface and Blackness," 20–21. *Uncle Tom's Cabin* premiered on July 18, 1852, with an all-white cast. Gerlyn E. Austin, "The Advent of the Negro Actor on the Legitimate Stage in America," *Journal of Negro Education* 35, no. 3 (1966): 237; Thomas L. Riis, "The Music and Musicians in Nineteenth-Century Productions of Uncle Tom's Cabin," *American Music* 4, no. 3 (Autumn 1986): 268–86.

The work was widely disseminated, and even translated into Yiddish: Isaac Meir Dik and Eli Rosenblatt, translation, "די שקלאַפֿערײַ אָדער די לײַב־אײגנשאַפֿט": Slavery or Serfdom" [a Yiddish translation of Harriet Beecher Stowe's *Uncle Tom's Cabin*] *In geveb: A Journal of Yiddish Studies* (December 2015), 1–21 https://ingeveb.org/texts-and-translations/slavery-or-serfdom. Many of the characters from this work spun off as independent characters: see Brown, *Babylon Girls*, 56–91.

37. "...bend your back joyfully and hopefully to the burden." Hartman, *Scenes of Subjection*, 135 cites Isaac W. Brinckerhoff, *Advice to Freedmen* (New York: American Tract Society, 1864).

38. Hartman, *Scenes of Subjection*, 32.

39. Hartman, *Scenes of Subjection*, 32; Cotarelo, *Entremeses*, cxcii–ciii, clxxxix.

40. Lavaur, "Teoría romántica," 17. On the economics of the slave trade in Spain, see *Negreros y esclavos Barcelona y la esclavitud atlántica (siglos XVI–XIX)*, edited by Lizbeth J. Chaviano Pérez and Martín Rodrigo y Alharilla (Barcelona: Icaria Editorial, 2017).

41. Lavaur, "Teoría romántica," 19–20, cites Antonio Machado y Álvarez, "Demófilo," *Colección de cantes flamencos recogidos y anotados* (Sevilla, 1881); Felipe Pedrell, *Por nuestra música* (Barcelona: Tip. de V. Berdós y Feliu, 1897); and Felipe Pedrell, *Cancionero musical popular español* (Valls: Eduardo Castells, 1922). Pedrell's appendix in the *Cancionero* on "Los cantos flamencos" (83–86) lays out this era's problematic identification of flamenco either with the "Bohemians" (Roma), the Flemish troops who came to Spain during the reign of Carlos V (1516–1556)—the explanation which Pedrell favors—or the Orientalizing explanation that flamenco derives from the music of "African Arabs." For more on these dynamics, see Mora and Goldberg, "Spain in the Basement."

42. Antonio Machado y Álvarez, "Demófilo," *Primeros Escritos Flamencos (1869–70–71)* (Fernán Núñez, Córdoba: Ediciones Demófilo, 1981), 10.

43. Jill Lane, *Blackface Cuba, 1840–1895* (Philadelphia: University of Pennsylvania Press, 2005), 70–71. Arderius was also known for his parody of a Mexican character, "Pancho." Víctor Sánchez Sánchez, "La habanera en la zarzuela española del siglo diecinueve: idealización marinera de un mundo tropical," *Cuadernos de Música, Artes Visuales y Artes Escénicas* 3, no. 1 (Octubre–Marzo, 2007): 12.

44. *La España musical*, no. 34 (Barcelona: September 6, 1866), 2.

45. Valentín Gómez, "Los Bufos Madrileños," *El Pensamiento español* (Madrid, September 20, 1866), 4.

46. See del Campo and Cáceres, "Los Morenos Andaluces," in *Historia cultural del flamenco*, 121–39.

47. Lavaur, "Teoría romántica," 12.

48. Zoido, *La ilustración contra los gitanos*, 17, 18, 20. See also Roger Bartra, *Cultura y melancolía: Las enfermedades del alma en la España del Siglo de Oro* (Barcelona: Editorial Anagrama, 2001).

49. Lavaur, "Teoría romántica," 14, 22–24; cites Hugo Schuchardt, *Die Cantes Flamencos* (Halle: E. Karras, 1881).

50. Hartman, *Scenes of Subjection*, 7, cites Morrison, *Playing in the Dark*, 17.

51. Lott, "Blackface and Blackness," 13.

52. Luis Olona (libretto) and Francisco Asenjo Barbieri (score), *Entre mi mujer y el negro. Zarzuela–disparate en dos actos. Representada por primera vez en el teatro de la Zarzuela en octubre de 1859* (Madrid: José Rodriguez, 1859) http://bdh-rd.bne.es/viewer.vm?id=0000104604&page=1, page 5.

53. E. V. de M. "Revista Coreográfica Musical—Crucistas y Circuistas—Muerte de la ópera española antes de haber nacido." *La España* (Madrid: April 30, 1848), 4.

54. On *zapitusé*, see Mora, *"Bailable,"* 113, 115.

55. "Leemos en La España," *La Esperanza* (June 30, 1848), 4; "La población entera canta," *El Observador*, no. 136 (June 30, 1848), 3; "Observaciones de la *España*," *El Heraldo* (July 1, 1848), 4; "El ayuntamiento empedrador de esta capital ha prohibido *El Tango Americano*," *El Papamoscas y su tío* (August 4, 1848), 8.

56. "La flor de la canela," "Gisela y las Wilis," *Diario oficial de avisos de Madrid* (April 5 and 6, 1850), 4; "Teatro de la Comedia," "Teatro de la Ópera," *La Nación* (April 6, 1850), 4; Mora, *"Bailable,"* 113. Guy-Stéphan had accompanied illustrious ballet choreographer Marius Petipa to Spain in 1843, and been "baptized" as "Andalusian" at a flamenco party in Triana in 1846. Marius Petipa, *Russian Ballet Master: The Memoirs of Marius Petipa*, edited by Lillian Moore, translated by Helen Whittaker (London: Adam and Charles Black, 1958), 14–15; Serafín Estébanez Calderón, "El Solitario," "Asamblea General de los Caballeros y Damas de Triana y toma el hábito de la órden de cierta rubia bailadora," in *Escenas andaluzas*, 243–72.

57. "Teatros," *El Observador*, no. 113 (June 3, 1848), 4: tango danced by four couples; "El Tango Americano," *Diario oficial de avisos de Madrid* (June 4, 1848), 4: six couples dance; "El que de ageno [*sic*] se viste," *Diario oficial de avisos de Madrid* (December 25, 1849), 4.

58. Mora, *"Bailable,"* 105–7, 112. One of the first mentions of flamenco as a form of music and dance is in an article by Eduardo Velaz de Medrano in the Madrid *Gacetilla* dated February 18, 1853. Faustino Núñez, "Música flamenca, Madrid 1853 y 54," *El Afinador de Noticias*, July 25, 2011, http://elafinadordenoticias.blogspot.com/2011/06/musica-flamenca-madrid-1853.html.

59. Eusebio Rioja, *El arte flamenco de Málaga—Los cafés cantantes (V): Una aproximación a sus historias y a sus ambientes*, part 2 (Málaga: Jondoweb.com, 2014), 12, cites *El Avisador Malagueño*, September 20 and 31, 1849, http://www.jondoweb.com/archivospdf/loscafescantantesdemalaga5_2.pdf.

60. Rafael Marín y Reus, *Método para guitarra: aires andaluces (flamenco): Único en su género* (Madrid: Sociedad de Autores Españoles, 1902), 177–78, cited in Rioja, *Flamenco en Málaga*, part 2, 14–15.

61. The *gracioso* is a comic character which emerged in the work of Lope de Vega at the turn of the seventeenth century. Some scholars have argued this figure derives from Harlequin (who arrived in Spain ca. 1579) and from the pastor bobo. Edwin B. Place, "Does Lope de Vega's Gracioso Stem in Part from Harlequin?" *Hispania* 17, no. 3 (October 1934): 257–70; Brotherton, *The Pastor-Bobo*; F. William Forbes, "The 'Gracioso:' Toward a Functional Re-Evaluation," *Hispania*, 61, no. 1 (March, 1978): 78–83; Cazal, "Del pastor bobo al gracioso," 7–18.

62. José Antonio Lacárcel Fernández, "El Tío Canyitas: La zarzuela andaluza y la presencia de Andalucía en la prensa musical española," *Música Oral del Sur*, no. 11 (2014): 208–209; cites Mariano Soriano Fuertes, *Historia de la música española*, vol. 4 (Madrid: Ediciones del ICCMU, [1859] 2007), 389.

63. Emilio Cotarelo y Mori, *Historia de la Zarzuela o sea el drama lírico en España, desde su origen a fines del siglo XIX* (Madrid: Tipografía de Archivos, Ozólaga, 1934), 299–303, quoted in José Lacárcel, "El Tío Canyitas," 210.

64. Lacárcel, "El Tío Canyitas," 207.

65. Steingress, "La Aparición del Cante Flamenco," 351.

66. José Sanz Pérez, (libretto), and Mariano Soriano Fuertes, (music), *El Tío Caniyitas o El Mundo nuevo de Cádiz: Ópera cómica española, en dos actos* (Cádiz: Imprenta, Librería y Litografía de la Revista Médica, á cargo de D. Juan de Gaona, 1850), scene 1, p. 8, http://www.bibliotecavirtualdeandalucia.es/catalogo/es/consulta/registro.cmd?id=1000443.

67. Davillier, *Spain*, 404.

68. Steingress records *Caniyitas* performances in Córdoba in 1854, 1863, 1866, 1867, 1868, 1869—at which performance a young woman sang "Las malagueñas," 1871, 1872—the year before "El Negro Meri" sang flamenco for the first time recorded in that city, and 1876. Gerhard Steingress, *La presencia del género flamenco en la prensa local de Granada y Córdoba desde mitades del siglo XIX hasta el año de la publicación de Los Cantes Flamencos de Antonio Machado y Álvarez (1881)* (Sevilla: Libro Blanco del Flamenco, August 2008), 20, 88, 117, 124, 128, 132, 136, 142, 145, 152, https://www.juntadeandalucia.es/cultura/redportales/comunidadprofesional/sites/default/files/presenciaflamencoprensagranadacordoba.pdf.

69. Lacárcel, "El Tío Canyitas," 207–14.

70. Sanz Pérez and Soriano Fuertes, *El Tío Caniyitas*, scene 1, p. 7.

71. On *cucurucucu*: Posner, "Sfessania," 205–207; On *gurumbé* in Francisco de Avellaneda's 1663 *Bayle entremesado de negros*: Martín Casares and Barranco, "Black African Weddings," 109.

72. Sanz Pérez and Soriano Fuertes, *El Tío Caniyitas*, scene 1, p. 8.

73. Pastora Pavón sang this tag in the rhythm of tangos. Puentesiete, "Flamenco.—La Niña de los Peines: Al Gurugú: Tangos," *YouTube* (Jan. 30, 2011), https://www.

youtube.com/watch?v=rWtYV1Q5Zkg. See Cristina Cruces Roldán, *La Niña de los Peines: El mundo flamenco de Pastora Pavón* (Córdoba: Almuzara, 2009), 542. On Pepe de la Matrona: Mora, *"Bailable,"* 113.

74. bell hooks (Gloria Watkins), "Eating the Other—Desire and Resistance," *Black Looks: Race and Representation* (Boston, MA: South End Press, 1992), 25.

75. Gaspar María de Nava Álvarez, Conde de Noroña, "La Quicayda—Canto VII," in *Poesías*, vol. 1 (Madrid: Por Vega y Compañía, 1799), 318, cited in Ángel Álvarez Caballero, *Historia del cante flamenco* (Madrid: Alianza Editorial, S.A., 1981), 27.

76. Gustavo Adolfo Bécquer "La Feria de Sevilla," *El Museo Universal*, April 25, 1869. Reproduced in Mario Penna, "Las 'rimas' de Bécquer y la poesía popular," *Revista de Filologia Española* 52 (1969): 200.

77. Hartman, *Scenes of Subjection*, 35–36, quotes Gilroy, *The Black Atlantic*, 37.

78. See Ta-Nehisi Coates, "The Miscegenation Ball," *The Atlantic Monthly*, June 24, 2010, http://www.theatlantic.com/national/archive/2010/06/the-miscegenation-ball/58149/.

Chapter 4

Note to Epigraph: "...vista la ridícula figura de los criados cuando dan a beber a sus señores, haciendo el Coliseo, el Guineo, inclinando con notable peligro y asco todo el cuerpo demasiado; y siendo mudos de boca, son habladores de pies..." Francisco de Quevedo, "Premática del tiempo," *Obras satíricas y festivas*, edited by José M. Salaverría (Madrid: Espasa Calpe, 1965 [1627]), 59.

1. Horacio J. Becco, *El tema del negro en cantos, bailes y villancicos de los siglos XVI y XVII* (Buenos Aires: Ollantay, 1951), 15.

2. Liu, *Medieval Joke Poetry*, 7, cites Émile Benveniste, "La blasphémie et l'euphémie," *Problemes de linguistique générale*, vol. 2 (Paris: Gallimard, 1966–1974), 255–57.

3. Pedrosa, "Zangorromangos," 138–42.

4. *"[D]ango, dingo...tráxolo el mio Mingo."* Pedrosa, "Zangorromangos," 158–59, cites Aurelio de Llano Roza de Ampudia, *Del folklore asturiano: mitos, supersticiones, creencias* (Oviedo: Instituto De Estudios Asturianos, 1972), 246–47.

5. Liu, *Medieval Joke Poetry*, 12; cites María Ana Ramos "La satire dans les Cantigas d'escarnho e de mal dizer: Les péchés de la langue," *Atalaya* 5 (1994): 67–84.

6. Stern, "Fray Iñigo," 205; Stein, "Eros, Erato, Terpsíchore," 668–70.

7. Liu, *Medieval Joke Poetry*, 22, cites Cantigas D'Escarnho e de Mal Dizir (CEM), 408.

8. Úbeda y Castelló, "Villancico IX"; Martín Casares and Barranco, "Popular Literary Depictions of Black African Weddings," 109. Skin color was not always ignored in early modern Spanish literature. For example, Quevedo, in his "Boda de negros" (Wedding of Blacks) compares black husband and wife in bed to the image of ink on cotton ("acostados parecerán sus dos cuerpos...algodones y tinteros"). Francisco de Quevedo, "Boda de negros," in *Obras festivas*, edited by Pablo Antonio de Tarsia (Madrid: F. de P. Mellado, 1844–45), 307, cited in Goldberg, "Sonidos Negros," 102.

9. "Encorvada...una dança descompuesta, que se haze torciendo el cuerpo y los miembros, 'ab incurbando.' A ésta sucedió la çaravanda [zarabanda], y parece ser nieta suya la chacona..." Covarrubias (1611), 349v; RAE, "descompuesto," http://dle.rae.es/?id=CgwifZ8.

10. *El Doctor Soleda*: Cotarelo, *Entremeses*, ccxliii; RAE, "endiablado," http://dle.rae.es/?id=FCvYfjU; "picazón," http://dle.rae.es/?id=SuoeRDW.

11. Esses, *Dance and Instrumental Diferencias*, 527–28, cites (among others) Caro, *Días geniales*. Esses does not provide a translation for the verse quoted above, which he also quotes, and there is no definition for *larenzado* in RAE. I wonder, however, whether the reference to putting on garlic may have something to do with protection against evil?

12. L[illian] H[all], "Harvard Library Notes. Some Early Black-face Performers and the First Minstrel Troupe," no. 2 (1920): 43–44, cites C. L. "An Old Actor's Memories—What Mr. Edmon S. Connor Recalls About his Career. An Old Stock Actor's Stories of the Days of Stock Companies—Joe Jefferson's Infancy—Early Days in Cincinnati—Hiram Power's Wax Works—Jim Crow Rice," *The New York Times* (June 5, 1881), 10.

13. Many excellent books deal with this subject matter. Among them: Fra Molinero, *La imagen de los negros* (1995); Martínez, *Genealogical Fictions* (2008); and Martínez, Nirenberg, and Hering Torres, *Race and Blood* (2012).

14. See Pierre Pellegrin, "Natural Slavery," translated by E. Zoli Filotas, in *The Cambridge Companion to Aristotle's Politics*, edited by Marguerite Deslauriers and Pierre Destrée (Cambridge, England: Cambridge University Press, 2013), 92–116.

15. Heuer, *The Discourse of the Ruffian*, 128, quotes Herrero, "Renaissance Poverty," 883–84.

16. Casas, *Destruction of the Indies*, 32.

17. Ned and Constance Sublette, *The American Slave Coast: A History of the Slave-Breeding Industry* (Chicago: Lawrence Hill Books, 2016).

18. Saidiya V. Hartman, *Scenes of Subjection: Terror, Slavery, and Self-Making in Nineteenth-Century America* (New York: Oxford University Press, 1997), 7; Ta-Nehisi Coates, *Between the World and Me* (New York: Spiegel & Grau, 2015), 21.

19. Hartman, *Scenes of Subjection*, 35–36, quotes Gilroy, *The Black Atlantic*, 37.

20. Frederick Douglass, John Stauffer, and Henry L. Gates, *The Portable Frederick Douglass* (New York: Penguin Books, 2016), 207.

21. George F. Rehin, "Harlequin Jim Crow: Continuity and Convergence in Blackface Clowning," *Journal of Popular Culture* 9, no. 3 (Winter 1975): 686.

22. Lemuel Johnson, *The Devil, the Gargoyle, and the Buffoon: The Negro As Metaphor in Western Literature* (Port Washington, NY: Kennikat Press, 1971), 36.

23. Kim Hall, *Things of Darkness: Economies of Race and Gender in Early Modern England* (Ithaca, NY: Cornell University Press, 1995), 138.

24. Rehin, "Harlequin Jim Crow," 686.

25. Rehin, "Harlequin Jim Crow," 696.

26. Luis Vélez de Guevara, edited and introduced by Adolfo Bonilla y San Martin, *El diablo cojuelo por Luis Vélez de Guevara–reproducción de la edición príncipe de Madrid, 1641* (Vigo: Librería de Eugenio Krapf, 1902), 12 (f. 5v).

27. Vélez de Guevara and Bonilla y San Martin, *El diablo cojuelo*, 13–14 (f. 7v); cited in Marcella Trambaioli, "Apuntes sobre el guineo o baile de negros: tipologías y funciones dramáticas," edited by María Luisa Lobato y Francisco Domínguez Matito, *Actas de los Congresos de la Asociación Internacional Siglo de Oro (1987–2005)* 6, no. 2 (2004): 1775–76.

28. Joellen A. Meglin, "Le Diable Boiteux: French Society behind a Spanish Façade," *Dance Chronicle* 17, no. 3 (1994): 264.

29. Jules Perrot's *La Esmeralda*, named for the Roma protagonist in Hugo's novel, premiered in 1844. Théophile Gautier, "Fanny Elssler in 'Le Diable Boiteux' " (1845), in *The Romantic Ballet as Seen by Théophile Gautier*, translated and edited by Cyril Beaumont (New York: Books for Libraries, 1980), 15; cited in Goldberg, "Sonidos," 92. For a wonderful compilation and translation of Gautier's writing on Spanish dance, see Théophile Gautier and Ivor F. Guest, "Théophile Gautier on Spanish Dancing," *Dance Chronicle* 10, no. 1 (1987): 1–104.

30. Meglin, "Le Diable Boiteux," 267. See also Bonilla's discussion of the Lesage *Diable Boiteux* in Vélez de Guevara and Bonilla y San Martin, *El diablo cojuelo*, xxxii–iv.

31. Tomko, "Magri's *Grotteschi*," 162, cites Mikhail Bakhtin, *Rabelais and His World* (Bloomington: Indiana University Press, 1984), 323, 319.

32. Rebecca Harris-Warrick and Carol G. Marsh, *Musical Theatre at the Court of Louis XIV: Le Mariage de la Grosse Cathos* (Cambridge, England: Cambridge University Press, 1994), 153.

33. Bruce Alan Brown, "Magri in Vienna," in *The Grotesque Dancer*, 63, quotes Gasparo Angiolini, *Lettere di Gasparo Angiolini a Monsieur Noverre sopra i balli pantomimi* (Milan: G. B. Bianchi, 1773), 12–14.

34. S. Foster Damon, "The Negro in Early American Songsters," *Papers of the Bibliographical Society of America* 28 (1934): 133, cites George C. D. Odell, *Annals of the New York Stage*, vol. 1 (New York: Columbia University Press, 1927), 103, 151.

35. Damon, "The Negro in Early American Songsters," 133; and Nathan, "Negro Impersonation," 252; Hutton, *Curiosities*, 94.

36. Hans Nathan, "The activities of the English Composer Charles Dibdin," in Hans Nathan, *Dan Emmett and the Rise of Early Negro Minstrelsy* (Norman: University of Oklahoma Press, 1962), 20–31; and Nathan, "Negro Impersonation," in Nathan, *Dan Emmett*, 252. See also Thomas Davies, *Memoirs of the Life of David Garrick, Esq: Interspersed with Characters and Anecdotes of His Theatrical Contemporaries. The Whole Forming a History of the Stage, Which Includes a Period of Thirty-Six Years.* (London: printed for the author, and sold at his shop, 1780), 169–70.

37. Miguel de Cervantes, "El celoso extremeño," *Novelas Ejemplares*, (Colombia: Panamericana Editorial, [1613] 1993), 131–64.

38. Stevenson, "The Afro-American Musical Legacy," 485.

39. Howard Mancing, *The Cervantes Encyclopedia, A–K* (Westport, CT: Greenwood Press, 2004), 118.

40. Querol, *La música en la obra de Cervantes*, 35–37, 42–43, 86–89.

41. Rehin, "Harlequin Jim Crow," 683; H[all], "Some Early Black-face Performers," 39–45; Damon, "The Negro in Early American Songsters," 133; Nathan, "Negro Impersonation," 252–53.

42. Nathan, *Dan Emmett*, 15, 34, cites Damon, "The Negro in Early American Songsters," 134–35, and on Sambo: [Hall] "Some Early Black-Face Performers," 41–42. Katzew, *Casta Painting*, 44.

43. Hutton, *Curiosities*, 93.

44. Nathan, "Negro Impersonation," 252, cites Charles Dibdin and Anker Smith, *The Professional Life of Mr. Dibdin, Written by Himself. Together with the Words of Six Hundred Songs Selected from His Works and Sixty Small Prints Taken from the Subjects of the Songs, and Invented, Etched, and Prepared for the Aqua Tint by Miss Dibdin*, vol. 1 (London: Published by the author, 1803), 69. See also Peter A. Tasch, *The Dramatic*

Cobbler: The Life and Works of Isaac Bickerstaff (Lewisburg: Bucknell University Press, 1972), 154.

45. "Reading Ira Aldridge," *Houghton Library Blog*, August 13, 2013, https://blogs.harvard.edu/houghton/2013/08/13/reading-ira-aldridge/.

46. James H. Dorman, "The Strange Career of Jim Crow Rice (with Apologies to Professor Woodward)," *Journal of Social History* 3, no. 2 (1969): 114, cites *American Songster* (New York, 1788); also in Damon, "The Negro in Early American Songsters," 134.

47. Nathan, *Dan Emmett*, 6. The paradoxical relations between late-eighteenth century British sentimentalism, slavery, and U.S. blackface minstrelsy are also discussed in Dorman, "Jim Crow Rice," 113.

48. Nandini Bhattacharya, "Family Jewels: George Colman's Inkle and Yarico and Connoisseurship," *Eighteenth-Century Studies* 34, no. 2 (2001): 220.

49. Nathan, *Dan Emmett*, 5–7.

50. Dorman, "Jim Crow Rice," 114, cites "Humming Bird" (Baltimore, 1809), also in Damon, "The Negro in Early American Songsters," 138–39, 142; and Nathan, *Dan Emmett*, 34.

51. Bhattacharya, "Family Jewels," 226; Rehin, "Harlequin Jim Crow," 688.

52. Dorman, "Jim Crow Rice," 114, cites "Humming Bird" (Baltimore, 1809), also in Damon, "The Negro in Early American Songsters," 142; and Nathan, *Dan Emmett*, 34.

53. Nathan, "Negro Impersonation," 253; Nathan, *Dan Emmett*, 22.

54. Nathan, "Negro Impersonation," 250.

55. Nathan, *Dan Emmett*, 20–31.

56. Dillon, *New World Drama*, 156, cites Richard Brinsley Sheridan, *A Short Account of the Situations and Incidents Exhibited in the Pantomime of Robinson Crusoe, at the Theatre-Royal, Drury-Lane* (London T. Becket, 1781), 20.

57. Dillon, *New World Drama*, 156.

58. David Worrall, *Harlequin Empire: Race, Ethnicity and the Drama of the Popular Enlightenment* (London: Pickering & Chatto, 2007), 24.

59. "Pantos," *Encyclopedia of Christmas and New Year's Celebrations*, 2nd ed. (Omnigraphics, Inc., 2003) http://encyclopedia2.thefreedictionary.com/Pantos.

60. Lillian Moore, "John Durang, the First American Dancer," in *Chronicles of the American Dance*, edited by Paul Magriel (New York: Henry Holt and Company, 1978), 20–21.

61. John O'Brien, *Harlequin Britain: Pantomime and Entertainment, 1690–1760* (Baltimore: Johns Hopkins University Press, 2004), 135.

62. Rehin, "Harlequin Jim Crow," 691–92, cites " 'Dans L'Armée de La Fayette,' Souvenirs Inédits du Comte de Charlus," *Revue de Paris*, LXIV (1957), 107.

63. Hutton, *Curiosities*, 94–95.

64. Lincoln Kirstein, *The Book of the Dance: A Short History of Classic Theatrical Dancing* (Garden City, NY: Garden City Publishing Co., Inc, [1935] 1942), 341–42; cited in Moore, "John Durang," 22; Rehin, "Harlequin Jim Crow," 691–92.

65. Worrall, *Harlequin Empire*, 25; Dillon, *New World Drama*, 156.

66. Henry Louis Gates Jr., *Figures in Black: Words, Signs, and the "Racial" Self* (New York: Oxford University Press, 1987), 52; Worrall, *Harlequin Empire*, 24.

67. Moore, "John Durang," 20–21.

68. Hutton, *Curiosities*, 96. See also John Durang and Alan S. Downer, *The Memoir of John Durang, American Actor, 1785–1816* (Pittsburgh: Published for the Historical

Society of York County and for the American Society for Theatre Research by the University of Pittsburgh Press, 1966); Chrystelle T. Bond, *A Chronicle of Dance in Baltimore, 1780–1814.* New York: M. Dekker, 1976; and Lynn M. Brooks, *John Durang: Man of the American Stage* (Amherst, NY: Cambria Press, 2011).

69. Moore, "John Durang," 21.

70. Brooks, *Durang*, 101.

71. Brooks, *Durang*, 100–101, cites Gregorio Lambranzi, *Neue und curieuse theatralische Tantz-Schul* (Nuremberg: 1716. Reprint, Leipzig: Edition Peters, 1716), also available in English: Gregorio Lambranzi, *New and Curious School of Theatrical Dancing*, translated by Friderica Derra de Moroda (New York: Dance horizons, 1972). Brooks's figure 15 (*Durang*, 100) is "Humpbacks'" dance. From Gregorio Lambranzi *Nuoua e curiosa scvola de' balli theatrali*, 1716, Courtesy of LPA; on Durang's "Dwarf dance": Brooks, *Durang*, 5.

72. Dillon, *New World Drama*, 159, cites *South-Carolina State Gazette and Timothy's Daily Adviser* (April 21, 1794). See also Moore ("John Durang," 24–29) on Alexander Placide, who participated in this performance, and on Fransiqui, both influential in Durang's development.

73. Dillon, *New World Drama*, 163, cites *City Gazette and Daily Advertiser* (December 16, 1803). "On the relation between the Harlequin figure and Jim Crow," cites Gates, *Figures in Black*, 51–53.

74. Robert Farris Thompson (*Tango*, 65) writes that New World "juba" is a creolization of the "Kongo body-striking dance, *zuba*."

75. Brooks, *Durang*, 101, 86–87.

76. Dillon, *New World Drama*, 157.

77. Dillon, *New World Drama*, 157, 155.

78. Worrall, *Harlequin Empire*, 24; Dillon, *New World Drama*, 155.

79. Isaac Bickerstaffe, *The Padlock: A Comic Opera: As It Is Perform'd by His Majesty's Servants, at the Theâtre-Royal in Drury-Lane* (London: printed for W. Griffin, 1768), http://name.umdl.umich.edu/004789151.0001.000.

80. Elisabeth Le Guin, "The Barber of Madrid: Spanish Music in Beaumarchais' Figaro Play," *Acta Musicologica* 79 (2007): 179–80. See also Craig H. Russell, "The Fandango in Mozart's the Marriage of Figaro: the Prism of Revolution in the Enlightenment," Goldberg and Pizà, *Fandango* (2015): 467–80; (2016): 418–43.

81. Worrall, *Harlequin Empire*, 24. See also Brooks, *John Durang*, "Off with the Circus," 107–31.

82. Tomko, "Magri's *Grotteschi*," 162; Harris-Warrick and Marsh, *Musical Theatre at the Court of Louis XIV*, 153.

83. Edward H. Sirich, "Lope de Vega and Praise of Simple Life," in *Romanic Review*, vol. 8, edited by Henry A. Todd (New York: Dept. of French and Romance Philology of Columbia University, 1917), 279.

84. N. D. Shergold, "Ganassa and the 'Commedia dell'arte' in Sixteenth-Century Spain," *The Modern Language Review* 51, no. 3 (July, 1956): 366.

85. Dillon, *New World Drama*, 159.

86. Lott, *Love and Theft*, 22.

87. Pierre-Louis Duchartre, *The Italian Comedy: The Improvisation, Scenarios, Lives, Attributes, Portraits, and Masks of the Illustrious Characters of the Commedia*

Dell'arte, translated by Randolph T. Weaver (New York: Dover Publications, 1966), 135, quoted in Rehin, "Harlequin Jim Crow," 692.

88. Rehin, "Harlequin Jim Crow," 690–92, quotes Marmontel, "Arlequin," 389.

89. Lott, *Love and Theft*, 18–19, cites Robert P. Nevin, "Stephen C. Foster and Negro Minstrelsy," *Atlantic Monthly* 20, no. 121 (1867): 608–16. This article is reproduced in its entirety in Edward Le Roy Rice, *Monarchs of Minstrelsy: From "Daddy" Rice to Date* (New York: Kenny Pub. Co, 1911), 7–10; Douglass, Stauffer, and Gates, *The Portable Frederick Douglass*, 207.

90. Lott, *Love and Theft*, 18–19, cites Nevin, "Stephen C. Foster and Negro Minstrelsy."

91. Hartman, *Scenes of Subjection*, 4.

92. Dillon, *New World Drama*, 151–52.

93. Aimé Cesairé's *A Tempest, Based on Shakespeare's The Tempest: Adaptation for a Black Theater* (New York: Ubu Repertory Theater Productions, 1969) is an important text in this reading. For an overview of re-readings of Caliban, see Trevor Griffiths, "'This Island's Mine'; Caliban and Colonialism," *The Yearbook of English Studies* 13 (1983): 159–80.

94. Shakespeare, *The Tempest*, edited by Rev. J. M. Jephson (London: Macmillan and Co., 1864), act 1, scene 2.

95. Shakespeare, *The Tempest*, act 2, scene 2; act 3, scene 2; act 1, scene 2.

96. Dillon, *New World Drama*, 151–52, cites Moten, *In the Break*, 6.

97. Liu, *Medieval Joke Poetry*, 6–7. See also "Acting the Wench," in Lott, *Love and Theft*, 159–68.

98. Dillon, *New World Drama*, 150.

99. Dillon, *New World Drama*, 153–54, cites Josiah Quincy, "Journal of Josiah Quincy, Junior, 1773," *Proceedings of the Massachusetts Historical Society*, vol. 49 (Oct. 1915–June 1916), 463.

100. hooks, *Black Looks*, 34.

101. Hartman, *Scenes of Subjection*, 33.

102. Dillon, *New World Drama*, 154, cites Quincy, "Journal, 1773."

103. See David Levinthal and Manthia Diawara, *Blackface* (Santa Fe, NM: Arena Editions, 1999).

104. I have written about Carmen Amaya's incorporation of the transgressive "Gypsy gaze" into flamenco dance in Goldberg, *Border Trespasses*, 394–407. Quotes are from Katherine Lee Bates, "The Gypsies of Spain," *New York Times* (May 14, 1899), 15.

105. See Ramón Soler Díaz and Antonio El Chaqueta, *Antonio El Chaqueta: Pasión por el cante* (Madrid: El Flamenco Vive, 2003), 234.

106. Marian H. Winter, "Juba and American Minstrelsy," in Magriel, *Chronicles of the American Dance*, 40.

107. Marshall W. Stearns and Jean Stearns, *Jazz Dance: The Story of American Vernacular Dance* (New York: Macmillan, 1968), 40, cite Odell, *Annals of the New York Stage*, vol. 4, 372; and C. L. "An Old Actor's Memories."

108. Stearns and Stearns, *Jazz Dance*, 41.

109. Stearns and Stearns, *Jazz Dance*, 41, quote Thomas W. Talley, *Negro Folk Rhymes: Wise and Otherwise* (New York: Macmillan, 1922), 296–7.

110. John F. Szwed and Morton Marks. "The Afro-American Transformation of European Set Dances and Dance Suites," *Dance Research Journal* 20, no.1 (1988): 33;

Henry E. Krehbiel, *Afro-American Folksongs. A Study in Racial and National Music. [with Musical Notes.]* (New York: G. Schirmer, 1913), 32–33; Samuel A. Floyd, "Ring Shout! Literary Studies, Historical Studies, and Black Music Inquiry," *Black Music Research Journal* 22 (2002 [1991]): 49–70.

111. Charles Dickens on William Henry Lane "Master Juba:" "Chapter VI—New York," in *The Works of Charles Dickens* (London: Oxford, 1957), 90–91.

112. Quoted in Winter, "Juba and American Minstrelsy," 42–43; See also Mark Knowles, *Tap Roots: The Early History of Tap Dancing* (Jefferson, NC: McFarland, 2002), 103.

113. On "dishevelment": Krehbiel, *Afro-American Folksongs*, 32, quoting Julien Tiersot, "La Musique chez les Peuples indigenes de l'Amerique du Nord."

114. Jayna Brown, *Babylon Girls: Black Women Performers and the Shaping of the Modern* (Durham, NC: Duke University Press, 2008), 6; Houston A. Baker, *Modernism and the Harlem Renaissance* (Chicago: University of Chicago Press, 1987), 50, 56.

115. Constance Valis Hill, *Tap Dancing America: A Cultural History* (New York: Oxford University Press, 2010), 7, cites Moore, "John Durang," 15–37.

116. Nathan, *Dan Emmett*, 84, on the double shuffle: cites W. T. Thompson, "Great Attraction," *Chronicles of Pineville* (Philadelphia, 1843), Eugene V. Smalley, "Sugar Making in Louisiana," *Country Magazine* (November 1887), Augustus Baldwin Longstreet, "The Dance" (1833) and *Georgia Scenes* (New York, 1840), and Henry Howe, *Historical Collections of Ohio* (Cincinnati, 1847), 274. On "knocking:" cites *Sketches and Eccentricities of Col. David Crockett of West Tennessee* (New York, 1833), 39: "[B]oth began to shuffle. Soon the whole house was knocking it off."

117. Nathan, *Dan Emmett*, 84–85, cites Crockett, *Sketches and Eccentricities*, 40, J. H. Clifford, "8th Step—Shuffle," *The Art of Jig and Clog Dancing Without a Master* (New York: T. B. Harrison & Co., 1864), and Henry Tucker, *Clog Dancing Made Easy* (New York: R. M. De Witt, 1874), 2.

118. Moore, "John Durang," 21–22.

119. Elizabeth Aldrich, Sandra Noll Hammond, and Armand Russell, *The Extraordinary Dance Book T. B. 1826: An Anonymous Manuscript in Facsimile* (Stuyvesant, NY: Pendragon Press, 2000), 5–6, 11.

120. Hill (*Tap Dancing America*, 7) observes that Durang's hornpipe on eggs was "one of the first soft-shoe dances." Brooks, *Durang*, on rope: 87, on Hornpipe on Eggs: 83 (cites *Pennsylvania Packet* [6 and 7 November, 1789]), on Durang dancing a fandango, which was also danced on eggs during this era: 85–86, cites *Federal Gazette and Philadelphia Evening Post* (July 1, 1791), and, on egg version of the fandango, Bond, *A Chronicle of Dance*, 26.

121. Moore, "John Durang," 21–22, cites "Pas de Matelot. A Sailor's Hornpipe—Old Style," in Charles Durang, *The Ball-Room Bijou, and Art of Dancing. Containing the Figures of the Polkas, Mazurkas, and Other Popular New Dances, with Rules for Polite Behaviour* (Philadelphia, Baltimore, and New York: Fisher & Brother, 1850), 156, http://www.unz.org/Pub/DurangCharles-1850.

122. Moore, "John Durang," 21.

123. Nathan, *Dan Emmett*, 85, cites *Dictionary of American English*, edited by Sir William A. Craigie and James R. Hulbert (Chicago, 1938–44), Bacon, *Complete Dancing Instructions*, 2nd step, and Tucker, *Clog Dancing*, 11th step.

124. Debra Craine and Judith Mackrell, *The Oxford Dictionary of Dance* (Oxford: Oxford University Press, 2010), 6.

125. Thomas Baird, email communication, January 24, 2016.

126. Magri, Berry, Fox, and Skeaping (translation), *Theoretical and Practical Treatise*, 84; cited in Harris-Warrick and Brown, *Gennaro Magri and His World*, 355, 350.

127. "Matteo," with Carola Goya, *The Language of Spanish Dance*, 177; Gail Grant, *Technical Manual and Dictionary of Classical Ballet* (New York: Dover Publications, 1982), 64.

128. Plaza, "Spanish Dance in Europe," 77; Ivor F. Guest, *Fanny Elssler* (Middletown, CT: Wesleyan University Press, 1970), 74; Gerhard Steingress, ...*y Carmen se fue a París: Un estudio sobre la construcción artística del género flamenco (1833–1865)* (Córdoba: Almuzara, 2005), 88–147.

129. Nathan, *Dan Emmett*, 86, cites Washington Irving, *Salmagundi*, Chaps. 1 and 5.

130. Nathan, *Dan Emmett*, 72, cites "Sich a Gitting Up Stairs" (Baltimore, n.d. [1930s]).

131. Fra Molinero, *La imagen de los negros*.

132. Baker, *Modernism and the Harlem Renaissance*, 15.

Chapter 5

1. For a semiotic analysis of the production of these two films, and for dance analysis of the classical dance recorded in the second film, "Quadro Flamenco" (1124), see Mora and Goldberg, "Spain in the Basement."

2. "Carmencita," Library of Congress, Motion Picture, Broadcasting, and Recorded Sound Division, http://www.loc.gov/item/00694116/; see Kiko Mora, "Carmencita *on the road*: Baile español y vaudeville en Los Estados Unidos de América (1889–1895)," Asociación Lumière (2011), http://www.elumiere.net/exclusivo_web/carmencita/carmencita_on_the_road.php; and Bennahum, "Early Spanish Dancers." The 1898 Lumière films are: "El Vito" (843), "Estrella de Andalucía" (844), "La Jota" (845), "Boleras Robadas" (846), "Bolero de Medio Paso" (847), "Las Peteneras" (848), "Las Manchegas" (849), "Boleras Robadas" (850), "La Malagueña y El Torero" (851), "Bolero de Medio Paso" (852), "La Sal de Andalucía" (853), and "El Ole de la Curra" (854); more information, and images from each clip, can be found in the Lumière catalog, https://catalogue-lumiere.com/?s=1er+mai+1898+seville.

3. José Luis Ortiz Nuevo, *Coraje. Del maestro Otero y su paso por el baile* (Sevilla: Libros con duende, 2013), 9; José Luis Navarro García, *La danza y el cine*, vol. 1 (Sevilla: Libros con Duende, 2014), 28; Otero, *Tratado*.

4. See, for example, the photo of Otero, at the bottom right of the frame, dancing in Lumière no. 851 "La Malagueña y el Torero," 1898, https://catalogue-lumiere.com/la-malaguena-y-el-torero/.

5. Mora, "¡Y dale con Otero!"

6. Moore, "John Durang," 24–25; Dillon, *New World Drama*, 159.

7. Moore, "John Durang," 31–32.

8. "...*porque danzaban en una cuerda floxa y en cuerda tirada.*" Roxo de Flores, *Tratado*, 83.

9. Rodriguez Calderón, *Bolerología*, 8.

10. Moore, "John Durang," 24–25.

11. Brooks, *Durang*, 89.

12. Worrall, *Harlequin Empire*, 23.

13. T. A. Brown and Charles Day, "Black Musicians and Early Ethiopian Minstrelsy," *The Black Perspective in Music* 3, no. 1 (1975): 78. This is a reproduction of Charles H. Day, *Fun in Black; or, Sketches of Minstrel Life, with the Origin of Minstrelsy, by Colonel T. Allston Brown* (New York: Robert M. DeWitt, 1874); Hutton, *Curiosities*, 122.

14. Winter, "Juba and American Minstrelsy," 40.

15. Hutton, *Curiosities*, 118–19, 115, quotes C. L. "An Old Actor's Memories"; Rice, *Monarchs of Minstrelsy*, 7, quotes Nevin, *Atlantic Monthly* (1867).

16. Carl F. Wittke, *Tambo and Bones: A History of the American Minstrel Stage* (New York: Greenwood Press, 1968 [1930]), 17; Rice, *Monarchs of Minstrelsy*, 6; H[all], "Some Early Black-face Performers," 42; William L. Slout, *Burnt Cork and Tambourines: A Source Book of Negro Minstrelsy* (San Bernardino, CA: Borgo Press, 2007), 6; Brown and Day, "Black Musicians," 78.

17. Wittke, *Tambo and Bones*, 17.

18. Nathan, *Dan Emmett*, 110, cites circus manager C. J. Rogers' letter to the editor of *The New York Clipper* (June 20, 1874).

19. Nathan, *Dan Emmett*, 109.

20. Nathan, *Dan Emmett*, 111, cites playbill of 1842 as republished in *The New York Clipper* (September 6, 1884).

21. Nathan, *Dan Emmett*, 118, cites *The New York Herald* (February 6–11, 1843), 121, and playbill of the Great Olympic Circus, March 29, 1843.

22. Nathan, *Dan Emmett*, on instruments: 153, cites Dorothy Scarborough, *On the Trail of Negro Folk-Songs* (Cambridge, MA: Harvard University Press, 1925), 101; Nicholas Cresswell, *The Journal of Nicholas Cresswell, 1774–1777* (London: J. Cape, 1974), 18–19; Walter Jekyll, *Jamaican Song and Story...* (Nendeln/Liechtenstein: Kraus Reprint, 1967), 283; on London debut: 122, 135, 183, 185, cites *The Morning Courier and New York Enquirer* (April 21, 1843), and *The New York Clipper* (August 8, 1874), which quotes from a letter by Pelham published in *Hague's Minstrel and Dramatic Journal* (Liverpool).

23. Rehin, "Harlequin Jim Crow," 688.

24. "...caras tiznadas, por supuesto...": Sánchez, "La habanera en la zarzuela española," 7, cites a letter sent from Madrid by the archivist of the Casa de Osuna to Barbieri in Paris, commenting on the zarzuela *Los piratas*, with music by Luis Cepeda and a libretto by Luis Rivera, which had premiered on September 1, 1860: José López de la Flor, "A F. A. Barbieri," 2 de septiembre de 1860, Legado Barbieri, Ms 14079, in Emilio Casares Rodicio, *Francisco Asenjo Barbieri*, vol. 2, *Escritos* (Madrid: ICCMU, 1994), 99.

25. Nathan, *Dan Emmett*, 137, cites *The Era* (June 25, 1843), as quoted in Harry Reynolds, *Minstrel Memories* (London, 1928), 84.

26. Nathan, *Dan Emmett*, 111, 113, cites a letter to the editor published in *The New York Clipper* (June 20, 1874) and signed "C. J. R." [C. J. Rogers], a playbill of the Cincinnati Circus (Cincinnati, April 23, 1841), and "Negro Minstrels and their Dances," *The New York Herald* (August 11, 1895).

27. Nathan, *Dan Emmett*, 154, citing Percival R. Kirby, *The Musical Instruments of the Native Races of South Africa* (London: Oxford University Press, 1934), 10, and Shakespeare's *Midsummer Night's Dream*, act IV, scene 1.

28. Cotarelo, *Entremeses*, cclxv–ix, cites Barbieri's translation of El Marini's poem "Adonis": Francisco A. Barbieri, *Las castañuelas: Estudio jocoso dedicado á todos los boleros y danzantes, por uno de tantos* (Madrid: Imp. de J.M. Ducazcal, 1879), 27. See also Cummings, "The Moresca," 55; and Victoria Cavia Naya, *La castañuela española y la danza: Baile, música e identidad* (Valencia, España: Mahali, 2013).

29. Nathan, *Dan Emmett*, 123. I have noted the similarity between the flamenco *esquina'ores* (corner men) and the "corner men" or "end men" of blackface minstrelsy, who likewise played percussion instruments: the tamborine and the bones (Goldberg,

Border Trespasses, 75). On end men and bone castanets, see Wittke, *Tambo and Bones*, 43–46.

30. Winter, "Juba and American Minstrelsy," 48–51.

31. Stephen B. Johnson, *Burnt Cork: Traditions and Legacies of Blackface Minstrelsy* (Amherst: University of Massachusetts Press, 2012), 79–80.

32. Johnson, *Burnt Cork*, 78–79.

Note to epigraph: Rioja, *El arte flamenco en Málaga*, part 1, 42, 44–45, cites *Ecos de la Juventud* (June 17, 1877); on *salto*: cites Francisco Bejarano Robles, (*Paco Percheles*), *Cafés de Málaga* (...*y otros establecimientos)* (Editorial Bobastro, Málaga, 1989), 514.

33. As noted above, the research on Jacinto Padilla was undertaken in collaboration with Kiko Mora, and the pivotal identification of the dancer in this film as Jacinto Padilla "El Negro Meri" is Mora's, not mine. The following section is based to a significant degree on Mora's research; I have been a grateful participant in the historiographic research, and have contributed the dance analysis. The Lumière clip featuring El Negro Meri can be seen most clearly at the Forum des Images http://collections.forumdesimages.fr/CogniTellUI/faces/details.xhtml?id=VDP13353. For an in-depth examination of the cast of performers, see Kiko Mora, "Who Is Who in the Lumière's Films of Spanish Song and Dance at the Paris Exposition, 1900," Le Grimh (Groupe de reflèxion sur l'image dans le monde hispanique, 2017), https://www.grimh.org/index.php?option=com_content&view=article&layout=edit&id=2745&lang=fr#4.

34. For more on the early filmography of Spanish dance, see José Luis Navarro García, *La danza y el cine*, vol. 1 (Sevilla: Libros con Duende, 2014); Mora, "Carmencita on the Road," and "Carmen Dauset Moreno, primera musa del cine estadounidense," *ZER* 19, no. 36 (2014): 13–35; and Cristina Cruces Roldán, "Presencias flamencas en los Archivos Gaumont-Pathé. Registros callejeros en la Granada de 1905," in *Presumes que eres la ciencia* (Sevilla: Libros con duende, 2015), 15–43. Edison's film: "Carmencita," http://www.loc.gov/item/00694116/.

35. On the "fashionable" La Feria: "À L'Exposition," *Le Journal* (July 27, 1900), 2; "À L'Exposition," *Le Journal* (September 11, 1900), 3. For a detailed study of the location of these films, see Kiko Mora, "Flamencos en la Exposición de París 1900 (II): el lugar de filmación de las películas de Lumière," *Cadáver Paraíso* (blog), June 3, 2016, https://goo.gl/kcSAOf.

36. Giovanni Boldini painted a portrait of "Anita de la Ferie" in 1900: https://commons.wikimedia.org/wiki/File:Boldini_-_Anita_de_la_Ferie_-_The_Spanish_Dancer.jpg.

37. Mora thinks that the seated women may be sisters, either Juana and Felisa Peña, or Margarita and Amparo Aguilera. For more, and for more on José Fernández, see Mora, "Who is Who." For more on the Spanish Students' tour in the United States, see Kiko Mora, "Sounds of Spain in the Nineteenth Century USA: An Introduction," in Goldberg and Pizà, *The Global Reach of the Fandango* (Spanish Edition 2015): 333–62; (2016): 270–309. For more on the *estudiantinas*, see Félix Martín Sárraga, *Mitos y evidencia histórica sobre las tunas y estudiantinas* (Lima: Cauce, 2016). For a dance analysis of the classical clip (1124), see Mora and Goldberg, "Spain in the Basement."

38. This is in the manner of Silverio Franconetti, who in turn followed the great flamenco singers "El Loco Mateo" and "El Nitri." Pineda Novo, *Silverio Franconetti: noticias inéditas* (Sevilla: Giralda, 2000), 71.

39. Examples are Antonio García Matos "Antonio Triana" (1906–1989) and his childhood partner Francisca González Martínez "La Quica" (1905–1967). See Clara Mora Chinoy, "The First Academy of Flamenco Dance: Flamenco and the 'Broken Dance' of the Gitanos," in Goldberg, Bennahum, and Hayes, *Flamenco on the Global Stage*, 143–56.

40. I explored stylistic differences in posture as signifying race and authenticity in flamenco in a presentation given in June 1998 at the Second Biennial Flamenco History Conference, University of New Mexico: "From Gautier to Hurok: The International Public and Notions of Authenticity in Flamenco."

41. "Christmas at the Belasco," *New York Times* (December 25, 1906); Mora, "Who is Who."

42. Jacinto Padilla was called "El Negro Meric," "El Negro Meri," "El Mulato Meric," "El Mulato Meri," "El Americano Merit," etc. in the press. For consistency, I refer to him by his given name, as "El Negro Meri," or "El Meri."

43. For more on the way six-beat measures work in bulerías, and a proposal for recognizing this music-dance syntax in eighteenth-century fandango dances, see Baird, Goldberg, and Newman, "Changing Places," (2015): 638–42, (2016): 589–94; and Goldberg, "Sonidos Negros," 102.

44. Mora, in "¡Y dale con Otero!," cites Santiago Romo-Jara, "La Exposición de París," *El álbum iberoamericano* (July 22, 1900), 314, and "La Exposición de París," *La Opinión* (May 6, 1900), 2.

45. Eusebio Rioja, "Un pinturero personaje del Flamenco decimonónico: EL NEGRO MERI" (Málaga: April, 2004), http://documents.mx/documents/el-negro-meri.html.

46. José Blas Vega y Manuel Ríos Ruiz, *Diccionario enciclopédico ilustrado del flamenco y maestros del flamenco* (Madrid: Cinterco, 1988), 488.

47. José Cruz Gutiérrez, *La Córdoba flamenca (1866–1900)* (Córdoba: El Páramo, 2010), 9, 27–28, 80; Steingress, *La presencia del género flamenco*, 145.

48. Eusebio Rioja, *El arte flamenco en Málaga*, part 1, 42–43; and José Gelardo Navarro, "Dime con quién andas y te diré quién eres: Silverio, La Cuenca, Juan Breva, El Rojo y otras malas compañas," *Revista de Investigación sobre Flamenco La Madrugá*, n° 2, (Junio 2010): 12.

49. Eusebio Rioja *El arte flamenco en Málaga*, part 1, 43, cites *El Avisador Malagueño* (September 11, 1872), 3–4, and *El Avisador Malagueño* (September 13, 1872), 3.

50. Cruz Gutiérrez, *La Córdoba flamenca*, 67; Eusebio Rioja, *El arte flamenco en Málaga*, part 1, 46.

51. Eusebio Rioja *El arte flamenco en Málaga*, 43, cites *El Avisador Malagueño* (September 13, 1872), 3.

52. Cruz Gutiérrez, *La Córdoba Flamenca*, 27–28.

53. Rioja, *El arte flamenco en Málaga*, part 1, 43–45, cites *El Avisador Malagueño* (July 5, 1874).

54. For more on mojigangas, see Kiko Mora, "El romance de Carmen y Escamillo o 'The Lady Bullfighter' en Nueva York, 1888," in José Luis Ortiz Nuevo, Ángeles Cruzado, and Kiko Mora, *La valiente: Trinidad Huertas "La Cuenca"* (Sevilla: Libros con Duende, 2016), 211–70. On the connections between the blackface equestrian clowns

of the nineteenth century and the rodeo clowns of today, see John H. Towsen, *Clowns* (New York: Hawthorn Books, 1976), 94.

55. Davillier and Thomson, *Spain*, 328–32.

56. Del Campo Tejedor and Cáceres Feria, *Historia cultural del flamenco*, 348.

57. "…colocó dos pares y medio al cuarteo, delantero uno y mejor el otro, sin cuadrar el bicho ni cosa que lo valga…" del Campo Tejedor and Cáceres Feria, *Historia cultural del flamenco*, 348, cite *Suplemento Nacional* (1877), 2.

58. Rioja, *Flamenco en Málaga*, part 1, 37, cites Manuel Martínez Barrionuevo, *El Padre Eterno. Novelas españolas* (Madrid: Impr. de Fortanet, 1887), 123–24. Rioja adds that on May 7, 1886, Martínez Barrionuevo related anecdotes related to El Negro Meri in *El Avisador Malagueño*. On "*baratero*," a "man of the dregs of society who has acquired extraordinary skill in handling knives, and who exploits the terror he inspires to demand of gamblers a share of the purse," Rioja cites Charles Davillier and Gustave Doré, *Viaje por España*, vol. 1 (Madrid: Grech, S. A., 1988 [1st edition: 1874]), 327. See Mariano de Rementería y Fica, *Manual del baratero: Ó arte de manejar la navaja, el cuchillo y la tijera de los jitanos* (Madrid: Imp. de A. Goya, 1849); English translation: James Loriega, *Manual of the Baratero, Or, the Art of Handling the Navaja, the Knife, and the Scissors of the Gypsies* (Boulder, CO: Paladin Press, 2005).

59. Rioja, *El arte flamenco en Málaga*, part 1, 42, 44–45, cites *Ecos de la Juventud* (June 17, 1877).

60. "Toros y Novillos," *Boletín de Loterias y Toros* (January 2, 1882), 1; and "Becerros y Novillos" (January 9, 1882), 1.

61. "Toros y Novillos," *Boletín de Loterias y Toros* (January 2, 1882).

62. Del Campo Tejedor and Cáceres Feria, *Historia cultural del flamenco*, 348, cite *El Toreo* (January 2, 1882), 1; "Toros y Novillos," *Boletín de Loterias y Toros* (January 2, 1882).

63. *El Toreo* (January 2, 1882), in del Campo Tejedor and Cáceres Feria, *Historia cultural del flamenco*, 348; "Toros y Novillos," *Boletín de Loterias y Toros* (January 2, 1882).

64. "Toros y Novillos," *Boletín de Loterias y Toros* (January 2, 1882).

65. "Plaza de Toros de Murcia. Las provincias de Levante" (June 10, 1887), 4. El Negro Meri's proper name, Jacinto Padilla, was first published in Mora, "¡Y dale con Otero!"

66. Rioja thinks Meri had Cuban roots (*Arte flamenco en Málaga*, part 1, 46). And Mora has unearthed evidence that Meri at least toured and was known in Cuba as a bullfighter: "Cuba Negra," *Correo español* (México, May 10, 1896), 1.

67. "Circo Ecuestre Barcelonés," *La Dinastía* (November 29, 1888), 4.

68. "Circo de Madrid—Bajo la dirección de Mr. Paul," *Diario de Avisos de Madrid* (June 2, 1847), 2.

69. "Diversiones Públicas—Circo de Madrid," *El Clamor Público* (July 27, 1847), 4.

70. "Circo de Madrid de Paul," *Diario Oficial de Avisos de Madrid* (March 6, 1848), 4; "Circo de Madrid, de Mr. Paul," *Diario de Avisos de Madrid* (June 16, 1847), 4.

71. This can be tricky to establish in the Spanish press, which often assiduously avoids any mention of race, or the use of blackface. For example, the expression "caras tiznadas, por supuesto" (in blackface, of course) in the above-cited 1860 letter to Barbieri, would seem to indicate that blackface was a commonplace on the mid-nineteenth century Spanish stage, but few Spanish sources of this period address this directly.

72. For example, "Circo de Mr. Paul," *El Heraldo* (September 2, 1847), 4; "Circo de Madrid de Mr. Paul," *Diario Oficial de Avisos de Madrid* (February 22, 1848), 4.

73. Steingress, "La aparición del çante flamenco," 357, cites *El Guadalete* (November 26, 1874, and January 15, 1875).

74. *El Guadalete* (November 26, 1874), 3, in Steingress, "La aparición del cante flamenco," 357.

75. Cruz Gutiérrez, *La Córdoba flamenca*, 9, 27–28, 80; Steingress, *La presencia del género flamenco*, 145.

76. *El Guadalete* (January 15, 1875), 3, in Steingress, "La aparición del cante flamenco," 357.

77. "Mañana tendremos…" *El Guadalete* (January 15, 1875). On *festeros*, see Estela Zatania, "El flamenco, las panderetas, y el bon sauvage: meditaciones sobre el flamenco festero," *Sinfonía Virtual*, no. 27 (July 2014), http://www.sinfoniavirtual.com/flamenco/panderetas_sauvage.php.

78. Marín, *Método para guitarra*, 70, cited in José M. Gamboa, *Una historia del flamenco* (Madrid: Espasa, 2011), 310–11. On nineteenth-century rondeñas and malagueñas, see Mª Luisa Martínez Martínez and Peter Manuel, "El Murciano's 'Rondeña' and Early Flamenco Guitar Music: New Findings and Perspectives," in Goldberg and Pizà, *Fandango* (2015): 249–72; (2016): 153–81.

79. José Blas Vega, *Los cafés cantantes de Sevilla* (Madrid: Cinterco, 1987), 17.

80. Alberto Rodríguez Peñafuerte, "EL CHATA DE VICÁLVARO—JABERAS," *YouTube* (April 27, 2009), https://www.youtube.com/watch?v=mEGtOtiCj-Q.

81. Adela Perujo Ortega, "Cantes rondeño-gaditanos VII- SOLEARES (2ª Parte) - Los Negros de Ronda," cites Pedro Peña Fernández, *Los gitanos flamencos* (Córdoba: Almuzara, 2013), 29, https://www.scribd.com/document/282530675/Cantes-de-Ronda-y-Cadiz-7. On La Andonda: Loren Chuse, *Cantaoras: Music, Gender and Identity in Flamenco Song* (Hoboken: Taylor and Francis, 2013), 63.

82. Pineda Novo, *Silverio Franconetti*, 78; Miguel López, Esteban Cabello, Rubén Molina, Mª Antonia Molina, Manuela Martín, Ana Fuentes y Pedro José Bonilla del colegio Virgen del Rosario de Totalán (Málaga) "La masculinidad y feminidad patriarcal desde 'La Jabera' como proyecto integrador," *Junta de Andalucía*, July 2, 2010, http://agrega.juntade-andalucia.es/repositorio/19032013/e2/es-an_2013031912_9133029/2009_02/c04.pdf.

83. Soler Díaz, "Del origen cubano de algunas letras flamencas," 2946.

84. Ramón Soler Díaz and Antonio El Chaqueta, *Antonio El Chaqueta: Pasión por el cante* (Madrid: El Flamenco Vive, 2003), 231–32. Cited in Rioja, *El arte flamenco en Málaga*, 45. Antonio "El Chaqueta" – Topic, "Los Números Cabales (Cantes del Piyayo)," *YouTube*, March 4, 2015, https://www.youtube.com/watch?v=R_b-tuxELc8.

85. Soler and Antonio el Chaqueta, *Antonio El Chaqueta*, 235. With his father, Soler is the author of an authoritative study of Mairena's discography: Luis Soler Guevera, and Ramón Soler Díaz, *Los cantes de Antonio Mairena: Comentarios a su obra discográfica* (Sevilla: Ediciones Tartessos, 2004). The cited recording is Antonio Cruz, singer, and Paco Aguilera and Moraíto, guitars, "Tangos malagueños: 'Tierra de tanta alegría,'" *Cantes de Antonio Mairena*, Columbia CCLP 31.010 (33 rpm, 1958).

86. Soler Díaz, *Antonio El Chaqueta*, 235–36; Ramón Soler Díaz, "Del origen cubano de algunas letras flamencas," *Candil*, nº 114 (Peña Flamenca de Jaén, Enero-Febrero 1998): 2937–60.

87. Rioja, *El arte flamenco en Málaga*, part 1, 46–47.

88. Javier Osuna García documents the intriguing notice in the *Diario Mercantíl de Cádiz* of a performance in the Teatro Principál of Cádiz on January 8, 1829, in which "celebrated bolero Luis Alonso, brother of [legendary flamenco singer] El Planeta," dances zapateados, the *Petenera Americana*, *el fricasé*, and *zapitusé de costa firme* (present day Venezuela). Javier Osuna García, "Luis Alonso y Lázaro Quintana, arte en el Teatro Principal," *Los fardos de pericón (1512)*, February 21, 2013, http://losfardos. blogspot.com/2013/02/luis-alonso-y-lazaro-quintana-arte-en.html.

89. "Echos des Teatres," *La Justice* (October 19, 1889), 3.

90. "Chocolat (clown)" *Wikipedia*, https://en.wikipedia.org/wiki/Chocolat_ (clown)#CITEREFNoiriel2016 and https://fr.wikipedia.org/wiki/Chocolat_(clown). See also Maurice Franc-Nohain, *Les Mémoires de Foottit et Chocolat* (Paris: Pierre Lafitte et Cie, 1907), https://gallica.bnf.fr/ark:/12148/bpt6k312620x/f5.image.

91. Ortiz Nuevo, Cruzado, and Mora, *La valiente*, 133, cite *El Día*, (September 26, 1886). See also Towsen, *Clowns*, 216–23; and "Foottit et Chocolat," *Circopedia: The Free Encyclopedia of the International Circus*, http://www.circopedia.org/Chocolat# Chocolat.E2.80.99s_Legacy.

92. Ortiz Nuevo, Cruzado, and Mora, *La valiente*, 198, cite *La Crónica de Huesca* (December 23, 1892).

93. On Oller: "Chocolat (clown)," *Wikipedia*; on *La feria de Sevilla*: Ortiz Nuevo, Cruzado, and Mora, *La valiente*, 122–23, 133, cite *La Correspondencia de España* (February 23, 1887).

94. Ortiz Nuevo, Cruzado, and Mora, *La valiente*, 139, cite *La Andalucía* (March 27, 1887).

95. Ortiz Nuevo, Cruzado, and Mora, *La valiente*, 148, 150, cite "La Soirée Théâtrale—Au Nouveau Cirque" *Le Figaro* (March 22, 1889), 3, and *L'Intransigeant* (May 19, 1889).

96. The Lumière films are: "Foottit et Chocolat, I. Boxeurs" (1138), "Foottit et Chocolat, II. Acrobates sur la chaise" (1139), "Foottit et Chocolat, III. Chaise en bascule" (1140), "Foottit et Chocolat, IV. Guillaume Tell" (1141), "Foottit et Chocolat, V. Le policeman" (1142), "Foottit et Chocolat, VI. La Mort de Chocolat" (1143), https://catalogue-lumiere.com/?s=+Foottit+et+Chocolat+vue+no+1141+.

97. On *Joyeux Nègres*, see Goldberg, "*Jaleo de Jerez* and *Tumulte Noir*." See also Davinia Caddy, "Parisian Cake Walks," *19th Century Music* 30, no. 3 (Spring 2007): 297–98.

98. Rae Beth Gordon, *Dances with Darwin, 1875–1910: Vernacular modernity in France* (Farnham, Surrey, England: Ashgate, 2009), 161–62, cites *Le Rire* (April 16, 1898), 2, and Willette, Advertisement for Pihan Chocolate, *Courrier Français* (January 17, 1889).

99. Gérard Noiriel, "Épilogue—Considérations sur le nom, le mémoire, et l'usure du temps," *Chocolat: La Véritable Histoire D'un Homme Sans Nom* (Montrouge: Bayard, 2016).

100. Goldberg, "*Jaleo de Jerez* and *Tumulte Noir*," 134, cites John Martin, "The Dance: A New Spanish Invasion," *New York Times* (July 28, 1929), x7.

101. Antonio Rivas Bonillo, "El espectáculo inefable: El circo visto por Ramón Gómez de la Serna," in *Intermedios: La cultura escénica en el primer tercio del siglo XX*

español, curated by Aurora Herrera, and edited by Elvira Marco Martínez (Madrid: AC/E Acción Cultural Española, 2016), 20–25.

102. For a deeper dive into these issues, see Mora and Goldberg, "Spain in the Basement."

103. Antonio J. Pradel, " 'Dju-Dju' o los orígenes bastardos del flamenco: Danza, superstición, terror y negritud," *El Estado Mental*, November 10, 2016, https://elestadomental.com/diario/dju-dju-o-los-origenes-bastardos-del-flamenco.

104. See, for example, Farruco dancing in this gathering of Triana's flamenco elite (00:19–00:36): Ilitur-gitano Lisardo, "El gran Farruco. (Bulerías con duende) Lope de Vega-Sevilla-1983," *YouTube* (April 2, 2014) https://www.youtube.com/watch?v=e8eplddNv9E. Farruco's grandsons Juan Manuel "Farruquito," Antonio "Farru," and Manuel "Carpeta" Fernández Montoya are among those carrying Farruco's style into this generation: Veo Flamenco, *YouTube*, January 29, 2017, https://www.youtube.com/watch?v=GijUWiZHYpo.

105. In a fascinating moment of dance genealogy, Susana Lupiañez "La Lupi" identified a high jump lifting two knees and landing on one foot at a time, which, with a strong hip swivel, became the signature jump of Antonio Montoya Flores "El Farruco," as being the invention of "El Herejía," a flamenco from the old Roma community of Triana. Class with Lupi, Flamenco Vivo Studios, New York City, March 7, 2016. For more on this community, see Ricardo Pachón, *Triana Pura y Pura* (R.T.V.Ed y Productora Andaluza de Programas, S.A. 1984). See also erjuaquini, "Triana Pura y su compás, gracia y pureza de ese tiempo que no volverá," *YouTube* (December 30, 2008), http://www.youtube.com/watch?v=WVOB7AbBBQE, 4:15–4:53. The guitarist is Manolo Domínguez "El Rubio," Rafael "El Negro," famed dancer and husband of Matilde Coral, is standing in the doorway. Seated at the large table is "El Coco," and seated to his left is "El Herejía." The dancer is Pepa "La Calzona." I am grateful to Estela Zatania for making these identifications.

Chapter 6

Note to Epigraph: Pablillos de Valladolid, "El conservatorio del flamenquismo—Baila la 'Macarrona,' " *Por Esos Mundos* 15, no. 238 (November, 1914), 525–26.

1. Jovino Ruiz, Frasquillo's close friend and father of the well-known bailaor Joaquín Ruiz, used this term to describe the Gitano style of dance. Chinoy, "Flamenco and the 'Broken Dance' of the Gitanos," 143–56.

2. Brown, *Babylon Girls*, 1.

3. This is why the advent of Carmen Amaya in Buenos Aires in 1936 and New York 1941 was so important. See K. Meira Goldberg, "A Heart of Darkness in the New World: Carmen Amaya's Flamenco Dance in South American Vaudeville," *Choreography and Dance*, no. 3 (1994): 95–107; K. Meira Goldberg, "The Latin Craze and the Gypsy Mask: Carmen Amaya and the Flamenco Aesthetic, 1913–1963," in Bennahum and Goldberg, *100 Years of Flamenco*, 80–121; and Montse Madrilejos Mora, "Carmen Amaya, 1947: The (Gypsy) Beloved of America Conquers Europe," in Goldberg, Bennahum, and Hayes, *Flamenco on the Global Stage*, 178–86.

4. For a version of this argument vis-à-vis the 1902 arrival of the cakewalk in Spain, see Goldberg, "*Jaleo de Jerez* and *Tumulte Noir*."

5. I began studying Macarrona in 2012 while co-curating the exhibit *100 Years of Flamenco in New York City*, and I wrote about Macarrona in my chapter on Carmen

Amaya for that catalog: "The Latin Craze and the Gypsy Mask." I also wrote about Macarrona in "*Jaleo de Jerez* and *Tumulte Noir*," and in K. Meira Goldberg, "Juana Vargas, 'La Macarrona:' A Flamenco Treasure." New York Public Library, Blogs, January 21, 2015, https://www.nypl.org/blog/2015/01/21/juana-vargas-la-macarrona-flamenco.

6. Léonide Massine, *My Life in Ballet* (London: Macmillan, 1968), 89.

7. In *Massine: A Biography*, Vicente García-Márquez explains: "Massine's autobiography is not accurate in its chronology of events. It was during the 1916 trip that he met Félix in Seville; he re-encountered him in Madrid in 1917, the year Félix joined the company" (New York: Knopf, 1995), 400, note 14.

8. For more on the complicated response of the "Generation of '98" to flamenco, see Mora and Goldberg, "Spain in the Basement."

9. Maurer and Soria Olmedo, *Back Tomorrow*, 4.

10. Pastora Imperio, considered the founder of the Sevilla School of flamenco dance, was a child of the heyday of the cafés: her mother was the renowned singer-dancer Rosario Monje "La Mejorana" (b. 1862). See María Estévez and Héctor Dona, *Reina del duende* (Barcelona: Roca Editorial, 2012). In 1925, Antonia Mercé "La Argentina" (1890–1936) would reinterpret this work. See Ninotchka Devorah Bennahum, *Antonia Mercé, "La Argentina": Flamenco and the Spanish Avant Garde* (Hanover, NH: University Press of New England, 2000), 76–102.

11. See Blas Vega, *Los cafés cantantes de Sevilla* and *Los cafés cantantes de Madrid*.

12. Massine, *My Life*, 101; García-Márquez, *Massine*, 80–81.

13. Massine, *My Life*, 101, 106.

14. While in Rome that winter, "eager to learn more of the background and history of choreography," Massine acquired first editions of eighteenth and nineteenth-century dance treatises by Raoul Feuillet (*Chorégraphie*, 1700), Louis Pécour (*Recueil de danses*, 1700), Philippe Rameau (*Le Maître à danser*, 1725), Jean Malpied (*Traité sur l'art de la danse*, 1770), and Carlo Blasis (*The Code of Terpsichore*, 1830). García-Márquez, *Massine*, 82.

15. See Vicente García-Márquez, Yvan Nommick, and Antonio Álvarez Cañibano, eds., *Los Ballets Russes de Diaghilev y España*. (Granada: Archivo Manuel de Falla, 2012).

16. Miguel Manzano Alonso, "Fuentes populares en la música de 'El sombrero de tres picos' de Manuel de Falla," in García-Márquez, Nommick, and Álvarez Cañibano, *Diaghilev y España*, 73–88.

17. García-Márquez, *Massine*, 111; Daniel Pineda Novo, *Juana, "la Macarrona" y el baile en los cafés cantantes* (Cornellà de Llobregat, Barcelona: Aquí + Más Multimedia, 1996), 43; Massine, *My Life*, 117–18; Alfonso Puig et al., *El arte del baile flamenco* (Barcelona: Ed. Poligrafa, 1977) 68; El de Triana, *Arte y artistas flamencos* (Madrid: Editoriales Andaluzas Unidas, S.A., 1986 [1935])173, 222, 224. The Victoria & Albert Museum holds Massine's Notebook (S.193-2008) from this period, although the July trip during which Massine filmed Macarrona is missing. The Archivo Manuel de Falla (AMF) in Granada holds Falla's correspondence with both Diaghilev and Massine.

18. Carol Hess "'Un alarde de modernismo y dislocación': Los Ballets Russes en España 1916–1921," in García-Márquez, Nommick, and Álvarez Cañibano, *Diaghilev y España*, 336–37.

19. García-Márquez, *Massine*, 111; Massine, *My Life*, 117.

20. Pineda, *Macarrona*, 9; Daniel Pineda Novo, *Antonio Ramírez, el baile gitano de Jerez* (Jerez de la Frontera: Centro Andaluz de Flamenco, 2005), 21, 23.

21. Encarnación López Júlvez "La Argentinita" (1898–1945) appeared in the 1916 *Flor de Otoño*, directed by Mario Caserini. By the 1920s and 1930s, there is a much more extensive filmography, including recordings of Argentinita, Vicente Escudero (1888–1980), Antonia Mercé "La Argentina" (1890–1936), Pastora Imperio, (1887–1979), and Carmen Amaya (1918–1963). José Luis Navarro García, *La danza y el cine*, vol. 1 (Sevilla: Libros con Duende, 2013), on Argentina and Argentinita: 88–92, on Escudero: 58–60, 62, on Amaya: 72–88. For a discussion of Spanish dance in silent films 1894–1910, see Cristina Cruces Roldán, "Bailes boleros y flamencos en los primeros cortometrajes mudos. Narrativas y arquetipos sobre 'lo español' en los albores del siglo XX," *Revista de Dialectología* 71, no. 2 (Julio–Diciembre 2016): 441–65.

22. A donation of the Léonide Massine Estate, the footage is held in the collection of the Jerome Robbins Dance Division at the New York Public Library for the Performing Arts.

23. Cristina Cruces speculates that the film was shot in front of the brick wall outside Los Altos Colegios, still a functioning elementary school in the Macarena neighborhood of Sevilla, near where Macarrona lived. "Altos Colegios Macarena," http://ceipaltoscolegiosmacarena.blogspot.com/p/historia-del-colegio.html

24. Eugenio Cobo "La Barcelona Flamenca de los años veinte," *La Caña: Revista de Flamenco*, no. 1 (1991): 18; Blas Vega and Ríos Ruiz, *Diccionario*, 111, 210, 651, 759.

25. Blas Vega, *Los cafés cantantes de Madrid*, 126–27, 254, 258–59, cites Carlos Miranda, *La caída de Isabel II (De las Memorias de Cleto Regúlez*, June 29, 1884), in *El Libro Popular* no. 15 (Madrid, April 14, 1914), and Miguel Pérez Ferrero, *Vida de Antonio Machado y Manuel* (Madrid, Rialp, 1947), 64.

26. "Fernando el de Triana," *Arte y artistas*, 72–73, 75, 148, 150. The only photo of which I am aware that positively identifies María is that in El de Triana, *Arte y artistas*, 75.

27. I am grateful for this identification to Rafael Estévez, director of the Ballet Nacional de Andalucía.

28. Pineda Novo (*Macarrona*, 43–45) writes that Macarrona and Ramírez were supposed to have been but were not finally included in the cast of Diaghilev's *Cuadro Flamenco* (1921). On "Mate Sin Pies" and Diaghilev's *Cuadro Flamenco*: Blas Vega, *Los cafés cantantes de Madrid*, 312–13, including two photographs; Blas Vega and Ríos Ruiz, *Diccionario*, 472; Lynn Garafola and Nancy V. N. Baer, *The Ballets Russes and Its World* (New Haven, CT: Yale University Press, 1999) 335; Francis E. Barrett, "The Russian Ballet," *The Musical Times* (London, July 1, 1921), 497. On the development of the garrotín in response to the 1902 arrival of the cakewalk in Spain: Goldberg, "*Jaleo de Jerez* and *Tumulte Noir*," 130–33.

29. Guitarist Curro de María, looking the guitarists' hands, helped me identify the rhythms and tonalities: clip 1 is in *mi* and *la* minor, clip 2 is in a major key, consistent with alegrías or *cantiñas*, and clip 3, in duple meter, is in *la* minor, consistent with farruca, tangos de Málaga or tangos del Piyayo (discussed in Chapter 5), and *tangos del Titi*.

30. As part of my research, I have added a rhythm soundtrack of palmas and a visual box showing the counts to the first and third Macarrona clips, at both 50 percent and 100 percent speed (which is slowed down slightly to compensate for the fewer frames per second in 1917 film technology). The modified clips have been donated and will be available at the New York Library for the Performing Arts.

31. On jerezana: "Matteo," with Carola Goya, *The Language of Spanish Dance*, 121–22; Grut et al., *The Bolero School*, 159; and Eulalia Pablo Lozano and José Luis

Navarro García, *Figuras, pasos y mudanzas: claves para conocer el baile flamenco* (Córdoba: Almuzara, 2007), 72. On carrerilla: Brooks, *Esquivel*, 101–102, Spanish: 228, English: 280 (ff. 18–18v); "Matteo," with Carola Goya, *The Language of Spanish Dance*, 52, 119; Pablo Lozano and Navarro García, *Figuras, pasos y mudanzas*, 54. On panaderos: "Matteo," with Carola Goya, *The Language of Spanish Dance*, 142–44; and Grut et al., *The Bolero School*, 142. On seasé: for those readers who dance sevillanas, this is the first step of the second verse: "Matteo," with Carola Goya, *The Language of Spanish Dance*, 223–24.

32. The jazz hands appear at timestamps 00:43–00:49 and 00:53–1:02 of the third clip.

33. In the New York Public Library's 1937 film of Massine and Tamara Toumanova dancing *The Three-Cornered Hat* with Col. W. de Basil's Ballet Russe de Monte Carlo at the Chicago Opera House, Massine performs this gesture in his *Farruca del Molinero*, at 15:00 and again at 15:25, and again, after defeating the Corregidor, at 21:40. *MGZHB 12-1000, no. 291–293. Many thanks to David Vaughn for showing me this film.

34. Goldberg, "*Jaleo de Jerez* and *Tumulte Noir*," 128–30.

35. Woods, *White Gypsies*, 112.

36. Joan Acocella, "The Critical Reception of *Le Tricorne*," in García-Márquez, Nommick, and Alvarez Cañibano, *Los Ballets Russes*, 109 (129 in the revision of this article in Goldberg, Bennahum, and Hayes, *Flamenco on the Global Stage*); Acocella quotes Edward Dent, "Manuel de Falla," *The Nation & Athenaeum* (May 28, 1921), 335.

37. Woods Peiró, *White Gypsies*.

38. Otero, *Tratado*, 211–13, 219–20, 226.

39. Goldberg, "*Jaleo de Jerez* and *Tumulte Noir*," 130–33, citing Otero, *Tratado*, 223–25.

40. See José María García Martínez, *Del fox-trot al jazz flamenco: El jazz en España [1919–1996]* (Madrid: Alianza, 1996).

Note to epigraph: Isidoro Fernández Flórez, "Fernanflor," "Seño José—Soledad—El Boyardo," in *La Ilustración Ibérica* (November 23, 1889), in *La ilustración ibérica*, volume 7 (México: Sres. Ballescá y Ca.: 1883), 738–39. Reproduced in David Pérez Merinero, "La Macarrona con Edison," October 12, 2012, http://www.papelesflamencos.com/2012/10/la-macarrona-con-edison.html.

41. This was one of the few of such fairs to make a profit. "Paris Exposition of 1889: Overview," Library of Congress Prints and Photographs Division, https://www.loc.gov/rr/print/coll/250_paris.html. For more on Spain in European world's fairs, see Mora and Goldberg, "Spain in the Basement."

42. Emilia Pardo Bazán, "Carta XXIII Diversiones—Gente Rara, Paris, septiembre 28," in *A los pies de la torre Eiffel, Obras completas*, vol. 19 (1891), 284, cited in Annegret Fauser, *Musical Encounters at the 1889 Paris World's Fair* (Rochester: University of Rochester Press, 2005), 261; and in Luis Sazatornil Ruiz and Ana Belén Lasheras Peña, "París y la españolada—Casticismo y estereotipos nacionales en las exposiciones universales (1855–1900)," *Mélanges de la Casa de Velázquez Nouvelle série* 35, no. 2 (2005): 279.

43. Parakilas, "How Spain Got a Soul," 172; Massine would choreograph *Capriccio espagnol* in 1939, with La Argentinita. Massine, *My Life*, 286.

44. Fauser, *Musical Encounters*, 79.

45. Lynn Garafola, *Legacies of Twentieth-Century Dance* (Middletown, CT: Wesleyan University Press, 2005), 91.

46. Manuel Viera de Miguel, "El imaginario visual español en la Exposición Universal de París de 1889: 'España de moda,'" *Anales de Historia del Arte*, no. 537 (2011): 544.

47. Julien Tiersot, *Musiques pittoresques: promenades musicales a l'Exposition de 1889* (Paris: Librairie Fischbacher, 1889), 72, cited in Fauser, *Musical Encounters*, 263, note 109.

48. Fauser, *Musical Encounters*, 261.

49. Zeynep Çelik and Leila Kinney, "Ethnography and Exhibitionism at the Expositions Universelles," *Assemblage: A Critical Journal of Architecture and Design Culture*, no. 13 (December, 1990): 50; Charles Castle, *The Folies Bergère* (London: Methuen, 1982), 49–55.

50. Fauser, *Musical Encounters*, 145; José Luis Navarro García, "Algunas novedades en torno a La Cuenca," *Revista de Investigación sobre Flamenco La Madrugá*, no. 2 (June 2010): 4–8; Alberto Rodriguez Peñafuerte, "Les Espagnols de la rue des Martyrs, 1880 (II/III)," *Flamenco de Papel*, November 9, 2009, http://flamencodepapel.blogspot.com/search?q=Les+Espagnols+de+la+rue+des+Martyrs, cites *La Iberia* (December 20, 1879), *La Iberia* (January 25, 1880), and Yorick, "España en París," *El Imparcial* (March 8, 1880), 4.

51. Parakilas, "How Spain Got a Soul," 174.

52. Parakilas, "How Spain Got a Soul," 167–68.

53. Parakilas, "How Spain Got a Soul," 148, 167.

54. Parakilas, "How Spain Got a Soul," 148, cites Théophile Gautier, *Voyage en Espagne, suivi de España*, edited by Patrick Berthier (Paris: Gallimard, 1981), 45; translated to English in Théophile Gautier, and Henry Christie Steel, *Voyage en Espagne* (Boston: D.C. Heath & Co., 1900), 32.

55. Edward W. Said, *Orientalism* (New York: Vintage Books, 1979), 137–38, 150; cites Ernest Renan, *De l'origine du langage,* in *Oeuvres completes*, vol. 8, 122, 102; *Histoire générale des langues sémitiques*, 180; and Edgar Quinet, *Le Génie des religions,* in *Ouvres completes* (Paris: Paguerre, [1832] 1857).

56. Arthur Gobineau and Adrian Collins (translation), *The Inequality of Human Races* (New York: G. P. Putnam's Sons, 1915).

57. Said, *Orientalism*, 138–40.

58. Estébanez Calderón, *Escenas andaluzas*, 204–205; Said, *Orientalism*, 138–40.

59. Navarro García, "La Cuenca," 6–7.

60. "Scenes and Characters in 'The Land of Joy,'" *Theatre Magazine* 27, no. 203 (January, 1918), 9.

61. Frimousse, "Le Soirée Parisienne—Les Danseuses Espagnoles," *Le Gaulois* (January 10, 1880), 3. I am grateful to Kiko Mora for this reference.

62. Heuer, *The Discourse of the Ruffian*, 106–107, cites Quevedo, *Los nadadores*, in *Poësias*, 248–50; Cotarelo, *Entremeses*, cxcii–iii, clxxxix.

63. Frimousse, "Le Soirée Parisienne," 3.

64. El de Triana, *Arte y artistas*, 146; Navarro García, "La Cuenca," 11, 9, 2; cites Yorick, "España en París," and Un Monsieur de l'orchestre, "La Soiré Théâtral: Les Espagnols de la rue des Martyrs," *Le Figaro* (January 15, 1880); Ortiz Nuevo, Cruzado, and Mora, *La valiente*.

65. Navarro García, "La Cuenca," 11, cites Yorick "España en París."

66. Henry Christie Steel, "Introduction," in Gautier and Steel, *Voyage en Espagne*, 5.

67. Parakilas, "How Spain Got a Soul," 139–40.

68. Parakilas, "How Spain Got a Soul," 147, cites Gautier, *Voyage en Espagne* (Paris: Gallimard, 1981), 43.

69. Yorick, "España en París," cited in Navarro García, "La Cuenca," 12.

70. Parakilas, "How Spain Got a Soul," 168; Fauser, *Musical Encounters*, 144.

71. Pardo Bazán, "Diversiones," 289–90.

72. See "Performing Bizet's *Carmen*: John Singer Sargent, *El Jaleo*, and the *Cigarreras* of Seville," in Mary Elizabeth Boone, *Vistas de España: American Views of Art and Life in Spain, 1860–1914* (New Haven, CT: Yale University Press, 2007), 115–46.

73. Pedro van der Lee, "Zarabanda: Esquemas rítmicos de acompañamiento en $\frac{6}{8}$," *Latin American Music Review* 16, no. 2 (Fall–Winter 1995): 205; Mora, "*Bailable*," 106–107; Parakilas, "How Spain Got a Soul," 154–55, 158–59.

74. Parakilas, "How Spain Got a Soul," 166–67, cites and translates Letter to Wilhelm Enoch and Georges Costallat, October 21, 1882, in Emmanuel Chabrier, *Correspondence*, ed. Roger Delage and Frans Durif with Thierry Bodin (n.p.: Klincksieck, 1994), 166–67.

75. If one counts the first *palmada* (clap) as a flamenco "12" (easily visualized on the face of a clock), then the accents in this little rhythm (which, as Chabrier described, would have been one line of a complex polyrhythmic texture of palmas) were 12, 4, 8, 2–3–4, 8, 2–3–4, 6–7–8–10, 2. The beginning on 12 and repeated groupings of 2–3–4 describe for me a fandango feel, and this rolling rhythm is finished off by the 6–8–10 hemiola of the penultimate measure. I also feel the 8 of the second measure and the 2 of the last measure as interesting and strong counter-accents, indicative of what would have been the music's syncopated fabric.

76. Blas Vega identifies this photo, no. 142 by Emilio Beauchy Cano, as "the performing group from the café El Burrero." The woman stage right of the central figure is readily identifiable as Concha la Carbonera (see, for example, her photograph in El de Triana, *Arte y artistas*, 40), known for dancing in the Burrero. I think the person in the middle may be Macarrona herself: in 1888, when Macarrona was dancing at the Burrero, Beauchy's studio was on the Calle Sierpes (on the same long street as the Burrero), and he photographed many flamenco artists. The date for this photo is often given as ca. 1888, though not always: Miguel Ángel Yáñez Polo, an authority on photography of this period, dates it ca. 1900. Blas Vega, *Los cafés cantantes de Sevilla*, 32–54, on Beauchy no. 142: 51. On Concha la Carbonera: El de Triana, *Arte y artistas*, 40. Miguel Ángel Yáñez Polo, "Historia de la fotografía en Andalucía," in *Historia de la fotografía española 1839–1986. Actas del primer congreso de Historia de la fotografía española* (Sevilla: Sociedad de Historia de la Fotografía Española, 1986), 41–63, cited in Noemí Espinosa Fernández, *La fotografía en los fondos de La Hispanic Society of America: Ruth Matilda Anderson* (doctoral dissertation, Universidad de Castilla La Mancha, 2010), 148. See also Miguel Angel Yáñez Polo, "Cien fotografos sevillanos insignes: Emilio Beauchy Cano," *ABC Sevilla* (April 26, 1984), 87.

77. Fauser, *Musical Encounters*, 144.

78. Parakilas, "How Spain Got a Soul," 168, 145–46, cites François René de Chateaubriand, "Avertissement" to *Les aventures du dernier Abencérage*, in Chateaubriand, *Oeuvres romanesques et voyages*, ed. Maurice Regard, vol. 2 (Paris: Gallimard, 1969), 1359, 1373–74.

79. Lemuel Johnson, *The Devil, the Gargoyle and the Buffoon*, 75; Joseph Conrad, *The Heart of Darkness* ([Edinburgh]: [W. Blackwood] 1899).

80. Çelik and Kinney, "Ethnography and Exhibitionism," 39.

81. Fauser, *Musical Encounters*, 142, 223–24.

82. It is fascinating to note how different Anita Reguera's technique and vocabulary, recorded in the 1900 Lumière films, is from that of Carmencita, filmed in 1894, or the

dancers filmed by Lumière in 1898 Sevilla. Mariano Parra, a protégé of Luisa Pericet, scion of the Pericet bolero dynasty, firmly identifies Carmencita's movement vocabulary as falling within that of the escuela bolera: *balanceado, rondezán, gorgollata, destaque, rondezán en vuelta con quebrada*. K. Meira Goldberg, interview with Mariano Parra, December 11, 2012; Matteo with Goya, *Language of Spanish Dance*, balanceado: 26, rondezán: 215, gorgollata: 93, destaque: 71, vuelta quebrada: 261–63. For a discussion of the iconography of the 1898 Lumière films, see "Introduction. *Sones de barco viejo*: Transatlantic Malagueñas and Zapateados," in Goldberg, Clark, and Pizà, eds., *Transatlantic Malagueñas and Zapateados in Music, Song, and Dance*.

83. Fauser, *Musical Encounters*, 216–17, cites Oscar Comettant, *La Musique, les musiciens et les instruments de musique chez les peuples du monde... 1869*, 282–90; Çelik and Kinney, "Ethnography and Exhibitionism," 39.

84. Said, *Orientalism*, 119–20.

85. Fauser, *Musical Encounters*, 223.

86. Fauser, *Musical Encounters*, 218, 224–25, cites Edmond de Goncourt, Jules de Goncourt, and Robert Ricatte, ed., *Journal: Memoires de la vie littéraire*, vol. 3 (Paris: Robert Laffront, 1989), 271.

87. Said, *Orientalism*, 137.

88. Pardo Bazán, "Diversiones," 276–77.

89. Fauser, *Musical Encounters*, 225.

90. Pardo Bazán, "Diversiones," 284, 288, 278–80. Nubia is located in present-day southern Egypt and northern Sudan, but in classical Greek usage was categorized, along with "Ethiopian," as "black." In early modern Spain, Gitanos were known not only as "Egyptians," but also as "Ethiopians," and "ethigitanos" (Ethiopian Gitanos). José Francisco Ortega Castejón, "Una carta latina de deán Martí no bien entendida" *Myrtia: Revista de Filología Clásica*, vol. 29 (University of Murcia, 2014): 307–308, cites Margarita Torrione, "Del viajero ilustrado al viajero romántico. Visión del folclore gitano-andaluz," in Ángel Caballero et al., "Los intelectuales ante el flamenco," *Cuadernos Hispanoamericanos. Los Complementarios*, 9–10 (1992): 9–30.

91. Pardo Bazán, "Diversiones," 285, Fauser, *Musical Encounters*, 227, 345.

92. Fauser, *Musical Encounters*, 238, cites Tiersot, "Promenades musicales à l'Exposition," 308; "Les Aissaoua," *Le Matin* (July 1, 1889), 1–2; and Émile Michelet, "Autour de l'Esposition," *Paris illustré* (July 20, 1889), 529.

93. Pardo Bazán, "Diversiones," 284–85.

94. Fauser, *Musical Encounters*, 242–43, cites Christopher L. Miller, *Blank Darkness: Africanist Discourse in French* (Chicago: University of Chicago Press 1985), 3–65.

95. Pardo Bazán, "Diversiones," 288.

96. Fauser, *Musical Encounters*, 242–43, quotes and translates François de Nion, "Theatre," *Revue Indépendante*, September 1889, 504.

97. See, for example, Gautier, "Fanny Elssler in 'Le Diable Boiteux,'" 15.

98. Pardo Bazán, "Diversiones," 288.

99. Theophile Gautier, "Mademoiselle Fanny Elssler," *Le Figaro* (October 19, 1837), cited in Nicole Haitzinger, "Female Bodies as the Other: Alterity on Stage," in Jeschke, Vettermann, and Haitzinger, *Les Choses Espagnoles*, 95.

100. Parakilas, "How Spain Got a Soul," 162–63. For more on the tension between emergent forms of flamenco and the escuela bolera in the first half of the nineteenth

century, see Mora, "*Bailable*;" and Mora, "Pepita Soto: una historia del sueño americano (1852–1859)," *Revista de investigación sobre flamenco La Madrugá*, no. 8 (Junio 2013): 177–230.

101. The ostinato is in Mehúl's comic opera *Les deux aveugles de Tolède* (The two blind men of Toledo): Parakilas, "How Spain Got a Soul," 143.

102. Pineda Novo, *Macarrona*, 3, 12.

103. El de Triana, *Arte y artistas*, 148.

104. Gil Gómez Bajuelo, "Evocación de Juana la 'Macarrona,'" *ABC Sevilla* (December 15, 1945). In David Pérez Merinero, *Papeles Flamencos*, December 16, 2009, http://www.papelesflamencos.com/2009/12/entrevista-la-macarrona.html.

105. Antonio Machado y Álvarez "Demófilo," in his list of "Cantadores de flamenco: Jerez de la Frontera," includes "Tío Vicente Macarrón" and "Tío Juan Macarrón, *cantador general.*" Antonio Machado y Álvarez, "Demófilo," and Enrique Jesús Rodríguez Baltanás, *Colección de cantes flamencos: recogidos y anotados por Demófilo* (Sevilla: Signatura Ediciones, [1881] 1999), 285; Manuel Ríos Ruiz, *De cantes y cantaores de Jerez* (Madrid: Editorial Cinterco, 1989), 42–43; Juan de la Plata, *Los gitanos de Jerez: historias, dinastías, oficios y tradiciones* (Jerez de la Frontera: Universidad de Cádiz, Cátedra de Flamencología, 2001), 121.

106. Felipe Picatoste y Rodríguez, *Diccionario popular de la lengua castellana* (Madrid: Dirección y administración, 1882), 673.

107. Pardo, "Diversiones," 290–91.

108. Brown, *Babylon Girls*, 7.

109. Pineda, *Macarrona*, 11, cites Juan de la Plata, *Flamencos de Jerez* (Jerez de la Frontera: Editorial Jerez Industrial, 1961), 88; Miguel de Cervantes, *Novelas ejemplares* (Colombia: Panamericana Editorial, [1613] 1993), *La gitanilla*, 7–68.

110. Blas Vega and Ríos Ruiz, *Diccionario*, 434–35. El de Triana, *Arte y artistas*, 148; Pineda Novo, *Macarrona,* 19, cites Francisco Vallecillo, "Las Cantiñas y sus derivaciones," *Candil*, no. 36 (1984): 7–9.

111. A *real*, meaning "royal," was a Spanish unit of currency. Pineda, *Macarrona*, 11.

112. Pineda, *Silverio*, 71–75.

113. Davillier, *Spain*, 308–309; Blas Vega, *Los cafés cantantes de Sevilla*, 12–13. El de Triana, *Arte y artistas,* 128; Otero Aranda, *Tratado de Bailes*, 201.

114. Blas Vega, *Los cafés cantantes de Sevilla*, 16, 18–19, 32, 35; Pineda, *Macarrona*, 11; Pineda, *Silverio*, 71–76; Davillier, *Spain*, 308–15.

115. Pineda, *Silverio Franconetti*, 71–75, cites Agustín Moyano ("Onayomnitsuga"), "EL SALON SILVERIO," *Boletín Gaditano*, no. 10 (June 1878), 81, https://archive.org/stream/CASGA_100415/CASGA_100415_djvu.txt.

116. Blas Vega, *Los cafés cantantes de Sevilla*, 35, 32.

117. Pineda *Macarrona*, 12.

118. Gómez Bajuelo, "Evocación de Juana la 'Macarrona;'" Blas Vega, *Los cafés cantantes de Madrid*, 190–91, cites Gonzalo Rojo Guerrero, *Joaquin José Vargas Soto "El Cojo de Málaga"* (Estepona, 1994), 64.

119. Pineda, *Macarrona*, 21; Blas Vega, *Los cafés cantantes de Sevilla*, 47.

120. Blas Vega, *Los cafés cantantes de Sevilla*, 47; El de Triana, *Arte y artistas*, 128; Otero Aranda, *Tratado de Bailes*, 201.

121. Blas Vega, *Los cafés cantantes de Sevilla*, 51.

122. Gómez Bajuelo, "Evocación de Juana la 'Macarrona.'"

123. Arthur Pougin, *Le Théatre à l'Exposition universelle de 1889, notes et descriptions, historire et souvenirs* (Paris: Librairie Fischbacher, 1890), 105.

124. "Dicen de Granada," *El Pais* (June 30, 1889), 2; "Ya han salido de Granada," *La Época* (July 2, 1889), 2; *El Progreso* (July 12, 1889), reproduced in José Luis Ortiz Nuevo, *¿Se sabe algo? Viaje al conocimiento del arte flamenco según los testimonios de la prensa sevillana del XIX. Desde comienzos del siglo hasta el año en que murió Silverio Franconetti (1812–1889)* (Sevilla: Ediciones el Carro de la Nieve, 1990), 330; "Nos escribe nuestra corresponsal..." *La Correspondencia de España* (July 28, 1889), 2.

125. *El Progreso* (July 12, 1889).

126. "Hors Paris," *Le Figaro* (August 1, 1889).

127. "La reine des gitanas," *La Lanterne*, August 5, 1889.

128. Pougin, *Le Théatre à l'Exposition*, 105.

129. "La fiesta en Granada—una 'troupe' de gitanos." *La Época* (July 2, 1889).

130. Pougin's listing of Macarrona and also "Juana" is tantalizing, seeming to imply that they are not the same person. Might this suggest that María came as well? I have not come across any mention of this possibility in any of the sources I have consulted. There are definitely two women dancing in the Massine footage at the New York Public Library, but the catalog (whose source I assume to be Massine himself) lists only "Macarrona," and Massine in his memoir speaks of only one Macarrona. In the 1945 *ABC* interview, Macarrona does say that her father accompanied her (and does not mention her sister). The July 12, 1889, article in *El Progresso* says "several couples": Pougin mentions Macarrona and Pichiri, Sanchez and Concepcion, Zola (man or woman?)...and who would the last person have been? Pougin, *Le Théatre à l'Exposition*, 105.

131. Might Pepa be La Castañeta? *Le Monde illustré* (August 31, 1889), cover, reproduced in Fauser, *Musical Encounters*, 265.

132. *Le Figaro* (August 7, 1889), 1.

133. "La journée du chah," *La Lanterne* (August 8, 1889).

134. "Chez les gitanas," *Le Radical* (August 10, 1889).

135. Pougin, *Le Théatre à l'Exposition*, 106.

136. "Courrier de l'Exposition—XVII—Les Gitanes," *Le Monde illustré*, August 31, 1889, 131.

137. Pougin, *Le Théatre à l'Exposition universelle de 1889*, 107–108. We have briefly discussed the footwork of seated *esquina'ores* (corner men) in Chapter 5.

138. Pougin, *Le Théatre à l'Exposition*, 108, 105–106.

139. Pougin, *Le Théatre à l'Exposition*, 107.

140. *Le Monde illustre* (August 31, 1889), 131.

141. Pougin, *Le Théatre à l'Exposition*, 106–107.

142. Pougin, *Le Théatre à l'Exposition*, 106–107.

143. *Le Monde illustré*, August 31, 1889, 131.

144. Blas Vega and Ríos Ruiz, *Diccionario enciclopédico*, 603.

145. *Boletín de Loterias y Toros* (January 2, 1882), 1.

146. Roberto de Palacio, "Los flamencos: bailaoras, cantaoras, y cantaores célebres," *Alrededor del mundo*, no. 5 (November 21, 1901), 325–26.

147. Palacio, "Los flamencos," 326. On *couplet*: Daniel Pineda Novo, *Las folklóricas* (Sevilla: J. Rodríguez Castillejo, 1990).

148. On *baile inglés*: Mora and Goldberg, "Spain in the Basement."

149. See José Gelardo Navarro, with María Amparo Fernández Darós, *¡Viva la Ópera Flamenca! Flamenco y Andalucía en la prensa murciana (1900–1939)* (Murcia: Universidad de Murcia, 2014).

150. Goldberg, "*Jaleo de Jerez* and *Tumulte Noir*;" Otero, *Tratado*, 211–13, 219–20, 226.

151. "Les gitanas," *La Lanterne* (August 18, 1889).

152. Pougin, *Le Théatre à l'Exposition*, 107. Fauser, *Musical Encounters*, 227, note 32, cites Çelik and Kinney, "Ethnography and exhibitionism," 43.

153. *Le Monde illustre* (August 31, 1889), 131.

154. Pougin, *Le Théatre à l'Exposition*, 108–109.

155. *Gil Blas* (September 3, 1889), 1.

156. Gautier, "Fanny Elssler in 'Le Diable Boiteux,'" 15. "La Cachucha (1836), by Fanny Elssler, excerpt B" danced by Margaret Barbieri, based on the Labanotation score in Ann Hutchinson Guest and Friedrich Albert Zorn, *Fanny Elssler's Cachucha* (New York: Theatre Arts Books, 1981) 42–43; *YouTube*, July 27, 2012, https://www.youtube.com/watch?v=7xfudtM8a4o, timestamp 1:09. The cachucha is not part of today's flamenco repertoire, but it was long preserved, including this drop to the knee with bend of the upper body, in the Gitano zambras of Granada. See José Luis Navarro García, *Cantes y bailes de Granada* (Málaga: Editorial Arguval, 1993); Willyrives, "Danzas del Sacromonte," *YouTube*, March 25, 2012, https://www.youtube.com/watch?v=ik6qp4 AaFs4: the cachucha starts at 4:00, and the drop to the knee is at 4:30 and 5:08. See also *Flamenco: encuentro con los gitanos españoles* by Dan Grenholm and Linnart Olson, excerpt: Granada Antigua, *YouTube*, February 9, 2014, https://www.youtube.com/watch?v=lVkMsFp24OM; see the drop to the knee in the opening sequence, and at 7:19. I am grateful to Estela Zatania for identifying El Millonario, the dancer in the opening scene.

157. Pougin, *Le Théatre à l'Exposition*, 108–109.

158. Pougin, *Le Théatre à l'Exposition*, 108–109.

159. Pineda, *Macarrona*, 19, 29–30, cites Francisco Vallecillo, "Las Cantiñas y sus derivaciones"; and José Blas Vega, *Vida y cante de Don Antonio Chacón: La Edad de Oro del flamenco (1869–1929)* (Madrid: Editorial Cinterco, 1990), 55–56.

160. Parakilas, "How Spain got a Soul," 167, cites Chabrier, *Correspondence*, 166–67; Marín, *Método para guitarra*, 177–78, cited in Rioja, *Flamenco en Málaga*, part 2, 14–15.

161. Pougin, *Le Théatre à l'Exposition*, 107.

162. Pougin, *Le Théatre à l'Exposition*, 109.

163. Parisian audiences knew the *Jaleo de Jerez*, an ancestor of today's bulerías, which was part of the Spanish repertoire on the mid-nineteenth-century ballet stage. See Goldberg, "Sonidos Negros," 95, 100–101, 106–107.

164. Pougin curiously uses "Maccarona" and "Juana" in the same passage. Pougin, *Le Théatre à l'Exposition Universelle de 1889*, 108–109; Gómez Bajuelo, "Evocación de Juana la 'Macarrona.'"

165. Pougin commented that not only did "all of Paris arts and letters" turn out for a long rendezvous at the Grand Theatre de l'Exposition, but "the Spanish-born *étoile*, Rosita Mauri" and "the entire *corps de ballet*" of the Paris Opera came "to watch the

lovely Soledad and the astounding Maccarona [*sic*]." Pougin, *Le Théatre à l'Exposition*, 109, cited in Fauser, *Musical Encounters*, 265–66, note 118. The Henriot caricature is reproduced in Fauser, *Musical Encounters*, 265, figure 5.16.

166. Pardo Bazán, "Diversiones," 291.

167. Alice Guy's 1905 footage of "Danse Gitane" in Granada is a fascinating document in this regard, especially because it records a performance of the repertoire from which the Gitanos of Granada would have drawn for their 1889 Paris appearances. A girl dances (00:42–2:20) with a *sombrero cordobés* (a man's hat) in a traditional circle of women playing palmas. Her movement is traditional (for example, at 1:16 she performs the side-to-side step that Reguera does), but movements feel to me like "quotations" in the manner of María La Macarrona's jazz hands. For example, she stands in place wiggling her hips while drumming fingers upon her hat, and wiggles down to the floor and back up (1:46–1:58)—not out of the bounds of tradition (Chuny Amaya does this step in tangos), but less "distinguished" than Reguera's 1900 and the Macarronas' 1917 performances. LookingForAlice, "GYPSY DANCE 1905 Alice Guy Blanche Cinema Pioneer Whitney Museum 2009," *YouTube*, August 23, 2008, https://www.youtube.com/watch?v=u19uY-iN6L4.

168. Fauser, *Musical Encounters*, 242–43, note 56: cites and translates François de Nion, "Theatre," *Revue Indépendante*, September 1889, 504.

169. Matilde Coral, Angel Álvarez Caballero, Juan Valdés,and Rocío Coral, *Tratado de la bata de cola: Matilde Coral, una vida de arte y magisterio* (Madrid: Alianza, cD. L. 2003), 152.

170. Aguardiente, or firewater, is a Spanish hard liquor.

171. Pardo's emphasis. Pardo, "Diversiones," 290–91.

172. Félix Grande, "Lo flamenco en 'La Lola se va a los puertos,'" *Boletín de la Real Academia Sevillana de Buenas Letras: Minervae baeticae*, no. 38 (2010), 351.

173. Alberto Rodríguez, "María la Bonita (y II)," *Flamenco de papel*, June 12, 2010, http://flamencodepapel.blogspot.com/search?q=macarrona, reproduces Monday, "París, 13 de Junio" *El Imparcial*, June 15, 1891.

174. Ortiz Nuevo, *¿Se sabe algo?* 330.

175. Pineda Novo quotes from an article in the *Diario de Cádiz* writing that Macarrona had achieved a resounding success Paris and repeating the shah of Persia's remark comparing her with the *almées* of Teheran (*Macarrona*, 25, 35, note 8). But Pineda gives the date of the periodical as January 12, 1889, which is clearly an error. "El director del Gran Teatro de la Exposición de París, Mr. Grasset..." *El Progreso* (July 12, 1889); "La España alegre," *El Español* (July 24, 1889); "España en París," *El Cronista*, (July 25, 1889); "...los príncipes de Sarigreno...," *El Español* (July 10, 1889), all in Ortiz Nuevo, *¿Se sabe algo?*, 330–35.

176. "...[O]ur Paris correspondent writes..." *La Correspondencia de España* (July 28, 1889), 2.

177. "Crónicas de la Exposición de París," *La Ilustración española y americana* (August 15, 1889), 6. The Spanish press did take notice of an off-stage event: at the end of the Paris run, Soledad was "kidnapped"—that is, she ran off with—a Russian nobleman. Isidoro Fernández Flórez, "Fernanflor," recounted the event in a bitingly sarcastic piece in *La Ilustración Ibérica* of November 23, 1889. The following year, in his hagiographic monograph on *Carmencita, the pearl of Seville*, Professor James

Ramirez included a bizarre chapter entitled "The Abduction," echoing similar themes (New York: Press of the Law and Trade Printing Company, 1890), 50–62. On July 6–7 of 1893, the Spanish press reported that Macarrona herself had been carried off by a capitalist millionaire—in the 1945 *ABC* interview, she says that she was "kidnapped" with a broad wink. *La Ilustración Ibérica* of November 23, 1889; *El Imparcial*, July 7, 1893; *La Iberia*, July 7, 1893 reproduced in Faustino Núñez, "Los Raptos de Juana la Macarrona," *El afinador de noticias*, February 8, 2012, http://elafinadordenoticias.blogspot.com/2012/02/los-raptos-de-juana-la-macarrona.html; Gómez Bajuelo, "Evocación de Juana la 'Macarrona.'"

178. "La Maccarona," *Le Figaro* (August 8, 1889).

179. Even during the fair, impersonating these "bohemian dances" was not limited to theaters. For example, on October 31, 1889, *Gil Blas* reported that the Marquis de Pothuau was "*un succes de fou*" impersonating Macarrona in a cachucha. "La province est en avance sur Paris, et les château sur les thèâtres." *Gil Blas* (October 31, 1889).

180. "Mme Granier ne fait qu'une apparition," *La Lanterne* (November 22, 1889).

181. This also occurred with Carmen Dauset, "Carmencita": at the end of the nineteenth century there were several "Carmencitas" dancing in Paris (Kiko Mora, personal communication April 9, 2014). Mora is researching Carmencita burlesques in the United States: see for example his reference to Susan Brown, "The Colored Carmencita": Kiko Mora, "Carmencita en cinco fragmentos y una coda," *España Contemporánea. Revista de Literatura y Cultura* 24, no. 2; and 25, nos. 1 & 2, (2015): 229. Emma Sears, a New Orleans prostitute, also performed as "the colored Carmencita": Joseph R. Roach, "Slave Spectacles and Tragic Octoroons: A Cultural Genealogy of Antebellum Performance," in *Exceptional Spaces: Essays in Performance and History*, edited by Della Pollock (Chapel Hill: University of North Carolina Press, 1998), 67.

182. "Le principal 'clou' de *Paris-Exposition*," *Le Monde illustré*, November 30, 1889.

183. G. B., "Petit Nouvelles," *Le Figaro* (December 11, 1889), 3; "Un petit détail pittoresque," *Le Figaro* (January 10, 1890), reproduced in David Pérez Merinero, "La Cuenca en la Macar(r)ona," *Papeles Flamencos*, September 21, 2012, http://www.papelesflamencos.com/2012/09/la-cuenca-en-la-macarrona.html. See also Otero, *Tratado*, 155; and "Paris flamenco," *La Andalucia* (March 27, 1887), reproduced in Ortíz Nuevo, *¿Se Sabe Algo?* 327–29.

184. "La charmante artiste obtient tous les soirs un succès," *La Lanterne* (December 29, 1889).

185. "Jeanne Granier," *La Rampe Illustré* (January 4, 1890).

186. "M. Zidler, directeur (empresario) du Moulin Rouge" *La Lanterne* (March 15, 1890).

187. "Les Miettes de l'année," *Le Radical* (March 25, 1890).

188. *Fol* is crazy, *arçon* is a climbing vine, and *enlèvement* is abduction. Folarçon, "L'enlèvement de la Sole" *Supplément litteraire de La Lanterne* (May 10, 1891), 1. Faustino Núñez ("Los Raptos de Juana la Macarrona") mentions the three-act opera by Fabrice Carré, *L'Enlèvement de La Toledad*, with music by Edmond Audran (Paris: Choudens, ca. 1894), http://catalog.hathitrust.org/Record/008874872/Home.

189. "Idylle," *Le Supplément* (Sept. 16, 1897).

190. Alberto Rodríguez Peñafuerte, "María la Bonita (y II)," June 12, 2010, http://flamencodepapel.blogspot.com/search?q=macarrona, reproduces Monday, "París, 13 de Junio" *El Imparcial,* June 15, 1891.

Afterword

1. Bates, "The Gypsies of Spain."

2. Francisco Lucientes, "La vida del negro en la tierra del blanco," *Nuevo Mundo*, January 4, 1929, 40–41. For a penetrating analysis of this complicated moment, see Woods Peiró, "Racing for Modernity: From Black Jazz to White Gypsy Folklore," Peiró in *White Gypsies*, 101–44. For more on Faíco and the absorption of the cakewalk into flamenco, see Goldberg, "*Jaleo de Jerez* and *Tumulte Noir*."

3. Chabrier, *Correspondance*, 166–67; Parakilas, "How Spain Got a Soul," 167; Pougin, *Le Théâtre à l'Exposition*, 106.

4. John Martin, "The Dance: A New Spanish Invasion," *The New York Times* (July 28, 1929), x7.

5. Pardo Bazán, "Diversiones," 276–77; Maurer and Soria Olmedo, *Back Tomorrow: Federico García Lorca/Poet in New York*, exhibit brochure, 7.

6. Harney and Moten, *The Undercommons*, 137.

7. Stuart Hall, Kobena Mercer, and Henry Louis Gates, Jr., *The Fateful Triangle: Race, Ethnicity, Nation* (Cambridge, Mass: Harvard University Press, 2017), xvi–viii.

8. Brown, *Babylon Girls*, 125.

9. Alfredo Mañas "Carmen Amaya," *La caña: revista de flamenco*, no. 1 (Madrid: Asociacion Cultural La Caña y España Abierta, December, 1991): 12–17, cited in Goldberg, *Border Trespasses*, 195.

10. Woods, *White Gypsies*, 117.

11. Pardo Bazán, "Diversiones," 276–77.

SELECTED BIBLIOGRAPHY

Acuña, Maria Virginia. *The Spanish Lamento: Discourses of Love, Power, and Gender in the Musical Theatre (1696–1718)*. Doctoral dissertation, University of Toronto, 2016.

Aguirre Beltrán, Gonzalo. *La población negra de México: Estudio etnohistórico*. México: Fuente Cultural, 1946.

Aldrich, Elizabeth, Sandra Noll Hammond, and Armand Russell. *The Extraordinary Dance Book T. B. 1826: An Anonymous Manuscript in Facsimile*. Stuyvesant, NY: Pendragon Press, 2000.

Allen, William Francis, Charles Pickard Ware, and Lucy McKim Garrison. *Slave Songs of the United States*. New York: P. Smith, 1867.

Alvar, Manuel. *Villancicos dieciochescos (la colección malagueña de 1734 a 1770): [editados con un estudio de] Manuel Alvar*. Málaga: Delegación de cultura excmo ayuntamiento de Málaga, 1973.

Álvarez Caballero, Ángel. *Historia del cante flamenco*. Madrid: Alianza Editorial, S.A., 1981.

Amira, John, and Steven L. Cornelius. *The Music of Santería: Traditional Rhythms of the Batá Drums*. Reno, NV: White Cliffs Media, 1999.

Anidjar, Gil. *Blood: A Critique of Christianity*. New York: Columbia University Press, 2016.

Antón Solé, Pablo. *Los villancicos de la Catedral de Cádiz*. Cádiz: Universidad de Cádiz, Servicio de Publicaciones, 1986, 117–38.

Arbeau, Thoinot. *Orchesography*. Translated by Mary Stewart Evans. New York: Dover Publications, Inc., 1967 [1589].

Arellano, Ignacio. "La poesía burlesca áurea, ejercicio de lectura conceptista y apostillas al romance 'Boda de negros' de Quevedo." *Filología Románica*, vol. 5 (Madrid: Editorial Universidad Complutense, 1987–1988): 259–76.

Armona y Murga, José Antonio, Charles Davis, and J. E. Varey. *Memorias cronológicas sobre el origen de la representación de comedias en España (año de 1785)*. Woodbridge, UK: Tamesis, 2007.

Asensio, Eugenio, and V. F. G. Quevedo. *Itinerario del entremés: Desde Lope de Rueda a Quiñones de Benavente*. Madrid: Gredos, 1971.

Aste, Richard. *Behind Closed Doors: Art in the Spanish American Home, 1492–1898*. Brooklyn, NY: Brooklyn Museum; New York: Monacelli Press, 2013.

Attali, Jacques. *Noise: The Political Economy of Music*. Minneapolis: University of Minnesota Press, 1985.

Aulnoy, Marie Catherine Le Jumel de Barneville, Comtesse d'. *The Ingenious and Diverting Letters of the Lady's Travels into Spain Describing the Devotions, Nunneries, Humours, Customs, Laws, Militia, Trade, Diet, and Recreations of that People*. London: Printed for S. Crouch, 1692.

Auserón, Santiago. *El ritmo perdido: Sobre el influjo negro en la canción española*. Barcelona: Ediciones Península, 2012.

Austin, Gerlyn E. "The Advent of the Negro Actor on the Legitimate Stage in America." *Journal of Negro Education* 35, no. 3 (1966): 237–45.

Azorín Fernández, María Dolores. *El diablo cojuelo de L. Vélez de Guevara: Glosario*. Alicante: Fundación Biblioteca Virtual Miguel de Cervantes, 2002.

Ayguals de Izco, D. Wenceslao. *El Fandango. Madrid—Sociedad Literaria—1845. Imprenta de D. Wenceslao Ayguals de Izco, calle de S. Roque*. Facsimile. Sevilla: Extramuros Edición, S. L., 2007.

"El bachiller revoltoso" (Jerónimo de Alba y Diéguez). *Libro de la gitanería de Triana de los años 1740 a 1750 que escribió el bachiller revoltoso para que no se imprimiera*. Edited by Antonio Castro Carrasco. Seville: Coria Gráfica, S. L., 1995.

Baird, Thomas, K. Meira Goldberg, and Paul Jared Newman. "Changing Places: Toward the Reconstruction of an Eighteenth Century Danced Fandango." In *Españoles, indios, africanos y gitanos. El alcance global del fandango en música, canto y baile*, edited by K. Meira Goldberg and Antoni Pizà. *Música Oral Del Sur*, no. 12 (2015): 619–56. Also published in *The Global Reach of the Fandango in Music, Song and Dance: Spaniards, Indians, Africans and Gypsies*, edited by K. Meira Goldberg and Antoni Pizà. Castle-upon-Tyne: Cambridge Scholars Publishing, 2016, 579–621.

Baker Jr., Houston A. *Modernism and the Harlem Renaissance*. Chicago and London: University of Chicago Press, 1987.

Barbieri, Francisco A. *Las castañuelas: Estudio jocoso dedicado á todos los boleros y danzantes, por uno de tantos*. Madrid: Imp. de J.M. Ducazcal, 1879.

Barletta, Vincent. *Covert Gestures: Crypto-Islamic Literature as Cultural Practice in Early Modern Spain*. Minneapolis: University of Minnesota Press, 2005.

Barrios, Manuel. *Gitanos, moriscos y cante flamenco*. Sevilla: RC Editor, 1989.

Bartra, Roger. *Cultura y melancolía: Las enfermedades del alma en la España del Siglo de Oro*. Barcelona: Editorial Anagrama, 2001.

Bates, Katherine Lee. "The Gypsies of Spain: Gitanas Sing and Dance, Beguiling Tourists with Coquetry—The Beggars are Persistent—Young and Old Alike are Irresistible in their Clamour for Pennies—the Fair at Seville." *New York Times* (May 14, 1899), 15.

Baudot, Georges, and M. Águeda Méndez. "El Chuchumbé, Un Son Jácarandoso Del México Virreinal." *Cahiers Du Monde Hispanique Et Luso-Brésilien*, no. 48 (1987): 163–71.

Baudot, Georges, and M. Águeda Méndez. *Amores prohibidos: La palabra condenada en el México de los virreyes: Antología de coplas y versos censurados por la Inquisición de México*. México: Siglo Veintiuno, 1997.

Becco, Horacio J. *El tema del negro en cantos, bailes y villancicos de los siglos XVI y XVII*. Buenos Aires: Ollantay, 1951.

Becker, Danièle. "El teatro palaciego y la música en la segunda mitad del siglo XVII." In *Actas del IX Congreso de la Asociación Internacional de Hispanistas*, edited by Sebastián Neumeister. AIH, Actas vol. 9 (1986): 353–64, http://cvc.cervantes.es/literatura/aih/aih_ix.htm.

Bécquer, Gustavo Adolfo. "La Feria de Sevilla," *El Museo Universal*, April 25, 1869.

Bean, Annemarie, James V. Hatch, and Brooks McNamara, eds. *Inside the Minstrel Mask: Readings in Nineteenth-Century Blackface Minstrelsy*. Hanover, NH: Wesleyan University Press, 1996.

Bennahum, Ninotchka Devorah. *Antonia Mercé, "La Argentina": Flamenco and the Spanish Avant Garde*. Hanover, NH: University Press of New England, 2000.

Bennahum, Ninotchka, and K. Meira Goldberg. *100 Years of Flamenco in New York City*. New York: New York Public Library for the Performing Arts, 2013.

Bentley, W. H. *Dictionary and Grammar of the Kongo Language, As Spoken at San Salvador, the Ancient Capital of the Old Kongo Empire, West Afrika [and Appendix] Compiled and Prepared for the Baptist Mission on the Kongo River, West Africa*. London: Baptist Missionary Society, and Trübner & Co., 1887.

Bergman, Ted L. L. *The Art of Humour in the Teatro Breve and Comedias of Calderón de la Barca*. Woodbridge, UK: Tamesis, 2003.

Beusterien, John. *An Eye on Race: Perspectives from Theater in Imperial Spain*. Lewisburg, PA: Bucknell University Press, 2006.

Bickerstaffe, Isaac. *The Padlock: A Comic Opera: As It Is Perform'd by His Majesty's Servants, at the Theatre-Royal in Drury-Lane*. London: printed for W. Griffin, 1768.

Blake, Jody. *Le Tumulte Noir: Modernist Art and Popular Entertainment in Jazz-Age Paris, 1900–1930*. University Park: Pennsylvania State University Press, 1999.

Blas Vega, José. *Los cafés cantantes de Madrid: (1846–1936)*. Madrid: Ediciones Guillermo Blázquez, 2006.

Blas Vega, José. *Los cafés cantantes de Sevilla*. Madrid: Cinterco, 1987.

Blas Vega, José. *Vida y cante de Don Antonio Chacón: La Edad de Oro del flamenco (1869–1929)*. Madrid: Editorial Cinterco, 1990.

Blasis, Carlo, and R. Barton. *Notes upon Dancing, Historical and Practical*. London: M. Delaporte, 1847.

Blight, David W. *Race and Reunion: The Civil War in American Memory*. Cambridge, MA: Belknap Press of Harvard University Press, 2001.

Bond, Chrystelle T. *A Chronicle of Dance in Baltimore, 1780–1814*. New York: M. Dekker, 1976.

Boone, Mary Elizabeth. *Vistas de España: American Views of Art and Life in Spain, 1860–1914*. New Haven, CT: Yale University Press, 2007.

Bourdieu, Pierre. *Distinction: A Social Critique of the Judgement of Taste*. London: Routledge & Kegan Paul, 1979.

Borrow, George. *The Zincali, or, An Account of the Gypsies of Spain with an Original Collection of Their Songs and Poetry, and a Copious Dictionary of Their Language*. London and New York: John Lane, 1902 [1841].

Brading, D. A. *The First America: The Spanish Monarchy, Creole Patriots, and the Liberal State, 1492–1867*. Cambridge: Cambridge University Press, 1991.

Briceño, Luis. *Método muy facilisimo para aprender a tañer la guitarra á lo español.* Paris: Pedro Ballard, 1626.

Brooks, Lynn Matluck. *The Art of Dancing in Seventeenth-Century Spain: Juan de Esquivel Navarro and His World.* Lewisburg, PA: Bucknell University Press, 2003.

Brooks, Lynn Matluck. *The Dances of the Processions of Seville in Spain's Golden Age.* Kassel: Ed. Reichenberger, 1988.

Brooks, Lynn Matluck. *John Durang: Man of the American Stage.* Amherst, NY: Cambria Press, 2011.

Brotherton, John. *The Pastor-Bobo in the Spanish Theatre, before the Time of Lope de Vega.* London: Tamesis, 1975.

Brown, Howard Mayer. *Music in the French Secular Theater, 1400–1550.* Cambridge, MA: Harvard University Press, 1963.

Brown, Jayna. *Babylon Girls: Black Women Performers and the Shaping of the Modern.* Durham, NC: Duke University Press, 2008.

de Cadalso, Don José. *Cartas marruecas, por el Coronel Don José de Cadalso, Caballero del Hábito de Santiago, nueva edición, revista y cuidadosamente corregida.* Paris: J. Smith, 1827 [1789].

C. L. "An Old Actor's Memories—What Mr. Edmon S. Connor Recalls About his Career. An Old Stock Actor's Stories of the Days of Stock Companies—Joe Jefferson's Infancy—Early Days in Cincinnati—Hiram Power's Wax Works—Jim Crow Rice." *New York Times* (June 5, 1881), 10.

Caddy, Davinia. "Parisian Cake Walks." *19th Century Music* 30, no. 3 (Spring 2007): 288–317.

Cairón, Antonio. *Compendio de las principales reglas del baile.* Madrid: Repullés, 1820.

Cairón, Antonio. *El encuentro feliz o Los americanos o La espada del mago.* Biblioteca Histórica Municipal de Madrid, BHM MUS, 1818, 605–7.

del Campo Tejedor, Alberto, and Rafael Cáceres Feria. *Historia cultural del flamenco (1546–1910): El barbero y la guitarra.* Córdoba: Almuzara, 2013.

Campóo Schelotto, Diana. "Danza y educación nobiliaria en el siglo XVIII: El *Método* de la escuela de baile en el Real Seminario de Nobles de Madrid." *Ars Bilduma* (2015): 157–73.

Capmany, Aurelio. "El baile y la danza." In *Folklore y costumbres de España: II*, edited by Francesch Carreras y Candi. Barcelona: Casa Editorial Alberto Martin, 1931, 161–418.

Carlson, Marvin. *Performance: A Critical Introduction.* London: Routledge, 1996.

Caro, Rodrigo. *Dias geniales ó Lúdicros, libro expósito dedicado á Don Fadrique Enrriquez Afan de Rivera.* Sevilla: Impr. de El Mercantil Sevillano, 1884 [ca. 1626].

Caro Baroja, Julio. *Temas castizos*, Madrid: Ediciones Istmo, 1980.

Caroso, Fabritio. *Courtly Dance of the Renaissance.* Translated and edited by Julia Sutton. Music transcribed and edited by F. Marian Walker. New York: Dover, 1995.

Carpentier, Alejo. *La música en Cuba.* México: Fondo de Cultura Económica, 1946.

Carpentier, Alejo. *Music in Cuba.* Translated by Timothy Brennan and Alan West-Durán. Minneapolis: University of Minnesota Press, 2001 [Spanish edition: 1946].

Carroll, James. *Constantine's Sword: The Church and the Jews; A History.* Boston: Houghton Mifflin, 2002.

de las Casas, Bartolomé. *A Short Account of the Destruction of the Indies: Or, a Faithful Narrative of the Horrid and Unexampled Massacres, Butcheries, and All Manner of*

Cruelties,...the Time of Its First Discovery by Them. Great Britain: Pantianos Classics, 2016.

Castellanos de Losada, Basilio Sebastián, Félix de Azara, and Agustín de Azara. *Glorias de Azara en el siglo XIX. Acta de la solemne inauguracion del monumento erigido en Barbuñales de Aragón, El 27 de noviembre de 1850, Al célebre diplomático...Don José Nicolás de Azara y Perera, Primer Marqués de Nibbiano, por Don Agustín de Azara, Tercer Marqués del Mismo Titulo...Corona (poético-Musical) que los poetas, orientalistas, hombres políticos, y artistas españoles, consagran al espresado señor. Obra escrita en parte y dirigida en lo demás por Don B.S. Castellanos de Losada.* Madrid, 1852.

Castle, Charles. *The Folies Bergère.* London: Methuen, 1982.

Cátedra, Pedro M., ed. *La literatura popular impresa en España y en la América colonial. Formas & temas, géneros, funciones, difusión, historia y teoría.* Salamanca: Seminario de Estudios Medievales y Renacentistas—Instituto de Historia del Libro y de la Lectura, 2006, 162.

Cavia Naya, Victoria. *La castañuela española y la danza: Baile, música e identidad.* Valencia, España: Mahali, 2013.

Cazal, Françoise. "Del pastor bobo al gracioso: El pastor de Diego Sánchez de Badajoz." *Criticón,* no. 60 (1994): 7–18.

Çelik, Zeynep, and Leila Kinney. "Ethnography and Exhibitionism at the Expositions Universelles," *Assemblage : A Critical Journal of Architecture and Design Culture,* no. 13 (December 1990): 34–59.

de Certeau, Michel. *The Practice of Everyday Life.* Translated by Steven Rendall. Berkeley: University of California Press, 1984.

Cervantes Saavedra, Miguel de. *El celoso extremeño.* In *Novelas ejemplares,* 131–64. Colombia: Panamericana Editorial, 1993 [1613].

Cervantes Saavedra, Miguel de. *El coloquio de los perros.* In *Novelas ejemplares,* 263–314. Colombia: Panamericana Editorial, 1993 [1613].

Cervantes Saavedra, Miguel de. *La gitanilla.* In *Novelas ejemplares,* 7–68. Colombia: Panamericana Editorial, 1993 [1613].

Cervantes Saavedra, Miguel de. *La ilustre fregona.* In *Novelas ejemplares,* 165–214. Colombia: Panamericana Editorial, 1993 [1613].

Cesairé, Aimé. *A Tempest, Based on Shakespeare's The Tempest: Adaptation for a Black Theater.* New York: Ubu Repertory Theater Productions, 1969.

Chacón Carmona, Vicente. "Singing Shepherds, Discordant Devils: Music and Song in Medieval Pastoral Plays." *Medieval English Theatre,* no. 32 (2010): 62–80.

Chaviano Pérez, Lizbeth J. and Martín Rodrigo y Alharilla, eds. *Negreros y esclavos Barcelona y la esclavitud atlántica (siglos XVI–XIX).* Barcelona: Icaria Editorial, 2017.

Chevalier, Maxime. *Quevedo y su tiempo: La agudeza verbal.* Barcelona: Editorial crítica, 1992.

Chuse, Loren. *Cantaoras: Music, Gender and Identity in Flamenco Song.* Hoboken, NJ: Taylor and Francis, 2013.

Clavería, Carlos. "Contribución a la semántica de Belén," *Hispanic Review* 27, no. 3, *Joseph E. Gillet Memorial Volume, Part III* (July 1959): 345–60.

Clavería, Carlos. *Estudios sobre los gitanismos del español.* Madrid: Anejo LIII R. F. E, 1951.

Coates, Ta-Nehisi. *Between the World and Me.* New York: Spiegel & Grau, 2015.

Cockrell, Dale. *Demons of Disorder: Early Blackface Minstrels and Their World.* Cambridge: Cambridge University Press, 1997.

Cohen, Albert. "Spanish National Character in the Court Ballets of J.-B. Lully." *Revista de Musicología* 16, no. 5 (1993): 2977–87.

Connelly, Frances S. *The Sleep of Reason: Primitivism in Modern European Art and Aesthetics, 1725–1907.* University Park: Pennsylvania State University Press, 1999.

Coral, Matilde, Angel Álvarez Caballero, Juan Valdés, and Rocío Coral. *Tratado de la bata de cola: Matilde Coral, una vida de arte y magisterio.* Madrid: Alianza, D. L. 2003.

Coolen, Michael T. "Senegambian Influences on Afro-American Musical Culture." *Black Music Research Journal* 11, no. 1 (1991): 1–18.

Correas, Gonzalo, and Cipriano Muñoz y Manzano Viñaza. *Arte grande de la lengua castellana: Compuesto en 1626 Por El Maestro Gonzalo Correas, Catedrático De Salamanca; Publícalo por primera ves El Conde de La Viñaza.* Madrid, 1903.

Cortés Alonso, Vicenta. *La esclavitud en Valencia durante el reinado de los Reyes Católicos (1479–1516).* Valencia: Excmo. Ayuntamiento, 1964.

Cortés López, José Luis. *La esclavitud negra en la España peninsular del siglo XVI.* Salamanca: Ed. Universidad de Salamanca, 1989.

Cosano Prieto, Jesús. *Los invisibles. Hechos y cosas de los negros de Sevilla.* Sevilla: Aconcagua, 2017.

Cotarelo y Mori, Emilio. *Bibliografía de las controversias sobre la licitud del teatro en España.* Madrid: Revista de Archivos, Bibliotecas y Museos, 1904.

Cotarelo y Mori, Emilio. *Colección de entremeses, loas, bailes, jácaras y mojigangas desde fines del siglo XVI à mediados del XVIII,* Madrid: Bailly Ballière, 1911.

Cotarelo y Mori, Emilio. *Historia de la Zarzuela o sea el drama lírico en España, desde su origen a fines del siglo XIX.* Madrid: Tipografía de Archivos, Ozólaga, 1934.

Covarrubias Orozco, Sebastián de. *Tesoro de la Lengua Castellana o Española.* Madrid: Luis Sanchez, impressor del Rey N.S., 1611.

Craun, Edwin D. *Lies, Slander, and Obscenity in Medieval English Literature: Pastoral Rhetoric and the Deviant Speaker.* Cambridge: Cambridge University Press, 1997.

Crawford, James Pyle Wickersham. "The Pastor and Bobo in the Spanish Religious Drama of the Sixteenth Century." *The Romanic Review*, no. 2 (1911): 376–401.

Cruces Roldán, Cristina. *La Niña de los Peines: El mundo flamenco de Pastora Pavón.* Córdoba: Almuzara, 2009.

Cruces Roldán, Cristina. *Más alla de la música (II). Antropología y flamenco: Identidad, género y trabajo.* Sevilla: Signatura, 2003.

Cruz Gutiérrez, José. *La Córdoba flamenca (1866–1900).* Córdoba: El Páramo, 2010.

Cummings, Anthony M. "Dance and 'The Other': The Moresca." In *Seventeenth-Century Ballet: A Multi-Art Spectacle,* edited by Barbara Grammeniati. Bloomington, IN: Xlibris Corporation, 2011, 39–60.

Curtin, Philip D. *The Atlantic Slave Trade: A Census.* Madison: University of Wisconsin Press, 1969.

Damon, S. Foster. "The Negro in Early American Songsters." *Papers of the Bibliographical Society of America,* no. 28 (1934): 132–63.

Daniel, Yvonne. *Caribbean and Atlantic Diaspora Dance: Igniting Citizenship.* Urbana: University of Illinois Press, 2011.

Daniel, Yvonne. *Rumba: Dance and Social Change in Contemporary Cuba.* Bloomington: Indiana University Press, 1995.

Davillier, Jean-Charles, and John Thomson. *Spain, by the Baron Ch. Davillier, illustrated by Gustave Doré.* Translated by J. Thomson. London: S. Low, Marston, Low and Searle, 1876.

Davis, Susan G. "'Making Night Hideous': Christmas Revelry and Public Order in Nineteenth-Century Philadelphia." *American Quarterly* 34, no. 2 (1982): 185–99.

Day, Charles H. *Fun in Black; or, Sketches of Minstrel Life, with the Origin of Minstrelsy, by Colonel T. Allston Brown.* New York: Robert M. DeWitt, 1874. Republished as Brown, T. Allston, and Charles Day. "Black Musicians and Early Ethiopian Minstrelsy." *The Black Perspective in Music* 3, no. 1 (1975 [1874]): 77–99.

Deanda-Camacho, Elena. "'El chuchumbé te he de soplar': Sobre obscenidad, censura y memoria oral en el primer 'son de la tierra' novohispano." *Mester* 36, no. 1 (2007): 53–71.

DeCosta-Willis, Miriam, ed. *Blacks in Hispanic Literature: Critical Essays.* Port Washington, NY: Kennikat Press, 1977.

Deren, Maya. *Divine Horsemen: The Living Gods of Haiti.* New Paltz, NY: McPherson, 1983.

Díez Borque, José María. "Liturgia-fiesta-teatro: Órbitas concéntricas de teatralidad en el siglo XVI." *Dicenda*, no. 6 (1987): 485–500.

Díez Borque, José María. *Sociología de la comedia española del siglo XVII.* Madrid: Cátedra, 1976.

Dillon, Elizabeth Maddock. *New World Drama: The Performative Commons in the Atlantic World, 1649–1849.* Durham, NC: Duke University Press, 2014.

Dolmetsch, Mabel. *Dances of Spain and Italy from 1400 to 1600.* New York: Da Capo Press, 1975.

Domínguez Ortiz, Antonio. *La esclavitud en Castilla en la Edad Moderna y otros estudios de marginados.* Granada: Editorial Comares, 2003 [1952].

Dorman, James H. "The Strange Career of Jim Crow Rice (with Apologies to Professor Woodward)." *Journal of Social History* 3, no. 2 (1969): 109–22.

Du Bois, W. E. B. *The Souls of Black Folk.* New York: Vintage Books/Library of America, 1990 [1903].

Duchartre, Pierre-Louis. *The Italian Comedy: The Improvisation, Scenarios, Lives, Attributes, Portraits, and Masks of the Illustrious Characters of the Commedia Dell'arte.* Translated by Randolph T. Weaver. New York: Dover Publications, 1966 [1929].

Durang, Charles. *The Ball-Room Bijou, and Art of Dancing. Containing the Figures of the Polkas, Mazurkas, and Other Popular New Dances, with Rules for Polite Behaviour.* Philadelphia, Baltimore, and New York: Fisher & Brother, 1850, http://www.unz.org/Pub/DurangCharles-1850.

Durang, John. *The Memoir of John Durang, American Actor, 1785–1816.* Edited by Alan S. Downer. Pittsburgh: Published for the Historical Society of York County and for the American Society for Theatre Research by the University of Pittsburgh Press, 1966.

Earle, Thomas Foster, and K. J. P. Lowe, eds. *Black Africans in Renaissance Europe,* Cambridge: Cambridge University Press, 2005.

Edminster, Warren. "Foolish Shepherds and Priestly Folly: Festive Influence in Prima Pastorum," *Medieval Perspectives* 15 (2000): 57–73.

Eli Rodríguez, Victoria, and María de los Ángeles Alfonso Rodríguez. *La música entre Cuba y España: Tradición e innovación*. Madrid: Fundación Autor, 1999.

Eliav-Feldon, Miriam, Benjamin Isaac, and Joseph Ziegler. *The Origins of Racism in the West*. Cambridge: Cambridge University Press, 2013.

Ellison, Ralph. "Change the Joke and Slip the Yoke." *Partisan Review* 25 (spring 1958): 212–22. Reprinted in Ralph Ellison, *Shadow and Act* (New York: Random House, 1964), 45–59.

Esquivel Navarro, Juan de. *Discursos sobre el arte del dançado y sus excelencias y primer origen, reprobando las acciones deshonestas [Texto impreso]/compuesto por Iuan de Esquiuel Nauarro...* Impressos en Seuilla: por Iuan Gomez de Blas, 1642.

Esses, Maurice. *Dance and Instrumental Diferencias in Spain during the 17th and Early 18th Centuries*. Stuyvesant, NY: Pendragon Press, 1992.

Estébanez Calderón, Serafín, "El Solitario," illustrated by Francisco Lameyer. *Escenas andaluzas: Bizarrías de la tierra, alardes de toros, rasgos populares, cuadros de costumbres y artículos varios... Edicion de lujo adornada con 125 dibujos por Lameyer*. Madrid: Baltasar González, 1847.

Etzion, Judith. "The Spanish Fandango from Eighteenth-Century 'Lasciviousness' to Nineteenth-Century Exoticism." *Anuario Musical*, no. 48 (1993): 229–50.

Etzion, Judith. "Spanish Music as Perceived in Western Music Historiography: A Case of the Black Legend?" *International Review of the Aesthetics and Sociology of Music* 29, no. 2 (1998): 93–120.

Eze, Emmanuel Chukwudi, ed., *Race and the Enlightenment*. Malden, MA, and Oxford: Blackwell Publishers, 1997.

Fanon, Frantz. *Black Skin, White Masks*. New York: Grove Press, 1967.

Faulín Hidalgo, Ignacio. *¡Bienvenido Mr. USA! La música norteamericana en España antes del rock and roll, 1865–1955*. Lleida: Milenio, 2016.

Fauser, Annegret. *Musical Encounters at the 1889 Paris World's Fair*. Rochester, NY: University of Rochester Press, 2005.

Fernández, Manuel F., and Rafael M. Pérez García. *En los márgenes de la ciudad de Dios: Moriscos en Sevilla*. Valencia: Universidad de Valencia, 2009.

Fernández-Armesto, Felipe. *1492: The Year the World Began*. New York: HarperOne, 2009.

Fernández Chaves, Manuel F., and Rafael M. Pérez García. "La esclavitud en la Sevilla del Quinientos: Una propuesta metodológica en base de documentación parroquial (1568–1590)," and "Reflexión historica (1540–1570)." In *Marginados y minorías sociales en la España moderna y otros estudios sobre Extremadura*, edited by F. Lorenzana de la Puente and F. J. Mateos Ascacíbar, 113–33. Llerena: Sociedad Extremeña de Historia, 2005.

Fernández Manzano, Reynaldo. "La Granada de Glinka (1845–1846)." *Los papeles españoles de Glinka*. Madrid: Consejería de Educación y Cultura, Comunidad de Madrid, 1996, 19–24.

"Fernando el de Triana" (Fernando Rodríguez Gómez). *Arte y artistas flamencos*. Madrid: Editoriales Andaluzas Unidas, S.A., 1986 [1935].

Ferriol y Boxeraus, Bartolomé, Joseph Testore, and Santiago Perez Junquera. *Reglas útiles para los aficionados a danzar: provechoso divertimiento de los que gustan tocar instrumentos: y polyticas advertencias a todo genero de personas: adornado con varias laminas: dedicado a la S. M. el Rey de las Dos Sicilias, & c.* Capoa: A costa de Joseph Testore, mercador de libros, à la Calle Nueva, 1745.

Flinn, Frank. "The Phenomenology of Symbol: Genesis I and II." In *Phenomenology in Practice and Theory: Essays for Herbert Spiegelberg*, edited by William S. Hamrick. Dordrecht: Springer Netherlands, 1984, 223–49.

Floyd, Samuel A. "Ring Shout! Literary Studies, Historical Studies, and Black Music Inquiry." *Black Music Research Journal* 22 (2002 [1991]): 49–70.

Forbes, F. William. "The 'Gracioso:' Toward a Functional Re-Evaluation." *Hispania* 61, no. 1 (March 1978): 78–83.

Forrest, John. *The History of Morris Dancing, 1483–1750.* Cambridge: Clarke, 1999.

Fra Molinero, Baltasar. *La imagen de los negros en el teatro del Siglo de Oro.* Madrid: Siglo XXI de España, 1995.

Franc-Nohain, Maurice. *Les Mémoires de Foottit et Chocolat.* Paris: Pierre Lafitte et Cie, 1907.

Franco Silva, Alfonso. *La esclavitud en Andalucía, 1450–1550.* Granada: University of Granada, 1992.

Franko, Mark. *Dance as Text: Ideologies of the Baroque Body.* Cambridge: Cambridge University Press, 1993.

Frenk Alatorre, Margit, and Mariana Masera. *La otra Nueva España: la palabra marginada en la colonia.* Barcelona: Azul, 2002.

Frenk Alatorre, Margit. *Nuevo corpus de la antigua lírica popular hispánica, Siglos XV a XVII.* México, D.F: Facultad de Filosofía y Letras, Universidad Nacional Autónoma de México, 2003.

Fuchs, Barbara. *Exotic Nation: Maurophilia and the Construction of Early Modern Spain.* Philadelphia: University of Pennsylvania Press, 2009.

de la Fuente Ballesteros, Ricardo. "Los gitanos en la tonadilla escénica." *Revista de Folklore* 4A, no. 40 (1984): 122–26.

de la Fuente Ballesteros, Ricardo. "El moro en la tonadilla escénica." *Revista de Folklore* 5A, no. 49 (1985): 32–36.

de la Fuente Ballesteros, Ricardo. "El personaje negro en la tonadilla escénica del siglo XVIII." *Revista de Folklore* 4B, no. 48 (1984): 190–96.

Gallego, José Andrés. *La esclavitud en la América española.* Madrid: Ed. Encuentro, 2005.

Gamboa, José Manuel. *Una historia del flamenco.* Madrid: Espasa, 2011.

Garafola, Lynn. *Diaghilev's Ballets Russes.* New York: Oxford University Press, 1989.

Garafola, Lynn. *Legacies of Twentieth-Century Dance.* Middletown, CT: Wesleyan University Press, 2005.

Garafola, Lynn, and Nancy V. N. Baer. *The Ballets Russes and Its World.* New Haven, CT: Yale University Press, 1999.

García de León Griego, Antonio. *El mar de los deseos: El Caribe hispano musical historia y contrapunto.* Coyoacán, México y Buenos Aires, Argentina: Siglo Veintiuno Editores, S.A. de C.V., 2002.

García Lorca, Federico. *Obras.* Edited by Miguel García-Posada. Madrid: Akal, 1980.

García Lorca, Federico. *In Search of Duende.* Edited and translated by Christopher Maurer. New York: New Directions, 1998.

García-Márquez, Vicente. *Massine: A Biography.* New York: Knopf, 1995. García Martínez, José María. *Del fox-trot al jazz flamenco: El jazz en España 1919–1996.* Madrid: Alianza, 1996.

García-Márquez, Vicente, Yvan Nommick, and Antonio Álvarez Cañibano, eds. *Los Ballets Russes de Diaghilev y España*. Granada: Archivo Manuel de Falla, 2012.

Gautier, Théophile. *A Romantic in Spain*. Translated by Catherine Allison Phillips. New York: Interlink Books, 2001[1926].

Gautier, Théophile. *Voyage en Espagne*. Translated by Henry Christie Steel. Boston: D.C. Heath & Co., 1900.

Gautier, Théophile, and Ivor F. Guest. "Théophile Gautier on Spanish Dancing." *Dance Chronicle* 10, no. 1 (1987): 1–104.

Gelardo Navarro, José, and María Amparo Fernández Darós. *¡Viva la Ópera Flamenca! Flamenco y Andalucía en la prensa murciana (1900–1939)*. Murcia: Universidad de Murcia, 2014.

Gerstin, Julian. "Tangled Roots: Kalenda and Other Neo-African Dances in the Circum-Caribbean." *New West Indian Guide/Nieuwe West-Indische Gids* 78, no. 1/2 (2004): 5–41.

Gilroy, Paul. *The Black Atlantic: Modernity and Double Consciousness*. Cambridge, MA: Harvard University Press, 1993.

Gobineau, Arthur. *The Inequality of Human Races*. Translated by Adrian Collins. New York: G. P. Putnam's Sons, 1915.

Goldberg, K. Meira. *Border Trespasses: The Gypsy Mask and Carmen Amaya's Flamenco Dance*. Doctoral dissertation, Temple University, 1995.

Goldberg, K. Meira. "A Heart of Darkness in the New World: Carmen Amaya's Flamenco Dance in South American Vaudeville." *Choreography and Dance*, no. 3 (1994): 95–107.

Goldberg, K. Meira. "*Jaleo de Jerez* and *Tumulte Noir*: Primitivist Modernism and Cakewalk in Flamenco, 1902–1917," 124–42. In *Flamenco on the Global Stage: Historical, Critical, and Theoretical Perspectives*. Edited by K. Meira Goldberg, Ninotchka D. Bennahum, and Michelle Heffner Hayes. Jefferson, NC: McFarland Publishing, 2015.

Goldberg, K. Meira. "The Latin Craze and the Gypsy Mask: Carmen Amaya and the Flamenco Aesthetic, 1913–1963." In Ninotchka D. Bennahum and K. Meira Goldberg, *100 Years of Flamenco*. New York: New York Public Library for the Performing Arts, 2013, 80–121.

Goldberg, K. Meira. "Sonidos Negros: On the Blackness of Flamenco." *Dance Chronicle* 37, no. 1 (2014): 85–113.

Goldberg, K. Meira, Ninotchka Bennahum, and Michelle Heffner Hayes, eds. *Flamenco on the Global Stage: Historical, Critical, and Theoretical Perspectives*. Jefferson, NC: McFarland, 2015.

Goldberg, K. Meira, Walter Clark, and Antoni Pizà, eds. *Spaniards, Natives, Africans, and Roma: Transatlantic Malagueñas and Zapateados in Music, Song, and Dance*. Castle upon Tyne: Cambridge Scholars Publishing, forthcoming 2018.

Goldberg, K. Meira, and Antoni Pizà, eds. "Españoles, indios, africanos y gitanos. El alcance global del fandango en música, canto y baile." *Música Oral del Sur*, no. 12 (2015).

Goldberg, K. Meira, and Antoni Pizà, eds. *The Global Reach of the Fandango in Music, Song and Dance: Spaniards, Indians, Africans and Gypsies*. Castle-upon-Tyne: Cambridge Scholars Publishing, 2016.

Goldenberg, David M. *The Curse of Ham: Race and Slavery in Early Judaism, Christianity, and Islam*. Princeton, NJ: Princeton University Press, 2005.

González, Domingo. *Escuela por lo vajo de Domingo González*. Real Academia de Bellas Artes San Fernando, Signatura A/1736 (2).

González Echevarría, Roberto. *Celestina's Brood: Continuities of the Baroque in Spanish and Latin American Literatures*. Durham, NC: Duke University Press, 1993.

Gordon, Rae Beth. *Dances with Darwin, 1875–1910: Vernacular Modernity in France*. Farnham, Surrey, England: Ashgate, 2009.

Gottschild, Brenda Dixon. *The Black Dancing Body: A Geography from Coon to Cool*. New York: Palgrave Macmillan, 2003.

Gottschild, Brenda Dixon. *Digging the Africanist Presence in American Performance: Dance and Other Contexts*. Westport, CT: Greenwood Press, 1996.

Griffiths, Trevor. " 'This Island's Mine'; Caliban and Colonialism." *The Yearbook of English Studies* 13 (1983): 159–80.

Grut, Marina, Alberto Lorca, Ángel Pericet Carmona, Eloy Pericet, and Ivor Forbes Guest. *The Bolero School: An Illustrated History of the Bolero, the Seguidillas and the Escuela Bolera: Syllabus and Dances*. Alton, Hampshire, UK: Dance Books, 2002.

Gruzinski, Serge. *Images at War: Mexico from Columbus to Blade Runner (1492–2019)*. Translated by Heather MacLean. Durham, NC: Duke University Press, 2001.

Guest, Ann Hutchinson, and Friedrich Albert Zorn. *Fanny Elssler's Cachucha*. New York: Theatre Arts Books, 1981.

Guest, Ivor F. *Fanny Elssler*. Middletown, CT: Wesleyan University Press, 1970.

Haidt, Rebecca. *Embodying Enlightenment: Knowing the Body in Eighteenth-Century Spanish Literature and Culture*. New York: Macmillan, 1998.

Haidt, Rebecca. "Los Majos, el 'españolísimo gremio' del teatro popular dieciochesco: sobre casticismo, inestabilidad y abyección." *Cuadernos de Historia Moderna, Anejo X: Los extranjeros y la Nación en España y la América española*. Madrid: Universidad Complutense, 2011: 155–73.

Halberstam, Jack. "The Wild Beyond: With and For the Undercommons." In Stefano Harney and Fred Moten, *The Undercommons: Fugitive Planning and Black Study*. Wivenhoe, New York, Port Watson: Minor Compositions, 2013, 2–13.

Hall, Kim F. *Things of Darkness: Economies of Race and Gender in Early Modern England*. Ithaca, NY: Cornell University Press, 1995.

H[all], L[illian]. "Harvard Library Notes. Some Early Black-face Performers and the First Minstrel Troupe," no. 2 (1920): 39–45.

Hall, Stuart. "The After-Life of Frantz Fanon: Why Fanon? Why Now? Why *Black Skin, White Masks*?" 12–37. In *The Fact of Blackness: Frantz Fanon and Visual Representation*, edited by Alan Read. London: Institute of Contemporary Arts, 1996.

Hall, Stuart. *The Fateful Triangle: Race, Ethnicity, Nation*. Edited by Kobena Mercer and Henry Louis Gates, Jr. Cambridge, MA: Harvard University Press, 2017.

Hargreaves-Mawdsley, W. N. *Spain Under the Bourbons, 1700–1833: A Collection of Documents, Edited and Translated with a Critical Introduction*. Columbia: University of South Carolina Press, 1973.

Harney, Stefano, and Fred Moten. *The Undercommons: Fugitive Planning and Black Study*. Wivenhoe, New York, Port Watson: Minor Compositions, 2013.

Harris, Max. *Aztecs, Moors, and Christians: Festivals of Reconquest in Mexico and Spain*. Austin: University of Texas Press, 2010.

Harris-Warrick, Rebecca, and Bruce A. Brown. *The Grotesque Dancer on the Eighteenth-Century Stage: Gennaro Magri and His World*. Madison: University of Wisconsin Press, 2005.

Harris-Warrick, Rebecca, and Carol G. Marsh. *Musical Theatre at the Court of Louis XIV: Le Mariage de la Grosse Cathos*. Cambridge: Cambridge University Press, 1994.

Hartman, Saidiya V. *Scenes of Subjection: Terror, Slavery, and Self-Making in Nineteenth-Century America*. New York: Oxford University Press, 1997.

Hayes, Michelle Heffner. *Flamenco: Conflicting Histories of the Dance*. Jefferson, NC: McFarland, 2009.

Hendrix, William S. *Some Native Comic Types in the Early Spanish Drama*. Doctoral dissertation, University of Chicago, 1922.

Heuer, Bronwen Jean. *The Discourse of the Ruffian in Quevedo's "Jácaras."* Doctoral dissertation, State University of New York at Stony Brook, 1991.

Hill, Constance Valis. *Tap Dancing America: A Cultural History*. New York: Oxford University Press, 2010.

hooks, bell (Gloria Watkins). *Black Looks: Race and Representation*. Boston: South End Press, 1992.

Huerta Calvo, Javier. "Comicidad y marginalidad en el sainete dieciochesco." *Scriptura* 10, no. 15 (1999): 51–76.

Huerta Calvo, Javier, Harm den Boer, and Fermín Sierra Martínez, eds. *Diálogos hispánicos de Amsterdam 8/I—El teatro español a fines del siglo XVII—Historia, cultura y teatro en la España de Carlos II*. Amsterdam, Atlanta, Georgia: Rodipi, 1989.

Hughes, Robert. *Goya*. New York: Knopf, 2006.

Hutton, Laurence. *Curiosities of the American Stage*. New York: Harper & Brothers, 1891.

Infante, Blas. *Orígenes de lo flamenco y secreto del cante jondo (1929–1933)*. Sevilla: Junta de Andalucía, Consejería de Cultura, 1980.

Irigoyen-García, Javier. *The Spanish Arcadia: Sheep Herding, Pastoral Discourse, and Ethnicity in Early Modern Spain*. Toronto: University of Toronto Press, 2014.

Jaque, Juan Antonio. *Libro de danzar de Don Baltasar de Rojas Pantoja compuesto por el Maestro Juan Antonio Jaque*. Copia de Francisco Asenjo Barbieri. BNE MSS/18580/5, nineteenth-century [ca. 1680]. http://bdh-rd.bne.es/viewer.vm?id=0000068465&page=1.

Jaque, Juan Antonio, and José Subirá. "*Libro de danzar de Don Baltasar de Rojas Pantoja*, compuesto por el maestro Juan Antonio Jaque." *Anuario Musical*, vol. 5. Barcelona: Consejo Superior de Investigaciones Científicas, Instituto Español de Musicología, 1950 [ca. 1680], 190–98.

Jeschke, Claudia, Gabi Vettermann, and Nicole Haitzinger. *Les Choses Espagnoles: Research into the Hispanomania of 19th Century Dance*. Múnchen: epodium, 2009.

Johnson, Lemuel A. *The Devil, the Gargoyle, and the Buffoon: The Negro as Metaphor in Western Literature*. Port Washington, NY: Kennikat Press, 1971.

Johnson, Stephen B. *Burnt Cork: Traditions and Legacies of Blackface Minstrelsy*. Amherst: University of Massachusetts Press, 2012.

Jones, Nicholas. *Lumbe, Lumbe! Radical Performances of Habla de negros in Early Modern Spain*. University Park: Pennsylvania State University Press, forthcoming.

Joyce, James, Hans Walter Gabler, Wolfhard Steppe, and Claus Melchior, *Ulysses: The Corrected Text* (London: Bodley Head, 1986), 23.

Kamen, Henry. *Spain, 1469–1714: A Society of Conflict.* London: Routledge, 2005.

Katzew, Ilona. *Casta Painting: Images of Race in Eighteenth-Century Mexico.* New Haven, CT: Yale University Press, 2004.

Kirstein, Lincoln. *The Book of the Dance: A Short History of Classic Theatrical Dancing.* Garden City, NY: Garden City Publishing, 1942 [1935].

Kleinertz, Rainer. "Music Theatre in Spain," 402–419. In *The Cambridge History of Eighteenth-Century Music,* edited by Simon P. Keefe. Cambridge: Cambridge University Press, 2011.

Knighton, Tess, and Álvaro Torrente. *Devotional Music in the Iberian World, 1450–1800: The Villancico and Related Genres.* Aldershot, Hants, England: Ashgate, 2007.

Knowles, Mark. *Tap Roots: The Early History of Tap Dancing.* Jefferson, NC: McFarland, 2002.

Krehbiel, Henry E. *Afro-American Folksongs. A Study in Racial and National Music [with Musical Notes].* New York: G. Schirmer, 1913.

Labrador Herraiz, José Julián, and Ralph A. DiFranco. "Villancicos de negros y otros testimonios al caso en manuscritos del Siglo de Oro." In *De la canción de amor medieval a las soleares: Profesor Manuel Alvar "In Memorian."* Edited by Pedro Manuel Piñero Ramírez. (Actas del Congreso Internacional "Lyra minima oral III," Sevilla, 26–28 de noviembre de 2001), 2004, 163–88.

Lacárcel Fernández, José Antonio. "El Tío Canyitas: La zarzuela andaluza y la presencia de Andalucía en la prensa musical española." *Música Oral del Sur,* no. 11 (2014): 207–14.

Laird, Paul R. *Towards a History of the Spanish Villancico.* Warren, MI: Harmonie Park Press, 1997.

Lambranzi, Gregorio. *Neue und curieuse theatralische Tantz-Schul.* Nuremberg: 1716; Reprint, Leipzig: Edition Peters, 1716.

Lambranzi, Gregorio. *New and Curious School of Theatrical Dancing.* Translated by Friderica Derra de Moroda. New York: Dance Horizons, 1972.

Lane, Jill. *Blackface Cuba, 1840–1895.* Philadelphia: University of Pennsylvania Press, 2005.

Lavaur, Luis. "Teoría romántica del cante flamenco." *Revista de Ideas Estéticas,* no. 107 (July–September 1969): 17.

Lavaur, Luis. *Teoría romántica del cante flamenco.* Madrid: Editora Nacional, 1976.

Leblon, Bernard. *El cante flamenco: Entre las músicas gitanas y las tradiciones andaluzas,* Madrid: Editorial Cinterco, 1991.

Le Guin, Elisabeth. "The Barber of Madrid: Spanish Music in Beaumarchais' Figaro Play." *Acta Musicologica* 79 (2007): 151–93.

Le Guin, Elisabeth. *The Tonadilla in Performance: Lyric Comedy in Enlightenment Spain.* Berkeley: University of California Press, 2014.

Lemke, Sieglinde. *Primitivist Modernism.* New York: Oxford University Press, 1998.

Levinthal, David, and Manthia Diawara. *Blackface.* Santa Fe, NM: Arena Editions, 1999.

Leza, José Máximo. "El mestizaje ilustrado: influencias francesas e italianas en el teatro musical madrileño (1760–1780)." *Revista de Musicología* 32, no. 2 (July 2009): 503–46.

Lhamon, W. T. *Raising Cain: Blackface Performance from Jim Crow to Hip Hop.* Cambridge, MA: Harvard University Press, 1998.

Lipski, John M. *A History of Afro-Hispanic Language: Five Centuries, Five Continents.* Cambridge: Cambridge University Press, 2010.

Liu, Benjamin. *Medieval Joke Poetry: The Cantigas d'Escarnho e de Mal Dizer*. Cambridge, MA: Harvard University Press, 2004.

Lobato, María Luisa, and Bègue, Alain, eds. *Literatura y música del hampa en los Siglos de Oro*. Madrid: Visor Libros, 2014.

López Alemany, Ignacio. "'En música italiana/y castellana en la letra': El camino hacia la ópera italianizante en el teatro palaciego de Felipe V." *Dieciocho* 31, no. 1 (2008): 7–22.

López Alemany, Ignacio, and John E. Varey. *El teatro palaciego en Madrid: 1707–1724; Estudio y documentos*. Woodbridge, UK: Támesis, 2006.

Lott, Eric. *Love and Theft: Blackface Minstrelsy and the American Working Class*. New York: Oxford University Press, 1993.

Lotz, Rainer E. "The 'Louisiana Troupes' in Europe." *The Black Perspective in Music* 11, no. 2 (Autumn 1983): 133–42.

Machado y Álvarez, Antonio (Demófilo). *Colección de cantes flamencos: recogidos y anotados por Demófilo*. Edited by Enrique Jesús Rodríguez Baltanás. Sevilla: Signatura Ediciones, 1999 [1881].

Machado y Álvarez, Antonio (Demófilo). *Primeros Escritos Flamencos (1869–70–71)*. Edited by Andrés Raya. Córdoba: Ediciones Demófilo, 1981.

Magri, Gennaro. *Theoretical and Practical Treatise on Dancing*. Translated by Mary Skeaping, with Anna Ivanova and Irmgard E. Berry; edited by Irmgard E. Berry and Annalisa Fox. London: Dance Books, 1988.

Mahar, William J. *Behind the Burnt Cork Mask: Early Blackface Minstrelsy and Antebellum American Popular Culture*. Urbana: University of Illinois Press, 1999.

Marcellus Vittucci, Matteo (Matteo), with Carola Goya. *The Language of Spanish Dance*. Norman: University of Oklahoma Press, 1990.

Marchante-Aragón, Lucas. "The King, the Nation, and the Moor: Imperial Spectacle and the Rejection of Hybridity in *The Masque of the Expulsion of the Moriscos*." *Journal for Early Modern Cultural Studies* 8, no. 1 (2008): 98–133.

de Mariana, Padre Juan. "Del baile y cantar llamado zarabanda." *Obras del Padre Juan de Mariana: Historia de España, tratado contra los juegos públicos*, vol. 2, Madrid: M. Rivadeneyra, 1854 [ca. 1601], 432–34. The original work is available online: BNE Mss/5735, ff. 55–8 (61–4 digital page numbers), http://bdh-rd.bne.es/viewer. vm?id=0000080960&page=1.

Marín y Reus, Rafael. *Método para guitarra: aires andaluces (flamenco): Único en su género*. Madrid: Sociedad de Autores Españoles, 1902.

Martín Casares, Aurelia. "Evolution of the Origin of Slaves Sold in Spain from the Late Middle Ages till the 18th Century," 409–30. In *Serfdom and Slavery in the European Economy, 11th–18th Centuries*, edited by Simonetta Cavaciocchi and E. Schiavitù. Firenze: Firenze University Press, 2014.

Martín Casares, Aurelia, and Marga G. Barranco, eds. *La esclavitud negroafricana en la historia de España siglos XVI y XVII*. Granada: Editorial Comares, S. L., 2010.

Martín Casares, Aurelia, and Marga G. Barranco. "Popular Literary Depictions of Black African Weddings in Early Modern Spain." *Sub-Saharan Africa and Renaissance and Reformation Europe: New Findings and New Perspectives: Renaissance et Réforme* 31, no. 2, Special issue edited by Kate J. P. Lowe (Spring 2008): 107–21.

Martín Marcos, Antonia. "El actor en la representación barroca: Verosimilitud, gesto y ademán." In *Diálogos hispánicos de Amsterdam 8/I—El teatro español a fines del siglo XVII—Historia, cultura y teatro en la España de Carlos II, vol. 3, Representaciones y fiestas*, edited by Javier Huerta Calvo, Harm den Boer, and Fermín Sierra Martínez. Amsterdam, Atlanta, Georgia: Rodipi, 1989, 763–74.

Martínez, María Elena. "The Black Blood of New Spain: Limpieza de Sangre, Racial Violence, and Gendered Power in Early Colonial Mexico." *William and Mary Quarterly* 61, no. 3 (July2004): 479–520.

Martínez, María Elena. *Genealogical Fictions: Limpieza de Sangre, Religion, and Gender in Colonial Mexico*. Stanford, CA: Stanford University Press, 2008.

Martínez, María Elena, David Nirenberg, and Max-Sebastián Hering Torres, eds. *Race and Blood in the Iberian World*. Zürich, Berlin: Lit, 2012.

Martínez-Góngora, Mar. "La problemática producción de la diferencia étnica: Imágenes de belleza petrarquista y génesis bíblica en la *Expulsion de los moros de España* de Gaspar Aguilar." *Revista de estudios hispánicos* 36, no. 3 (2002): 501–22.

Massine, Léonide. *My Life in Ballet*. London: Macmillan, 1968.

Matthews, Brander. "The Rise and Fall of Negro-Minstrelsy." *Scribner's* 57, no. 6 (June 1915): 754–59.

Mayo, Francisco S. *Diccionario gitano*. Madrid: Oficina Tipográfica del Hospicio, 1867.

McGowan, Margaret M. *Dance in the Renaissance: European Fashion, French Obsession*. New Haven, CT: Yale University Press, 2008.

Meglin, Joellen A. "Le Diable Boiteux: French Society behind a Spanish Façade." *Dance Chronicle* 17, no. 3 (1994): 263–302.

Mérimée, Prosper. *Carmen*. Paris: M. Lévy frères, 1846.

Mérimée, Prosper. *Carmen and Other Stories*. Translated and with an introduction and notes by Nicholas Jotcham. Oxford: Oxford University Press, 1990 [1846].

Mesonero Romanos, D. Ramón de. *El antiguo Madrid, paseos históricos-anecdóticos por las calles y casas de esta villa*. Madrid: Don F. de P. Mellado, 1861.

de Miguel, Manuel Viera. "El imaginario visual español en la Exposición Universal de París de 1889: 'España de moda.'" *Anales de Historia del Arte* 537 (2011): 537–50.

Minguet é Irol, Pablo. *Arte de danzar a la francesa, adornado con quarenta figuras, que enseñan el modo de hacer todos los diferentes passos de la danza del minuete, con todas sus reglas, y de conducir los brazos en cada passo: Y en quatro figuras, el modo de danzar los tres passapies. Tambien están escritos en solfa, para que qualquier musico los sepa tañer. Su autor Pablo Minguet e Irol...Añadido en esta tercera impression todos los passos, ó movimientos del danzar à la española...*Madrid, P. Minguet, en su casa, 1758 [1737?], 1–36; published with *Explicacion del danzar a la española*, 37–72, https://www.loc.gov/item/13019257/.

Minguet é Irol, Pablo. *Breue tratado de los passos del danzar a la española [Texto impreso]: que oy se estilan en las seguidillas, fandango, y otros tañidos*. Madrid: Imprenta del autor, 1764, http://bdh-rd.bne.es/viewer.vm?id=0000061855&page=1.

Minguet é Irol, Pablo. *El noble arte de danzar a la francesa, y española adornado con LX láminas finas...*Madrid: P. Minguet, en su casa, 1755, http://bdh-rd.bne.es/viewer.vm?id=0000175380&page=1.

Misón, Luis. *Tonadilla de los negros*. Musical score, 1761. http://www.memoriademadrid.es/buscador.php?accion=VerFicha&id=20810&num_id=1&num_total=244&voto=5.

Moore, Lillian. "John Durang, the First American Dancer," 15–37. In *Chronicles of the American Dance*, edited by Paul Magriel. New York: Henry Holt and Company, 1978.

Mora, Kiko. "Pepita Soto: una historia del sueño americano (1852–1859)." *Revista de investigación sobre flamenco La Madrugá*, no. 8 (Junio 2013): 177–230.

Mora, Kiko. "Sounds of Spain in the Nineteenth Century USA: An Introduction." In *Españoles, indios, africanos y gitanos. El alcance global del fandango en música, canto y baile*, edited by K. Meira Goldberg and Antoni Pizà. *Música Oral Del Sur*, no. 12 (2015): 333–62. Also published in *The Global Reach of the Fandango in Music, Song and Dance: Spaniards, Indians, Africans and Gypsies*. Edited by K. Meira Goldberg and Antoni Pizà. Castle-upon-Tyne: Cambridge Scholars Publishing, 2016, 292–96.

Mora, Kiko. "Who Is Who in the Lumière's Films of Spanish Song and Dance at the Paris Exposition, 1900." Le Grimh, Groupe de reflèxion sur l'image dans le monde hispanique, 2017, https://www.grimh.org/index.php?option=com_content&view=article&layout=edit&id=2745&lang=fr#4.

Mora, Kiko. "¡Y dale con Otero!…Flamencos en la Exposición Universal de París de 1900." *Cadáver Paraíso* (blog), June 11, 2016, https://goo.gl/YCTtSJ.

Mora, Kiko, and K. Meira Goldberg. "Spain in the Basement: Dance, Race, and Nation at the Paris Exposition, 1900." In *Writing the Body; Staging the Other: Essays on Corporeal Marking, Creating, and Resisting*, edited by Brynn Shiovitz. Jefferson, NC: McFarland, forthcoming, 2018.

Moreno Navarro, Isidoro. *La antigua hermandad de los negros de Sevilla: Etnicidad, poder y sociedad en 600 años de historia*. Sevilla: Universidad de Sevilla y Consejería de Cultura de la Junta de Andalucía, 1997.

Morrison, Toni. *Playing in the Dark: Whiteness and the Literary Imagination*. Cambridge, MA: Harvard University Press, 1992.

Moten, Fred. *In the Break: The Aesthetics of the Black Radical Tradition*. Minneapolis: University of Minnesota Press, 2003.

Mulcahy, F. David. *Comedic Treatment of the Flamenco Subculture, 1882–1889*. Doctoral dissertation, Brooklyn Polytechnic University, 1988.

Nathan, Hans. *Dan Emmett and the Rise of Early Negro Minstrelsy*. Norman: University of Oklahoma Press, 1962.

Nathan, Hans. "Negro Impersonation in Eighteenth Century England." *Notes, Second Series* 2, no. 4 (September 1945): 245–54.

de Nava Álvarez, Conde de Noroña, Gaspar María. *Poesías*, vol. 1. Madrid: Por Vega y Compañía, 1799.

Navarro García, José Luis. *Cantes y bailes de Granada*. Málaga: Editorial Arguval, 1993.

Navarro García, José Luis. *La danza y el cine*, vol. 1. Sevilla: Libros con Duende, 2014.

Navarro García, José Luis. *Semillas de ébano: El elemento negro y afroamericano en el baile flamenco*. Sevilla: Portada Editorial, S. L., 1998.

Negri, Cesare, Rovere G. M. Della, and Leone Pallavicini. *Nuove inventioni di balli: Opera Vaghissima nella quale si danno i giusti modi del ben portar la vita, et di accommodarsi con ogni leggiadria di mouimento alle creanze et gratie d'amore. Conueneuoli a tutti i cavalieri, & dame, per ogni sorte di ballo, balletto, & brando d'Italia, di Spagna & di Francia. Con figure…in rame et regole della musica et intauolatura quali si richieggono al suono et al canto. Divisa in tre trattati*. Milano: G. Bordone, 1604.

Nietzsche, Frederich. *Thus Spoke Zarathustra: The Portable Nietzsche*, translated by Walter Kaufman (New York: Penguin Books, 1976), 129.

Noiriel, Gérard. *Chocolat: La véritable histoire d'un homme sans nom.* Montrouge: Bayard, 2016.

Noveli, Rodrigo. *Chorégraphie figurativa y demostrativa del arte de danzar en la forma española.* MS. Madrid, 1708.

Núñez, Faustino. *Guía comentada de música y baile preflamencos (1750–1808).* Barcelona: Ediciones Carena, 2008.

O'Brien, John. *Harlequin Britain: Pantomime and Entertainment, 1690–1760.* Baltimore, MD: Johns Hopkins University Press, 2004.

Olmedo, Federico. "Canciones populares de la guerra de la independencia española." *La Ilustración Española y Americana* 32 (August 30, 1908): 129–32.

Olona, Luis (libretto) and Barbieri, Francisco Asenjo (score). *Entre mi mujer y el negro. Zarzuela–disparate en dos actos. Representada por primera vez en el teatro de la Zarzuela en Octubre de 1859.* Madrid: Jose Rodriguez, 1859, http://bdh-rd.bne.es/viewer.vm?id=0000104604&page=1.

Ortega Castejón, José Francisco "Una carta latina de deán Martí no bien entendida." University of Murcia, *Myrtia: Revista de Filología Clásica,* vol. 29 (2014): 301–14.

Ortiz, Fernando. *La antigua fiesta afrocubana del "Día de Reyes,"* La Habana: República de Cuba, Ministerio de Relaciones Exteriores, Dep. de Asuntos Culturales, División de Publ, 1960.

Ortiz, Fernando. *Cuban Counterpoint: Tobacco and Sugar.* Translated by Harriet de Onís. Introduction by Bronislaw Malinowski. Prologue by Herminio Portell Vila. New York: Random House, 1970 [1947].

Ortiz, Fernando. *Glosario de afronegrismos: con un prologo por Juan M. Dihigo.* Habana, 1924.

Ortiz, Fernando. *Los instrumentos de la música afrocubana* (5 volumes). Habana: Publicaciones de la Dirección de Cultura del Ministerio de Educación, 1952.

Ortiz, Fernando and Diana Iznaga. *Los negros curros.* La Habana: Editorial de Ciencias Sociales, 1986.

Ortiz Nuevo, José Luis. *Coraje. Del maestro Otero y su paso por el baile.* Sevilla: Libros con duende, 2013.

Ortiz Nuevo, José Luis. *¿Se sabe algo? Viaje al conocimiento del arte flamenco según los testimonios de la prensa sevillana del XIX. Desde comienzos del siglo hasta el año en que murió Silverio Franconetti (1812–1889).* Sevilla: Ediciones el Carro de la Nieve, 1990.

Ortiz Nuevo, José Luis. *Tremendo asombro.* Sevilla: Libros con Duende, S.A., 2012.

Ortiz Nuevo, José Luis, Ángeles Cruzado, and Kiko Mora. *La valiente: Trinidad Huertas "La Cuenca."* Sevilla: Libros con Duende, 2016.

Ortiz Nuevo, José Luis, y Faustino Núñez. *La rabia del placer: El nacimiento cubano del tango y su desembarco en España (1823–1923).* Sevilla: Diputación de Sevilla, Área de Cultura y Ecología, 1999.

Otero Aranda, José. *Tratado de Bailes de Sociedad, regionales españoles, especialmente andaluces, con su historia y modo de ejecutarlos.* Seville: Tip. de la Guía Oficial, Lista núm. 1, 1912.

Pablillos de Valladolid, "El conservatorio del flamenquismo—Baila la 'Macarrona,'" *Por Esos Mundos* 15, no. 238 (November 1914): 524–28.

Pablo Lozano, Eulalia and José Luis Navarro García. *Figuras, pasos y mudanzas: claves para conocer el baile flamenco.* Córdoba: Almuzara, 2007.

Padre Juan de Mariana, Francisco Pi y Margall. *Obras del Padre Juan de Mariana: Historia de España, tratado contra los juegos públicos*, Vol. 2. Madrid: M. Rivadeneyra, 1854 [ca. 1601].

Parakilas, James. "How Spain Got a Soul," 137–93. In *The Exoticism in Western Music*, edited by Jonathan Bellman. Boston: Northeastern University Press, 1998.

Pardo Bazán, Emilia. "Carta XXIII Diversiones—Gente Rara, Paris, Septiembre 28." In *A los pies de la torre Eiffel, Obras completas*, vol. 19 (1891), 276–91, http://cdigital.dgb.uanl.mx/la/1020027895/1020027895.PDF.

Patterson, Cecil Lloyd. *A Different Drum: The Image of the Negro in the Nineteenth Century Popular Song Books*. Doctoral dissertation, University of Pennsylvania, 1961.

Pedraza Jiménez, Felipe. "De Quevedo a Cervantes: La génesis de la jácara," 77–88. In *La comedia de caballerías: Actas de las XXVIII jornadas de teatro clásico de Almagro, 12, 13 y 14 de julio de 2005*, edited by Felipe B. Pedraza Jiménez, Elena E. Marcello, and Rafael González Cañal. Almagro: Ed. de la Univ. de Castilla–La Mancha, 2006.

Pedrell, Felipe. *Cancionero musical popular español*. Valls: Eduardo Castells, 1922.

Pedrell, Felipe. *Por nuestra música*. Barcelona: Tip. de V. Berdós y Feliu, 1897.

Pedrosa José Manuel. "Zangorromangos, bimbilindrones, chuchumbés y otros eufemismos líricos populares." *Olivar* 18 (2012): 135–75.

Pellicer, Casiano. *Tratado histórico sobre el origen y progresos de la comedia y del histrionismo en España: y con la noticia de algunos célebres comediantes y comediantas así antiguos como modernos*. Madrid: Imprenta de la Administración del Real Arbitrio de Beneficiencia, 1804.

Peña Fernández, Pedro. *Los gitanos flamencos*. Córdoba: Almuzara, 2013.

Pérez Fernández, Rolando Antonio. *La música afromestiza mexicana*. Xalapa: Universidad Veracruzana, 1990.

Perry, Mary Elizabeth. *The Handless Maiden: Moriscos and the Politics of Religion in Early Modern Spain*. Princeton, NJ: Princeton University Press, 2005.

Pfandl, Ludwig. *Cultura y costumbres del pueblo español de los siglos XVI y XVII: Introducción al estudio del Siglo de Oro*. Madrid: Visor, 1994 [1929].

Phillips, William D. *Slavery in Medieval and Early Modern Iberia*. Philadelphia: University of Pennsylvania Press, 2014.

Pike, Ruth. *Penal Servitude in Early Modern Spain*. Madison: University of Wisconsin Press, 1983.

Pineda Novo, Daniel. *Antonio Ramírez, el baile Gitano de Jerez*. Jerez de la Frontera: Centro Andaluz de Flamenco, 2005.

Pineda Novo, Daniel. *Las folklóricas*. Sevilla: J. Rodríguez Castillejo, 1990.

Pineda Novo, Daniel. *Juana, "La Macarrona" y el baile en los cafés cantantes*. Cornellà de Llobregat, Barcelona: Aquí + Más Multimedia, 1996.

Pineda Novo, Daniel. *Silverio Franconetti: noticias inéditas*. Sevilla: Giralda, 2000.

Place, Edwin B. "Does Lope de Vega's Gracioso Stem in Part from Harlequin?" *Hispania* 17, no. 3 (October 1934): 257–70.

de la Plata, Juan. "Esclavos, moriscos, y gitanos: La etapa hermética del flamenco." *Páginas*, no. 3, (Jerez, 1990): 76–84. Also published in *Revista de Flamencología*, Cátedra de Flamencología de la Universidad de Cádiz, Año II, núm. 3 (1r semester 1996), 45–53.

Poché, Christian. *La música arábigo-andaluza*. Translated by Beatríz Martínez del Fresno. Madrid: Akal, 2006.

Posner, Donald. "Jacques Callot and the Dances Called Sfessania." *The Art Bulletin* 59, no. 2 (June 1977): 203–16.

Pougin, Arthur. *Le Théâtre à l'Exposition universelle de 1889, notes et descriptions, historire et souvenirs*. Paris: Librairie Fischbacher, 1890.

"Don Preciso," Juan Antonio de Iza Zamácola. *Colección de las mejores coplas de seguidillas, tiranas y polos que se han compuesto para cantar a la guitarra. Vol. 1*. Madrid: Imprenta de Villalpando, 1799. *Vol. 2*. Madrid: Imprenta de Repullés, 1816.

Puig, Alfonso, Flora Albaicín, Sebastià Gasch, Kenneth Lyons, Robert Marrast, Ursula Patzies, and Ramón Vives. *El arte del baile flamenco*. Barcelona: Ed. Poligrafa, 1977.

Pym, Richard. *The Gypsies of Early Modern Spain, 1425–1783*. Basingstoke, England: Palgrave Macmillan, 2007.

Querol Gavaldá, Miguel. *La música en la obra de Cervantes*. Alcalá de Henares (Madrid: Ed. del Centro de Estudios Cervantinos, 2005 [1948]).

Querol Gavaldá, Miguel. "El villano de la época de Cervantes y Lope de Vega y su supervivencia en el folklore contemporáneo." *Anuario Musical* 11, no. 25 (1956): 25–36.

Quevedo, Francisco de. "Premática del tiempo." *Obras satíricas y festivas*. Edited by José M. Salaverría. Madrid: Espasa Calpe, 1965 [1627]), 59.

Quiñones de Benavente, Luis. *El Amolador*. Madrid, 1643. Biblioteca Nacional de España, Ms. 14851, available online, http://bdh-rd.bne.es/viewer.vm?id=0000214150&page=1, digital page numbers 17–20.

Rabassó, Carlos A. *Granada–Nueva York–La Habana. Federico García Lorca entre el flamenco, el jazz y el afrocubanismo*. Madrid: Libertarias-Prodhufi, 1998.

Read, Alan, ed. *The Fact of Blackness: Frantz Fanon and Visual Representation*. London: Institute of Contemporary Arts, 1996.

Read, Malcolm K. *Visions in Exile: The Body in Spanish Literature and Linguistics: 1500–1800*. Amsterdam: John Benjamins, 1990.

Real Academia Española (RAE). *Diccionario de la lengua castellana en que se explica el verdadero sentido de las voces . . . con las phrases o modos de hablar, los proverbios o refranes y otras cosas convenientes al uso de la lengua*. Madrid: Francisco del Hierro. Vol. 1 (A, B), 1726, vol. 2 (C), 1729, vol. 3 (D, E, F), 1732, vol. 4 (G, H, I, J, K, L, M, N), 1734, vol. 5 (O, P, Q, R), 1737, vol. 6 (S, T, V, S, Y, Z), 1739.

Rehin, George F. "Harlequin Jim Crow: Continuity and Convergence in Blackface Clowning." *Journal of Popular Culture* 9, no. 3 (Winter 1975): 682–701.

de Rementería y Fica, Mariano. *Manual del baratero: Ó arte de manejar la navaja, el cuchillo y la tijera de los jitanos*. Madrid: Imp. de A. Goya, 1849. Translated by James Loriega, *Manual of the Baratero, Or, the Art of Handling the Navaja, the Knife, and the Scissors of the Gypsies*. Boulder, CO: Paladin Press, 2005.

Rey, Juan José. *Danzas cantadas del Renacimiento Español*. Madrid: SedeM, 1978.

Rice, Edward Le Roy. *Monarchs of Minstrelsy: From "Daddy" Rice to Date*. New York: Kenny Pub. Co, 1911.

Rico Osés, Clara. "French Dance in Eighteenth-Century Spain." *Dance Chronicle* 35, no. 2 (2012): 133–72.

Riis, Thomas L. "The Experience and Impact of Black Entertainers in England, 1895–1920." *American Music* 4, no. 1, *British-American Musical Interactions* (Spring 1986): 50–58.

Riis, Thomas L. "The Music and Musicians in Nineteenth-Century Productions of Uncle Tom's Cabin." *American Music* 4, no. 3 (Autumn 1986): 268–86.

Rioja, Eusebio. *El arte flamenco de Málaga—Los cafés cantantes (V): Una aproximación a sus historias y a sus ambientes, part 2*. Málaga: Jondoweb.com, 2014.

Rioja, Eusebio. "Un pinturero personaje del Flamenco decimonónico: *EL NEGRO MERI*." Málaga: April, 2004. Published on documents.mx July 15, 2015 http://documents.mx/documents/el-negro-meri.html.

Ríos Ruiz, Manuel. *De cantes y cantaores de Jerez*. Madrid: Editorial Cinterco, 1989.

Roach, Joseph R. *Cities of the Dead: Circum-Atlantic Performance*. New York: Columbia University Press, 1996.

Rodríguez, Raúl. *Razón de son: Antropomúsica creativa de los cantes de ida y vuelta, cuadernos de trabajo (1992–2014)*. Madrid: Fol Música, 2014.

Rodríguez Calderón, Juan Jacinto. *La bolerología o quadro de las escuelas del baile bolero, tales cuales eran en 1794 y 1795 en la corte de España*. Philadelphia: Zacarias Poulson, 1993 [1807].

Rodríguez Demorizi, Emilio. *Música y baile en Santo Domingo*. Santo Domingo: Librería Hispaniola, 1971.

Romero Peña, María Mercedes. *El teatro en Madrid a principios del siglo XIX (1808–1814), en especial el de la guerra de la independencia*. Doctoral dissertation, Universidad Complutense de Madrid, 2006.

Roxo de Flores, Felipe. *Tratado de recreacion instructiva sobre la danza: su invencion y diferencias*. Madrid: En la Imprenta Real, 1793.

Ruiz Mayordomo, María José. "Danza impresa durante el siglo XVIII en España: ¿inversión o bien de consumo?" 131–44. In *Imprenta y edición musical en España (SS. XVIII–XX)*, edited by Begoña Lolo and Carlos José Gosálvez Lara. Madrid: Universidad Autónoma de Madrid, Ministerio de Economía y Competitividad, 2012.

Ruiz Mayordomo, María José. "Los maestros de danzar en la corte de los Austrias," 63–78. In *La memoria de la dansa: Colloqui internacional d'historiadores de la dansa*. Barcelona, October 27–30, 1994.

Ruiz Mayordomo, María José. "El papel de la danza en la tonadilla escénica," 60–71. In *Paisajes sonoros en el Madrid del S. 18. La tonadilla escénica: Museo de San Isidro, Madrid, Mayo–Julio 2003*, edited by Begoña Lolo and Andrés Amorós. Madrid: Ayuntamiento de Madrid, 2003.

Rumeu de Armas, Antonio. *España en el África Atlántica*. Madrid: Consejo Superior de Investigaciones Científicas. Instituto de Estudios Africanos, 1956.

Russell, Craig H. *Santiago de Murcia's "Códice Saldívar No. 4": A Treasury of Secular Guitar Music from Baroque Mexico*. 2 volumes. Urbana: University of Illinois Press, 1995.

Said, Edward W. *Orientalism*. New York: Random House, 1978.

Saint Amour, Sister Mary Paulina. *A Study of the Villancico*. New York: AMS Press, 1969.

Saldívar, Gabriel, with Elena Osorio Bolio. *Historia de la música en México (Épocas precortesiana y colonial) [with Musical Notes]*. México, 1934.

Sales Mayo, Francisco, and Francisco Quindalé. *El gitanismo: Historia, costumbres y dialecto de los gitanos…; Con un Epítome de gramática gitana…Y un diccionario caló-castellano…Por Francisco Quindalé*. Madrid: Suarez, 1870.

Salillas, Rafael. *El lenguage: (estudio filológico, psicológico y sociológico); Con 2 vocabularios jergales*. Madrid: Suárez, 1896.

Salomon, Noël. *Lo villano en el teatro del Siglo de Oro.* Madrid: Castalia, 1985.

Sánchez Ortega, María Elena. "Evolucion y contexto historico de los gitanos espanoles." In *Entre la marginación y el racismo: Reflexiones sobre la vida de los gitanos,* edited by Teresa San Roman. Madrid: Alianza Editorial S. A., 1986, 13–60.

Sánchez Romeralo, Antonio. *El villancico: Estudios sobre la lírica popular en los siglos XV y XVI.* Madrid: Gredos, 1970.

Sánchez Sánchez, Víctor. "La habanera en la zarzuela española del siglo diecinueve: idealización marinera de un mundo tropical." *Cuadernos de Música, Artes Visuales y Artes Escénicas* 3, núm. 1 (Octubre–Marzo, 2007): 4–26.

Sanz Pérez, José (libretto), and Mariano Soriano Fuertes (music). *El Tío Caniyitas o El mundo nuevo de Cádiz: Opera cómica española, en dos actos.* Cádiz: Imprenta, Librería y Litografía de la Revista Médica, á cargo de D. Juan de Gaona, 1850.

Saunders, A. C. C. M. *A Social History of Black Slaves and Freedmen in Portugal: 1441–1555.* Cambridge: Cambridge University Press, 2010 [1982].

Sazatornil Ruiz, Luis and Ana Belén Lasheras Peña. "París y la españolada—Casticismo y estereotipos nacionales en las exposiciones universales (1855–1900)." *Mélanges de la Casa de Velázquez Nouvelle* 35, no. 2 (2005): 265–90.

Schaffer, Matt. "Bound to Africa: the Mandinka Legacy in the New World." *History in Africa* 32, no.1 (2005): 321–69.

Schaub, Jean-Frédéric. *Pour une histoire politique de la race.* Paris: Seuil, 2015.

Schuchardt, Hugo. *Die Cantes Flamencos.* Halle: E. Karras, 1881.

Schuchardt, Hugo. *Los Cantes Flamencos: (die Cantes Flamencos, 1881).* Translated by Gerhard Steingress, Eva Feenstra, and Michaela Wolf. Sevilla: Fundación Machado, 1990.

Selva, Juan B., "Sufijos americanos." *Thesaurus: boletín del Instituto Caro y Cuervo* 5, nos. 1–3 (1949): 192–213.

Shergold, N. D. "Ganassa and the 'Commedia dell'arte' in Sixteenth-Century Spain." *Modern Language Review* 51, no. 3 (July, 1956): 359–68.

Sheridan, Richard Brinsley. *Robinson Crusoe; or, Harlequin Friday. A Grand Pantomime, in Two Acts, as Performed at the Theatre-Royal, Newcastle upon Tyne, in 1791…* Newcastle, Printed by Hall and Elliot [1791].

Shiloah, Amnon. *Music in the World of Islam: A Socio-Cultural Study.* Detroit: Wayne State University Press, 1995.

Slout, William L. *Burnt Cork and Tambourines: A Source Book of Negro Minstrelsy.* San Bernardino, CA: Borgo Press, 2007.

Soler Díaz, Ramón. "Del origen cubano de algunas letras flamencas." *Candil,* n° 114. Peña Flamenca de Jaén (Enero–Febrero 1998): 2937–60.

Soler Díaz, Ramón and Antonio El Chaqueta. *Antonio El Chaqueta: Pasión por el cante.* Madrid: El Flamenco Vive, 2003.

Soler Guevera, Luis, and Ramón Soler Díaz. *Los cantes de Antonio Mairena: Comentarios a su obra discográfica.* Sevilla: Ediciones Tartessos, 2004.

Spadaccini, Nicholas, and Jenaro Taléns. *Through the Shattering Glass: Cervantes and the Self-Made World.* Minneapolis: University of Minnesota Press, 1993.

Sparti, Barbara. "Style and Performance in the Social Dances of the Italian Renaissance: Ornamentation, Improvisation, Variation, and Virtuosity." *Proceedings, 9th Annual Conference of the Society of Dance History Scholars,* 1986, 31–52.

Stearns, Marshall W., and Jean Stearns. *Jazz Dance: The Story of American Vernacular Dance.* New York: Macmillan, 1968.

Stein, Louise K. "Eros, Erato, Terpsíchore, and the Hearing of Music in Early Modern Spain." Special issue: *Music as Heard: Musical Quarterly* 82, no. 3/4 (Autumn–Winter 1998): 668–70.

Stein, Louise K. "The Origins and Character of *recitado.*" *Journal of Seventeenth-Century Music* 9, no. 1 (2003), 3.3, http://sscm-jscm.org/v9/no1/stein.html#ch3.

Steingress, Gerhard. "La Aparición del Cante Flamenco en el Teatro Jerezano del Siglo XIX." In *Dos Siglos de Flamenco: Actas de la Conferencia Internacional. Jerez 21–25 junio, 1988*. Jerez de la Frontera: Fundación Andaluza de Flamenco, 1989, 343–80.

Steingress, Gerhard. *La presencia del género flamenco en la prensa local de Granada y Córdoba desde mitades del siglo XIX hasta el año de la publicación de Los Cantes Flamencos de Antonio Machado y Álvarez (1881)*. Sevilla: Libro Blanco del Flamenco, August 2008, https://www.juntadeandalucia.es/cultura/redportales/comunidadprofesional/sites/default/files/presenciaflamencoprensagranadacordoba.pdf.

Steingress, Gerhard. *Sociología del cante flamenco*. Jerez: Centro Andaluz del Flamenco, 1991.

Steingress, Gerhard....*y Carmen se fue a París: Un estudio sobre la construcción artística del género flamenco (1833–1865)*. Córdoba: Almuzara, 2005.

Stern, Charlotte. "The Coplas de Mingo Revulgo and the Early Spanish Drama." *Hispanic Review* 44, no. 4 (1976): 311–32.

Stern, Charlotte. "Fray Iñigo de Mendoza and Medieval Dramatic Ritual." *Hispanic Review* 33, no. 3 (1965): 197–245.

Stern, Charlotte. "The Genesis of the Spanish Pastoral: From Lyric to Drama." *Kentucky Romance Quarterly* 25, no. 4 (1978): 413–34.

Stevenson, Robert. "The Afro-American Musical Legacy to 1800." *Musical Quarterly* 54, no. 4 (1968): 475–502.

Suárez Ávila, Luis. "Jaleos, Gilianas, versus Bulerías." *Revista de Flamencología* 10, no. 20 (2004): 3–18.

Suárez-Pajares, Javier, and Xoan M. Carreira, eds. *The Origins of the Bolero School: Studies in Dance History*, vol. 4, no. 1. New Jersey: Society of Dance History Scholars, 1993.

Subirá, José. *La tonadilla escénica*. Three volumes: 1. *Concepto, fuentes y juicios. Origen e historia*. 2. *Morfología literaria. Morfologa musical*. 3. *Transcripciones musicales y libretos. Noticias biográficas y apéndices*. Madrid: Tipografía de Archivos, 1928–1930.

Subirá, José. *Tonadillas teatrales inéditas. Libretos y partituras, con una descripción sinóptica de nuestra música lírica*. Madrid, 1932, 348.

Sublette, Ned. *Cuba and Its Music: From the First Drums to the Mambo*. Chicago: Chicago Review Press, 2004.

Sublette, Ned. *The World That Made New Orleans: From Spanish Silver to Congo Square*. Chicago: Lawrence Hill Books, 2008.

Sublette, Ned, and Constance Sublette. *The American Slave Coast: A History of the Slave-Breeding Industry*. Chicago: Lawrence Hill Books, 2016.

Surtz, Ronald E. *The Birth of a Theater: Dramatic Convention in the Spanish Theater from Juan del Encina to Lope de Vega*. Madrid: Castalia, 1979.

Swiadon Martínez, Glenn. *Los villancicos de negro en el Siglo XVII*. Doctoral dissertation, Universidad Nacional Autónoma de México, 2000.

Swinburne, Henry. *Travels through Spain, in the Years 1775 and 1776*, vol. 1. Dublin: S. Price, R. Cross, J. Williams, et al., 1779.

Szwed, John F. "Race and the Embodiment of Culture." *Ethnicity* 2, no. 1 (1975): 19–33.

Szwed, John F., and Morton Marks. "The Afro-American Transformation of European Set Dances and Dance Suites." *Dance Research Journal* 20, no.1 (1988): 29–36.

Talley, Thomas W. *Negro Folk Rhymes: Wise and Otherwise*. New York: Macmillan, 1922.

Taylor, Diana. *The Archive and the Repertoire: Performing Cultural Memory in the Americas*. Durham, NC: Duke University Press, 2003.

Thomas, Hugh. *Beaumarchais in Seville: An Intermezzo*. New Haven, CT: Yale University Press, 2006.

Thompson, Robert Farris. *Flash of the Spirit: African and Afro-American Art and Philosophy*. New York: Vintage Books, 1984.

Thompson, Robert Farris. *Tango: The Art History of Love*. New York: Vintage Books, a Division of Random House, 2005.

Thornton, John K. *Africa and Africans in the Making of the Atlantic World, 1400–1680*. Cambridge: Cambridge University Press, 1999.

Towsen, John H. *Clowns*. New York: Hawthorn Books, 1976.

Trambaioli, Marcella. "Apuntes sobre el guineo o baile de negros: tipologías y funciones dramáticas," 1773–83. In *Actas de los Congresos de la Asociación Internacional Siglo de Oro (1987–2005)* vol. 6, no. 2. Edited by María Luisa Lobato and Francisco Domínguez Matito, 2004.

Tucker, Henry. *Clog Dancing Made Easy*. New York: R. M. De Witt, 1874.

Twiss, Richard. *Travels Through Portugal and Spain in 1772 and 1773*. London: Printed for the author, and sold by G. Robinson, T. Becket, and J. Robson, 1775.

Úbeda y Castelló, Gaspar. *Letras de los villancicos, que se cantaron en la Iglesia Cathedral de Cadiz, en la kalenda, noche, y dias del nacimiento de N. Sr. Iesu-Christo este año de 1709*. 1709. BNE R/34199/40.

Unamuno, Miguel. *En torno al casticismo*. Madrid: F. Fé, 1902.

Vélez de Guevara, Luis, and Adolfo Bonilla y San Martín. *El diablo cojuelo por Luis Vélez de Guevara—Reproducción de la edición príncipe de Madrid, 1641*. Vigo: Librería de Eugenio Krapf, 1902.

Viqueira Albán, Juan Pedro, Sonya Lipsett-Rivera, and Ayala S. Rivera. *Propriety and Permissiveness in Bourbon Mexico*. Wilmington, DE: Scholarly Resources, 2004.

Vizuete Picón, P. *Diccionario enciclopédico hispano-americano de literatura, ciencias y artes: edicion profusamente ilustrada con miles de pequeños grabados intercalados en el texto y tirados aparte, que reproducen las diferentes especies de los reinos animal, vegetal y mineral*. Barcelona: Montaner y Simón, 1888.

Vodovozova, Natalie. *A Contribution to the History of the Villancico de Negros*. Master's thesis, University of British Columbia, 1996.

Weber de Kurlat, Frida. "El tipo del negro en el teatro de Lope de Vega: Tradición y creación." In *Actas del II Congreso de la Asociación Internacional de Hispanistas: celebrado en Nijmegen del 20 al 25 de agosto de 1965*, Nijmegen (Holanda): Asociación Internacional de Hispanistas, Instituto Español de la Universidad de Nimega, 1967, 695–704.

Weinberg, Meyer. *A Short History of American Capitalism*. New History Press, 2002.

Welsh-Asante, Kariamu. *African Dance: An Artistic, Historical, and Philosophical Inquiry*. Trenton, NJ: Africa World Press, 1998.

Winter, Marian H. "Juba and American Minstrelsy," 39–64. In *Chronicles of the American Dance,* edited by Paul Magriel. New York: Henry Holt and Company, 1978.

Wittke, Carl F. *Tambo and Bones: A History of the American Minstrel Stage*. New York: Greenwood Press, 1968 [1930].

Woods Peiró, Eva. *White Gypsies: Race and Stardom in Spanish Musical Films*. Minneapolis: University of Minnesota Press, 2012.

Worrall, David. *Harlequin Empire: Race, Ethnicity and the Drama of the Popular Enlightenment*. London: Pickering & Chatto, 2007.

Wynne, Shirley Spackman. *The Charms of Complaisance: The Dance in England in the Early Eighteenth Century*. Doctoral dissertation, Ohio State University, 1967.

Zatania, Estela. *Flamencos de gañanía: Una mirada al flamenco en los cortijos históricos del bajo Guadalquivir*. Sevilla: Giralda, 2008.

Zoido Naranjo, Antonio. *La Ilustración contra los gitanos: Antecendentes, historia y consecuencias de la Prisión General*. Sevilla: Signatura Ediciones de Andalucía. 2009.

Zugasti, Julián. *El bandolerismo: Estudio social y memorias históricas*. Madrid: Impr. de T. Fortanet, 1876.

INDEX